Managing the Congregation

Managing the Congregation

Building Effective Systems to Serve People

Norman Shawchuck
Roger Heuser

Abingdon Press
Nashville

Managing the Congregation

This book is printed on recycled, acid-free paper.

Library of Congress Cataloging-in-Publication Data

Shawchuck, Norman, 1935-
Managing the congregation : building effective systems to serve people / Norman Shawchuck, Roger Heuser.
p. cm.
Includes bibliographical references and index.
ISBN 0-687-23072-1
1. Church management. I. Heuser, Roger. II. Title.
BV652.S456 1996
254—dc20 95-26561
CIP

The authors gratefully acknowledge the following for permission to reprint:

Bantam Books for excerpts from *A World Waiting to Be Born: Civility Rediscovered* by M. Scott Peck, 1993, Bantam Books.

Berrett-Koehler Publishers, Inc. for excerpts from *Stewardship: Choosing Service over Self-Interest,* copyright © 1993 by Peter Block, Berrett-Koehler Publishers, Inc., San Francisco, CA. All rights reserved.

Doubleday Currency for excerpts from *The Fifth Discipline: The Art and Practice of the Learning Organization* by Peter Senge, 1990, Doubleday Currency.

Unless otherwise noted Scripture quotations are from the New Revised Standard Version Bible. Copyright 1989 by the Division of Christian Education of the National Council of the Churches of Christ in the USA. Used by permission.

Scripture quotations designated NASB are from the New American Standard Bible, © The Lockman Foundation 1960, 1962, 1968, 1971, 1972, 1973, 1975, 1977.

96 97 98 99 00 01 02 03 04— 10 9 8 7 6 5 4 3 2 1

MANUFACTURED IN THE UNITED STATES OF AMERICA

Contents

Acknowledgments

To Alvin Lindgren; friend, professor, mentor. Alvin extended to me the highest honor I ever was accorded by a professor when, as his student, he invited me to write with him. Two books resulted from our effort: *Management for Your Church: A Systems Approach*, and *Let My People Go: Empowering Laity for Ministry*.

With his book, *Foundations for Purposeful Church Administration*, published in 1965, Alvin Lindgren set the standard for all writing in the field of management for religious organizations. With this book I trust that Roger Heuser and I have met that standard.

To Verna, Carita, Melody and Kay; the four women in my life.
To Jacqueline; without whom work projects would get out of hand quicker than they do.
To Pacer, Amy, Aslan and Buck; Doñã, Aloe and Velvet; true friends who have companioned me in my writing activities spanning twenty years.

Norm Shawchuck

To Gayle, whose companionship of emotional support and sacrifice of time has enabled long hours of work late at night and early in the morning—she continues to be a gift from God.

To the following graduate students at Southern California College—J. David Trotter whose editing and reflection questions within chapters and whose summaries and "how to" ideas at the end of each chapter made a significant contribution; Jonathan Renker and Mark Merrick whose "eagle eyes" and discerning minds helped in proofreading and constructing the index. And, to Phyllis Burns, Coordinator of Graduate Studies in Religion at SCC, whose mind for details and heart for relationships helped to give me breathing room for this project.

Roger Hueser

Preface

This is the third book in a series dedicated to those who serve in congregations and religious organizations. The first book, *Marketing for Congregations: Choosing to Serve People More Effectively,* by Norman Shawchuck, et al., provides a comprehensive guide to building responsive organizations. While not a substitute for spirituality and vision, marketing is a tool that makes the minister and ministry more effective. The second book, *Leading the Congregation: Caring for Yourself While Serving the People,* by Norman Shawchuck and Roger Heuser, explores the interior life of the leader; what the leader brings to the congregation in terms of spirituality, vision, renewal, and change; and the changing paradigms for today's church leader. This third book, *Managing the Congregation: Building Systems to Serve People More Effectively,* is an in-depth look at the inner workings of the congregation as a system.

This is not a book about developing policy manuals, leading committee meetings, maintaining financial record keeping, or performing many of the other things that a manager must do.[1] This book is about recognizing the waves of cultural change that are rolling over all institutions, and understanding how to manage a congregation in the wake of these all-pervasive changes. One thing is clear; yesterday's methods won't work any longer.

PART ONE

The Manager

Introduction

Consider this parable of how religious organizations grow:

A Guru was so impressed by the spiritual progress of his disciple that, judging he needed no further guidance, he left him on his own in a little hut on the banks of a river.

Each morning after his ablutions the disciple would hang his loincloth to dry. It was his only possession! One day he was dismayed to find it torn to shreds by rats. So he had to beg for another from the villagers. When the rats nibbled holes in this one, too, he got himself a kitten. He had no more trouble with the rats; but now, in addition to begging for his own food, he had to beg for milk as well.

"Too much trouble begging," he thought, "and too much of a burden on the villagers. I shall keep a cow." When he got the cow, he had to beg for fodder. "Easier to till the land around my hut," he thought. But that proved troublesome too, for it left him little time for meditation. So he employed laborers to till the land for him. Now overseeing the laborers became a chore, so he married a wife who would share this task with him. Before long, of course, he was one of the wealthiest men in the village. Years later his Guru happened to drop by and was surprised to see a palatial mansion where once a hut had stood. He said to one of the servants, "Isn't this where a disciple of mine used to live?"

Before he got a reply, the disciple himself emerged. "What's the meaning of all this, my son?" asked the Guru.

"You're not going to believe this, sir," said the man, "but there was no other way I could keep my loincloth!"[1]

Like the disciple in the above parable, we scramble to find excuses. We find ourselves burdened by all of the trappings that accumulate in church management. For example, we sorely want (and need) the latest versions of computer hardware or software and, after an installation that breaks down and ruins our schedule for several days, we wish we had the old system. As the parable suggests, it is far easier to add another layer of activity and responsibility than it is to remove one. With advances in our efficiency, there is a price.

Yet, amidst all the complications in our lives, there remains a desire, a longing, to stay true to the biblical vision of ministry and caring. The challenge for any church management team is to keep up with the latest technology and environmental opportunities, but not at the neglect of the more simple "tools of the trade" introduced by Jesus, with which he intended the church to get things done—the towel and basin.[2] The symbol of tools is important because one's tools define the manager's trade. Yet, however powerful our management "tools" become, they cannot replace the power of the towel and basin.

Defining our ministry through the symbol of towel and basin is difficult because these tools call us to intimacy. Walter Brueggemann points out that the towel is something we use on ourselves, but not on other people (except our kids before they go to bed). The towel is not firm and manageable but flexible, receiving shape only as it wraps around the feet and dries them. More important is the positioning that takes place in this relationship; the role of a slave "positions" the other as master. The only ministers who can assume this caring posture are those who are strong enough to be vulnerable, those "who have had their lives empowered by the gospel, who have been freed enough to live their lives out of a very different value system. Thus the towel and basin drastically call into question our sense of identity."[3]

The religious managers who will not surrender the simple tools of the trade are the ones who will help the church navigate troubled waters. What are seen as troubled waters by many of us are seen as opportunities by those who know who they are, and who tend to the interior life of the Spirit in order to keep Christ's awareness alive and vital.

In chapter 1 we will consider the identity and role of the manager as a steward in a special partnership with God. In chapter 2, we explore the spirituality of the manager; a person before God, who must tend to the inner life in order to meet the demands of ministry. In chapter 3, we explore "what the manager manages." This chapter will introduce a systems approach to understanding the dynamic relationships of forces inside the congregation, as well as the interdynamic relationship between the church and its environment.

1

The Manager as Steward

The role of the manager is the most stressful of all roles, and the profession of management the most complex and demanding of professions. I can assure you that it is infinitely more difficult to be a good hospital administrator than it is to be a good physician. . . . God calls some people to be managers and definitely does not call others. A few of us are ideally suited to be managers. Most of us are ill-suited.[1]

M. Scott Peck

Management is all consuming. It is never completed and put away. An architect sees the finished construction; the doctor says goodbye to his patient who checks out of the hospital; the painter finishes the house and moves on. But not so with the church manager. The responsibilities of management go on and on. Continuously rushing toward the pastor is the next Sunday, the next board meeting, and the next telephone call to be returned. John Sanford relays the story of a ministering person who remarked, "Well, how many blood transfusions a day can you give to people?" That is what a person does when she ministers to someone in need: her energy is used up in supplying energy to the other person. This is so even if the person in need is a fine person whom we like; it is all the more so if the needy person is difficult, demanding, or clinging.[2]

Disciplining Oneself to Function Effectively

Managers of religious organizations are not without conflicting personal and professional interests and demands. The manager, like everyone else, has her share of personal problems. The healthy manager, however, faces up to these realities, and does whatever it takes to function effectively. If she is unable to manage herself and her priorities, she will get the help she needs to do so. This may mean going back to school, beginning a disciplined home study program, or finding a mentor. Whatever she needs, the healthy manager will find it.

The Dysfunctional Manager

Many observers of theological institutions are noticing that "the vocation of ordained clergy may be getting an overload of people with deep emotional and psychological problems."[3] Entering into ministry as a psychologically and spiritually infirm person is not the same as the person whom Henri Nouwen discusses as the "wounded healer." The wounded healer is someone who has experienced God's healing of body, mind, and soul and is thus able to serve others. It is not good news when persons enter the seminary unconsciously wanting the school to meet their spiritual or psychological deficiencies.[4] The seminary is an educational institution, not a healing station.

> God calls very broken people to enter the ministry, for, once healed, it is out of brokenness that we accomplish our greatest ministry of healing toward others.

Dysfunctional seminary students, failing to be healed, graduate and enter into ministry, bringing deep psychological disturbances with them. Should then dysfunctional persons not present themselves for ministry? Dysfunctional persons should present themselves for ministry, but they should be healed before they harm others. Once dysfunctional persons are healed and well trained, they are equipped for a ministry of unusually sensitive and effective dimensions—made possible because they have experienced what it means to be a deeply hurting person.

Nonetheless, to realize their highest calling, they must be healed. And for this the dysfunctional person must assume full responsibility, because seminaries cannot, and most ordaining agencies will not. We hear a great deal about dysfunctional persons coming into ministry today. Perhaps too much. Because such worrying can become a ploy to excuse church officials from dealing with a far greater problem—the malfunctioning and the nonfunctioning pastors that are already in ministry, some for a lifetime.

The Malfunctional Manager

A malfunctioning manager is one who functions—perhaps overfunctions—but almost always leaves the congregation smaller, weaker, or more discouraged than before he functioned. What causes a religious manager consistently to malfunction? At the root of malfunction is the fact that the manager is not a learner and is not reflective. He takes no time or effort to further his professional growth. He makes no effort to plan and organize for effective ministry. He does not reflect on his experience, therefore he malfunctions in the same ways, over and over again, without knowing it.

There is a much quoted myth that says "experience is the best teacher." This is not so. Many people learn nothing from experience. They simply plow ahead, committing the same mistakes again and again. Experience is only a good teacher when one reflects deeply upon her experience and projects her learning onto her future experiences.

Malfunctional managers are not learners. They are doers—but learn little or nothing from their doing. There is a spiritual dimension at work in the life of the manager who refuses to study, to pray, to assess the results of his actions. There are probably more malfunctioning pastors in our midst than there are dysfunctional. Nonetheless, one word of commendation can be given to the malfunctional manager; at least he is doing something, even if it makes matters worse.

God often calls malfunctional persons into the ministry. Consider Saul (later to become Paul, the apostle). Saul was someone who was busy doing things *to* the church! However, none of these things were the right things. Saul was persecutor of the church and killer of the saints, yet it was he whom God called to evangelize the gentile world. The lesson here is that God prefers to work with persons who are already doing something—even if it is the wrong thing—rather than to work with people who are doing nothing, who choose to "play it safe," and to conserve what is already there.

The Nonfunctional Manager

Perhaps the larger segment of benign or damaging religious managers is not comprised of the dysfunctional and malfunctional persons combined. A larger number is comprised of those who choose to do nothing at all. The Navy chaplains have a term for this type of person: "Retired while still on active duty." Church leaders sometimes refer to other pastors as R.I.P.: "Retired in Place." There is always the chance that the dysfunctional pastor will be healed, or that the malfunctional pastor will learn something from her mistakes. But God cannot help the nonfunctional pastor at all, because she gives God nothing with which to work.

The desert fathers had a great deal of experience with nonfunctional monks and disciples, and their assessment of them was scathing. The fathers coined a term for the nonfunctional monks who roamed the land begging for food, fleecing people of their meager possessions, or otherwise causing harm. The term is *acedia*—spiritual boredom, or spiritual sunstroke.[5] Too lazy to earn their keep, they relied upon the goodwill of others to provide them excitement and provisions for another day. The fathers viewed their laziness and lethargy as a spiritual disorder—their boredom was a spiritual derangement; their indifference toward spiritual matters was a sick condition of soul.

All pastors must develop the holy habits that amount to resting in God. Failing to do this, the essential spiritual reserves for withstanding the many temptations inherent in the work of the ministry, and for carrying its heavy demands and burdens, will soon be depleted. Then, when the pastor sees diminishing returns for his efforts, he finds himself afflicted with nervous agitation and fills every minute either with sleep or meaningless noise and activity. More regretfully, some having spent all of their spiritual, physical, and mental reserves, will sell their souls for a mess of pottage.

Ministry born out of acedia is fruitless and unsatisfying. We cannot ignore the standards of our profession or avoid doing what is required of our vocation. There is no other way to experience effective and soul-satisfying ministry. So Christ encourages us, "Abide in me as I abide in you. Just as the branch cannot bear fruit by itself unless it abides in the vine, neither can you unless you abide in me. . . . Those who abide in me and I in them bear much fruit" (John 15:4-5).

There is an alternative to the manager who is dysfunctional, malfunctional, or nonfunctional; it is to see oneself and so behave as one who is steward and partner with Christ.

QUESTIONS FOR REFLECTION UPON HOW YOU FUNCTION AS A MANAGER

1. Truthfully, would you describe your own management in the church as dysfunctional, malfunctional, or nonfunctional?
2. Which areas of your life need to be changed in order to become a more effective, functioning minister? What is holding you back from working through these changes?
3. What recent or past experiences do you need to reflect upon in order to learn from them?
4. What requirements of stewardship ministry have you been ignoring because of acedia?

The Minister as Steward

Our word *manager* was never used by Jesus. Rather he used the term steward. The root of the word *steward (oikonomos)* is the same as the root for manager or guardian of a household, and it is the same root that gives us the modern *economist.* Jesus made many references to the steward as one who manages only at the volition of another, the owner. The steward-as-manager owned nothing, but his reputation was made with the ability to manage with integrity, or at least with prudence (Luke 16:1-8).

The steward served under orders; he was always accountable to the owner. At any moment he could be removed from his station and called to give an account of his management: "So [the owner] summoned him and said to him, . . . 'Give me an accounting of your management, because you cannot be my manager any longer' " (Luke 16:2-3). There is an eschatological reality attached to management in the church; the manager will give an accounting.

Church management is a stewardship responsibility. The steward is accountable to God for his actions and results. An account will be called for, and an account will be given; there is no escaping the reality of this judgment. The false manager manages for her own self-interest. If she is a faithful steward, she manages at the behest of God, and throughout scripture this commission is a very sober matter before God.

As managers, because we do not own the congregation and can be removed, we should hold our position loosely. We should, however, take our responsibility very seriously, for there will be an accounting. It is in this spirit of service that the pastor is to take up his task.

Jesus Depends upon the Church

As hard as it is for some of us to believe, Jesus depends upon those who will cooperate with him to achieve God's purposes in the world. Jesus told Philip his disciple, "Very truly, I tell you, the one who believes in me will also do the works that I do and, in fact, will do greater works than these" (John 14:12*a*); the departing words of Jesus, according to Matthew, were "And remember, I am with you always, to the end of the age" (Matt. 28:20*b*). Evelyn Underhill expresses the dynamic working relationship between God and servants:

> Some people suppose that the spiritual life mainly consists in watching God work. God provides the spectacle. We gaze with reverent appreciation from our comfortable seats. . . . [However] our place is not the auditorium but the stage—or, as the case may be, the field, workshop, study, laboratory—because we ourselves form part of the creative apparatus of God, or at least are meant to form part of the creative apparatus of God. He made us in order to use us, and use us in a most profitable way; for [God's] purpose, not ours. To live a spiritual life means subordinating all other interests to this single fact.[6]

Underhill reminds us that we are called not to be spectators but to be partners with Christ in the Kingdom's work. This partnership with Christ is expressed in two dimensions: first, Jesus calls upon all who believe to do what he cannot do; and second, this energizes Jesus to do what they can never do.

Raising Lazarus from the Dead

Can faith and action energize Jesus to act on our behalf? The Scriptures repeatedly answer this question in the affirmative. Perhaps the most telling example of Jesus' dependence upon others to do what he cannot is given in the account of the raising of Lazarus from the dead.

> This, we think, was the moment the Church was born; from that crowd, some persons separated themselves from the milieu of unbelief and joined Jesus in the act of raising Lazarus from his death experience. In this moment a great separation occurred between those who dared to believe and act, and those who did not.

In the account of Lazarus' resurrection, John takes pains to convince us that Jesus was greatly impressed by the death of his beloved friend, Lazarus. Twice we are told that Jesus was grieved to the point of weeping at the sorrow of Lazarus' family and again, when he encountered the great obstacle (the stone) that barred the door to Lazarus' tomb. Yet, when confronted with the obstacle, Jesus did not rush forward to roll it away. Rather, he looked to the crowd and said, "You must roll the stone away!"

Some rolled the stone away, and their faith-in-action energized Jesus to do what they could never do. We see the powerful effect their participation had upon him, first in his prayer, "Father, I thank you for having heard me"; and second, in the strength of his voice to penetrate the deadness of Lazarus' tomb, to shatter his death and call him to life.

When Lazarus appeared, however, he came dragging all of his grave clothes with him. Once again Jesus did not act but stood in the place where he was, and said to those who had dared to roll the stone away, "Unbind him, and let him go." Imagine the outcome of this story if no one there would have stepped forward to roll the stone away, or to free Lazarus from the binding effects of his dying experience.

From this incident we derive some important principles for ministry. First, ministry is often a stinky business (John 11:38-44); and second, people can emerge from their deadening life experiences alive, but still bound by the grave clothes of wounded memories, damaged relationships in need of repair, and in need of the Church to nurse them. And, third, for all God's omnipotence, God will not accomplish God's work on earth magically. There are those times when God must depend upon our participation. In such times, failing to receive our participation, God cannot accomplish what God wishes to do on our behalf.

> It is assumed that if God is omnipotent he can do anything; but this is not strictly true. What God's omnipotence means is that nothing can obstruct him, nothing can prevent his being fully and eternally himself.
>
> But this means that it is actually a part of his omnipotence that God does not contradict himself. He is free to determine the manner of his own working; and, in fact, as we know from revelation, he has chosen to work in such a way that we can interfere, and interfere very drastically, with his creation. God made man such that man could rebel against him, and set up his own "world" in opposition to God. Of course, God is not without allies even in "our" world; he knows that we can never really be satisfied with any world of our own devising, so that we will always be vulnerable to his influence in one way or another; and God exploits this to the full. But he always respects the freedom and independence that he has given us.[7]

The minister who finds this freedom intoxicating must learn that this partnership with God depends upon our admission of weakness.

> Before we get too carried away with thoughts of God's power, we should listen attentively to what St. Paul says about the "weakness of God" (1 Cor. 1:25), which is a vital part of God's self-revelation. If we look at the way in which he discloses himself in Jesus Christ we have to acknowledge that he does not come in to our world with a great display of superi-

> or power; in fact, this was one of the temptations which our Lord had to resist as being contrary to his mission, contrary to his true nature (Matt. 4:5-7). He does not come in strength but in weakness, and he chooses the foolish and weak and unimportant things of the world, things that are nothing at all, to overthrow the strength and impressiveness of the world. . . . he is like the judo expert who uses the strength of his opponent to bring him to the ground; it is the art of self-defense proper to the weak.
>
> This is why, if we keep clamoring for things we want from God, we may find ourselves disappointed, because we have forgotten the weakness of God and what we may call the poverty of God. We had thought of God as the dispenser of all the good things we would possibly desire, but in a very real sense God chooses to give God's self.[8]

Partnering with Christ

"I do not call you servants any longer, because the servant does not know what the master is doing; but I have called you friends" (John 15:15*a*).

The difference between being a servant and a friend is so transparent that we often miss it. The servant does not have the big picture of what the master is doing, does not ask questions, but unthinkingly does the "assigned piece of work."[9] In contrast, the friend knows what the master is up to and why.

> To be a friend of the one who dies and is risen does not mean to be his buddy or his casual acquaintance, but to be his confidant, to share his intent, perhaps to be in on the planning, to invest in his dreams and his anxieties. Imagine that! Taken into God's dreams for the world which the world itself rejects and fears. To be in on a secret that to know is to be a doomed person in the eyes of the world.
>
> I don't know about you. As for me, I would rather be a servant—go through the motions, finish the clearly defined day, and go home and not worry about it all. But this other relationship is burdensome. It means to be there with him through it all.[10]

The manager as steward is accountable for her part of the partnership—with Christ and others. It might be less stressful to be a servant to those who would manage us as their slaves. Ironically, Christ asks us to become slaves or servants of our neighbors; while in relationship to Christ, we are invited to be friends and partners.

The Essence of Stewardship

1. God has called you to serve out of the deep well of God's grace which is continuously made available to you.
2. Experience is not always the best teacher!
   - Experience + Reflection = Learning
   - Without reflection, one will simply plow ahead, committing the same mistakes over and over.
3. Stewardship has standards and requirements that God and your parishioners trust you to keep.
   - Is ministry any less demanding than other professions? For example, if you are going to the hospital for surgery, would you not hope that the doctor has been keeping to the standards of her profession?
4. The business of a manager is not to burden, watch over, or dominate a congregation, but to set persons free to grow in their own ministry effectiveness.

How You Can Implement Stewardship

1. Take the next step in addressing the important issues in your life and congregation that can change dysfunctional, malfunctional, and nonfunctional management to effective management. This will happen through disciplines such as daily reflection, resting in God, becoming a member of a covenant group, sharing serious conversation with others in spiritual direction, or perhaps counseling.

2. "Heighten" your awareness of individuals and groups who are holding on to a calm and predictable status quo.
   - With your provision of safety, others will be able to handle the rough waters of change!

3. Respond to God's desire to live in partnership with you.
   - Partnership with God is found in your own admission of weakness!
   - God has chosen you to be a partner by allowing you to have a dramatic influence upon God's movement and actions!
   - Specifically, what actions is Christ compelling me to carry out on his behalf, and what things am I completely reliant on Christ to do?

2

The Manager as a Person Before God

For too long we have thought of the essential Christian life as either organized involvement in political, economic, or social concerns (which tend to wear us out or result in depression) or activity which keeps the church machinery intact or the depository of beliefs doctrinally pure. To avoid this kind of thinking in the religious manager, our primary orientation cannot be the activities of an institution or some great cause or even other people, but our attention must be directed first and forever to God. Unless our identity as a religious manager is hid in God we will never know who we are or what we are to do. Our first act must be prayer, or Oratio, which is the discipline that the contemplative or reflective manager should cultivate. To be human is to pray. To manage process in a religious organization is to meditate both day and night on the love and activity of God. Through prayer we are continuously formed and transformed by the thought of God within us. Prayer is a disciplined dedication to paying attention. Without the single-minded attentiveness of prayer we will rarely hear anything worth repeating or catch a vision worth asking anyone else to gaze upon.[1]

John H. Westerhoff III and John D. Eusden

We define spirituality as "the means by which persons enter into an awareness of the presence of God in their lives, and how they nurture that awareness to keep it fresh and vital." The apostle Paul believed that one's spirituality was a formative process (not a static condition), and that it involved a birthing process. To the church in Galatia he wrote, "I am again in the *pain of childbirth* until Christ is *formed* in you" (Gal. 4:19, *emphasis added*).

There are religious traditions which believe, contrary to Paul, that one's spirituality is not so much a process as it is an accomplished fact at some point in the person's life; for example, some religious traditions believe that the work is completed at the moment of baptism, or upon being born again, or upon being saved and sanctified.

The drama about the children of Israel in the Old Testament is a story of journey and formation much more than "arrival" and an accomplished condition. The Israelites journeyed first as a sperm in Abraham's body, and a fetus in Sarah's womb. Later, driven by starvation, they journeyed into Egypt and into slavery. Years after that, they journeyed out of Egypt and into the wilderness. Finally, they journeyed across the river Jordan and into the Promised Land. By all these experiences they were formed; that is, their experience of God (their spirituality) was conditioned by each and all of these circumstances and events. The same can be said about the early disciples, the apostles, the apostolic church, the church of Christendom, the early reformers, Billy Graham, Martin Luther King, Jr., and so on.

From the examples given in the Old and New Testaments and from ancient to modern history, we can deduce that a person's spirituality is conditioned by many converging factors in a person's life experience: family history and traditions, nodal events in one's life, religious experiences, the history, traditions, theology, and practices of the church one attended at formative stages of life, examples of persons who were/are highly respected (professors, pastors, neighbors), one's private religious journey, spiritual disciplines, and life's work, to name a few.

The weakness in our argument to this point is that one may conclude that our spirituality and spiritual formation are experienced passively; that we play a small part in our spiritual formation. The truth is, however, that we are active participants in the development of our spirituality and in our spiritual formation process. For the purposes of this text on religious management, we want to say that your management experiences influence your spirituality (the passive element) and, on the other hand, your spirituality influences the results of your management (the active element). It is this narrow focus on the dynamic relationship of your spirituality and your work as a religious manager that we will focus on throughout the rest of this chapter.

The Elements of the Manager's Spirituality

The contrasting spiritualities for the religious manager include two major expressions of Christianity: the apostolic church and the church of Christendom.[2] We enter into this discussion of the two spiritualities of the Christian church not as a study in history but as a means to assist you in assessing which most characterizes your own spiritual attitudes and experiences as a religious manager. We can, each of us, locate ourselves somewhere in these two spiritualities, and we can see how expressions of these spiritualities are manifested in our lives and work.

The Spirituality of the Apostolic Church: Downward Mobility.[3]

Jesus proclaimed a message of sacrifice and self-denial—out of which, he claimed, would come joy and fruitfulness. While there were some who wanted to make him a political ruler, and argue where each would sit in his kingdom, Jesus resisted such voices and pointed to the downward way of service. He eventually died like a criminal.[4] From humble beginnings he traveled downward to a most ignominious end. The spirituality of the ancient Church was one of joy, humility, meekness, sacrifice, and suffering. The spirituality of downward mobility is not some masochistic choice for the Christian manager. It is the way chosen by God (see Philippians 2). The invitation to journey with Christ into downward mobility is extended to us that we might be able to find God in the midst of our struggles and suffering. Then we are transformed by the Spirit, being formed into Christ's likeness. The fruit of this spirituality blesses the world: love, joy, peace, patience, kindness, goodness, trustfulness, gentleness, and self-control (Gal. 5:22-23). All these stand in sharp contrast to societies torn apart by idolatry, envy, greed, sexual irresponsibility, strife, and other sins (Gal. 5:19-21).[5] The Church that came into being at the raising of Lazarus from the dead, at Pentecost, and in the days following, was a church whose spirituality was influenced by their experiences, rejection by the status quo, persecution, poverty, and torture. The apostolic congregation also experienced the living presence of Christ, the rich blessings of God upon their evangelistic efforts, a fiery baptism in the Holy Spirit, and an infectious joy and freedom.

The church of downward mobility in its infancy was known as the Church of the Apostles, most of whom were summarily slaughtered by the powerful monarchs and kings, who viewed their message as a challenge to the prevailing religions and gods.

The Spirituality of Christendom: Upward Mobility

Christendom, the label for a powerful religious monarchy, did not emerge until the fourth century with the conversion of the mighty emperor Constantine. Upon his conversion to Christianity, Constantine decreed that all his subjects were to be Christian—or else! By that decree Christendom was born. Now the Church, far from being tortured and killed could, itself, arrest, torture, and kill anyone who did not blindly swallow the party line. From Christendom came the inquisitions, burnings at the stake, wars to subdue heathen kingdoms—all in the name of Christ. Christendom ascended to its highest pinnacle of power with the advent of the papacy. Then, two powerful sovereigns reigned side by side—the monarch and the Pope—as the king of the secular order and the sovereign of the religious order.

The managers and poets of Christendom wrote, preached, and sang about its invincible power in military terms: "Onward, Christian soldiers! Marching as to war, with the cross of Jesus going on before. Like a mighty army moves the Church of God. . . ." The spirituality of Christendom was one of power, adulation, conquest, and victory. The economic goal was upward mobility, identifying with the successful and the powerful.

The Temptations of Upward Mobility

Henri J.M. Nouwen poignantly describes the temptations of Jesus in the wilderness (Matt. 4:1-11) as the temptations with which all managers must do business. These include: (1) the temptation to be relevant (turning stones into bread), (2) the temptation to be spectacular (to coerce God), and (3) the temptation to be powerful (to rule the whole world).[6] These temptations are a result of our relentless desire to join the ranks of the upwardly mobile. M. Scott Peck says that the temptations Jesus faced in the wilderness are illustrative of the temptations inherent in managing an organization.[7]

> To me it is clear that Jesus went into the desert to wrestle with the problem of authority. In being baptized by John, he is essentially told by both John and God that he is the Messiah. "Me, the Messiah?" he must have asked himself. "Where do I come off being the Messiah? I'd better go off alone and think this one over."
>
> So into the wilderness he went to face the issues. They were three. The first was the temptation to use power for food, for money and security. The second was to use it for what I call "spiritual flashiness." The third was to use it for the pleasure and glory of rulership. And then, having rejected these temptations, having emptied himself of all ambition, he immediately came out of that empty place to preach, full of godly authority.[8]

The temptation for an abundant supply of bread is the temptation to guarantee our own security. This temptation is universal. Bread is the symbol of having enough of whatever we need in order to have total relief from the fear of coming to the end of our ministry in poverty. How much do you need to feel secure in your ministry? Will you sleep well and with a secure sense of accomplishment if you have a large salary? Have your home paid for? Have a nest egg laid in store awaiting your retirement?

The temptation to cast one's self down is to feel that we have to prove our worth. "Satan is saying to Jesus: 'Prove it. Prove your greatness to me. Prove it to yourself and to others.' "[9] Herein lies the most insidious temptation for all pastors: to feel that I must prove my greatness as the manager of this congregation. Only then will I be free of the lurking fear that I am really not good enough, not bright enough to lead this congregation. Then people will recognize my abilities and accept me as their equal, or even as more than their equal.

The temptation to "glory" is the desire to manage with a sense of spiritual flashiness. This is the temptation to show people just how spectacular we are, to be the star attraction, or to manage the best program. This temptation pushes us to abuse our power and our calling in order to reach the top.

In positioning ourselves as managers before God, we must do business with these bribes. The temptations to be secure, to prove our worth, and to be master of more people are unavoidable aspects of the authority that is ours as the leader and/or manager of the congregation.

QUESTIONS FOR REFLECTION UPON YOUR SPIRITUAL JOURNEY

1. Make a list of the aspirations you have held for your ministry, and of the major career decisions you have made in the past ten years. Do these aspirations and decisions characterize more of the spirit of downward mobility or upward mobility?
2. List five or ten of the most predominant concerns of pastors in your denomination. Are these concerns indicative of the apostolic church or Christendom? Of a desire for downward mobility or upward mobility?
3. Which of the spiritualities most nearly describe your managerial attitudes and behaviors in your present ministry? What are the long-term results for you and for the ministry?

How, then, do we successfully confront the temptations of being the one in authority? Our advantage lies in the practice of the same spiritual exercises that Jesus employed to confront the relentless temptations of his own ministry and authority.

The Essential Spiritual Disciplines for the Religious Manager

The essential spiritual disciplines, we believe, include availing oneself to the means of grace, journaling, the examination of consciousness, living in covenant community and under accountability, care of the physical body, care of the family, and lifelong learning.

The Means of Grace

The "means of grace" are commonly understood to be those spiritual exercises that were modeled in the life of Jesus. They include: "prayer, searching the scriptures, fasting, the Lord's Supper, serious spiritual conversation, and acts of mercy."[10] The means of grace are well termed as "spiritual exercises," because they constitute the staples of our daily spiritual workout routine. We exercise ourselves in them to avoid becoming weak and flabby, mentally and spiritually, and to avert carrying extra weight, as God helps us to lay aside the extra baggage that otherwise impedes our progress in work and right thinking.

It is very difficult to separate oneself from the relentless management responsibilities which are always clamoring for immediate attention. To deliberately turn aside from these in order to spend daily time in the sweatshop of the spiritual exercises requires an act of deliberate will. It has never been any different. This is a lesson that each of us must learn as a solitary. No one can force us to pray, and no one can do our spiritual exercises for us. But we can take our cue from the saints and reformers who have gone before us. Consider Luther, who at the height of the reformation declared that, "I am so busy, that unless I pray four hours a day I can't get my work done."

But why should a busy religious manager consider making prayer such a priority? Does not God see our good intentions and count these for something, even as we bury ourselves in our management responsibilities? The desert fathers, and the spiritual writers of the Russian Orthodox church in the 1800s, consistently urged prayer upon us, not as an additional burden but as a secret to fruitful ministry:

> When you undertake some special endeavor, do not concentrate your attention and heart on it, but look upon it as something secondary; and by entire surrender to God open yourself up to God's grace, like a vessel laid out ready to receive it. Whoever finds grace finds it by means of faith and zeal, says St. Gregory of Sinai, and not by zeal alone. However painstaking our work, so long as we omit to surrender ourselves to God while performing it, we fail to attract God's grace, and our efforts build up within us not so much a true spirit of grace but a spirit of pride and arrogance. . . . If we are self-satisfied and contented with our efforts, it is a sign that they are not performed in the right way, or that we lack wisdom.
>
> So long as you hold on to even a little hope of achieving something by your powers, the Lord does not interfere. It is as though he says: "You hope to succeed by yourself—very well, go on trying! But however long you try you will achieve nothing."[11]

M. Scott Peck gives his assent to the idea that prayer is essential to fruitful work. He says:

> I have a very full and busy life and occasionally am asked, "Scotty, how can you do all that you do?" The most telling response I can give is: "Because I spend at least two hours a day doing nothing." Ironically, the questioner usually responds by saying he's too busy to do that.
>
> My two hours doing nothing are the most important hours of the day for me. I do not take them all in one gulp. Usually they are distributed into three forty-minute periods. They are "alone" times, times of quiet and solitude. I could not survive without them.
>
> I refer to these periods as my "prayer time." It's another one of the benefits of being a "religious person."[12]

Many religious managers, however, claim to be too busy to pray. They have too many needs to attend to, too many meetings, too many people demanding immediate attention. Observing this inclination in our own lives, and in our students and clients, we are led to believe that the toughest job confronting most religious managers is to manage oneself, to achieve the necessary balance and rhythm between one's public ministry and one's spiritual exercises.

A busy Methodist lay pastor once complained to John Wesley that his many demands left no time for the means of grace. John Wesley responded, "Oh, Begin! Fix some time each day for prayer and Scripture, whether you like it or not. It is for your life. Else you will be a trifler all your days."[13] To learn the balance between engagement in work and experiencing the means of grace will make our lives ultimately more satisfying and effective. When Hercules wrestled with Antaeus he threw him again and again upon the ground. But each time Hercules threw him down, Antaeus rose up stronger than before. Finally realizing that Antaeus was gaining renewed strength from the earth, Hercules changed his tactics and held Antaeus high in the air, away from the source of his strength, and soon brought him under subjection. As with Antaeus, each time we throw ourselves back upon the means of grace, we gain new strength to carry on our managerial duties.

QUESTIONS FOR REFLECTION UPON THE MEANS OF GRACE

1. How well are you succeeding in striking a balance between your management work and the means of grace?
2. Make a list of the most common hindrances you experience to establishing a consistent "method" for making time for prayer and meditating upon the Scriptures. Which of these hindrances are in your control? Which are beyond your control?
3. What steps can you take, even now, to reduce these hindrances? What help, and from whom will you need it, in order to take these steps?
4. What specific differences do you think a more consistent prayer discipline might make in your ministry? Would these differences make the necessary efforts worthwhile?

Living in a Covenant Community

In the tradition of convenant communities, small groups of spiritual pilgrims journey together, each sharing the others' burdens, and each holding the other up—in the most intimate and private affairs of one's life and journey. Authentic community is a place where we can be our real selves with God in the presence of others. The community does for our own faith what we cannot do for it ourselves. It can be a place where we receive the acceptance from others that we often fail to provide for ourselves, as well as a place where we can embrace the challange, albeit reluctantly, to move beyond where we are at present. From whom do we receive the truth spoken in love? With whom can we express our deepest agony, share our heaviest of burdens, and confess the mysterious of our own temptations? We need to be with others who will neither be angered or appalled by our confessions, who will help us take the risk of gazing into our own souls.

Being a member of a covenant community may, at first glance, seem to be something unrelated and unusual for a manager; however, for a church manager, belonging to a covenant group may be the saving grace needed for discernment in decisions, vitality in endless projects, and care in some of ministry's loneliest moments. Living in a covenantal relationship with other people (it seems to us from our own experience) is both a means of grace and a stimulating aid to all of the other means of grace.

Keeping a Spiritual Journal and a Management Journal

One of the most effective, and most neglected, resources to the manager's spirituality is the practice of keeping a daily journal. Actually, not one journal but two should be kept; a spiritual journal and a management journal. The keeping of these two journals will cause you to reflect upon your experiences as a manager from two very different perspectives: your life with God, and your work as the manager of a congregation. Though the two journals are not the same, they are related. Together they provide a disciplined way of identifying and reflecting upon your experiences and feelings in both your private life and your public ministry. God will speak to you through both journals.

The Spiritual Journal

The intent of this journal is to help one become more transparent before God and oneself. The journal also helps us to listen more intently to what God is saying to us through the means of grace and our work.[14] Your spiritual journal contains feelings, prayers, quotations, decisions, and critical incidents that help you to integrate Christ's presence into your conciousness of life's experiences.

The key to journaling is honesty in your writing. Write for yourself and God alone. Resist every temptation to quote from your journal or to allow anyone else to read any part of it. Journals and lives in progress are not meant for publication. Your journal is to become a log of your spiritual journey with God. It will enable you to reflect upon the events and impulses of your life, to interpret their meanings, and to discover where God is leading you through these circumstances. Your journal will become a "travel log" and "road map" to help you recall and reflect on where you have been and where you are going as a spiritual pilgrim.

It would be difficult for us to suggest any other spiritual life resource that is more helpful to your spiritual journey than that of conversing with the Word, and journaling your spiritual experiences. By calling almost any retreat center, monastery, or convent, you will be able to discover workshops in spiritual reflection and journal writing.

The Management Journal

The management journal is a log of what you are experiencing in your work—the critical incidents that have happened in ministry — key people, conversations, decisions and experiences; and what you are thinking about these. Just as important is the expression of your feelings about these incidents. How do these experiences make you feel? Are you angry, frustrated, afraid, lonely, happy, sad? We discover that virtually all religious managers are able to describe their work climate and experiences, but many are thoroughly out of touch with their feelings. So when we ask someone to tell us about their ministry, they give us a list of events and problems. Usually they express very little about their feelings.

We recommend that you record in your two journals at different times of the day. One might, for example, keep his spiritual journal a morning prayer season, and his management journal toward the end of the day.

We also recommend that once a month or so you take time to read back over your written reflections for that month, and that you set aside some retreat days at the beginning of each year in which you read through all of your writing covering the past year. Much is gained by daily writing. Much more, however, is gained by reviewing your journal at monthly and yearly settings. Here is where you will discover the hunches and impulses that God has impressed upon you, as you see certain themes recurring again and again—themes that seemed almost insignificant as you wrote them. There is no magic in keeping these journals. The practice is simply a disciplined approach to more in-depth thinking about your spiritual journey and your management work.

In the preceding paragraph we introduced the idea of developing the ability to listen to your intuitions. Presently, much is being written about the manager's ability to listen to her intuition. The writers refer to this as listening to the divine center that is in each of us. Here we are speaking of modern secular writers and consultants to the managers of American secular institutions and corporations.

Listening to the Blessed Impulse

David Trickett is an educator who also serves as a consultant to major global corporations. One corporation executive recently told him that he often finds it necessary to make decisions that involve millions of dollars in a few minutes. This kind of short-term and instant pressure is leading many corporate leaders to place heavy emphasis upon the ability to listen to "the inner voice," which in secular parlance amounts to trusting their hunches. Warren Bennis puts it this way:

> A part of whole-brain thinking includes learning to trust what Emerson called the "blessed impulse," the hunch, the vision that shows you in a flash the absolutely right thing to do. Everyone has these visions, [managers] learn to trust them. . . . Emerson talks about listening to that inner voice and going with it, all voices to the contrary.

Then, quoting a television producer, Bennis says:

> "I don't know when I started to understand that there was something divine about the inner voice. . . . How is it possible that as a writer I can go to bed a thousand times with a [problem] and wake up with the answer? Some inner voice. To go with that . . . is the purest, truest thing we have. . . . When I've been most effective, I've followed that inner voice." . . . Following the "blessed impulse" is, I think, basic to [management]. This is how guiding visions are made real.[15]

The desert fathers, and later the reformers, had a different term for this phenomenon. They called it "the discerning heart," or discerning the mind of God. And they said that silence and prayer are the essential conditions for discerning (listening in to) the mind of God regarding the decisions we should make and the actions we should take. They made discernment a matter of spiritual discipline.

Perhaps all of us have had experiences in which God broke into our train of thought with a totally new idea, but we often fail to comprehend these "divine impulses" or "blessed hunches" because we are not conditioned to do so. Our Western models of theological and ministerial training condition us to accentuate the rational and analytical, and thus we are conditioned to distrust anything that smacks of intuition in our work. A compelling example of this comes out of the Inquisition.

The young Joan of Arc was brought before the inquisitors to defend herself of several supposed heresies, one of which was her claim that God spoke to her. "You are an ignorant peasant," the inquisitor growled, "how can God speak to you?" "God speaks to me through my imagination," came the reply. "Your imagination?" pressed the inquisitor. "How can God speak to you through your imagination?" "But, sir," she replied, "how else could God speak to me but through my imagination?"

God does not call us into ministry only to leave us to fend for ourselves in carrying out the work God assigns to us. For the most part we believe this, but what we find hard to believe is that God might actually speak to us about our work. The Western view of the spiritual world holds a view of God as being "out there." We find it hard to believe that God is also inside us, attempting to speak to us from within. Thus, we probably fail to comprehend many imaginations and intuitions that are from God.

These, then, are some of the major elements for a Christian spirituality of management: an attitude of downward mobility, the spiritual exercises, keeping a spiritual journal and a management journal, and learning to decipher from our many imaginations and intuitions those that are from God; the discerning heart.

But what happens when a religious manager fails to nurture

these conditions in his life and work? What happens when he is not being continuously formed in the nature of Christ, and manages out of other attitudes and conditions? At best his ministry will be insipid. At worst his aspirations and motivations will be unexamined, and he will manage out of a shadow side of his personality. In doing so he will tend to project his darksome inclinations upon the congregation, and will blame them for all of his personal and managerial problems.

A point of reference with which to begin our conversation of this phenomenon is to state that every religious manager experiences himself, God, and others uniquely through his or her management activities. This is what makes the manager's spirituality separate and unique from the spirituality of others. And it is expressed through the spirit that the manager projects upon the congregation and its ministries. The manager may, under certain interior conditions, project a spirit of love, joy, peace, hope, courage, and so on. Under other interior conditions, however, a manager may project a spirit of quite a different nature.

> We [religious managers] share a responsibility for creating the external world by projecting either a spirit of light or a spirit of shadow on that which is other than us. We project either a spirit of hope or a spirit of despair, either an inner confidence in wholeness and integration or an inner terror about life being diseased and ultimately terminal. We have a choice about what we are going to project, and in that choice we help create the world that is. Consciousness precedes being, and consciousness can help deform, or reform, our world.[16]

QUESTIONS FOR REFLECTION UPON THE SPIRITUAL EXERCISES

1. In what ways are you regularly throwing yourself upon the "Soil of God"? What activities, circumstances, people, and places rejuvenate you?
2. How are you cultivating an awareness of the "blessed impulse" in your daily life?
3. What activity or relationship is God's "still, small voice" nudging you to draw near to God? Which ones should you push away?

What Spirit Does the Manager Project upon the Congregation?

When managers are out of touch with their inner self, their shadow side will unconsciously increase its power, with conscious results on other individuals, groups, and organizations.[17] Projecting a shadow spirit upon a congregation is not a matter of denying or ignoring the reality of one's shadow side. For the most part, religious managers who project a shadow spirit upon the congregation are not aware of the clouded memories, emotions, and inclinations that reside in the unexamined recesses of their minds. In reality, many of us, however stable, may yet have less than healthy aspirations and motives that remain unrecognized or unexamined. When this is the case, then these infuse the spirit that we project upon our congregations.

Therefore, it is the responsibility of every religious manager to investigate the emotions and forces that take harbor on the inside, lest some be projected in less than healthy or responsible ways. There is no escape from the need for religious managers to explore and understand their interior conditions. The same can be said for the lay leaders and members of the congregation. However, no person in the congregation occupies a position of greater power and influence than the manager. Where the greater power and influence reside, there lies the greater possibility of inflicting damage upon the congregation and all its ministries.

Parker J. Palmer identifies five examples of the shadow sides common to religious managers. He says: "If [managers] are to create less shadow and more light, [they] need to ride certain monsters all the way down."[18] These five monsters include:

1. **A deep insecurity about the manager's own identity and self-worth.** Our identity is not in our titles, degrees, size of offices, or roles. Our identity is rooted in being God's child, a brother or sister of our coworkers. When managers know this and act upon this, relationships are different; committee and board meetings are different; the ministry setting is different, because managers no longer need to deprive others of their identity and value.
2. **Inside many managers is a perception that the world out there is hostile, one in which there must be winners and**

losers. This internal shadow is very different from the perception of one who manages by listening, sharing, and consensus.

3. **Some managers possess "functional atheism"—a fundamental belief that "everything depends upon me."** This shadow can often lead to dysfunctional behavior: out-of-whack priorities, workaholism, burnout, and relationships that mirror the image that we have of bombed cities, such as Beruit or Sarajevo. Dispelling this shadow requires learning how to share the task, to ask for help, and to rest, knowing that the task will be patiently waiting for us when we return.
4. **Some managers have a fear of chaos.** This shadow side is projected in an inordinate need to organize every detail so that there is no trace of disorder, dissent, or change. When this happens there is little chance for creativity since a precondition for creativity is chaos.
5. **The final shadow which the manager may project upon others is the denial of death.** Harboring great fear of public failure and negative feedback, we will continue in denial about those programs that should have died naturally a long time ago. But we keep putting energy into their life support systems. How different this is from those organizations that encourage risk, even at the possibility of failure, for they know that the best learning sometimes comes from failure. There are times when resurrection and new life, whether for persons or programs, only come out of death. Keeping something alive by our efforts may only prolong the advent of a life or ministry ready and waiting to be born.[19]

To confront our shadow side is to take our inner life seriously and understand the value of prayer, reflection, and living in covenant relationships with others. In addition, there may need to be a healing of one's internal world through spiritual guidance and professional therapy.

To cut corners in this important area of our lives will mean that we cut corners in our effectiveness. For when we manage from inner strength, hope, and trust, we create a context in which all the workers and the congregation grow stronger, are filled with hope, and are trustworthy.[20]

QUESTIONS FOR REFLECTION UPON THE SPIRIT YOU PROJECT

1. Do you like what you see in your congregation? If not, have you considered that the congregation may be reflecting a picture of your interior world?
2. Have you carefully explored the personalities, behaviors, and repeated illnesses, brokenness, and addictions in your preceding generations? In your spouse's generations? Have you made serious exploration as to how and what your preceding generations may have passed on to you? What do you see in the histories of your spouse's generations that attracted you to join your spouse's family tree?
3. Make a list of all the places you have served throughout your ministry. What are the most common critical incidents, relationships, and results of your ministry in these places? How did you contribute to these?
4. Have you ever thought that you might benefit from psychotherapy? What interior concerns and blockages keep you from availing yourself of it?

The Essence of the Manager's Spirituality

1. Management is not the manager's most essential work; it is to be seen as secondary to the manager's complete surrender to God, and opening his or her self to God's grace.
2. In the manager's context of endless tasks and incessant demands clamoring for immediate attention, the manager must learn to hear, trust, and act upon the inner voice, or intuition.
3. The temptations as manager—security, not being good enough, being "first in line"—are real and must be met head-on, as Jesus did in his wilderness experience.
4. "Downward Mobility" points toward the long road of journeying with God, it is not a shortcut to "instant success."
5. The manager is responsible for exploring and understanding his or her interior self, so as not to minimize the projection of unresolved issues onto the congregation.

How You Can Renew the Energy You Need to Manage the Congregation Effectively

1. Throw yourself upon the "Soil-of-God" continuously.
    - What activities, circumstances, people, or places rejuvenate you? These are probably the ways and places that you will begin to hear the "still, small voice."
    - Go beyond those daily times of reflection. Monthly or quarterly retreats provide an extended time of thought and prayer about long-term vision, people concerns, personal issues, and so on.
2. Begin keeping a spiritual journal and a management journal.
    - During your daily times of reflection, write down important experiences and feelings that are active in both areas of your life: personal and ministry.
    - Through this time of reflection and writing a "road map" will emerge, making it apparent where you have been and where you are going.
3. Lead by example!
    - The people whom you manage will begin to notice a difference in your decision making, conflict management, overall management style, and other areas as you delve into the shadow side of your interior life.
4. Live in community!
    - Do you have a small group of colleagues or friends with whom you discuss your life and ministry?
    - If not, are you willing to develop such relationships?
    - What are your next steps in doing this?

In this chapter we suggest that the religious manager has a particular and unique experience of God, that his spirituality is, in some dimensions, unique. We also say that the religious manager is responsible for knowing what is going on deep inside, even on the shadow side, so as not to project his own unresolved issues onto others. We will now shift to what the religious manager manages: the context and content of his work.

3

What the Manager Manages

A Systems Approach to Management

The churches, which once gave security and hope by presuming to mediate between God and [humankind], continue to function this way even though many persons, including faithful church attenders, now seek their values in their own experience. As a consequence, the alienated and purposeless have multiplied to devastating proportions for want of sufficient value-shaping influence that once was the churches' major role. And the large human (and material) resources of churches seem to be groping for a way to serve.[1]

Robert K. Greenleaf

Every congregation, in order to thrive, must continuously deal with three basic questions: (1) Who are we (within and apart from our denominational identity)? (2) What is our business (what are the unique features about our mission, ministry approaches, and services that uniquely distinguish us from all the other churches in the community)? (3) How do we get it done (what programs, services, structures, and resources do we need to carry on our work)?[2] These questions are important if we are to understand the mission of the congregation (we address these specific questions in chapter 5). One way to answer the question "what does the manager manage?" is to say that the manager of the congregation manages these important questions.

Virtually all congregations are facing formidable challenges today that congregations in previous generations did not encounter. These challenges come as a result of tremendous changes in the environment: global, national, local, social, political, and religious. Not a single congregation has escaped the effects of these changes. Many congregations, however, are proving that they cannot learn and adapt fast enough to survive the effects of such change, for about sixty congregations close each week. Another way to answer the question "what does the manager manage?" is to say that the manager of a congregation manages change.

Managing change always implies movement. Something has to move aside to make room for something new. In Christian practice there are four basic "movements" which individuals and congregations are invited to encounter. They are (1) to move from sin to salvation, darkness to light, brokenness to wholeness; (2) to step out into service; (3) to move closer to Jesus in order to share his sufferings; and (4) to "tie the knot" with Jesus—loving Christ intimately and unconditionally. These four movements are not static. They are dynamic experiences, which the Scriptures illustrate as a journey and questing. The church must be on a journey with Christ. If a congregation is not on a journey, if its only quest is to figure out how to meet the budget, then the journey will lead to despair, wherein all sense of joy and mission are sacrificed to the survival goals of "getting by for another year." Another way to answer the question of what the manager manages is to say that the manager manages the corporate journey of the congregation. Or put another way, the manager manages the soul of the congregation.

Many corporate leaders are becoming more intentional about nurturing the soul of their business. Many of these leaders look to the church to help them in this task, assuming that the church knows how to nurture its own soul, and is therefore in position to help them learn. However, too often the church has concentrated on understanding the human soul, and has done little to nurture its corporate soul—the center of its corporate spirituality and vision, its core mission, values and beliefs, and relationships. As a congregation begins to take seriously its corporate state of health, it must also pay attention to its corporate spiritual journey. And when this happens, the congregation will eventually be caught up by its vision, and its true mission will become clear and compelling.

Peter Senge, referring to non-learning organizations as having a learning disability, asserts that organizations today must become Life Long Learners.[3] There simply is no way out. The pastor who does not learn continuously will fail. The congregation which does not learn continuously is doomed. One way to answer the question of what the manager manages is to say that the manager of the congregation manages the corporate learning of the congregation.

QUESTIONS FOR REFLECTION UPON WHAT YOU MANAGE

1. Are you managing the crucial questions that relate to your congregation's future:
   - Who are we?
   - What is our business?
   - How do we get it done?
2. Are you managing congregational change? Or, are the changes managing you?
3. Are you promoting an awareness of the corporate journey of the congregation?
4. Are you helping to facilitate corporate learning within the congregation?

The Manager's Instrument Panel: A Systems Approach

In our book *Leading the Congregation,* we compared the systems model of an organization to the instrument panel of an airplane. The pilot must pay attention to many lights and gauges at the same time. The same is true for the manager of a congregation. The manager must take a holistic approach to understanding the congregation's life and ministry. Virtually all pastors instinctively look at circumstances and events as isolated incidents, and fail to see the influential connections one has with another.

Since the 1960s, however, advances in organizational theory have changed this isolationist thinking. Now we know that the only way to understand the workings of an organization is to view all of its pieces as a coordinated whole—to see it all at one time, recognizing that change in any one component will set in motion influences and changes in every other component. This is known as the Systems Theory of Organization.

A systems approach suggests that a congregation can be studied as a whole, considering the interrelationships of its parts as well as the relationship between the organization and its environment. Simply stated, "An organizational system is a set of coordinated components working together to accomplish an overall objective that is set within a sufficient boundary to distinguish it from its environment."[4] Whenever change occurs in any of the components, all of the other components are affected—each is changed to some degree. The most comprehensive response to the question "what does the manager manage?" is to say that the manager manages the congregation-as-a-whole. The manager manages all the components of the congregation—at the same time. The components of an organizational system are illustrated in Figure 3.1.

Figure 3.1

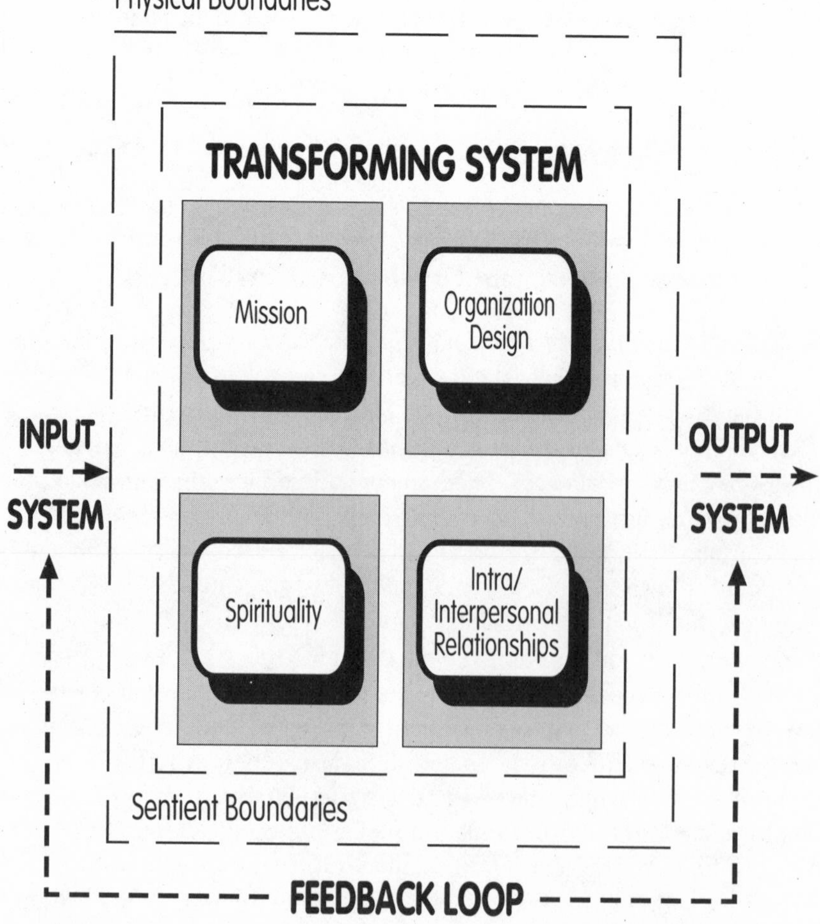

In the discussion that follows, we briefly describe the components of the congregation-as-a-system. We will then use the systems model to give structure to the chapters that follow. We find the systems model on page 46 to be helpful in suggesting and clarifying the activities of church management.

The Environment (see chapter 4)

The congregation's environment is comprised of other systems (political, economic, social, educational, religious), known or unknown, desired or undesired, which exert influence upon the congregation and its ministries. The environment also includes those systems upon which the congregation wishes to exert influence.

The congregation must seek exchanges with its environment in order to survive and, therefore, must be open to environmental influences—or else it will die. The lesson is clear: in order to thrive a congregation must be an open system, one that interacts with its environment. A closed system, on the other hand, assumes that there is no need to interact with the environment.

Inputs into the Congregation's Life and Ministry (see chapter 4)

The **input system** is comprised of the programs, ministries, and other efforts that the congregation puts together in order to import from the environment the resources it needs in order to achieve its mission and to survive. The "inputs" include such things as people, money, new leadership, and technology. The evangelism ministries of a congregation are a part of its input system. Likewise, the methods a congregation uses to attract a new pastor are also a part of its input system.

Without sufficient inputs from the environment, the congregation experiences entropy; it deteriorates, runs down, and eventually dies. It also becomes narcissistic, being preoccupied only with itself.

John A. Seiler identifies four major inputs which an open system imports from its environment: human inputs (e.g., new people, and the humor, politics, brokenness, and enthusiasm each new person brings), technical inputs (e.g., a new computer system), organizational inputs (e.g., hired personnel, leadership style), and social inputs (e.g., local, state, and federal laws, societal trends).[5]

The Boundary Region of the Congregation (see chapter 4)

The boundary region serves as a filter to let into the congregation that which the congregation wants to let in from the environment, and to keep out that which the congregation wants to keep out, whether consciously or unconsciously. In addition, the boundary filters also serve to keep inside that which the congregation wishes to keep from exiting back into the environment.

The boundary region is comprised of two components: the congregation's physical boundaries and its sentient boundaries. The physical boundaries are those which serve to tell where the congregation is. The sentient boundaries help define who the congregation is.

Physical Boundaries The physical boundaries comprise such things as the church's address, its real estate holdings, and the community in which the church is located. One might extend this understanding to view the physical boundaries to be wherever its members are (e.g., wherever they live, work, and play).

Sentient Boundaries The sentient boundary includes the history, values, mores, beliefs, emotions, and traditions which distinguish a particular system from all other systems. Sentient boundaries may be explicitly expressed, as in a church's creed, constitution, by-laws, or the particular history that gives a congregation its identity, unique from all others. Sentient boundaries may also be implicitly expressed as in the attitudes of members toward their neighborhood and the first-time visitor.

For example, the *explicit* sentiences of a mainstream Protestant church may include its traditional liturgy, following the lectionary, or celebrating the Eucharist every Sunday. These sentient boundaries distinguish this mainline church from the community church with its spontaneous worship style, following no particular worship theme, and where communion is served once a month.

Perhaps more influential upon the congregation are the *implicit* sentiences that separate it from all other systems in its environment. For example, the implicit dress code of one church may cause people to "dress up" to go to church, while in another church nearby a "dressed up" person feels out of place—with everyone else dressed in jeans, shorts, or sportswear.

The Transforming System

The fundamental purpose of the transforming system is to convert the raw materials taken in from the environment into energy, which the congregation needs to survive and to carry out its mission. If the congregation produces energy for outreach, then it can make an important difference in its environment. If the congregation uses more energy than it produces, it will eventually run out of stamina and slip into decline. If this condition continues too long, the congregation will die.

The transforming system is comprised of four components or subsystems: the congregation's mission, its spirituality and vision, its organizational design, and its human relationships.

The Congregation's Mission (see chapter 5)

The missional component of the transforming system is the congregation's understanding of its purpose and reason for being. This component includes the congregation's theological beliefs and values that give the congregation its sense of "call" to be God's people in the community and in the world.

The missional component and the environment are the two aspects that exert the most influence on the system's character and reason for being. In a rapidly changing environment, missional opportunities are also changing rapidly. The congregation that does not change to meet the opportunities in its environment will soon find itself cut off, irrelevant, and lost.

The Congregation's Vision and Spirit (see chapters 6–7)

The spirituality and vision component of the transforming process includes the programs, covenants, and disciplines by which the congregation seeks to order its life in a continual awareness of the presence of God in the congregation's affairs.

The congregation's spirituality becomes the wetlands for corporate vision—the passion and desire that capture the congregation's heart and soul, and coalesce their resources toward whatever is necessary to make the vision for the future a concrete reality.

The disciples of Jesus caught glimpses of Jesus' vision while following him around. However, the vision had not as yet "caught" them. It was only after they had time to reflect on their relationships with Christ from birth to resurrection and to experience an encounter of the Holy Spirit that they gave themselves fully to the vision Jesus consistently held up before them. Then they lived their vision for all the world to see. The Scriptures consistently demonstrate that vision comes only to people who are already doing something (A nonfunctional religious manager is not likely to be captured by vision.) and who have developed the capacity to reflect upon their actions and results.

In order to be possessed of a vision, the congregation must develop a "clear eye" toward their own situation and a "big ear" toward God. God does not speak to people out of a vacuum but out of their concrete realities.

Organizational Design (see chapters 8–10)

> The organizational component of the transforming system comprises the various combinations of people, properties, finances, by-laws, and policies that the congregation puts together in order to achieve its mission.

The organizational design is the skeletal component that holds together the different parts of the system. There are many different ways that a congregation may organize itself in order to accomplish its mission (e.g., professional clergy, committee structures, lay volunteers, volunteer pastors). As such, the organization's design gives form to the institution's mission, spirituality, vision, and relationships, which all come together (or fall apart) within the organization's design.

Over time, persons working in organizations arrive at an understanding of certain governance policies that give shape to their mutual expectations and relationships. These governance policies, once fully adopted, constitute an organization's belief system. In short, the organization's structure will be imbued with a governance process or belief system that defines the operating expectations by which the people relate to one another and to the system. The organization's structures and belief system together constitute the organization design. Currently, in order to deal with change, the traditional designs of bureaucracy are being replaced by partnership.

The Congregation's Relationships (see chapters 11–15)

The relational component of the transforming system includes the quality of human relationships within the congregation and the morale of the people. To what extent do people live together in covenant community? To what degree do persons share in one another's lives? Does the organization cause people to grow or to shrink?

Relationships within the congregation do not develop in a vacuum. If persons live and work in effective and growing structures, they experience a sense of growth, self-actualization, and worth. If the structures are inappropriate and ineffectual, persons experience themselves as disempowered, shrinking, and frustrated. Moreover, "a group in community will always demonstrate better task performance than a group that is not in community."6

M. Scott Peck gives us reassurance and a challenge when he states that "You don't just build community; you rebuild it and rebuild it and rebuild it for as long as you have reason to continue to be together."[7]

The Output System (see chapter 4)

Outputs are the influences and resources that the congregation wants to put out into its environment—in order to carry out its mission and to make society more reflective of the congregation's own values. The output system is comprised of the programs, ministries, and other efforts the congregation puts together in order to "export" its influences into its environment.

These "exports" are resources that the congregation hopes will cause the environment to reflect its own values and, in turn, be more willing to "contribute" back to the congregation the resources it needs in order to survive. Outputs such as food pantries, AA meetings, and global missionaries influence the environment in different ways.

Congregations often experience a "gap" between their desires to influence the environment (desired outputs) and their actual influences upon the environment (actual outputs). This gap is always symptomatic of a lack of congruity among the components (subsystems) comprising the transforming system. This rift between the desired and the actual is often experienced as "pain" or "illness."

Not all of the congregation's outputs stay in the environment; some outputs are "fed back" into the system, thus becoming inputs into the congregation.

The Feedback Loop (see chapter 16)

Two very different types of feedback are generated by the congregation through the mere fact that it exists and is operating. One type of feedback information is statistical and numerative: i.e., demographic trends of the congregation, the average attendance as compared to last year's attendance, financial patterns, growth patterns, staff and membership morale, average length of workers' tenure, the number of program ministries it is carrying, or the percentage of first-time visitors who return a second time. The other type of feedback is highly fluid and is expressed as amplifying or restricting processes.

Statistical or numerative feedback information requires no process or effort to generate since it is constantly being produced as the congregation goes about its life and work. This is the purest and least ambiguous information the congregation can possibly have, because it is always there, waiting to be used. Unfortunately, feedback information is generally cast off and lost, because the organization pays no attention to it.

Merging the Congregation's Divine and Human Efforts

The cooperation between human and divine effort must be viewed humbly by religious managers, for God covenants with individuals and families, and not with structures or positions. While God loves the individual unconditionally, God's love for an organization is conditional. Peck makes it very clear, "If the organization is sufficiently sinful, God will dump it, desert it, even if it is a church supposedly operating in God's name."[8] The religious manager has an opportunity to help the congregation merge its divine and human efforts—to be creative in helping the congregation love God and neighbor. Everything else is secondary.

> Destiny is not where we wait for God to push us. You know always in your heart that you need God . . . but do you not know, too, that God needs you—in the fullness of [God's] eternity needs you? . . . the world is not divine sport. It is divine destiny. . . . We take part in creation, meet the Creator, reach out to [God], helpers, and companions.[9]

One way to describe what the manager of a congregation manages is to say that the manager manages the congregation-as-system, assuring that all of the components work together to accomplish desired results.

Understanding Congregations Through Systems Theory

1. Problems are usually more complex than simple cause and effect relationships.
2. Systems theory views organizational components as being interrelated—both interdependently and interdynamically.
   - Each part depends upon all the others.
   - Change in one causes a change in all the others.
3. The congregation must be viewed as a total entity; its components are not to be seen in isolation.
4. The congregation's relationship with its environment is of prime importance.
   - It must be open to exchange of relationships and resources through inputs and outputs.
5. Though feedback is sometimes painful, it cannot be denied.

How You Can Implement the Systems Approach to Management

1. Recognize learning disabilities!
   - People must become learners, through your example (especially the "know-it-alls").
   - The traditional "cause and effect" model must be put aside.
2. Use the visual systems model (Figure 3.1) to "map out" problems and concerns.
   - After identifying the manifestation of the problem, pinpoint interrelated components that are connected to the concern.
   - From these connections, define the symptoms and the problem.
3. Before you examine the trees, take some time to gaze at the forest.
4. To receive feedback talk to a multitude of people, not just those closest to you.
5. Develop a "clear eye" toward the situation and a "big ear" toward God.

QUESTIONS FOR REFLECTION UPON YOUR APPROACH TO MANAGEMENT

1. In what ways do you continue to view problems as simply "cause and effect"?

2. How can you begin to view the congregation's components as being interrelated—both interdependently and interdynamically?

3. What boundaries—physical and sentient—have you and the congregation erected that serve as barriers to getting in?

4. Are you open to feedback from your parishioners and the community? If so, in what ways are you actively collecting and applying this feedback?

In Part One of this book we considered who the religious manager is before God, and what comprises his or her stewardship responsibilities, and we have introduced the systems model for understanding the responsibilities of religious management. In Part Two and following, we will focus more specifically upon the congregation as a system, especially the congregation's relationship to its environment, input system, boundary region, and its mission.

PART TWO

The Congregation and Its Environment

Introduction

The clash between British soldiers and Massachusetts colonists at the end of that night's long march is a story known to every American schoolchild. . . . How could it come to pass that people who spoke the same language; who shared the same traditions, values, and laws; and who until so recently had seen themselves as loyal subjects of the same king, would find themselves desperately sighting down musket barrels at each other on a fine April morning in 1775? Could no one have prevented it?[1]

Richard Luecke

It's really a wake-up call. With the galloping changes that are taking place—demographic, geopolitical, global—if you think you can run the business in the next 10 years the same way you did the last 10 years, you are crazy.[2]

Warren Bennis

Many observers believe that the North American Church is at the crossroads of its very existence. Imminent change is on the horizon. Loren B. Mead, founder of The Alban Institute, writes, "The storm is so serious, I believe, that it marks the end of 'business as usual' for the churches and marks a need for us to begin again building churches from the ground up."[3] While every generation of the Church seems to understand its mission as a defining moment in history, the present includes opportunities and threats which the Church has not faced before in its history. A growing number of churches (Lyle Schaller calls them "Seven-Day-A-Week" churches) have chosen a path of opportunity.[4] Among these churches and other trends of Protestant congregations is some good news! For many others, however, the situation may get worse before it gets better. It is clear for writers like Mead that when the storm clouds have cleared away, "our religious institutions may bear little resemblance to those with which we grew up."[5]

It is one thing to reflect about the changes that face religious institutions on a conceptual and national level; it is quite another thing to talk about change with a pastor who is not certain whether his church will survive another six months. When the storm clouds have been sighted over a particular congregation (among the thousands of small, rural and urban churches that are dying), they become more ominous.[6]

In Part Two we address the relationship between the congregation's mission and its environment. An understanding of these two key components of systems theory is absolutely necessary to fully understand change, organizational responsiveness, and effectiveness. Without an environment there is no mission, and without a mission there is no impact on the environment. Chapter 4 explores the environment, inputs, boundaries, and outputs of the congregation, and chapter 5 examines the organization's mission.

4

The Congregation's Environment

Inputs, Boundaries, and Outputs

A well-known scientist (some say it was Bertrand Russell) once gave a public lecture on astronomy. He described how the earth orbits around the sun and how the sun, in turn, orbits around the center of a vast collection of stars called our galaxy. At the end of the lecture, an old woman at the back of the room got up and said: "What you have told us is rubbish. The world is really a flat plate supported on the back of a giant tortoise." The scientist gave a superior smile before replying, "What is the tortoise standing on?" "You're very clever, young man, very clever," said the old woman. "But the truth is it's turtles. Turtles, all the way down!"[1]

Until World War Two, the environments of the major nations in the world moved along at about the same pace as turtles. However, World War One changed the pace, perhaps forever. Now the rate of change in our environment is rapid, radical, unpredictable, and uncontrollable. We, more than any generation in history, understand the old saying, "The faster I run, the more behind I get."

When the environment changes, the way the church thinks and acts must also change, or the congregation, still holding on to its outdated ways, will soon find itself sailing in a sea of irrelevancy and obsolescence.

Rapid, radical, and uncontrollable change is one thing judicatories and congregations neither want nor appreciate. Indeed, thousands of congregations today are expending large amounts of energy to ensure that nothing changes. But they cannot win at this game, and in the end will stand to lose it all.

A few years ago a Presbyterian researcher observed that at the present rate of decline, there would be no Presbyterian church nor a single Presbyterian member left in the Chicago Presbytery by the year 2050. Recently George Barna predicted that by the year 2050 sixty percent of the congregations in America today will have passed away.

The future does not bode well for those denominations that have thousands of "graying" and shrinking congregations—the mortality tables are relentless and can only be adjusted by the inclusion of new generations.[2] Two major factors will contribute to the demise of those congregations and denominations that do not survive to the year 2050: (1) resistance to environmental change that comes with new generations; or (2) the inability to take advantage of the new and unforeseen windows of opportunity that open up because of change.

> To make a fairly accurate prediction as to whether your congregation will be around in 2050, construct a line of the number of members in your church for the past twenty years and then project it ahead for fifty years. Next, construct a line of the median age of your congregation and project it ahead for fifty years. If your congregation is growing smaller or if it is growing older, it may not survive to 2050. If it is growing both older and smaller, and continues to do so, it almost certainly will close before 2050.

Actually the passing of resistant congregations is not all bad news in the scheme of things. The vast majority of these congregations served well in the environment in which they were brought into being. But now they have become inflexible and will not, or cannot, adapt to a new and different environment. Ministry effectiveness in a new environment points to the fact that reformation and life come with the organizing of new church plants, which find it easier to serve in the environment in which they are being planted.

Environmental Changes: Threats or Opportunities

Virtually all new opportunities for growth and ministry expansion arise out of changes in the social or community context in which the congregation is situated. Yet most congregations resist change, viewing it as a threat to what they already have, and to their traditions. Such congregations are usually blind to the changes in their environment, or they are in deep denial, or they feel overwhelmed by all the changes going on around them.

A congregation that is blind to the changes in its environment is also blind to the effects of these changes upon its ministries and membership. Such congregations either ignore the effects of these changes or predict a better tomorrow through pious platitudes, such as "God is on our side" or "there will always be a faithful remnant." Some believe that their problems can be solved by stressing the need for prayer alone, or sounding the call for a return to the things that made them successful in previous times—but without any idea of how to duplicate or even approach the successes of former days in the new environment in which they now are forced to carry out their ministries.

If there were no changes in the environment, there would be few, if any, new windows of opportunity for ministry and expansion. But windows of opportunity that open up because of rapid changes in the environment are always windows of fleeting opportunity. They never stay open very long, because the environment rushes on, and the windows close—always too soon for a slow-moving congregation to grasp.

Those congregations that do not learn to adjust to environmental change, and do not develop the necessary quickness to grasp fleeting windows of opportunity, will decline and ultimately die. However, those congregations which do develop the skills and intuition to discern changes in their environment are the first ones to see the windows of opportunity for evangelism, outreach, expansion, and growth. The necessary skill for the religious manager is to create methods for scanning the environment, in order to spot new windows of opportunity, and to take advantage of these opportunities with relative quickness.

Scanning the environment is being a curious learner about all the changes taking place (e.g., social and political movements, economic trends, religious movements, new worldviews, demographics). The method that you choose for this kind of scanning is not as important as your continuously doing it. Do it all the time. Else by the time you become aware of the changes that have opened new windows of opportunity, you may be too late to harvest the field of opportunity.

The Church's View of Its Environment

Burt Nanus points out that "modern organizations are being buffeted and shaped by many powerful forces in their external environments."[3] Since its inception, the church has been struggling with its identity and its relationship with its environment. In the title of his book *How the Church Can Minister to the World Without Losing Itself,* Langdon Gilkey describes a fundamental tension of the church in its relationship with the environment. At times the church's mission is seen as opposition to the world, while at the same time there is a need for the church's relevance in the world.[4] This is not something new, for "all through the centuries the church has in one way or another been conscious that, like its Lord, it is *in* but not *of* the world."[5] Jesus prayed that his disciples would not belong to the world, just as he does not belong to the world. And yet, even as God sent him into the world, so he sent them into the world (see John 17:16, 18). Herein lies a persistent dilemma for the church; to be in the world, but not of it; to relate to it, but not join it. The words of Jesus in John 17 raise issues that have to do with the relationship of the church with its environment. One of the most important questions that each congregation must ask itself is how to love and serve the world without belonging to the world and losing its soul in the process. This reality holds tremendous importance for our discussion of the church and its environment because the congregation's view of its environment, and the relationships it attempts to establish with it, exert a dynamic influence upon the types of ministries the church will offer, and upon the long-term results of those ministries.

The relationships between the church and its environment can take on two extremes. On one hand, if the church becomes too cozy with its environment, and seeks to be acclimated to its surrounding culture, it loses its distinct identity. Thus it becomes "the easiest club to enter and the hardest from which to be expelled."[6] On the other hand, if the church insulates itself from the environment so as to not become contaminated, not "to get its hands dirty," it forfeits its mission.[7] Earlier in this book we described two basic paradigms that have characterized Christianity since the beginning: the apostolic church and Christendom. We will now return to the two paradigms as examples of the church in relationship to its environment, and the boundaries that the church constructs as a result of its view of environment.[8]

The Apostolic Church: Ministering in a Hostile Environment

Loren Mead describes the apostolic paradigm of the early church as "conscious of itself as a faithful people surrounded by hostile environment to which each member was called to witness to God's love in Christ. . . . They were impelled to take the life they shared within the congregation and cross over the boundary into the hostile world outside. They called it 'witnessing,' the Greek word for which is 'martyr.' "[9] The environment was so hostile in many places that to even associate with a Christian was a capital offense.

If the environment "out there" was so antagonistic to their presence and message, why did the early Christians venture forth? We all know the answer: they crossed the boundaries of safety and put their lives at jeopardy because they believed that God loved the world, and they loved their lost neighbors—so much that they would risk life and limb to bring them back to God. They did all of this, we say, because of their view of the environment and how they were to relate to it.

The Sect-Type Congregation

The historical record is testimony to a number of groups who, just like the apostolic church, also believe that the world is lost. However their view of the environment is that it is not only hostile but it is also powerful and evil. This view of the environment causes them to withdraw and insulate themselves from the world. Contrary to the apostolic church, their view of the environment causes them to close their boundaries as tightly as possible—to keep the world from influencing its programs and traditions. They move their "faithful remnant" into walled and guarded compounds to keep the environment out.

In recent years we have seen that many of these groups have built up stockpiles of ammunition that they fully intend to use to destroy some part of this hostile, lost, evil environment. Again we see that the church's view of its environment is a dynamic influence upon the ministry and character of the congregation.

The Church in Christendom: Ministering to a Friendly Environment

After the conversion of Constantine, the church quickly revised its view of the environment. Contrary to the apostolic church, the Christendom church viewed its environment as friendly, even to be admired, and opened wide its boundaries to let in the environment. Those churches which fraternized most with the environment often became known as the state church, or were the most recognized religious institutions in the community; for example, Roman Catholicism, the Anglican Church, classic Lutheranism, the United Methodist Church, and the Presbyterian Church in the United States of America. The identity of these churches does not reside in the holiness of individual members so much as it does in sacraments, a creed, or apostolic authority.[10] The defining element of the Christendom paradigm is its view of the church as being linked with the Empire; serving as its religious arm. Since everyone in the state is Christian there is no need for evangelistic outreach. Loren Mead says that "With this view of the environment the missionary frontier disappeared from the doorstep of the congregation and became, in effect, the political boundary of the society itself, far away."[11] By "far away," Mead is saying that in the Christendom view of its environment, the church believes that the only true need for missionary activity lies "far away," beyond the boundaries of the church and its more immediate environment. The "far away" mentality of Christendom is still the paramount thinking of contemporary churches that expect their members to support missions with prayer, generous giving, and perhaps "encouraging the young people to go into 'full-time Christian service' (as employees of the denomination, preferably overseas)."[12] Another defining characteristic of Christendom is the concept of "Parish": a community with geographical boundaries in which all of the residents were expected to belong to the parish church. For the local congregation, the geographic bounds of a parish offered everyone living within those boundaries church membership by virtue of their residence. The pastor was the community's religious leader or local "holy person."[13]

While many congregations do behave as if these polar extremes—being like the world or hostile to the world—are definitive, most churches exhibit a mixed, inconsistent relationship to the environment. This inconsistency should prompt the church manager to observe carefully what type of influence the environment is having upon the ministries and attitudes of the church.

Exchange Relationships of the Congregation with Its Environment

In order to survive, every congregation must carry out "exchange" relationships with its environment. That is, the church must have some degree of influence upon its environment, and the environment must have some degree of influence upon the church. The environment is made up primarily of other social institutions—political, economic, educational, family, and religious—with which the congregation has an exchange relationship. For example, we recently heard of a congregation that offered single mothers free auto repair service. In exchange, however, the congregation hoped these single moms would send their children to events or attend certain events themselves.

A congregation without any exchange relationships with its environment could not continue to exist; it would inevitably die. What puts a congregation at risk is how it views and responds to the changes in its environment. (See Figure 4.1.)

Figure 4.1

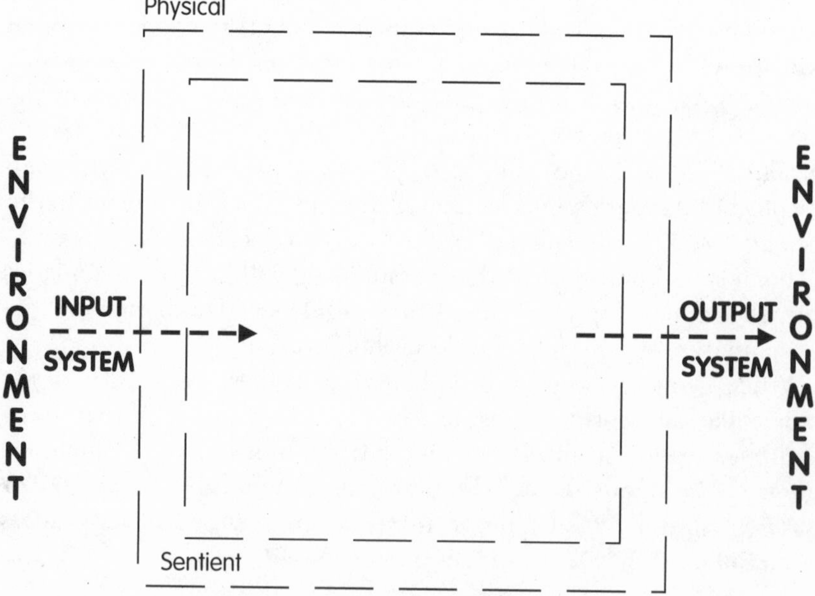

A congregation relates to its environment through its inputs and its outputs. Its outputs are what the church exports into its environment, exerting influence upon its environment. The congregation's inputs are what it takes in from its environment, exerting influence upon the church.

QUESTIONS FOR REFLECTION UPON YOUR CONGREGATION'S RELATIONSHIP WITH ITS ENVIRONMENT

1. Do you view environmental change as a threat or an opportunity?
2. In what specific ways do you "scan the environment"? Are you continuously seeking to understand the changes in your environment?
3. How do you view the changes that are taking place within your environment? How are you responding to them?
4. In what ways are you unable to take advantage of new and unforeseen windows of opportunity that open because of change?

Inputs from the Congregation's Environment

The mechanisms that the congregation puts together to capture resources from its environment are called (in systems language) the input system. All organizations, religious and secular, have difficulty coping with environmental change. The American automobile industry certainly struggled when Japan entered the American automobile environment. The mainline churches did not cope well when the baby boomer generation came upon the scene. Nonetheless, however awesome environmental change may appear, without receiving inputs from the environment, the congregation becomes entropic—it deteriorates, runs down, and eventually dies.[14]

The congregation's input system is comprised of the ministries, programs, and other efforts that the church puts together in order to bring in from the environment the resources it needs to achieve its mission, and to survive. Looking at it from another perspective, the input system is the congregation's effort to take advantage of the windows of opportunity for growth and expansion that open up as a result of changes in the environment. For example, evangelism is an input process designed to bring in new resources to achieve the mission that Jesus gave the church.

John A. Seiler has identified four major inputs which an open system imports from its environment:

1. **Human inputs:** new people and the humor, politics, brokenness, and enthusiasm each new person brings.
2. **Technical inputs:** a new computer system, video equipment, electronic musical instruments, and so on.
3. **Organizational inputs:** hired personnel, leadership style, a new accounting system, and so on.
4. **Social inputs:** local, state, and federal laws, societal trends, and other factors.[15]

Congregations survive, and ultimately succeed, because they link their mission with the new opportunities that environmental change opens up to them (without losing sight of the needs and interests of those people who are already in the congregation). Ironically, however, it is the success of a congregation in responding to its environment at some point in time that compels it to want to close its boundaries to new environmental changes. George Parsons and Speed B. Leas state that

> Many congregations are stuck in their successes. They can point to an earlier time of vitality and growth and subsequent efforts to build on their successes. They can often identify their strengths and the connection between those strengths and past success. But their successes led them to embrace organizational patterns and habits that no longer serve them well. They continue to exercise the same set of muscles while the rest of the body atrophies.[16]

The Congregation's Boundaries

Highly interactive with, and exerting great influence upon the success of the church's input processes, are the congregation's boundaries. In fact, however important the input system is, concentrating on inputs without addressing the congregation's boundaries will likely be an exercise in futility.

The *boundary region* of the congregation is comprised of two major components: the church's *physical boundaries* and the congregation's *sentient boundaries.* Physical boundaries tell *where* a congregation is (location). Sentient boundaries tell *who* the congregation is (identity). As such, the boundary region serves as a filter to let into the congregation that which it wants to take in from the environment, and filter out that which it wants to keep out.

Physical Boundaries

The physical boundaries tell where the congregation is—an address where the church is located, its main property and real estate holdings, the community in which the church is located, buildings, signs, landscaping, and parking. The physical boundaries are very often the congregation's first line of communication with the people they are attempting to reach. If one picture is worth a thousand words, then the picture that is presented to a first-time visitor as she looks at the church sign, lawn, and the exterior of the buildings is already feeding her some highly important subliminal messages about what to expect when once inside. And when these messages create a mental image, then perhaps even a thousand words of greetings and a cup of coffee will not change her initial impressions.

Sentient Boundaries

The sentient boundaries include the history, myths, values, mores, beliefs, emotions, and traditions which define the congregation's identity, and set it apart from all other systems—in a unique environment of its own. Explicit sentiences give the congregation an identity different from all others, which is explicitly expressed in the church's creed, constitution, by-laws, and its particular history. Perhaps more influential are the implicit sentiences that set a congregation apart from other churches in its environment, such as worship style, dress codes, and friendly or judgmental atmosphere.

In chapter 3 we said that each component of the system affects all the other components in the entire system. The congregation's boundaries affect its relations with the environment, positively or negatively influencing the ability of its input system to bring in the desired resources. This in turn affects the congregation's ability to achieve its mission. In this chapter we focus on the interdynamic and interdependent relationships between the church's input processes, its boundaries, and its environment (see Figure 4.2).

Figure 4.2

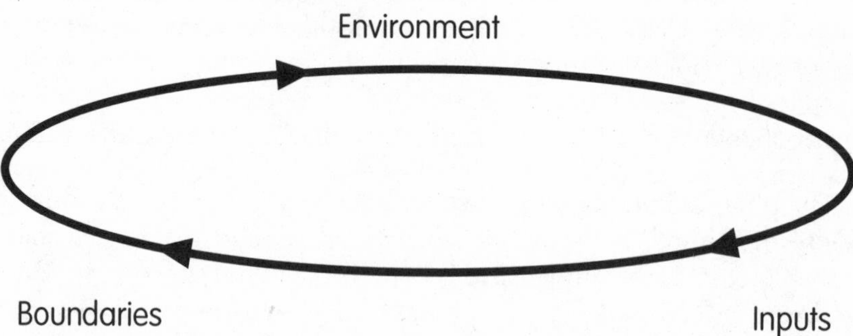

Many congregations are not utilizing high-tech or multimedia equipment; others would not think of new age jazz worship music. Therefore, these environmental developments will probably never make their way through the boundary filters of these churches. A new bookkeeper, yes! Computerized financial and member record keeping, no! New flannel boards for the elementary classrooms, yes! Computers in the classrooms allowing interactional teaching methods, no! A new circle in the women's organization, yes! A twelve-step program for sexual offenders—no! The list of boundaries is endless. What becomes clear is that we all have boundaries, and open boundaries are necessary for our survival. However, push us too far, and our boundaries will close.

More insidious than our boundaries, however, are the effects that our decisions and programs have upon the mental boundaries of the persons we are attempting to reach and serve.

The Boundary Regions of the Mind

As important as it is for the manager to understand the boundaries of the congregation, it is perhaps even more important to realize that, as individuals, we all filter information and experience through the filters (boundaries) of our minds. As persons come into contact with a congregation, their experience causes them either to open or close their mental boundaries—either letting the church in or shutting it out of their life. The functioning of one's "mental boundaries" is carried out consciously or unconsciously. Either way the results are the same. We review some actual examples.

Every Blade of Grass Is an Evangelist

The location and size of your church lawn constitute a physical boundary. However, the condition of the lawn may evoke mental images of your entire operation in the minds of a passerby or potential visitor. These mental images may serve to close the boundaries of their mind to you—their boundaries may serve to keep them out of your church, or to keep your church "out of them."

> When Charles Sineath was appointed as senior pastor of First UMC, Marietta, Georgia, the congregation was declining and looking for ways to cut expenses. A hallmark of the church was its beautiful lawns and flower gardens. At the first church board meeting he attended there was considerable debate as to whether the congregation should continue to make this expenditure. Charles said, "I have been thinking—every blade of grass is an evangelist."
>
> The board members pressed for an explanation. Charles replied, "Our church stands at a very busy and strategic intersection in the heart of this community. Thousands and thousands of automobiles pass by here every day. The appearance of our property is a very important front line witness to our love for our Lord, and the high esteem in which we hold him. The appearance of our lawn, gardens, and property makes a witness to all who drive by here. It shapes the opinions and impressions of all who choose to visit us—even before they enter our doors."
>
> That was twenty years ago. Today every square foot of property, inside and out, demonstrates tender loving care—and Marietta First UMC is one of the largest and healthiest churches in America. When we inquired of various members and workers regarding the secret to the congregation's success, always the reply was given, "Every blade of grass is an evangelist."

How Old Should the Sunday Morning Greeters Be?

The answer to this question depends a great deal upon the demographics of the people you are trying to reach through your evangelism efforts, and just exactly how you plan to reach them.

Windsor Village UMC established a Junior Usher Board of 3rd, 4th, and 5th graders. Pastor Kirbyjon Caldwell describes how they greet visitors, and are responsible for ushering duties at several services a month. This practice teaches them respect for one another, as well as respect for guests in the church. When they perform this task well, they are rewarded with a sense of self-esteem that prepares them for greater responsibility in the life of the congregation.

Imagine the impression these greeters must make upon children and parents who visit that church for the first time.

This is an example of boundaries in the mind, and it tells us something about the visitors who pass through the church doors. Eight-year-old greeters will symbolically open up the boundaries in the minds of young parents who enter the doors for the first time. Perhaps they enter with vivid memories of when as little children they attended church with their parents—where, even before they could read, they read the handwriting on the wall that "Children are welcome here, but not in the sanctuary; and if they must be seen, they are not to be heard." However these young greeters will instantly communicate to them that not only are children welcome here, they are front and center in the ministry of the congregation. This goes a long way toward opening the boundaries of their mind—to let the church in.

On the other hand, there may be a price to pay for having children as greeters (See Figure 4.3). There may also come through the door persons who still are of the opinion that children in church are an unwanted distraction. For them, the sight of children rushing forward to greet them might slam shut the boundaries of their mind to keep the church out. While you are imagining these boundaries, think what boundaries might be violated in some churches if women were allowed to serve on the official board or to be communion stewards?[17]

The Ghosts of Experiences Past

Let us suppose that a new family moves into your community. On their first opportunity they drive through the neighborhood to get a feel for their new home and community. Driving by your church, the

Figure 4.3

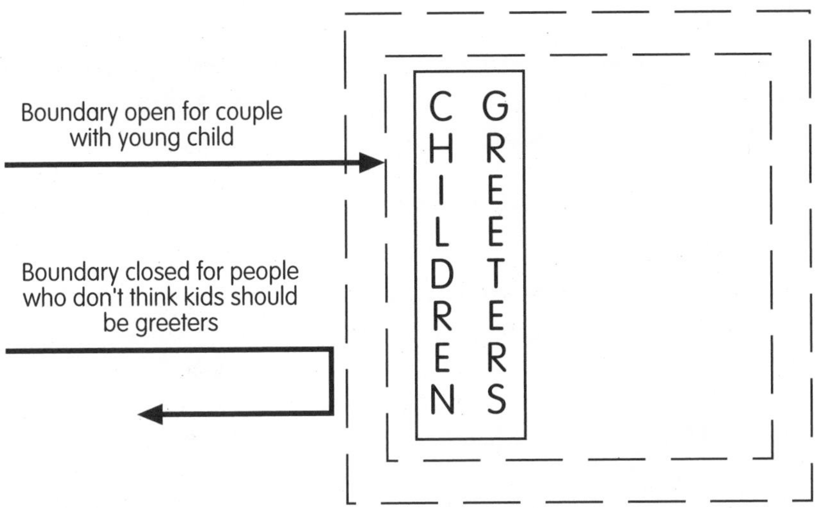

architecture of the building reminds them of the church home they left behind, and how dearly they loved that congregation. Now the physical boundary of your property becomes a boundary in their minds—a boundary that opens wide to let the new church in.

> In the church that he started two and one-half years ago in Courd'alene, Idaho, Pastor Bruce Miles includes in the Sunday celebration services ten-minute coffee and ice cream fellowship time. The church averages 1,800 people in its three Sunday morning services.

That same afternoon another person walks by your church and, reading the name of your denomination on the sign, is instantly repelled because he recalls former wounds inflicted during a bitter church fight where he once attended. The boundaries of his mind slam shut to keep you out.

Another example is that in many churches, drinking coffee or tea in the sanctuary during worship would be a definite infringement of the boundaries. However, an increasing number of churches welcome hot refreshments during the worship service. One visitor seeing coffee in the sanctuary may instantly feel at ease and open the boundaries of her mind to let you in. Another may be affronted by this sacrilege and slam shut the boundaries of his mind to keep you out. These all have to do with the congregation's boundaries and input system. Boundaries affect the congregation's input capabilities—for better or worse.

Persons make first impressions of your church within two minutes from the time they first encounter your boundaries. These first impressions tend to be lasting impressions, whether positive or negative.

The Boundary Region in Your Mind

As you manage the systems of a church, you have boundary regions in your mind also. You have mental images and strongly held presuppositions that exert strong influence upon the way you view the world and the systems that make up your ministry. It isn't merely those people "out there" who have mental and emotional boundaries: We do too. And it is our boundaries that exert the greater influence upon our success, not theirs.

If, for example, we think that having children as greeters is a crazy idea, then we won't have children as greeters. If we think that twelve-step programs will bring all sorts of unsavory characters into our building, we will rationalize such programs to be New Age psychobabble. The boundary regions of your mind exert great influence upon the way you see and relate to the world around your church. Even now many good ideas may languish just beyond your grasp, locked in the vice of the boundaries of your mind.

One of the first things a new pastor should do when coming to a congregation is to learn the history of the congregation; its inception and early years, successes, failures, major conflicts, problems, victories; and from these stories ferret out the explicit and implicit boundaries which give the congregation its unique sense of identity. This knowledge will serve the pastor well as the one responsible to keep the congregation's story alive, and to effect those changes which are necessary to move the organization to a more healthy relationship with its environment.

The Congregation's Outputs

The organization's outputs are the influences and resources that the organization wants to put out into its environment—in order to extend its influence farther into the world.[18] The congregation exports some things from its transforming process into the environment; for example, the recovered life of a person who was divorced, a youth member who decides to become a teacher, day camps for children, child care, short-term missionary trips, a soup kitchen, ministry among gang members. The congregation's outputs determine its level of "responsiveness" to its environment. We define a responsive congregation as "one that makes strong effort to sense, serve, and satisfy the needs and wants of its members, and those outside of its membership, within the constraints of its resources."[19]

The Gap Between the Congregation's Desired Outputs and Its Actual Outputs

No congregation is 100 percent effective in its intentions. There is always a gap between its intended outputs and its actual outputs (see Figure 4.4), between desired results and actual results, between what the congregation wants to accomplish and what it actually accomplishes. This gap is a symptom of a problem or neglected opportunity in the input system, boundaries, or transforming process. Perhaps the congregation's structures are not appropriate to the mission, or the congregation is lacking sufficient spirit to carry out the ministries, and so forth.

Figure 4.4

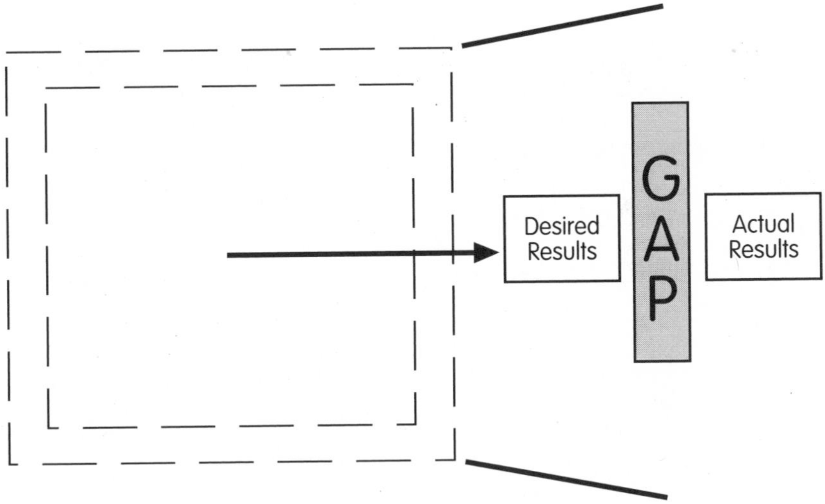

Desired Results

GAP

Actual Results

Trying harder to fix the gap, as if it were the problem, and not a symptom, will lead to frustration and make matters worse. What is important is to identify the underlying problem, and then to work on its solutions. In chapter 17 we will discuss the difference between "trying harder" and "removing barriers" that contribute to a problem or gap.

A key feature of open systems thinking is that the congregation always views all inputs from the environment (no matter how desired or necessary) as raw material. As they are, they are not fully suited to the congregation's purposes. In the following chapters we will address the ways by which a church goes about transforming its inputs (raw materials) into energy in order that it may survive and carry out its ministries.

QUESTIONS FOR REFLECTION UPON YOUR VIEW OF THE CONGREGATION'S RELATIONSHIP WITH ITS ENVIRONMENT

1. Is your congregation linking its mission to new opportunities that environmental change opens up? How are you drawing these opportunities to the forefront of the parishioners' minds?
2. Are you aware of the sentient boundaries that are at work within the congregation? If not, how can you find out what these boundaries look like?
3. What mental boundaries are holding you back as a leader-manager? How do your boundaries filter out good ideas and block your view to opportunities for ministry?
4. How do your mental boundaries "clog" the congregation's outputs into the environment?

The Essence of the Congregation's Relationship with Its Environment: Change and Exchange

1. When the environment changes, the way the church thinks and acts must also change, or the congregation will become irrelevant.
2. Environmental change is the spawning ground of new opportunities for ministry and growth.
3. Congregations survive and grow as they link their mission with arising opportunities out of environmental change.
4. In order to survive, every church must have an "exchange relationship" with its environment through inputs and outputs; without this relationship, the congregation dies.
5. Mental boundaries cause visitors and members to be open or closed to the ways in which you "do" church.

How You Can Implement Your Congregation's Exchange Relationships with Its Environment

1. Scan the environment.
   - Find out the needs of your community.
   - Create unique ways of linking your mission to the opportunities that these needs present to you.

2. Ask people in your community about the church.
   - Do they know where the church is located?
   - What are their impressions of the church (facilities, people)?
   - Have they heard "stories" about the church? If so, what?

3. Become aware of your mental boundaries!
   - Are these boundaries helping or hurting the congregation?
   - In light of the mission of the church, are these boundaries appropriate?

4. Stop thinking about the windows of opportunity that you missed yesterday! *Begin looking for the windows of opportunity that are coming tomorrow!*

5

The Congregation's Mission

One can visit congregations that seem to exist to preserve eighteenth- and nineteenth-century music. I love music enough to hope somebody takes on that task, but I'm not sure that's what I want congregations for—or that that is what they have to contribute. Do congregations exist so they can preserve genteel social structures? . . . Are they to preserve an ethnic heritage from the past? . . . Do we need them to provide meeting places for Alcoholics Anonymous? Do we need them so every community will have a paid pastoral counselor available to those who cannot pay for a therapist? Do we need them to provide a place for people concerned for community betterment? I have no quarrel with any of those as by-products of congregations, but none of them seems big enough, frankly. None of them carries—by itself—the kind of power that comes from connecting with God's purposes and intentions. They are nice enough in themselves, but they hardly provide the kind of energy that turns societies upside down.[1] Loren B. Mead

The church exists by mission as fire exists by burning.

Emil Brunner

Our search for mission is ultimately tied to the heritage of those men and women who left their footprints on the pages of Scripture as they, like us, grappled with the meaning and mission of their lives; e.g., Abraham and Sarah, Gideon, the prophets, Jesus, and the fledgling congregations that embodied the Apostolic Church. When we set about defining and pursuing our mission, we join ranks with a long and illustrious procession of men and women whose lives demonstrate the power of having clear missional intention. From them we have learned that mission, in order to have integrity, must relate to the identity of the congregation (who are we), to God's own mission (the reconciliation of the world God loves), and to the pressing needs that are going unmet in our communities (near and far).

A simple way to define the mission of the church is to say that the mission of the church is a transformed person—one whose life is changed through an encounter with God. Jesus accomplished his mission because his ministry was always received as Good News by the people to whom he ministered. They received his ministry as good news, because he allowed them to influence him in what Good News would mean for them. Jesus worked to accomplish his mission in the lives of very real people, in specific settings.

So when blind Bartimaeus asked for mercy, Jesus asked him more specifically, "What do you want me to do for you?" When the blind man asked for sight, Jesus gave him sight. To be sure, the blind man received sight as Good News. However, Jesus did not come into the world only to give sight to blind people. His mission was a transformed person. And so the writer says that immediately the blind man began to follow him in the Way (Mark 10:46-52). We are left with a sense that in the process of ministering to the man's felt needs, Jesus succeeded in his mission of bringing not only sight but transformation to Bartimaeus.

The mission of your church must be grounded in the contextual realities of specific people, as they define their needs, for when you respond to their genuinely felt needs they will take your actions as Good News, and thus become open to the influences of your mission. The only other way to accomplish your mission is through force or coercion; neither of which work since the collapse of Christendom.

Loren B. Mead summarizes how the actions of Jesus opened people to God's transcending mission, as well as the mission of the church:

> For Jesus, . . . Good news is profoundly contextual. For a blind man, good news is sight. For a lame person, good news is the ability to leap and dance or even walk. For the guilt ridden, good news is being forgiven. For the person in prison, good news is getting out of prison. For the lonely, good news is community. For the person—or society—crushed by oppression, good news is freedom. For a person possessed by demons, good news is to be released from their power. For hungry travelers, good news is food before they face the journey home. For a marriage running short of wine, good news is a few buckets of good wine. These stories lead me to think about Jesus' respect for boundaries. Each person is allowed freedom. . . . [H]e does not come with his bag of tricks to do his thing in spite of those around him. . . . He listens, and where

people open up their bad news, his good news is ready. He does not force or push his good news, but he never holds it back.[2]

God chose to accomplish God's divine mission by a *kenosis,* a mission of giving away, of emptying, in order that all who are human may be reconciled to Christ and share in God's glory (see Phil. 2:1-11). God's mission is expansive enough to include the entire globe as well as a cup of cold water, a prison visit, some clothing, and a welcome mat (see Matt. 25:42-45). The very nature of mission is to reach out; there is no such thing as an "internal mission."

Terry Fullam was ready to be questioned during his first interview as a potential candidate at St. Paul's Episcopal Church in Darien, Connecticut. Upon meeting with about twenty people from the church, no one seemed to have anything to ask. It appeared that quite a few had already made up their minds. He had written out a hundred questions he wanted to raise and, when no one was forthcoming, he asked the first one: "If this church were to disappear tomorrow, would anybody miss it?"

A ton of silence fell upon the room. No one breathed; all looked straight ahead for several seconds. Then they began to look at each other, seemingly embarrassed. Finally someone said, "Probably not much." Fullam then asked, "Do you really want to be a church, or are you actually looking for a chaplain for your club?" More silence.[3]

Fullam was inquiring into the missional understanding of St. Paul's leaders, and framed the concept of mission in stark relief by his use of two words, *church* and *club.* Every congregation could profit from asking the question, "If our church were to disappear tomorrow, would anybody miss it, and if so, who?" If the only ones who would miss it are already on the inside, then the congregation has probably settled down into being a nice, comfortable club.

On a dangerous seacoast where shipwrecks often occur there was once a crude little lifesaving station. The building was just a hut, and there was only one boat, but the few devoted members kept a constant watch

> over the sea, and with no thought of themselves went out day and night tirelessly searching for the lost. Many lives were saved by this wonderful little station, so that it became famous. Some of those who were saved, and various others in the surrounding area, wanted to become associated with the station and give of their time and money and effort for the support of its work. New boats were bought and new crews trained. The little lifesaving station grew.
>
> Some of the members of the lifesaving station were unhappy that the building was so crude and poorly equipped. They felt that a more comfortable place should be provided as the first refuge of those saved from the sea. So they replaced the emergency cots with beds and put better furniture in the enlarged building. Now the lifesaving station became a popular gathering place for its members, and they decorated it beautifully and furnished it exquisitely, because they used it as a sort of club. Fewer members were now interested in going to sea on lifesaving missions, so they hired lifeboat crews to do this work. The lifesaving motif still prevailed in this club's decorations, and there was a liturgical lifeboat in the room where the club initiations were held. About this time a large ship was wrecked off the coast, and the hired crews brought in boatloads of cold, wet, and half-drowned people. They were dirty and sick, and some of them had black skin and some had yellow skin. The beautiful new club was in chaos. So the property committee immediately had a shower house built outside the club where victims of shipwreck could be cleaned up before coming inside.
>
> At the next meeting, there was a split in the club membership. Most of the members wanted to stop the club's lifesaving activities as being unpleasant and a hindrance to the normal social life of the club. Some members insisted upon lifesaving as their primary purpose and pointed out that they were still called a lifesaving station. But they were finally voted down and told that if they wanted to save the lives of all the various kinds of people who were shipwrecked in those waters, they could begin their own lifesaving station down the coast. They did.
>
> As the years went by, the new station experienced the same changes that had occurred in the old. It evolved into a club, and yet another lifesaving station was founded. History continued to repeat itself, and if you visit that sea coast today, you will find a number of exclusive clubs along that shore. Shipwrecks are frequent in those waters, but most of the people drown! [4]

Again we iterate that, for the church, there is no such thing as an internal mission. Mission is for the congregation what the North Star was for the early mariners. Without it, every congregation stands in danger of losing its way.

Mission and the Church's Environment

Mission and the environment are the two most strategic components of the church's system (see Figure 5.1), in that the manner in which the two are brought into exchange relationships will largely determine the character of the congregation, and the extent to which it will ultimately succeed in its efforts. The relationship of mission and environment is a primary predictor of the system's ability to survive in the future.

Figure 5.1

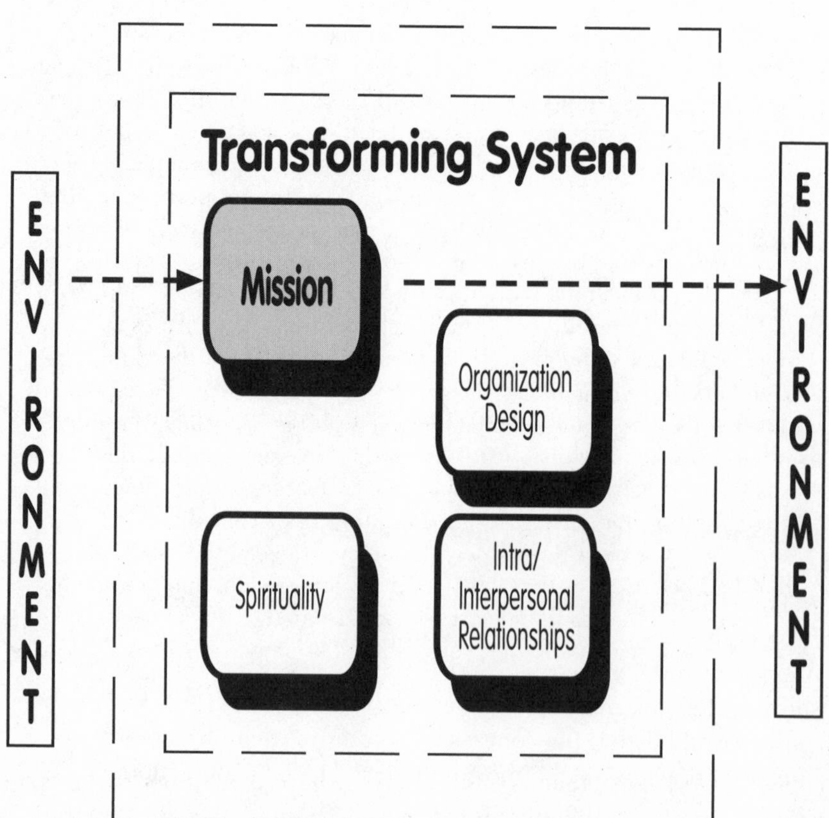

We should not allow ourselves to be deceived into believing that we can build strong congregations without understanding the realities of the congregation's environment—and then being able to define a clear and compelling mission.

> Every pastor should be a lay sociologist and understand how to interpret and apply demographics to ministry planning. We observe that growing numbers of pastors, who are accomplishing noteworthy results in ministry, are students of demographics, knowing how to do street research, and keeping up with the social and political developments in the community.

Richard Luecke suggests that Martin Luther succeeded in his complaints against the papacy, while all the earlier would-be reformers failed, because he understood his environment. "Luther shared much of the philosophy of these early reformers, yet he not only survived, he triumphed. How did he manage to succeed where others had failed? Why did his ideas take root while those of the others did not? One way to find the answer is to examine the environment in which he operated—the German states on the eve of the Reformation."[5] Luther understood his environment, and was therefore able to take the actions and communicate the message that was needed *at that point in time.*

No two churches share the exact same environment, and the congregation that defines its mission, paying no attention to its environment, or misreading the environment, is setting itself on a collision course with failure growing weaker from a lack of sufficient resources to sustain its life and ministry. Unless corrections are made, the congregation will eventually shrink, "gray," and die.

Discerning the Congregation's Mission

Three different lenses enable the congregation to discern its mission. First is the call of Christ to tend to the timeless and the timely needs present in the congregation's local environment: Second are the large shifts in the global or regional environments—those forces that happen in the world beyond the congregation's control that often open new and unexpected windows of opportunity. Third is the congregation's perception of God's call—the inner pull to move in a certain direction.

The Timeless and the Timely Aspects of Mission

The mission of the church is comprised of two streams (see Figure 5.2) that flow together to form a congregation's mission. One stream is timeless, the other is timely.[6]

Figure 5.2

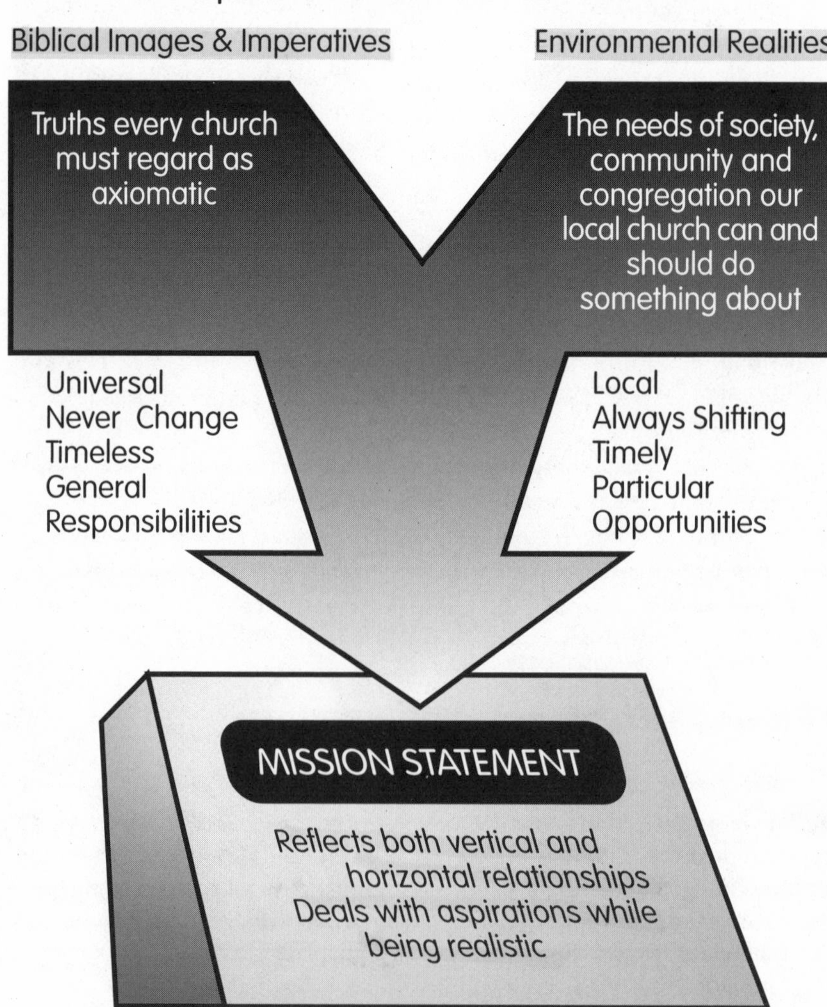

Components of the Church's Mission

The diagram illustrates that the mission of the church is determined by the needs and opportunities resident in its environment, and by the biblical imperatives. Some things about the mission never change. Other aspects of the mission are always changing.

The timeless aspects of mission are given to the church by Christ: "Go therefore and make disciples of all nations, baptizing them . . . and teaching them" (Matt. 28:19, 20). Following this stream we understand that the mission of the church is a transformed person. Every church, to be faithful to its mission, must take seriously its responsibility to evangelize, baptize, and teach those who have not yet made a serious and conscious commitment of their lives to Christ.

The timely aspects of mission are also suggested by Christ: feed the hungry, refresh the thirsty, welcome the stranger, clothe the naked, care for the sick and the prisoner (Matt. 25:42-45). Following this stream we understand that the mission of the church is to alleviate human needs that plague the body or crush the human spirit. These needs are more or less unique to every community. For example, there may be no persons in your community who are without food or shelter; however there may be many who need job training, counseling, release from drug addictions, help with knowing how to raise their children, financial counseling, or friendship.

QUESTIONS FOR REFLECTION UPON YOUR VIEW OF THE CONGREGATION'S MISSION

1. Where would you place your church on the following continuum in terms of the seacoast parable?

Seacoast Lifesaving Station — Seacoast Club

1 2 3 4 5 6 7 8 9 10

2. In what specific ways are you aiding the congregation in being "mission driven"?
3. How do you collect demographic information about your community?
4. What needs and opportunities within the community should you be pointing out to the congregation as you continue to reflect upon your mission?

The absolutely regrettable and quite unforgivable reality is that most churches have no sense of mission at all, while many others choose to focus on one of the streams, and to utterly neglect the others. The result is not mission. It is spiritual stubbornness and an abuse of the call of God to the congregation.

Large Environmental Shifts

Earlier, we considered the congregation's local environment. Now we call attention to the fact that the environment in which your church exists is larger, much larger, than the local context. There are global and societal forces that exert influence upon the life and success of your congregation. From time to time these global forces shift, sometimes with amazing speed. These global forces are often referred to as paradigms, and, when they shift, their displacement of the old paradigm is referred to as a *paradigm shift*. These global environments and their migrations are beyond the control of the congregation—yet some of them cause tremendous change in the congregation's local environment, changes which congregations often experience as bad news.

However, the church that is able to "read" these paradigm shifts may open new windows of opportunity for fresh and expansive ministries that can catapult the congregation to new horizons of growth and ministry effectiveness. As examples, we briefly discuss recent large environmental shifts, and how they are influencing the success or failure of congregations.

The Collapse of the Former Soviet Union

When the former Soviet Union collapsed, no one guessed the far-reaching effects this would have upon the churches in southern California. But today virtually every congregation in the area is painfully aware that when the fortunes of the Soviet Union shifted, theirs did also. Southern California was home to some of our largest military bases, war materials production plants, and much of our nation's military high tech research. Over the ensuing few short years following the collapse of the Soviet Union, the United States dismantled much of its defense industry—military bases were closed, many navy ships were mothballed, high tech contracts were canceled, and production facilities were shut down. In southern California thousands of military and civilian personnel were displaced. Hundreds of churches in that region found their financial fortunes dismantled also, as contributions nose-dived. Many churches were forced to close their doors; others were forced to curtail their ministries; professional staffs were reduced; and denominational plans for expansion were shelved. These rapid social shifts remind us that global and regional forces beyond our control nonetheless affect our congregations.

The Baby Boomers' Distrust of Large Institutions and Their Leaders

The baby boomers' distrust of large, bureaucratic institutions, which is often traced to the national conflicts that emerged around the Vietnam War, is another large scale environmental shift operating outside the control of religious institutions. This paradigm shift in our culture has spelled bad news for denominations and their local churches. However, it has been a harbinger of good news for the new independent, seeker-targeted congregations, and a few risk-oriented denominational churches, both large and small.

The bad news for denominations and their local churches: With the advent of the baby boomer generation, the denominations either slipped into decline or their ascending growth curves leveled off. Between 1964 and 1970 virtually every mainline denomination turned into deep decline. Was this because the denominations had suddenly all become inept? Was it something the mainline denominations could have controlled? The answer is probably no. Their sudden declines were in some part due to an environmental shift. Whereas previously every mainline denomination could count on their members' children to follow their parents into church membership and attendance, they now found that the baby boomers had broken step with tradition and were more likely not to join the churches of their parents—because they matured with a lively distrust of large, bureaucratic institutions.

The mainline denominations were unable to make the necessary, rapid structural changes to gain the baby boomers' trust, or the necessary changes in worship and program style to gain their interest. These denominational systems could not change because they are not designed to change. They are designed to go in one linear direction, and the baby boomers were not headed that way.

Some mainline congregations did succeed in making the necessary shifts, and have prospered even as their counterparts have withered. But for the local leaders who made the necessary shifts, it came by swimming upstream and against formidable denominational currents.

The good news for the new independent, seeker-targeted churches: Though the baby boomers eschewed bureaucratic institutions, they came on the scene with a high demand for quality, a questing for spiritual values, and tremendous pride and care for their (one, maybe two) children. It did not take long for some youth group leaders and pastors (most of them baby boomers, themselves) to recognize that the baby boomers had rejected the denominations, but were receptive to a local church that offered helps for everyday problems, cared deeply for their children, took Christian living and spiritual values seriously, and would challenge the seeker to study, service, and a serious Christian lifestyle. They provided the seeker a large menu of classes, programs, and services, that were custom-made as they listened to the needs and interests of the people they were seeking to serve. In virtually every urban and suburban community one or more large pastoral churches attracted these boomers (1,000+ in weekend worship/celebration services). Beyond these, many larger population areas now have mega-churches (3,000–20,000 in weekend worship/celebration services).

When the environment changes, our responses must change; or else we die—eventually.

What made the difference for these congregations? Why do they succeed even as denominations continue to fail? The answer in part lies in a fundamental difference of opinion regarding how the congregation should relate its mission to its environment. The new independent churches, and those few denominational churches who have shed the old skin in favor of the new, take their mission from the eternal axioms of Scripture (the primary source of authority) and from their immediate environment (the locus of ever-changing needs). The mainline churches take their mission from tradition handed down through hierarchies that were constructed by followers of founders, by responding to the quandries and conflicts of liberal democracies (such as disputes over sexuality), and from denominational polities which are revised by "win-lose" votes.

Responding to the Human Condition

Loren Mead describes a difference between Martin Luther King, Jr., and Billy Graham in how they assess the human condition. Both of these men came from Baptist roots and were fully grounded in the story of Jesus; however, they each experienced sin's alienating effects and the process of salvation in very different ways. This analogy might help us discuss the congregation's mission.[7] Graham views the "bad news" for humankind as individual alienation from God, which is the primary source of *pain in the person's life*. King, however, viewed the "bad news" as a corporate alienation from God, which is the primary source of *pain in society*. In response to the "bad news," both Graham and King announce the "good news," but from different perspectives. For Graham, the good news is, "knowing God in a personal, one-on-one relationship." King, on the other hand, views the good news as, "The only way to know God is in the midst of God's people, the church."

Mead points out, "Graham understands the response to the bad news of estrangement from God to be articulated and acted out in a 'religious' context and with religious language. Consequently he speaks of sin and salvation; his call to action is to make 'a decision for Christ'; the movement he urges is into religious community and sustenance."[8]

King, from a very similar religious tradition, came to a response to the bad news of estrangement from God to be articulated and lived out in the "secular" context with "secular" language. When he perceived systems oppressing the human spirit, he called for action mostly in the social arena, outside of religious institutions. Consequently, he spoke a language of oppression and freedom; his call to action was to meet violence with nonviolence on city streets; the movement he urged was within the secular social structures, the judicial systems—the political and economic realms.[9] In responding to the good news, there comes a sense of inner call. How one perceives the call is conditioned by one's interpretation of the bad news and the good news. For example, if one perceives the bad news and the good news as being intensely individualistic, then the sense of inner call will also tend to be individualistic; to live one's life in such a way as to be ready to meet God upon one's death.

On the other hand, if one perceives the bad news and the good news as being wrapped in the fabric of corporate and societal systems, then one's sense of inner call will tend to be within the context of a community, where one works with others to build a society in which all persons desire peace, justice, and love among all peoples. In Figure 5.3, below, we illustrate the two different interpretations of the bad and good news, and how each leads to a specific sense of mission.

In our perceptions above regarding the two different orientations to salvation and mission represented by Billy Graham and Martin Luther King, Jr., we defined the orientations in the extreme. However, many people and congregations would locate their position somewhere between the extremes or as a mix of extremes. We have inserted a numerical scale of one to ten beneath each item. You (or your staff or board) may want to find yourself on each of the scales.

Figure 5.3

Individual		***Corporate***
The pain of individual separation from God	***Bad news***	Corporate oppression; "Society's Sins"

1 2 3 4 5 6 7 8 9 10

You can be related to God through a one-on-one, direct relationship	***Good news***	You can know God in the midst of God's people, the church

1 2 3 4 5 6 7 8 9 10

The end and purpose of life is to live so that I am reunited with God at my death	***Mission***	The end and purpose of life is to participate with brothers and sisters in building a human society of shalom, where peace and justice and love reign

1 2 3 4 5 6 7 8 9 10

Both Graham and King felt called to their ministry—and they formulated their mission out of their perception of that call. Mead says: "I suggest that the inner pull to respond is much more than a pull or an attention grabber. It is no less than our perception of call. It is our open door to the good news we share." [10] When deciding our mission, our "inner pull" to respond toward one end of the continuum or the other is nothing less than our perception of Christ's call to us.

Becoming Clear About the Congregation's Mission

In the 1970s, writing a mission statement became a popular thing to do. The experience made a big difference in the ministries of many congregations.[11] For others, however, once the mission statement was written, practices reverted to "business as usual." For these congregations, writing a mission statement was an exercise; they did what they were supposed to do, and then got on with the "important stuff." For the former churches, the mission statement became a part of their operational belief system, if not their theology. It was utilized to define ministries and to target resources. For the latter, the mission statement became a part of their confessional theology. It was printed on their bulletins and occasionally read in the worship services—but it made no real difference in what they did, or how they spent their money.

The exercise of writing a mission statement may be a good and worthwhile process. However, we have come to understand that the most important thing for the congregation is to be always coming to clarity about the timeless and the timely needs in its community—and to regularly ask the question, "Which of these needs can we serve, and how?" Some aspects of the congregation's mission will never change, while other components of it will be changing—in order to keep the church relevant in its environment.

The Three Questions of Missional Clarity

The answers to three questions will bring the church to a clearer understanding of its mission: (1) Who are we? (2) What is our business? (3) How do we get it done? These questions were first suggested by Peter F. Drucker, who says that because "[these questions are] so rarely asked—at least in a clear and sharp form—and so rarely given adequate study and thought, is perhaps the most important single cause of [organizational] failure."[12] We will consider each question in order.

Who are we?

This is a question of being, and is, by far, the most difficult to decide, because the congregation and/or its leaders tend to think they already know who they are and, therefore, to spend time on this question is a waste. Do not be deceived, however, for this is one of those questions of which Peter Drucker says "the right answer is usually anything but obvious,"—to the congregation and its leaders. But to the community or to a chance visitor who has an ear to hear, the congregation's answer to the question is clear.

> Within twenty minutes of visiting with the pastor after arriving for the first time at a church, we heard the pastor's response to the "who are we" question: "We have the most famous organ in the United States. Many of the greatest artists come here when they want to make recordings." When we entered the sanctuary we were met by a man, who upon hearing that we were there to study the church, took us immediately to see the "famous" organ.
>
> Following the services, we were introduced to some people, who immediately asked what we thought about the organ music in the worship service.

The congregation's answer to the identity question is "We are the church with the famous organ." No one asked us whether we were helped by the sermon, or whether we found the congregation to be friendly (which they certainly were). But everyone wanted to know how we felt about the organ, because upon knowing our feelings about the organ, they assumed that they could also learn how we felt about them.

A corollary question follows the definition of who we are: *Is this who we want to be?* Again, finding the answer is usually anything but obvious. Judging from the comments made to us by members of the congregation discussed above, we might assume that, with the famous organ, they are who they want to be. But following the service we had an opportunity to interview several of the members privately. In the private conversations the organ was never mentioned. Instead we heard questions such as these: "Can you tell me, how can our church have so many wonderful people and still be so dead?" (I want the church to be more alive.) "You must know many bishops in the church. Can you tell us three or four to whom we can speak in confidence about getting a pastor with more life?" (We want to be the church that is alive and vibrant.) "Unless something happens to turn our church around I don't think we will be here after the older members pass away." (I want the church to survive this generation.)

Where did we get the more accurate assessment of the "who are we" question? Did it come from the people we met in the church, or was the question more correctly answered in response to the "is this who we want to be" question? No doubt both responses are accurate, but each alone is incomplete. The congregation does want to be known for its organ. On the other hand, however, it does not want to be known as the dying church with the famous organ.

There is, however, a third question that must be answered before the congregation can know the complete response to the question of identity. The question is: "Who do others say we are?" The congregation is not the only group with a perspective on who it is. Many constituencies in the community also feel that they know who the congregation is. For them, their impressions are valid, because they relate to the congregation out of their subjective impressions and objective experiences. They do not relate to the congregation out of who the congregation thinks it is.

So the answer to the "who are we" question needs to be supplemented by environmental responses to the "who do others say we are" question. Are we, for the outsiders, the church with the famous organ, the organ recording studio, the church with the empty (or full) parking lot, the church that cares for anyone who is in trouble, the church with the warm, gifted pastor? To discover the answer to this question, one must get outside of the church, into the community, to ask people who they say the church is.

The process of gathering community responses to the question will also make obvious any gap between whom you say you are and what influence you are having upon the community.

Recently, three pastors serving an Evangelical Free Church in southern California attended one of our marketing classes. They became interested in discovering the responses the community might give to the identity question. They asked the members of the congregation to invite friends who had never attended the church before to attend on a given Sunday, and to participate in a focus group the following Monday evening.

In the focus group, they asked the one-time visitors, "From everything you have ever heard about us, and your experiences in yesterday's services, how would you describe us?"

One of the participants, physically disabled and responding from a wheelchair, said she always thought the church was friendly, until she attended and found that the church had made no preparations for her coming, even though she was invited to come. She arrived alone only to discover that she could not get up on the sidewalk because there were no ramps. She visited the women's room to discover that the stall doors were too narrow to accommodate her wheelchair. She entered the sanctuary but no one told her where she might park her wheelchair.

Throughout the class the three pastors had maintained that theirs was a friendly church, conscious of persons' needs, and quick to accommodate visitors. They are responsive to most people, but there is much room for improvement, which became obvious when the congregation took intentional steps to set up exchange relationships with its environment. The answer to the "who are we" question seems deceptively simple, but often the answer is far from obvious.

What is our business?

Nothing may seem so obvious at first glance as the mission of a congregation. However, grappling seriously with the question "What is our business?" will soon demonstrate that the answer is not so simple or obvious. It can only be answered after much reflection and study. As an example of how easy it is to quickly arrive at the wrong conclusion regarding what our business is, Peter Drucker states that almost every hospital he has worked with has a mission statement that reads something like "Our mission is health care." But this is a misleading definition of the hospital's business, he says, because people enter the hospital only after health care has already broken down. A clear mission statement of an emergency room is "to give assurance to the afflicted."[13] Ford Motor Company makes cars; their business seems so obvious. But Henry Ford, the founder of the Ford Motor Company, did not take it as his mission to build cars. His mission was "to provide transportation for the common man." Building cars was a means of achieving the mission. And because these cars would be sold to common people, most of them far removed from the few automobile garages that were in existence, Ford stated a set of guiding principles for building and servicing the first car he built, the Model T. (These principles were heretofore unheard of among those who built cars.) The car would have to be reliable. The car would have to be simple in its design, so that the owner could service the car himself. Further, since the owners would generally live in rural areas, the parts must be available by mail order. And going beyond this, Ford said the car would have to be economical, since the buyers would be of meager income.

Reliable, simple, easy access to parts, economical; Ford's objectives became clear—after he had answered the question, "what is our business?" Ford allowed the "business" to be determined in large part by the marketplace, not by the producer.

Therefore, to answer the question "What is our business?" requires looking at the mission from the "outside-in." The users define the business. The name of the business, articles of incorporation, the buildings, and even its reputation cannot define the operational mission until the recipient is satisfied with the organization's product or service. The man who fell among thieves on the road from Jerusalem to Jericho fully understood this when he experienced the "mission" of the Good Samaritan in contrast to the "mission" of the priest and Levite (see Luke 10:25-37).

The story of Charles Simeon illustrates how he allowed the environment to help define the business of Holy Trinity Church, through his conversations with the poor in the church's neighborhood.

> In the later part of the 1700s, Charles Simeon was appointed vicar of Holy Trinity Church, whose congregation had dwindled to a handful of very unwilling parishioners. Simeon began his ministry by going from

door to door throughout his parish, repeating at every door these words, "My name is Simeon. I have called to inquire if I can do anything for your welfare." The poor and despised living in the bounds of his parish freely offered their suggestions, which Simeon gathered together into innovative ministries. Soon the poor and despised began to attend his church in ever-increasing numbers, and this caused the few rich members of the church to hate them even more. The rich members locked their pews during the morning service and hired a guest lecturer in the afternoon. Undaunted, Simeon made portable benches with money from his salary and placed them in the aisles and foyer. This went on for eleven years; in the twelfth year, the walls of conflict came down and the congregation was united. Simeon stayed for fifty-four years continuing to work with the poor.[14]

Others have taken the approach of interviewing persons in the marketplace to help articulate the mission of their church.[15] The mission of Jesus was outside of himself; its source was the Spirit and the needs of others (as they defined them) who were the recipients of his ministry. As with Jesus, the very existence of the church is not for itself; the integrity of its mission lies in reaching out to those who need good news, a message ultimately heard and received through loving deeds. His mission included both the eternal verities and the real human needs of those whom he served.

How do we get it done?

The church stands in the vortex of God's eternal purposes and human needs. Here the church is to do something—not for its own sake, but for the sake of others. If the church has "eyes to see and ears to hear," it will see its strategy for accomplishing its mission coming clear as it reflects upon the activities of God-through-Christ, as God seeks to achieve God's mission in the world—and by looking deeply into the human needs which are resident in its environment.

God has not chosen to prescribe a singular missional strategy for each and every congregation, because each congregation's environment, identity, and resources are uniquely a part of the dynamic mix that the congregation must put together to achieve its mission. God leaves it to each congregation to define its strategy—in the light of the timeless and the timely streams that flow together within its unique environment, and in the light of its resources.

If the congregation lacks the resources or the will to achieve its defined mission in its own community, it makes little sense to set out to save the world. Often congregations sing "We'll win the world for Jesus" as a dodge from going next door to see whether they can participate in the transformation of their unchurched neighbor. Your vision may be as big as the world, but your mission must be in sync with your resources: finances, goodwill, spirit, volunteer labor pool, and esprit de corps, to name a few.

Congregations should attempt a mission strategy that is as comprehensive as possible—because the surrounding needs are indeed, very great. However, a congregation must not try to do everything—at the expense of quality. It is far better to be excellent in one thing than mediocre in everything. Congregations can, however, encourage every member to stand "before an imaginary window, facing all the need and hurt of the world. Most, if not all, of us feel a pull to engage with some of that pain, whether it is physical pain or homelessness, ignorance or spitefulness, hunger or illness, guilt, a sense of lostness, hopelessness, or despair."[16] The congregation may then plan its mission strategy in the light of that to which the members feel the "inner call."

A part of the congregation's missional strategy should be to redefine the mission either when it is fully accomplished, or when changes call for a new mission—and not before. Drucker puts it this way:

> The basic rationale for the [congregation's mission will] be there for a very long time. As long as the human race is around, we'll be miserable sinners. . . . We will [however] have to look at the mission again and again to think through whether it needs to be refocused because demographics change, because we should abandon something that produces no results and eats up resources, or because we have accomplished an objective.[17]

In Part Two of this book we have discussed the importance of the congregation having a clear, distinctive sense of its mission. In doing this, we also discussed the congregation's environment as the "timely stream" which must flow into our understanding of mission—in the place where we are. We said that the relationship of the congregation's mission to its environment encompasses the two components of the congregation's system that most strongly influence the character of the congregation's systems. The congregation's boundaries by-and-large determine what the congregation will let in from its environment, and what it will keep out.

QUESTIONS FOR REFLECTION UPON MISSION CLARIFICATION

1. What large environmental shifts have affected your church in the last year? Has your mission been affected by any of these changes?
2. How has your "perception of call" pulled you toward a particular sense of mission? In what ways has this influenced the life and mission of your congregation?
3. How is your congregation approaching the three questions of mission clarification:
   - Who are we? (And, is this who we want to be?)
   - What is our business?
   - How do we get it done?
4. Is your mission helping you to respond effectively to the needs of your community? If not, how can you clarify the mission so that it can help you?

The Essence of Mission

1. Mission is invariably outward directed; there is no such thing as an "internal" (or introverted) mission.
2. The exchange relationship between the congregation's mission and its environment largely determines its future existence.
3. The congregation should devote special attention to three key areas while discerning its mission:
   - Include timeless and timely streams.
   - Pay attention to large environmental shifts.
   - Listen to God's call for its participation in the ministry of reconciliation.
4. The needs of the "user," coupled with the timeless nature of God, define the business of a congregation!

How You Can Implement Your Mission

1. Become a student of demographics!
   - Keep up with the social and political developments in the community and nation.
   - Begin executing "street research"!
2. Involve a team of people from the congregation in the process of mission clarification.
   - Without their involvement, the mission will only be "your" mission, not the congregation's mission.
3. Devote special attention to three key areas while discerning the mission.
   - Include timeless and timely streams.
   - Pay attention to large environmental shifts.
   - Listen to God's call for us to participate in the ministry of reconciliation.
4. Develop a clear sense of mission!
   - Eat, sleep, and breathe your mission.
   - It does not become "your" mission until you "own it" in your heart!

> Don't aim at success—the more you aim at it and make it a target, the more you are going to miss it. For success, like happiness, cannot be pursued; it must ensue, and it only does so as the unintended side effect of one's personal dedication to a cause greater than oneself.[18]
>
> Victor E. Frankl

> Make us worthy, Lord,
> to serve our fellow men throughout the world
> who live and die in poverty and hunger.
> Give them through our hands
> this day their daily bread,
> and by our understanding
> love, give peace and joy.
>
> Mother Teresa of Calcutta

In Part 3, following, we will address the congregation's energy source—the congregation's vision, the congregation's spirituality, and the congregation's spirit.

PART THREE

The Congregation's Energy Source

Introduction

> *What are the spiritual resources of ministers? What prevents them from becoming dull, sullen, lukewarm bureaucrats, people who have many projects, plans, and appointments but who have lost their heart somewhere in the midst of their activities? What keeps ministers vital, alive, energetic and full of zeal? What allows them to preach and teach, counsel and celebrate, with a continuing sense of wonder, joy, gratitude, and praise?*[1]
>
> Henri J.M. Nouwen

Organizational systems theory suggests that the transforming process of an organization has four strategic components which are interdependently and interdynamically related; that is, each depends upon the other to supply what it alone cannot. To cause change in any one of these will cause the others to change also. These components are: the mission of the organization, the structure of the organization, the intrapersonal and interpersonal relationships that persons experience as they live and work together in the organization, and the spirituality and spirit of the organization.

In the past decade corporations and institutions have recognized that there is a fourth strategic component that is active within the organization's transforming system. That is the vision, spirituality, and the spirit (esprit de corps) of the organization. Corporate America now recognizes that within the organization there is a spirit calling out, and a presence greater than the organization itself, and that management can draw on a spiritual force and cut through to a deeper level. It is now recognized that businesses and institutions (secular and sacred) each have a unique spirit about them—which fosters a corporate spirituality among people who work within the organization.

We quote one of corporate America's best known writers to give a flavor of what is being said regarding the spirituality of the secular organization. In his book *Stewardship: Choosing Service over Self-interest,* Peter Block addresses the subject:

> The revolution [in American business and industry] is also about the belief that spiritual values and the desire for economic success can be simultaneously fulfilled. Stewardship taken seriously is not just an economic strategy for a way to achieve higher levels of productivity or to succeed in a marketplace. It is also an answer to the spirit calling out. Spirituality is the process of living out a set of deeply held personal values, of honoring forces or a presence greater than ourselves.[2]

Dr. David Trickett, a theologian and scholar of organizational systems, assists corporations, governments, and nonprofit organizations in discovering and nurturing an appropriate spirituality for their organization, and assists the organization to recover its soul. *Spirituality* and *soul* are the words his clients used first as they came to him for help.

The relationship of the organization's spirituality and its spirit (esprit de corps), has an influence upon the mission, work, and relationships of the organization. This relationship can be simply defined: *mission and ministry consume energy, whereas spirituality generates energy*. And it is also true that no one thing—good structures, close relationships, a well-articulated mission, or all combined, can serve as a substitute for this divine presence and vital force. Spirituality and vision generate energy for the organization. Structures and mission consume energy. Without spirituality and vision, the organization will sooner or later run out of energy and wither.

Two types of religious organizations must pay attention to the spirituality of the workers (paid and volunteer), and to the spirit of the congregation or they will soon stagnate; those that are experiencing great success in their ministry, and those that are experiencing much disappointment and decline. For the former, spirituality is important to continually renew the vision and energies needed for carrying out ever-expanding ministries. For the latter, spirituality is important to bring new vision and new energy to launch the necessary ministries for renewal.

There is also a vital relationship between spirituality and vision.

Many congregations attempt to plan up a vision, which ends up printed somewhere on the bulletin, church stationery, or in the long-range planning document. The missing ingredient is the spirituality of waiting on God, spiritual conversation, prayer, covenant community, and the means of grace, all of which move the congregation and its leaders to be receptive to vision—God's dreaming God's vision of the Kingdom in the heart of a congregation.

God can indeed dream God's dreams in the hearts of receptive persons. However, no vision will be given to the congregation, or its leaders, if there be none there who are receptive to the word God is speaking to them. At some point, God's vision must be expressed and experienced by the congregation, and the key to this is that it is experienced by the congregation's leaders. While the seeds of vision may start anywhere, they must eventually be planted in the hearts of the congregation's leaders and managers.

This is where we begin Part Three, the vision of the congregation (chapter 6), followed by the spirit of the congregation (chapter 7).

6

The Congregation's Vision

Then the Lord *answered me and said: Write the vision; make it plain on tablets, so that a runner may read it. For there is still a vision for the appointed time; it speaks of the end, and does not lie. If it seems to tarry, wait for it; it will surely come, it will not delay* (Habakkuk 2:2-3).

There is such a thing as a "visible future." The seedlings of the twenty-first-century life are sprouting all around us if we have the wit to identify them. Most significant changes are preceded by a long train of premonitory events. Sometimes the events are readily observable.[1]

John W. Gardner

In the book *Leading the Congregation,* we discussed vision from two perspectives: the leader's vision and the leader as guardian of the corporate vision.[2] We encourage you to read what we wrote earlier in *Leading the Congregation,* as a supplement to what will follow. In this chapter we will discuss the various ways by which vision is expressed in a congregation.

The Difference Between Vision and Mission

Vision is not the same as mission. They are closely related, but they are not the same. Vision is a compelling image of a more desirable future; mission is "now." Vision generates energy, ignites passions; mission consumes energy, organizes passion into work. The mission of a congregation is practical, concrete, always in process because the organization is in an environment that is always in transition—a stable, static congregation is probably dead. The mission puts flesh and muscle on the vision, making it real.

Some examples that illustrate the difference between mission and vision are:

Jesus' vision was the kingdom of God.
Jesus' mission was to bring good news to the poor, release captives, recover the sight to the blind, and set free the oppressed.[3]

Figure 6.1

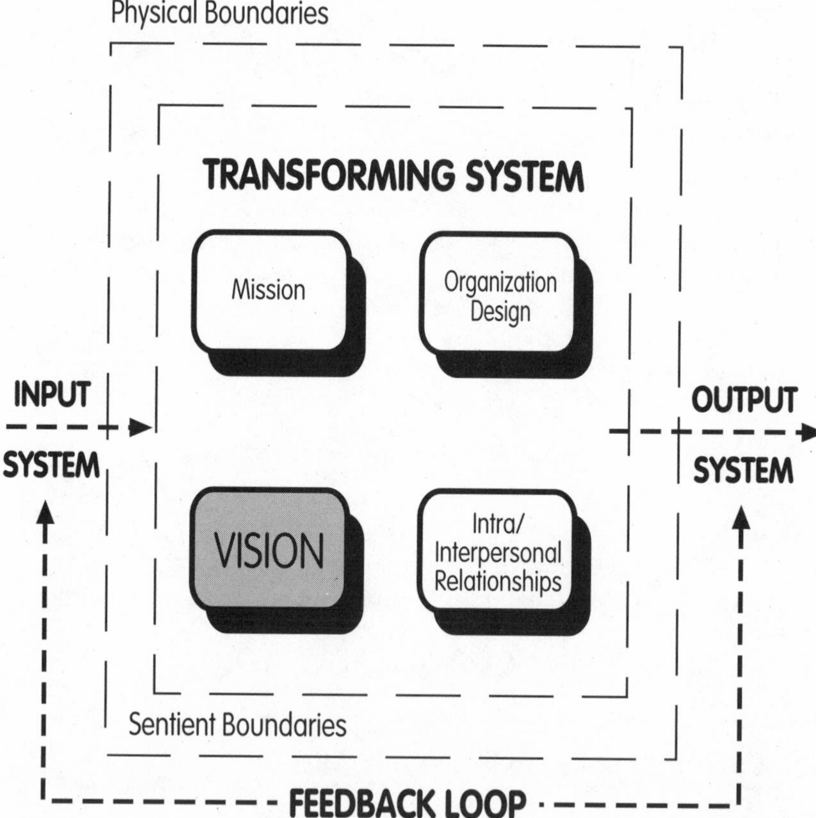

Moses' vision was the Promised Land.
His mission was to get the Children of Israel out of Egypt and into the Promised Land.

Paul's vision was people transformed by the mind of Christ.
His mission was to evangelize the Gentiles and to establish Christian churches throughout the Roman Empire.

John Wesley's vision was a renewed church.
His mission was "to spread scriptural holiness throughout the land."

Martin Luther King, Jr.'s vision was all people living together in equality and harmony.
His mission was racial integration and civil rights.[3]

A *corporate vision* is a recognition and an intense yearning for a more desirable future, shared in common among a group of people. Corporate vision is a desire that captures the heart and mind of a people, coalescing the resources of the group toward whatever action is necessary to cause the vision to become a concrete reality. Corporate vision coalesces the congregation's thinking, feeling, and doing into a common volition toward a destination—a future that in important ways is different from the present. Burt Nanus expresses it well when he says that "a vision portrays a fictitious world that cannot be observed or verified in advance and that, in fact, may never become reality. It is a world whose very existence requires an act of faith."[4] The visionary congregation is in sharp contrast to congregations that spend their day hoping for a better future, but that do nothing to make it happen.

How Vision May Come to a Congregation

There is no singular way to be captured by, or to create, a vision for the congregation. For some it seems to be a flash of insight, a revelation, a mystical and mysterious experience. For others it is a serendipitous circumstance, being at the right place at the right time with the right idea to create corporate commitment to a more desirable future. Yet for others it may be the ability to assist the congregation to see through a need, rather than simply seeing the condition and being paralyzed by it, or denying that it exists. Sometimes vision grows as persons talk together, sharing their hopes and dreams for the church. Following are some ways vision comes to a congregation.

Vision as a Result of Divine Encounter

The consistent portraiture of vision in the Old Testament is that of God communicating the vision to someone whom God has chosen to turn the vision into reality. The one to whom God has communicated the vision is then responsible to communicate the vision to the people. In these accounts God, or a chosen being, sometimes speaks to the chosen vision bearer; at other times God dreams the vision into the chosen vision bearer while the person is sleeping.

Scriptures give us no reason, whatsoever, to believe that God no longer communicates vision to chosen persons on behalf of the congregation. God still shares God's vision with congregations and with persons.

Many visions, however, are communicated in far less dramatic fashion, but are just as authentically from God. We will now consider some less spectacular means by which God communicates vision to the congregation. As you consider these approaches to vision, keep in mind that though we are discussing corporate vision, the same will hold true for individuals in the congregation.

A Divine Impulse, or a Blessed Hunch

In Scripture vision often came to persons who had come to a state of "nothingness" in which they could hear a "still small voice" or pay attention to an inner nudging. An example of this type is Elijah (1 Kings 19), who through much trouble, was reduced to utter solitary silence. Then, his head wrapped in his coat, a voice came to him.

Today, many authors writing to secular managers place heavy emphasis upon this type of "coming to vision." They call it *intuition*, or a *divine impulse*, or a *blessed hunch*. Out of these nudges, visions are sometimes born. Intuition must be practiced. Every person has an intuitive center inside him or her. However, most do not pay attention to it, and so they do not sense the impulse, or feel the hunch. And when they do, they do not trust it.

In history there are wonderful examples of priests and pastors who trained congregations to "see" God's vision for them through simple processes. One of these was Joseph Cardinal Cardijn, bishop of the Roman Catholic Church in Belgium.

Cardijn's tenure spanned 1906–1967. Cardijn was the founder of the Young Christian Workers Movement, which is one of the most powerful examples of lay ministry in history.

Cardijn first applied his method of assisting young persons to gain a vision of what God is calling them to do in 1912, working with a large group of girls and young women from 11–30 years of age. He divided them into "cells" according to their type or place of employment. He challenged each group to Christianize its place of work.

Cardijn utilized a simple method to help these groups to "see" what God wanted them to do to bring the spirit of Christ into their workplaces. The method contains a three-step process, and one very definite role for the priest or pastor.

The process was: First, the young women would look carefully at the work setting and the people who labored there —out of this relationship God helped them to identify a need to consider. Second, they would consider a Christian social teaching discussing this problem, and then the group would reflect seriously on a Gospel passage that addressed the issue in some way. Finally, the group would prepare a plan of action that provided a Christian solution to the problem.

The one and only role for the priest was that of chaplain or spiritual director. He taught them to pray and he taught them the Gospel stories. Nothing more. He insisted that the young, illiterate, inexperienced young people had to plan and carry out their ministries. "They have to be able to do it themselves," he insisted, "they have to fly on their own wings."

The Christian Youth Workers movement grew to 600,000 in Belgium, and into the millions in other countries. When Cardijn died, the Christian Youth Workers were in 109 countries.[5]

Cardijn's method is an excellent example of training a congregation, large or small, to come to vision through divine impulse or a blessed hunch. His story teaches us that the role of the religious manager is to teach the people how to look at things, how to pray, how to meditate upon Scripture and apply it to what they are "seeing," and finally to insist that they are to do God's bidding on their own. No advice, no expert opinion, no help except that the manager is consistently to hold the group in prayer for God's support and direction.

Seeing Through a Need

At times vision comes to a congregation as they see "through" a need to visualize a more desirable condition. The vision may come as an existential moment, a "flash" vision that is sparked out of an intense desire to do something to rectify a condition, or it may begin as a small, halting response and then "leapfrog" from a good idea to an encompassing vision.

This is probably one of the most common means by which congregations come to vision. By some means the group becomes aware of a pressing need or opportunity in the community and a vision is born within, compelling them to act.

We know of a group of pastors, all serving small congregations, who spent several days talking about the need to involve their congregations in ministry to their communities. Then without knowing the other pastors were doing so, each of them preached a sermon on Christian service, connecting his or her sermon to real needs in the community. Within three months, each and every one of the congregations had discovered a new and compelling vision for ministry—which transformed the life of every congregation.

John Bueno, founder of Latin America Child Care, a ministry of providing education, food, and health care to children throughout Latin America, describes the beginning of his vision when, one day, he walked out of the church he pastored in El Salvador, and observed the hopeless condition of the scores of children playing in the streets. He had seen the children many times before, but this time he was arrested by their great plight.

Then and there he asked himself, "How can I demonstrate the love of Jesus to these children in a tangible way?" Almost immediately, he was captured by a vision of a school for them with proper clothing, food, and medical care so that they could grow up as recipients of God's love.

Bueno saw a way to give these children of poverty a chance to grow up to be teachers, doctors, government workers, business leaders, pastors, and responsible citizens. The first school he started in El Salvador has grown to more than 250 schools in eighteen different countries with an organization of 1,500 teachers and staff serving over 75,000 children.

Vision as a Cloud 9 Experience

Another way for the congregation to come to vision is to define a "cloud 9" future for themselves. Vision is like the proverbial "cloud 9" in that it is always out there, beckoning us to hitch our wagons to it. If we ever succeed in achieving our cloud 9, viewing the future from that vantage point, we discover that our cloud 9 wasn't *the* cloud 9, for now we see another loftier and more desirable condition.

The analogy to cloud 9 is much like a "waking dream," a dream that comes to the congregation in expanding dimensions at various times during its journey. Each succeeding dimension does not invalidate the former dreams, rather they give a seal of authenticity to them.

Most of these persons have achieved earlier "cloud 9" goals in their lives, and now standing on top of their cloud 9s, they see another cloud 9 they never knew existed until they achieved their earlier lofty aspirations. These professionals would not say that their earlier visions were too small, but having accomplished them, it is now time to set their sights on a higher and more compelling cloud 9.

Administrators in higher education are reporting an increasing number of successful professionals in their 30s and 40s who are going back to school to retrain themselves for a new profession. They believe that this will open up new meanings of service to humanity.

There are many more thousands who wish they could do this or dream about doing it—but they never will. What makes the difference? Vision. People wish for many things, but believe their wishes can come true. Others dream of many things, but lack the inner fortitude and commitment to get up and make their dreams come true. Vision compels the people to get up and do something.

The Hopes and Dreams of the Members

God is speaking to persons in the congregation all the time. However, very few religious managers and lay boards take time to find out what dreams lie resident in the hearts of the people. However, when this is done, the results can be transforming. In attempting to form a corporate vision there are two possible approaches: (1) to listen through *discussion* and (2) to listen through *dialogue*.

Discussion: Usually when the managers and lay boards attempt to engage the congregation in discussion, they have already made up their minds regarding the future directions and programs of the church. They set up discussions with the congregation to sell them on the ideas—or at least to gain their compliance.

Discussion has the same root meaning as percussion and concussion—it is like a Ping-Pong game, where the ball goes back and forth over the net until it goes sailing off into space, or hits the net and drops down on the side of the one who last attempted to return it. The goal of discussion, like that of Ping-Pong, is winning, or wanting your particular point of view to prevail.[6]

> What makes dialogue successful is three basic conditions: (1) individuals must suspend their assumptions; (2) participants must see each other as colleagues; and (3) there must be a facilitator who "holds the context" of the dialogue.[7]

Dialogue: Dialogue takes its meaning from two Greek words; *dia,* meaning through, and *logos* meaning word—which suggests a discourse in which the full meaning is finally arrived at as persons seek to understand the ideas and feelings of others, building idea upon idea until the fuller meaning of all the ideas and feelings emerges. The result is a larger pool of understanding that cannot be claimed by any one of the persons as their own. In dialogue, no one is trying to win by having her ideas and desires prevail. Rather, all are supporting something beyond themselves, with the expectation that all will gain greater insight than that which could be gained by any one of them, alone. Peter M. Senge puts it this way, "In dialogue people become observers of their own thinking."[8]

So, a corporate vision can emerge as the management team listens to the personal aspirations and visions of those in the congregation. The corporate vision only matters to people to the extent that it reflects their hopes and dreams for the church, and blends their personal visions into the larger corporate vision.[9] In this type of vision casting, the manager functions as an orchestrator of the many personal visions resident in the congregation.

Some managers may be hoping for an even more simple form of vision casting. There are two that we will discuss.

Vision in Its Simplest Form

Sometimes the very thought of "having a great vision for the congregation," or of being a visionary person seems too overwhelming, too grand for our meager capacities. If this describes your feelings about vision, don't be discouraged. We can approach visioning by some very simple, and yet productive principles.

Just Make One Up

Get the congregation together in small groups or *in toto* to make up a desirable vision for the church. Then put it on and wear it for a while. How does it feel? How would it feel to the people if the congregation were to decide to pursue it for ten years? If the congregation seriously works at the vision for some time with decreasing passion and commitment from yourself and the people, you will have to get everyone together to decide whether this vision is real for the congregation or whether it is time to go back to the "drawing board."

Some managers would howl in protest about "making it up as you go." But we ask, "Why not?" If by the other means your group cannot arrive at a true and compelling vision for its future, what is wrong with the group pretending they have a vision—and then acting like it? "But," the rational manager asserts, "how can pretense be real?" To which we reply, "Visions aren't real. They are images of what will become real if the congregation gives its heart and soul to it." Furthermore, "In order to generate real vision, the vision must be conceived without reference to the apparent possibility or impossibility of its accomplishment. . . . Real vision is the conceptual crystallization of a result a creator wants to bring into reality."[10]

Vision is not about market trends, needs assessments, or brainstorming; it is about answering a very simple question, "What does God want to create through us?" Robert Fritz warns that many will believe this to be "drivel or heresy. And yet every professional creator, either consciously or intuitively, thoroughly understands the principle of how a creator conceives of a vision. The creator simply makes up the vision."[11]

Practice Foresight

Another simple and yet powerful way to create a vision is to practice foresight. Foresight is the ability to see what changes will most likely occur, and what the new ministry opportunities will be five or ten years from now. Foresight also is a point of view of the resources, competencies, and programs that will be needed to minister more effectively in the five or ten years ahead. Foresight gives a congregation the inner track to get to the future first, and to stake out effective ministries.

The way to begin practicing foresight is to practice forethought. Just think ahead five or ten years and ask yourself, "How can we get there first?" "First" here does not mean in terms of time, but in terms of "readiness." So the forethought questions are: "What will our community be like in five or ten years? What will be the most pressing social and human needs? How do we prepare ourselves to be ultimately effective with the new people, the new conditions, and the realities that are coming?"

The objective of foresight is to learn as quickly and as thoroughly as possible about the precise nature of "customer demand," the suitability and acceptance of ministry programs, and the need for adjustments in what you are now doing that will position you to minister effectively and productively five or ten years down the road.

There are many resources to help you practice foresight, most of which are available to you without cost—i.e., the local chamber of commerce, demographics journals in your local library, attending seminars given by pastors and churches who have proven their foresight ability, books on major cultural trends in your country and in the relationship between the congregation and its culture. One may raise a legitimate case for not having a vision, but there is no excuse for not practicing foresight.

Making up your vision, and practicing foresight, is still better than attempting to force a vision through a strategic planning process and Robert's Rules of Order. Vision will not submit itself to a planning process. Vision is caught, or it catches us. Vision may come in a flash. However, it also sometimes grows gently and without effort—like an apple ripening in the sun. From our discussion above we are now able to list several characteristics of vision in a congregation.

Characteristics of Vision

Often when historians or preachers talk about vision and visionary persons they do so in story form. This is because vision defies rational analysis or concrete form. From the discussion above, and from our observation and study, we will list some common characteristics of vision:

1. Vision is akin to "cloud 9." Achieving one vision gives the congregation the vantage point to see another.
2. Vision is suprarational. It defies rational defense, and is best communicated and understood through symbols and stories.
3. Vision is a mind and spirit altering experience. It aligns the congregation's energy, thinking, feeling, and doing into a coordinated, concerted volition—often described in the literature as a "journey" and a "search" for something that is difficult to find—and even more difficult to claim (e.g., the holy grail, the golden vial, the fountain of youth).
4. Vision is contagious. It has a way of drawing others into "questing" for it, sometimes spanning decades and generations.
5. Vision is always "bigger" than the congregation pursuing it, and its achievement comes at the expense of hard work, focused effort, and sometimes requires great sacrifice.
6. Vision calls the congregation out of its comfort zone. It calls the people to leave all the familiar and safe ways, and often leads into totally uncharted and untamed territory.
7. Vision burns the congregation's bridges behind it. Having once been captured by vision and setting out on the vision quest, there is no going back.
8. Vision and the "in-visioned" congregation will often appear as sheer madness to those who look in from the outside. Vision calls upon the congregation to undertake the impossible, often with insufficient visible resources. Thus vision is sometimes described as "the impossible dream."

The fact that so few congregations have a clear and compelling image of their future leads us to search for causes, or blockages, that keep congregations from being vision led.

Blockages to Vision

Announcing a Periodic Theme

The practice of promoting a cause or slogan that is thought up by some committee engaged in parliamentary process, which is then announced to the people as the "vision" for the next few years, is a serious blockage to true vision. Even the uninitiated member senses that vision does not come and go according to the calendar.

A suicide note once stated, "I could find nothing to die for, and so I had nothing to live for." Religious people sense that vision is something for which they would die. They know that vision calls for genuine sacrifice, persistent pursuit, and never giving up. Few people will invest such passion into a vision that they know will be replaced on schedule for another theme or program.

"God Told Me" Language

"God told me" language is taken too seriously to be bandied about lightly. Most of God's people take "God talk" seriously or, at least, they want to. Thus they remember vision talk when it is used in the context of a sermon or meeting. When a pastor announces, "God has given me a vision for this church," only to resign a year later in order to "answer God's call" to another place, the people remember. They remember that only a few months ago the pastor said, "God has given me a vision for this place." The people notice if the next call or appointment is to a bigger place and if it pays a better salary. They sense whether the pastor has accepted another call because he considers "these people too reprobate to support my ideas." The people remember, and any future visioning has been seriously damaged in that place for a long time.

When the pastor has, indeed, heard from God regarding the life of the church, she should say so in unambiguous terms, as should any member of the congregation. When the message is truly from God there will be at least some people who will recognize this, and immediately volunteer their energies to it.

In one congregation in the 1980's, a respected member of the church announced to the congregation that God had burned a message upon his mind: "Heal the sick." He confessed he had never had such an experience before and worried whether he had gone too far in this "prayer stuff." He asked that if anyone had ever had such an experience to please help him.

Before that day was over twelve people contacted him to

say, "Larry, if you are thinking about doing something for sick people who cannot afford treatment, count me in."

Out of one man's vision has grown a free clinic in that city that serves as a healing place for the poor. It has saved the lives of many children and adults. The clinic was nominated to a former President's 1,000 points of light.

On the other hand, the pastor must resist all pressures from the "more godly" in the congregation to force him into "announcing a vision," or to engage in "God told me" language merely "so our people can have a feeling that God has not given up on us," when, in fact, the pastor has not the faintest idea where the congregation is headed. This kind of false prophecy, to be distinguished from "making up or creating a vision," is an evil form of harassment.

We were called upon to intervene in a congregation that was taking great delight in attacking its pastor, who had been there less than a year. The criticisms were myriad and vicious. On our initial visit the first thing we did was attend a meeting of about seventy concerned members who had demanded a session with the pastor to voice their deep worries about the youth program. We walked in unannounced.

After hurling many accusations against the pastor for not caring about the youth, a concerned member slithered up to a microphone and said in a squeaky, melodramatic voice, "Pastor, you have been here several months, and you have never told us what your vision is for our youth program. What is your vision for our young people?"

The pastor replied, "I have only been here five months, and from the day I arrived I have been under a constant barrage of threats and accusations. To tell you the truth, I have not even thought about the youth program." "Well then," the accuser lamented, "if you don't have a complete vision for our young people, at least tell us your partial vision." Any hope for a compelling and burning vision in that place has been sabotaged for a long time.

Robert's Rules of Order

Perhaps the most damaging invention ever made to squelch creative group discernment is Robert's Rules of Order—and the vote. There is a place for the use of Robert's Rules of Order in the church; however, its appropriate place is not nearly so large and overwhelming as that which we have accorded to it. The debate and vote is an efficient way to make decisions, and should be used whenever the topic under consideration is of little consequence to the ministry, and is not heavily reliant upon the people's support; for example, when deciding whether to purchase a van from the Chrysler, Toyota, or Ford dealer.

However, when the major concern is the *effectiveness* of the decision, and not the *efficiency* of time, Robert's Rules of Order and the vote should be avoided. If the group cannot come to a corporate decision, it is far better to offer a serious matter into God's hands, asking that God point the way—and then draw straws, flip a coin, or cast lots.

We were called upon to work with a small but rapidly growing independent congregation. The growth had outstripped all of the group's spaces: sanctuary, Sunday school rooms, fellowship hall, parking. Over a period of a year and a half the board had appointed first one and then two building committees, each of which was charged with the responsibility to develop a plan that would address the issues facing the congregation. Each group took about six months to develop its plan. The congregation voted down each plan by a spread of less than 5 percent.

After the second committee failed in getting its plan approved, the board decided it would prepare a plan. The board worked on its plan for several months. Just before they were to present the plan to the congregation, one of the board members requested that the group vote, using a secret ballot. The group's vote split 50–50. They decided they could not present the plan to the congregation, fearing the people would do likewise. In the meantime two other plans were brought forward by members of the congregation, but were never formally presented or voted upon.

After some time, we were called upon to help the board resolve its dilemma. Upon hearing that the congregation had split on two votes, and the board on one, we decided that the group needed to learn a new decision-making approach. We met with the board only once, for about four hours. We never met the congregation.

We spent some time leading the board through a process to prioritize the space needs of the congregation, and looking at the five plans that had been considered formally or informally, to rank the plans in light of the board's priorities.

Then we spent some time preparing them to listen to God through Scripture and silence. Following this, we led the group into two sessions of extended silence, with conversation in-between. Then we asked each person to write on a piece of paper what they "heard" through the Scripture and the silence. Out of this, the group quickly came to full consensus around a totally new approach that was suggested in their writing.

The board presented the plan to the congregation; this time not calling for a vote. They led the entire congregation, of some 260 people, into an extended silence in which each one was to listen for God's leading. After the silence there was a time of sharing what persons had "heard" in the silence. After a while the board asked for a straw poll. The plan which the board "heard" in its silence was unanimously selected by the congregation.

The sense that God had indeed led them this way unleashed a dynamic that propelled the congregation into joy and much growth.

Debate and the vote are deadly mechanisms when the congregation is attempting to discern the mind of God for its vision, mission, and priority objectives. Debate is not likely to create an atmosphere in which everyone suspends their opinions in favor of discerning God's leading. Debate creates an atmosphere of contest, in which both parties are seeking to have their opinion prevail over the other's. The vote is simply the capstone to an already adversarial process. The vote creates winners and losers. In vision casting there must be no losers, for the success of the vision will depend upon the goodwill and sacrifice of all the people. We all know these things intuitively, and for this reason it often happens that when an important vote splits about 51 percent to 49 percent, someone who was numbered among the 51 percent will "move that we now cast a unanimous vote for the decision to show our solidarity."

Vision casting is not the same as planning. Plans are based on process—goals to be achieved, steps to be taken, deadlines, workers' responsibilities, and budgets. Planning is based upon a process. When people ask "Of all the alternatives, what do we want to do?" they are asking an appropriate question if they are in a planning process. However, if the group is seeking God's dream for the congregation, the question is inappropriate, for such processes reduce vision to one alternative among many, and it becomes a dead-end street that thwarts creativity and, ultimately, vision itself.[12]

QUESTIONS FOR REFLECTION UPON YOUR OWN SENSE OF VISION

1. What is your personal vision? How do you flesh out that vision in an understanding of your mission?
2. What stories do you associate with your own personal vision? With the congregation's vision?
3. How is your energy, thinking, feeling, and doing "fueled by" vision?

How Do You Know if You Need a New Vision?

There are some warning signs of problems in congregations that "speak louder than words." Many of these problems can be traced to a lack of direction, and the energy that vision inspires. Does your congregation need a new vision? To help you decide your answer to the question, we invite you to consider the following questions.

1. Are your key leaders and managers paralyzed because of frequent and often endless disagreement? Can you start no new ministries because the group cannot agree on anything? Does defensiveness and passive-aggressive behavior over hairsplitting issues prevent attention to important results?
2. Is there a spirit of goodwill, fun, excitement, and trust in your congregation? Or is there a spirit of cynicism about present ministries, a spirit of pessimism about the future?

3. Is your congregation declining while new congregations are springing up around you that are growing?
4. Is your congregation out of touch with the environmental changes surrounding your church? Do your leaders and managers feel threatened or excited about these changes?
5. Are there signs of declining pride in your congregation? Are people hesitant to bring friends, or tell other people about your congregation? Are paid staff working only for their weekly paychecks with little passion and excitement for the congregation's ministries?
6. Are people involved in the ministries of your congregation afraid to take risks? Do they only "go by the book," unwilling to initiate anything new, and resisting any type of change?
7. Do people dwell on the "good days" of the past? Are they paralyzed, believing that a bright future is "too good to be true?"
8. Do people talk about the future in the same way as they have for years, without ever doing anything about it—the platitudes being predictable and boring?
9. Is there a hyperactive rumor mill that majors on "pet" topics or insignificant issues—and drains off energy? Do people trust the church leaders and managers?[13]

Winston Churchill once said, "It is no use saying 'we are doing our *best.*' You have got to succeed in doing what is *necessary.*"[14] Nothing is more necessary for congregations who answered "yes" to the above questions than to have the right vision for leading them into a more desirable future.

QUESTIONS FOR REFLECTION UPON THE NEED FOR A NEW VISION

1. Does your congregation need a new corporate vision? Do you need a new personal vision?
2. Do you have enough room within yourself to be "caught" by a vision?
3. Are some of the ways of being caught by a vision outside your mental boundaries? If so, how can you help "make room" for these opportunities?
4. Do you have foresight skills that help you encourage the eagerness and aspiration of others? If not, how can you cultivate those skills within yourself?

The Essence of Vision

1. Vision produces energy; mission consumes energy.
    - This energy is created as the congregation's thinking, feeling, and doing are coordinated into a volition toward one's target.
2. Spirituality is the seedbed that spawns vision.
    - Within the disciplines of silence and journaling, we develop the courage to allow a vision to "catch us."
3. Vision can break out in the congregation in a thousand places. Every worker can have a vision of how his or her ministry will create a new condition or future (e.g., the Sunday school teacher can have a vision of what the students will become as a result of the class).
4. These many visions may come together to form a corporate vision for the congregation. As a result of all we do, a new future or condition will exist.
5. The congregation may be led on a Vision Quest—a search for the Golden Thread or Holy Grail.
    - The congregation's vision may be taken from the vision of the pastor and leaders.
    - What is required of the religious manager is that she be ethical and mature in witnessing to her vision. Do not force it, but announce it, and let the others respond to it in dialogue.
    - Visions grow in settings where people share their ideas, passions, hopes, and dreams.

How You Can Implement Your Vision

1. Understand what God wants to create through you.
    - Tap into the vision already created, but not yet apparent.
    - "Chisel" away the debris that encases the final object of beauty in your ministry and calling.
2. Develop an "attending ear" toward the inner voice and a "clear eye" of needs around you.
    - Spirituality must be the seedbed that spawns vision!
    - Through dialogue with God and the people, personal visions can be fused into a corporate vision.
    - You can perform the role of a conduit to funnel the many personal visions resident within the congregation.
3. When a vision catches you, don't look back!
    - Burn your bridges! Forget the farm! Scuttle your ships! Go for it!
4. Remember the seven different levels that describe the degree to which persons commit themselves to a corporate vision:

    Commitment: Those persons who really want the vision and will do whatever it takes to make it happen.

    Enrollment: Those persons who want the vision and will do whatever it takes within the "spirit of the law."

    Genuine compliance: The "good soldiers" who, seeing the benefit of the vision, will do what is expected of them (and perhaps even more).

    Formal compliance: The "pretty good soldiers" who will do what is expected (but nothing more).

    Grudging compliance: Those persons who do not see the benefits of the vision, but they also do not wish to lose their status or position. They do what they have to do, but make their resistance known.

    Noncompliance: Those persons who do not see the benefit of the vision and will not do what is expected of them. No one can make them become involved.

    Apathy: Those persons with no interest or energy who are neither for nor against the vision.[15]
5. Be mindful of the blockages to vision.
    - Scheduled themes of the "vision" for a period of time.
    - "God told me" language utilized to exert one's will over another.
    - Using Robert's Rules of Order as a funnel for "passing" or "denying" a vision.
    - Planning a vision.

7

The Spirit of the Congregation

> *Medical technology . . . can keep a patient alive under extraordinary circumstances, creating ethical and legal debates as to when a person is truly dead. If the heart or brain is "dead," yet the body lives with mechanical support, is the person alive?*[1]

Every congregation, like General Motors or the League of Women Voters, has its own "spirit." Like individuals, the congregation can make a difference, for better or worse, by the spirit it projects from the inside to the outer world. It is this spirit projected on the outer world that shares responsibility in creating that reality. The concept of organizational spirituality and spirit is not limited to religious institutions. In recent years corporate America has also recognized that businesses and institutions have a defining spirit about them—which fosters a corporate attitude and worldview among the people who work within the organization. In a chapter entitled "Spiritual Leadership," James A. Ritscher states:

> Spirit is the sense of vitality, energy, and vision which is at the heart of all organizations—with some organizations being more inspired than others in how they operate. One of the basic functions of leadership is to stimulate and focus the organization's spirit. . . . By spiritual leadership, I mean two things: (1) The leadership of spirit (in the sense of vitality or esprit de corps) in a business or other organization, (2) Transformational leadership: leadership that draws on a spiritual force and hence cuts through to a deeper level and is creating a vital and effective business.[2]

Jay A. Conger, in his provocative book *Spirit at Work*, describes how those communities that once served our needs for growth and connection—churches and temples, the extended family, and civic communities—no longer provide the help we need:

> Within a matter of a few decades, the ability of these other communities to provide satisfying links to others and to a greater good has lessened dramatically. Yet our needs and longings for spirituality, for community, and for contribution have not diminished. Instead they have, for most of us, simply slid into neglect. This neglect is in turn creating a growing hunger.[3]

So we see that secular corporations and institutions recognize that spirituality and spirit (esprit de corps) do have influence upon their mission, structures, and relationships. They recognize that there is a spirit calling out, and a presence greater than ourselves, and that leadership can draw on a spiritual force and cut through to a deeper level. The relationship of spirituality to mission, work, and relationships can be simply defined: mission and ministry consume energy; spirituality and a healthy esprit de corps generate energy.

This chapter discusses the spirit of the congregation-as-system. The word *spirit* as we use it is an amalgamation of two concepts of spirit. The first concept of the congregation's spirit is that Spirit which is promised in Acts 1:4-8. The Scriptures often use the word *pneuma* when referring to this Spirit. Pneuma in the original language has two meanings: one is the life's breath, or the breath of life. The other meaning is wind, or the force of the wind that blows.

The second concept of the congregation's spirit is its esprit de corps, translated "the spirit of the body," and defined as the common spirit of the group, or group spirit existing in the members of a group. The group spirit may inspire enthusiasm, devotion, high commitment to the group's purpose, and strong regard for relationships within the group. Or the group spirit may provoke quite the opposite: i.e., ennui, indifference, lethargy, and disregard for relationships in the group. When the common spirit of the congregation tends toward the latter, the spirit is expressed as a dark force which harms the congregation and repels people from becoming a part of it.

The Congregation's Common Spirit and Its Spirituality

Figure 7.1

The Congregation's Spirit

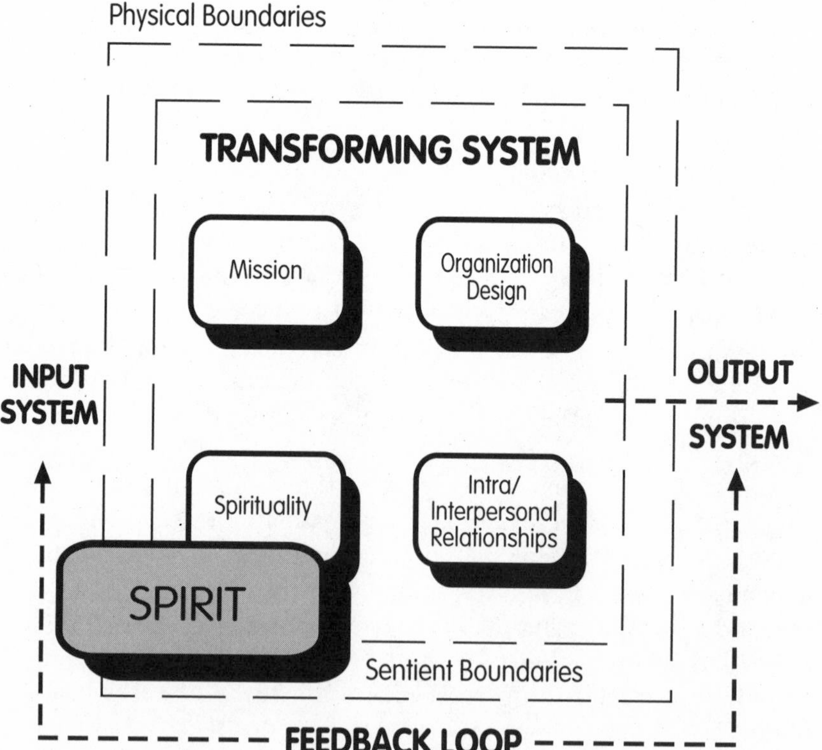

The Spirit of the Apostolic Church

The fifth book of the New Testament is called the Acts of the Apostles. It is a story of the actions of the followers of Jesus, and the congregations that came into being wherever they went throughout their world. The story begins with an interesting twist: The first thing they were to do after Jesus left them was nothing—until the promised Spirit came to them. Then in the power of this Spirit they went out and witnessed to the love of God, and tackled the domestic and social issues in their locale. They fed hungry people and gave clothes to those who had none. They started a ministry to care for the needs of widows, and when one of their congregations needed help, others sent them money.

Everywhere these people went with their simple witness and generous actions, people were attracted to them—by the thousands. Always they attracted their neighbors first, those who lived next door and down the street.

Luke describes the attraction that drew people into their communities as an almost irresistible force, much like the attractive force a magnet has upon a needle. He says: "None of the rest dared to join them, but the people held them in high esteem. Yet more than ever believers were added to the Lord, great numbers of both men and women" (Acts 5:13-14).

As we ponder the drawing power of these early congregations, we wonder:

> Why don't our [congregations] send out people in that way? Why aren't our own [congregations] more attractive? Why is our mission activity lacking in spirit? What has happened to us?
>
> Many of us have experienced entering a church for a Sunday service and noting that everything in the parish seems to be dead. There are people, but they all seem gray, even when dressed in bright colors. The singing seems muted—booklets are opened, so are some mouths, but no hymn is raised, no rhythm caught. The organ overpowers the few small voices. The minister does all he is supposed to do. The homily is well prepared. The collection baskets go around. The service is liturgically correct. . . . The service begins, continues, and ends without a whimper. Symbols are used, the word is spoken, bread broken, but the liturgy falls flat. The young are obviously bored; the older participants yawn behind their hands. After the service everyone moves out, some hands are shaken. The homily—some say—was interesting. Then they are on their way, the door of the church is firmly closed, and after a last look back, it is all over for the week. You decide never to come back, if you can help it. You want to find another community. A caricature? Maybe . . .
>
> And then you come into a community where everything breathes joy, hope, and spirit. You notice it when you come in; people welcome you with a smile here and a word there. The singing is taken up by all. The young sit with the old. Young people blow their trumpets and swing their tambourines, while the older solemnly beat their drums. Psalms

> are sung, and the hymns started by the choir are taken up by all. . . . Simplicity and utter seriousness seem to go hand in hand. It is a joy to have been there. You decide to join them again when possible. You leave a better and divinely inspired person. You know again what you are about, living your life and doing your work.
>
> Both types of parishes do exist. We all know them. It is not difficult to guess the difference. It is not the Spirit of Jesus as such. That Spirit is present in both. It is in the sharing of that Spirit that they differ.[4]

Every congregation has a common spirit of the body (esprit de corps) that attracts or repels, consoles or discourages, liberates or subjugates those who come into that "house."[5]

The Spirit of the Roman Church in the 12th–16th Centuries

It is easy for us to "see" the esprit de corps, the spirit of the body of other groups and congregations. To be outside of the group gives us an excellent vantage point from which to see, and know. For example, does anyone have difficulty in understanding the spirit that drove the Popes Alexander III, Lucius III, Innocent III, Honorius III, Gregory IX, Innocent IV, and their inquisitors, to charge as heretics and traitors those who disagreed with the Church's doctrine and practices, and to excommunicate, imprison, torture, and burn them at the stake? This was a spirit that expressed itself in repeated cycles from the 12th into the 16th centuries.

Contrast this with the spirit that inspired, encouraged, and compelled others who worked to reform the institutional church in those times; for example, Martin Luther, who at his own inquisition stood firm; the young Joan of Arc, who before the inquisitors also stood firm—and died for it.

So we see that not all religious groups have the same spirit about them. The esprit de corps of the early disciples was different from the spirit of the Jewish religious leaders. The spirit of the Inquisition was different from the spirit of the Reformation.

Even a cursory review of church history demonstrates that not all congregations, and not all leaders, have the same spirit. The same holds true for today; not all congregations or religious managers share the same common spirit.

QUESTIONS FOR REFLECTION UPON THE ESPRIT DE CORPS IN YOUR CONGREGATION

1. How would you describe the esprit de corps in your congregation?
2. What is the common spirit that defines your thinking, your actions, and your relationships with one another in your congregation, and in your community?

Unless you manage to maintain an attractive spirit, then everything the congregation does will bring disappointment.

The Spirit of the Pastor Projected upon the Congregation

The esprit de corps of the congregation is strongly influenced by its spirituality—and by the pastor's spirituality and the spirit that commonly characterizes her management. To a significant degree the common spirit of the congregation is a shadow reflection of the pastor's inner world. There cannot be a true, genuine spirituality and, at the same time, a darksome, shadowy common spirit of the body.

It is crucial, therefore, that the religious manager asks, "What is the condition of my spiritual life with God, and what common spirit am I projecting on the congregation?" Or conversely, if you have been the pastor of the church for four or five years and everything seems dark, conflicted and divided, you must consider whether this is a reflection of the spirit that you commonly project upon the congregation, the spirit that resides in the unexamined spaces of your mind.

Parker J. Palmer describes the spirit that the religious manager may project upon the congregation in these terms:

> [We] project either a spirit of light or a spirit of shadow on that which is other than us. We project either a spirit of hope or a spirit of despair, either an inner confidence in wholeness and integration or an inner terror about life being diseased and ultimately terminal. We have a choice about what we are going to project, and in that choice we help create the world that is. Consciousness precedes being, and consciousness can help deform, or reform, our world.[6]

It may be tempting to argue that the religious manager does not, and cannot, have such singular influence upon the spirituality and common spirit of the congregation, but history does not stand on our side when we do. Did the one man Martin Luther have any influence on the common spirit and the spirituality of the Reformation? Does Mother Teresa have any influence on the spirituality and the common spirit that define the experience of the sisters who work with her, and the afflicted whom they serve? Was not the spirit of the Reformation a reflection of the spirit of Martin Luther? Is not the joy and love that is commonly shared by the Sisters and the afflicted not a reflection of the spirit of Mother Teresa? Is not the spirit of your congregation a reflection of your spirit?

We said earlier that one of the most important things a religious manager manages is the common spirit of the congregation. Now we can amplify this premise to say that the most important thing a manager manages is also his or her own spiritual formation. In our earlier book *Leading the Congregation* (the second book in a trilogy, of which this book is the third), we identify the common spirits that pastors may project upon the congregation when they live unexamined lives.[7] We encourage you to read what we say about one's ministry when one is operating out of the dark side of his or her spiritual and common experience.

Organizations cannot be understood apart from a recognition and understanding of their spirituality and spirit which indwells it.

QUESTIONS FOR REFLECTION UPON YOUR CONGREGATION'S SPIRIT

1. What types of words do people (guests and members) use to describe their feelings about the church? Do they seem to gain energy or be burdened by their involvement?
2. What spirit do you see and feel that the congregation is nurturing? Do you want to continue to cultivate that spirit?
3. How will your congregation nurture the spirit that it desires?

Practical Conditions for Tending the Common Spirit of the Congregation

Three corporate abilities support, and are supported by, the common spirit of the congregation. They are: silence, timing, and discernment.

Silence and Stillness

> If you go away alone and find a tree and sit down with your back against it for only half an hour, listening inside yourself for the Word of the Lord—Jesus will speak to you.
>
> Robert Doherty, S.J.

Nothing is more important for a church board or ministry team than to learn how to sustain brief, and longer, periods of silence. Even brief periods of silence that allow the board members to listen to their own deeper intuitions, and to God's speaking from within during stressful or confusing sessions, will often help the group come to clarity and accord. When the discussion is over and it is time to decide, five or ten minutes of silence for the board members to listen to God's leading from within will often bring a sense of calmness and confidence to the vote.

Church groups often pray for God to "open the door" for them, or to come to them in their hour of deciding. Christ has something else to say about a door and Christ's coming: "Listen! I am standing at the door, knocking; if you hear my voice and open the door, I will come in to you and eat with you" (Rev. 3:20). Christ is always standing at our door, always knocking. But unless those inside the house are quiet and listening they will not hear the knocking, for Christ never knocks very loudly—just persistently.

Verna Shawchuck led a weekend planning retreat for the leadership team (volunteer and paid) of a very active, "go, go, go" congregation. For two days she listened as they planned new undertakings and worried whether the present ministries were accomplishing enough—but she sensed a spirit of tiredness and no celebration among the group. As the time drew near for the group to decide the church's ministry menu for the next year, Verna suggested that each one should go away alone for a half hour to sit by the lake, or stroll through the woods, or simply sit for a half hour with their backs against a tree.

When the group returned, she asked them what Word had come to them through the silence. To the last person they all said, "I heard God saying, 'Do not work so hard. Don't worry about not doing enough. The congregation is already too busy to simply enjoy my love.' " In a few minutes the group dropped all their new plans and began talking about the congregation having some fun times. The pastor later told Verna that the result was a highly fruitful and enjoyable year of ministry for the congregation.

This interior stillness is more than being still and letting your mind wander into various dusty closets of its choosing. Rather, it is a purposeful stillness—and an openness for metanoia. Just as the Queen's guard stands still—and yet fully attentive to hear Her Majesty's distant footfall—so the silence we suggest is an active listening in stillness.

Timing

In all of history nothing has proven more powerful than a good idea, acted upon at just the right time. But those who acted often went counter to all the current ideas of convention, and against the wishes of powerful rulers and forces. Nonetheless, again and again social history has been altered by the power of one good idea. How did these change agents know that their idea would succeed even when all outward circumstances seemed to point to the contrary?

They felt in their bones that the time had come. These now famous change agents all shared three things in common: first, they had a good idea. Second, they felt intuitively that the time had come to act on the idea. Third, they possessed the courage to act—all outward signs contradicting, and against formidable forces. A fourth characteristic shared by most of them is that they entered upon the scene of social history as relatively unknown and obscure individuals. Consider, for example, Mahatma Gandhi, Albert Einstein, Martin Luther, Martin Luther King, Jr., and W. Edwards Deming, to name a few.

Were these the only ones who had a good idea in their time? The answer is no. For every "great idea" they had, there must have been thousands of others who also had good ideas. In fact, we know that many had the same good idea; yet their efforts failed—either because they did not have a good sense of timing and acted at the wrong time, or because they did not possess the courage to act at all.

Those who did act at the right time were persons of great spirit, and they were in tune with *the Spirit*. They felt their idea to be something of a divine nudge. They acted on a blessed impulse. They were in tune with a divine center within. As examples of what we have here stated, we will briefly consider the ideas, timing, and courage of: Martin Luther and W. Edwards Deming.

Martin Luther

Martin Luther was a relatively obscure priest, a teacher in a newly founded university in the small, isolated city of Wittenberg, when he arose early one October day in 1517, walked the short distance to the church, and nailed his arguments against the powerful Roman papacy regarding the sale of indulgences (a form of trading money for the assurance of gaining a fast track to heaven) to the front door. "Wittenberg?" people must have asked, "Where is Wittenberg, and who is Martin Luther?" One would have expected that such courage might come from Cologne, or Augsburg, or Nuremberg, Germany's largest cities (each of them then having 30,000 to 50,000 residents). But Wittenberg?

Luther was not the first to have firmly held opinions against the sale of indulgences and all that they represented—a religious and national system gone mad in its quest for power over the rank and file in its gluttonous appetite for wealth. On the day Luther pounded his theses on the front doors of the palace church, the Church of Rome owned at least one-third of Germany's land and more of its wealth. The Roman church had succeeded in amassing such wealth across Europe by colluding with the lords and rulers of the European countries. They scratched each other's backs and all grew rich by standing upon the shoulders of the poor, and exacting backbreaking taxes from one and all.

But this was not new to Luther's day. It had gone on for at least a century, and many before Luther had complained about the religious system that made a farce of religion while enriching the gentry and the Church. Most of these had paid with their lives for their ideas, and all of the earlier reformers had been silenced. Consider, for example, Pope Innocent III's bloody crusade against the "heretics" of southern France; John Wycliffe, whom the Church forced underground for questioning the sacramental powers of the Church; John Hus, who was condemned and burned; and Girolamo Savonarola, who attempted to reform the Church's ways, and for this he was tortured and burned.

Then came Luther, who not only survived, but triumphed over all the religious and national powers of his day. What made the difference for Luther? Timing. Luther had two things going for him that the earlier reformers did not, and this made all the difference. First, Luther sensed correctly that the time had come in which a challenge made against the Roman Church's practices of selling indulgences and grabbing much of Germany's wealth might succeed. Second, the printing press had been invented and made operational.

During the times of the earlier reform attempts, the lords and princes of Europe were satisfied with Rome's behavior because they, too, were thereby enriched. But by 1500 the tides had turned, for now Rome was putting the squeeze on the nobles as well as the poor. So the leaders of the European countries quickly climbed on board Luther's bandwagon. Suddenly, Rome found itself in opposition by many, if not all, of its former allies throughout the continent.

This rapid spread of support for Luther's theses could not have been possible were it not for the printing press. Within days of Luther's pounding in Wittenberg, thousands of leaflets were printed and carried across Europe. Almost overnight, the European leaders, and growing numbers among the populace, knew of Luther's courageous act. Before the papacy could organize itself, Luther became too well known and supported by the populace for the Church to arrange a quick hearing and tidy disposal of him. Contrary to all of the earlier reformers, Luther found himself to have a growing support not only of the nobles but also the rising middle class, and among the peasants—who were not only prepared to oppose Rome, but also to rebel against their secular overlords.

Luther's reformation kept Europe at the boiling point for nearly a century. Ultimately, the priest in Wittenberg, armed with a good sense of timing and his good ideas, proved powerful enough to prevail over his archbishop, his pope, and the emperor.

W. Edwards Deming

In the 1920's Deming proved himself to be an outstanding student in engineering, physics, and mathematics, so much so that he was invited to study at Yale. There Deming met Walter Shewart, who was doing groundbreaking work around his new idea—quality control.

Shewart was becoming well known at AT&T and other American industrial institutions for his ideas of eliminating poor quality output. For Shewart, being good in some things but not good in everything was not good enough. What was needed was continuous improvement. These concepts Deming would later introduce to Japan at the end of World War Two. The Japanese coined the term *kaisen* for "continuous improvement." Kaisen means do it right the first time and to make at least one continuous improvement—every day.

Before Deming introduced these concepts to Japan, he was invited to help train the U.S. war industry in the application of high-quality concepts. The concepts worked. Even though the American factories were managed and operated by low-skilled and untrained workers (the managers and experienced workers were away fighting the war), they produced huge supplies of high-quality war materials.

Then the war ended, and the old managers returned to once again take control of American industry. The factories were remodeled to produce domestic products, and their coffers were overflowing with money. Deming and his ideas of quality were quickly thrown out in favor of emphasis on quantity. After all, the orders were rapidly coming; why slow them down? The old spirit of "anything will do" returned with a vengeance, for quality was not a habit of the old managers.

The spirit of the old managers was effused with the idea that the American consumers would buy anything, and by the fact that the war had obliterated all foreign competitors.

Then General Douglas MacArthur, who was commissioned by the U.S. government to oversee the restoration of Japan following the war, invited Deming to present his ideas to the Japanese. Deming went to Japan. The conditions that Deming observed upon his arrival were dismal. The Japanese industrial base was in complete shambles; their managers were ill equipped to face their daunting task; the factory buildings were torn apart from the bombing; and the workers were totally untrained. But because they had absolutely nothing to lose, the Japanese welcomed Deming's ideas with open arms. The rest is history. Quality became the Japanese standard. In less than a decade, the Japanese turned their entire industrial base around, and Japan stepped onto the map as a world competitor to be reckoned with. For the Japanese,

Deming's idea of quality was an idea whose time had fully come.

What was it that caused Deming to succeed so greatly in Japan, even as the Americans returned to their old ways of doing business? Timing. The American industrialists felt that quality would cost them too much money. However, the Japanese had absolutely nothing to lose, and so they had everything to gain.

The failure of the Americans to adopt quality caused them to lose their markets and to see the American industrial base decline. This has to do with the spirit and soul of American industrial managers. The people who had won the war became consumed with a spirit of greed, complacency, pride, and arrogance. For them, the time had not yet fully come to adopt quality as the standard.

In the late 1970s the Americans were taking a terrible beating from the Japanese in the world marketplace. Their time had now come. Deming, now in his late 70s, was welcomed back to preach his message of quality.

What caused Deming to succeed in America, when previously his message had been so sorely scorned? Timing. Now his message found a ready hearing. His great idea of quality succeeded because the environmental conditions in America were now most favorable to his ideas.[8]

The Discerning Heart

The voice of God that speaks to us from the interior silence is often referred to as the "inner voice," or "discernment." The reformers stressed the importance of listening for the inner voice so that one might discern the mind of God. This ability is often referred to as "the discerning heart."

The effectual qualities of discernment depend upon the religious managers and leaders to suspend their prior judgments, and to enter into a season of inner stillness and silence—that they may hear the still, small voice of God saying, "This is the way, walk in it." Also needed is the intuitive sense of timing, for even the best ideas will find little acceptance until the time has fully come for them to be birthed.

Discernment, however, is more than stillness and timing. Discernment is both a listening to the voice speaking from the divine center within, and a concrete management approach to planning. There are necessary steps and essential processes to be followed. We invite you to read about discernment and spirituality in our earlier book *Leading the Congregation.*[9]

QUESTIONS FOR REFLECTION UPON YOUR ROLE IN NURTURING THE CONGREGATION'S SPIRIT

1. Are you facilitating the three corporate abilities that are conditioned by the congregation's spirit (e.g., silence, timing, and discernment)? If not, how can you creatively foster them within the life of the church?
2. What spirit do you bring to the congregation through your leadership and management? Is this spirit energizing or burdening the church?
3. Does the congregation have an openness to metanoia? If not, how can you assist in providing an environment that is open to change?

The Essence of the Congregation's Spirit

1. Every congregation has a common spirit (esprit de corps) of some kind and to some measure, it is either within the realm of energizing or darksome.
2. Where there is no energizing spirit, there is no vision! Without a vision caught out of spirit, mission and ministry soon wither and die.
3. There are several indicators of the spirit of the congregation:
    - The temperament of the top leaders.
    - How they view and display their prominence.
    - How vulnerable they are about their inner life, including their shadow side.
    - How new ideas and paradigms are received.
    - The way people represent the organization.
4. Metanoia must be incorporated into the everyday life of the congregation.
    - The congregation's spirit provides the environment in which metanoia will or will not be fostered.
    - This openness toward metanoia (change) is seen as a major indicator of the congregation's spirit, whether energizing or darksome.
    - By embracing change, the congregation is energized; without that embrace, it soon becomes darksome.

At the height of the Reformation, Martin Luther said, "Unless I pray four hours a day I won't get my work done." This flies straight into the teeth of our busyness as we scurry about tending to the trivial burdens of our ministry—too hectic to be still and too busy to pay attention to the knocking on our interior door. Not so for Luther. He realized that unless he heard a voice saying, "This is the way, walk in it"; unless he heard instructions which transcended a rational planning process, he would never see the Reformation completed. Did it work for him? Toward the end of his sojourn Luther wrote, "All my life I never had a single plan. God led me, like a dumb ox, along." He heard the inner voice, he discerned the clues coming from his divine center.

How You Can Become Aware of Your Congregation's Energy Source—Its Esprit de Corps

1. Ask visitors, board members, staff, unchurched persons, and others how they feel about the church.
   - Do they describe the church in energizing or darksome terms?
   - Do they seem to be gaining energy through the conversation, or are they burdened?
2. Examine the indicators of the spirit of the congregation:
   - The temperament of the top leaders-managers.
   - How leaders-managers display their prominence.
   - How vulnerable leaders-managers are about their inner life, including their shadow side.
   - How new ideas and paradigms are received.
   - The way people represent the organization.
3. After coming to some idea of the spirit of the congregation, talk about it with your leaders-managers.
   - Do they want to continue to nurture the spirit? If so, how? If not, why not, and what will you and they do about it?
   - Model and foster honesty about the nature of the church; without honesty, change will most likely be stunted.
4. Concentrate on integrating the three corporate abilities: silence, timing, and discernment.
   - It is within these exercises that a congregation can be led by God into becoming a learning organization.

In this chapter we have considered the spirit of the congregation as a strategic component of the church's life, ministry, and results. The spirit of the congregation breathes life into organizational structures. A structure without spirit, whether it be the worship service or the finance committee meeting, is a deadening structure. When spirit is lacking, the relationships among persons are characterized by distance, distrust, and cool formality. If you walk into a church and the relationships you observe appear stiff, guarded, cliquish, or "clammy," you likely have entered a place where spirit has been lost.

Two characteristics of a congregation's life and work are essentially defined by its common spirit and its spirituality: the quality of its ministries and the energy level of the congregation and workers. We undertake a discussion of these important organizational concerns in chapter 17—"Quality and Continuous Improvement: The Ultimate Test of Management." You may choose to turn to that chapter now, or to read it later as you come to it in reading through the book.

In Part Four, we will consider the design of the congregation's organizational systems. We will look at organizational design which includes organizational structures, and belief systems.

PART FOUR

Designing the Congregation as System

Introduction

> *History books will describe the final two decades of this millennium as the period during which new organizational forms evolved.*[1]
>
> Jay R. Galbrith

Since the beginning of the industrial revolution, theorists and managers of organizations have been primarily concerned with the structures of the organization: the combinations of hardware, people, technologies, policies, real estate, manuals of procedures, rules, and regulations. Over the past thirty years, religious organizations, just like their secular counterparts, have also focused tightly on organizational structures as the source of their major problems. So when congregations get into trouble they almost always seek to apply structural remedies; i.e., firing the pastor, cutting the budget, excommunicating a few members, rewriting the church constitution and by-laws, or moving from a bicameral board system to a unicameral board.

When denominations get into trouble they, too, try to get out by applying structural changes; i.e., relocating the national offices, reducing national staff numbers, merging, realigning judicatory boundaries, establishing tenures for the service of bishops or superintendents.

If after thirty years of restructures, reallocations, and realignments, matters have gotten worse, why don't the leaders and planners of the denominations stop it? The answer is that from the advent of the industrial revolution it has been a basic premise that organizations are built upon structures, and when organizations fail to work well, it is a sign that the structures need to be changed.

Some of the problems of the denomination or of congregations are structural and require structural responses. The organization, however, is more than structure, and it will not produce results when leaders attempt to solve nonstructural problems with alterations to the structure. When this is done repeatedly, the casualties will increase.

The following analogy is not fully apropos, but the human being certainly includes a number of physical systems: the skeletal system, respiratory system, and digestive system, to name but a few. However, we all know that the human being also includes some things that are not physical: will, soul, consciousness, emotions, and spirit, to name a few. We know this of the human being and so we often refer to the totality of that which is the human being in shorthand fashion as: body, mind, and spirit.

These distinctions help us understand the human being, and when it is not functioning up to par, we decide the remedy based upon which particular system is malfunctioning. If it is the body, we see a physician or physical therapist; if it is the mind, we see a psychiatrist or psychologist; if it is the spirit, we see a pastor or spiritual counselor.

The organization-as-system is comprised of two highly related, but nonetheless distinct components: its structures and its organizational belief system. When stresses or problems are located in the organizational belief system, purely structural interventions are guaranteed to fail. As this continues, matters will get worse.

When referring to "belief systems" we are not talking about doctrine, theology, creed, or faith. We are referring to the belief systems that are imbedded in the organization's structures; those beliefs which define how people relate in the system, what the workers expect the leaders to do for them, what level of servitude the leader expects from the workers, and so on.

The idea and place of an organizational belief system in a religious system are, at first, confusing because the religious system operates within several other belief systems that function alongside the organizational belief system. The congregation has a body of beliefs that define its theology, a body of beliefs that define its spiritual experiences, and so on. All of these belief systems are highly related, and all of them influence the structures, and the structures influence all the belief systems. Put simply, the congregation is a system, and all its entities are interdependently and interdynamically related.

In Part Four we will focus only upon the congregation's organizational structures and its organizational belief system. We will do this under the rubric of *organizational design,* or *systems design.* The basic premise is that the organization is comprised of two components: the organization structures and the belief systems which are inherent in the structures. Designing an effective organization requires that we pay attention to its structures and to its belief systems.

As stated earlier in Parts Two and Three, the transforming system is comprised of four components: mission, spirituality, structure, and relationships. These are the machinery that work together to transform the raw materials into energy. *Organization design* refers to getting these four components into the best possible arrangement so that they work well together—to generate the maximum energy with a minimum of effort and consumption of energy. The organization design is intended to accomplish two things:

1. To bring the components of the transforming system into alignment; to get them all working harmoniously in order to narrow the gap between desired outputs and actual outputs.
2. To channel energies (programs, people, policies, and practices) toward desired results.

In religious organizations things do not always work harmoniously. Organizational energies often become blocked, or diverted into nonproductive pursuits. The major blockages of energy in an organization are:

1. **Treating symptoms as problems:** This diverts the organization from recognizing the real problems, wastes energy, and makes problems worse. The results of treating symptoms as problems are frustration and lack of confidence in the manager's abilities to run the operation.
2. **Bottlenecks:** Bottlenecks are individuals, committees, or policies that block energy from flowing through or around them. The bottleneck may be such persons as the pastor, a church power broker, or a committee. The result of bottlenecks is that energies are dammed up, imprisoned behind the "bottlenecker."
3. **Nonalignment:** Nonalignment wastes energy through much activity that goes nowhere. The old adage fits here: "The harder

we run the behinder we get." The results of nonalignment are that no reasonable results are achieved from all the energy expended.

4. **Self-defeating practices:** All congregations develop habits. Habits can enhance ministry and relationship, and this is desirable. On the other hand, habits can defeat ministry and shrink relationships.

Everything we talk about in Part Four has to do with producing and channeling energy into mission and ministry. Organization design has to do with energy, direction, and relationships. In the early 1960s, the idea of producing and aligning energy for a religious system was seen as a nice theory but not essential. After all, it seemed the denominations had enough energy to carry them full bloom into the next millennium. Then their fuel gauges tilted toward empty. For mainline and evangelical denominations, alike, the idea of religious systems running out of energy is no longer a theory but an existential reality.

8

The Basic Components of Organization Design

Structures and Belief Systems

Figure 8.1

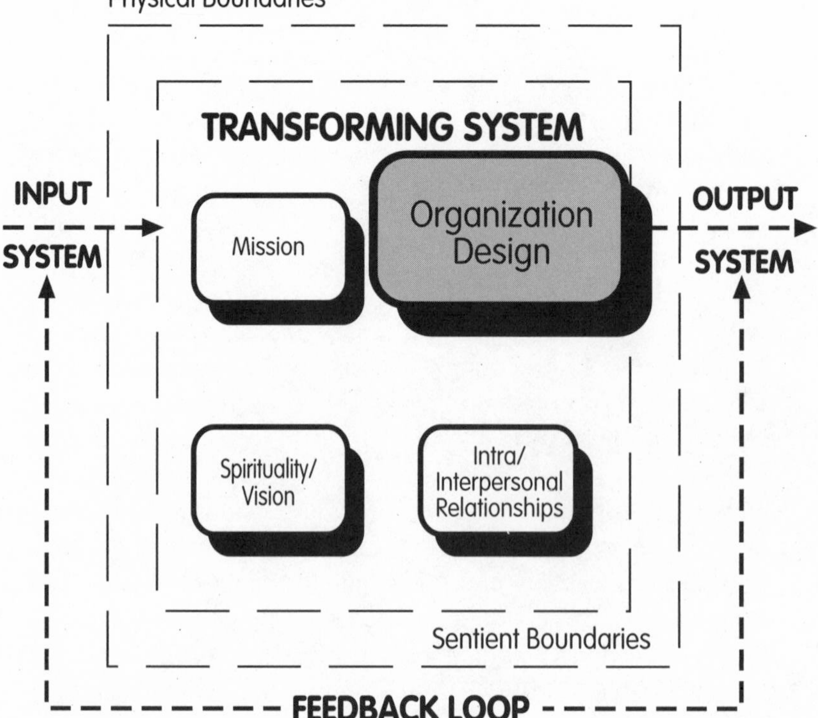

The championship sports teams and great jazz ensembles provide metaphors for acting in spontaneous yet coordinated ways. Outstanding teams in organizations develop the same sort of relationship—an operational "trust," where each team member remains conscious of other team members and can be counted on to act in ways that complement each other's actions.[1]

Peter M. Senge

The Organization's Design: Structures and Belief Systems

Designing an organization means much more than drawing little boxes connected by solid and dotted lines with impressive titles written inside the boxes. Organization design gives form and substance to the institution's mission, spirituality, vision, and relationships. They all come together (or fall apart) in the organization's design.

Organization design comprises two entities: the organization's structures and the belief systems that dictate what people expect from the organization, and how people relate in the organization.

1. **Structures** are the "sum total of the ways in which organizational effort is divided into distinct tasks and the means by which coordination is achieved among these tasks."[2] Structure includes the various combinations of people, properties, facilities, constitution and by-laws, policies, committees, and ministries, that are put together to achieve the congregation's purpose and goals. Structures are tangible; they can be seen, touched, or read.
2. A **belief system** is a widely shared mental model of how the organization governs its relationships, expectations that leaders have of the paid and volunteer workers, expectations that the workers have of the leaders, and so on. The belief system also includes deeply held, often unconscious, assumptions espoused by the people which strongly influence their actions and their expectations of one another.[3] The belief system goes both ways; it includes a person's assumptions about the congregation as well as the congregation's assumptions about its people. Belief systems are not obvious, and they are seldom written. Nonetheless, they are powerful motivators of expectations and behaviors.

Over time the congregation's members, paid and volunteer workers arrive at an understanding of certain governance policies that give shape to mutual expectations and relationships. Some of these expectations are explicitly stated in the organization's constitution and bylaws. Most, however, are unwritten and implicit (you have to be around for a while to learn what they are). These governance policies and relational expectations constitute the congregation's organizational belief system. In short, the congregation's structure is imbued with a belief system that defines the operative expectations by which the people relate to one another and to the system. More specifically, the belief system is comprised of the congregation's internal politics, what persons expect from one another, the expectations persons have of their leaders and managers, the view that leaders and managers have of the members and workers, and often repeated stories or myths of the leaders and/or followers.

Grouping Task, Structure, and Belief Systems

A perennial concern for the religious manager is: "How can we design our congregation to accomplish the desired goal with the best relationships among the people who are involved, and with the least amount of energy wasted in solving problems?"

At its simplest level, the two fundamental and opposing requirements for every organized human effort are "the total of the ways in which its labor is divided into distinct tasks and then its coordination achieved among those tasks."[4] Human effort requires the division of labor into various tasks to be performed and the coordination of those tasks to accomplish the activity.

Peter F. Drucker describes how the coordination of tasks takes place according to their grouping within an organization. There is *grouping by knowledge and skill* that members bring to an organization (e.g., surgeons, anesthetists, and lab technicians within a hospital; or music director, youth pastor, and pastoral care on a church staff). There is also *grouping by the functions* members perform within an organization (e.g., manufacturing, marketing, engineering, and finance; or pastoral staff, board of directors, and volunteer leaders for small groups within a church). *Grouping by time* refers to the time when the work is done (e.g., same work by different shifts in a factory; or volunteer nursery workers during different worship services in a congregation). *Grouping by output* is a structure that is concerned with the products or services rendered by the organization (e.g., a church that has a school connected with it may have different structures according to the outputs). *Grouping by client* is a structure that deals with different types of clients (e.g., churches that address unique needs of singles, senior citizens, single mothers, and so forth). *Grouping by place* (e.g., a church that provides a home for small groups in different locations, or volunteer ministry within a particular community).

Often the groupings are a combination. For example, schools are organized primarily by age, grade, and subject matter. Sometimes the structure can be frustrating—the department of motor vehicles in many states is organized around the one long line you stand in for forty-five minutes to learn in which other line you should be standing.[5]

Organization design is intended to deal with certain important attributes:

1. **Alignment:** Getting all the ducks in order so that they move along together instead of waddling around in every direction, quacking at everyone else to get out of the way.
2. **Energy flow:** Getting all the energies flowing toward the vision or desired results so that energy "a" isn't smashing into energy "b" and knocking it directly into the path of energy "c." Just as hurtful is when all the energies of the congregation are flying out from the center into a widening arc, as though they are being cast away from some centrifugal force.
3. **Habitual patterns** that cause the ducks to break ranks without realizing that they are once again waddling over one another; this wastes enormous amounts of time and energy without the ducks ever learning anything from their experiences. Poorly aligned congregations, once they become habitual, produce notoriously poor learners.

Another factor exerting singular sway over organization effectiveness is mistaking symptoms as problems, then treating the symptoms but never getting around to dealing with the underlying problems. This condition is prevalent in religious organizations and is a scandalous waste of immense amounts of time and energy. But religious managers just keep doing it because the symptoms are obvious and demand urgent attention, whereas the problems are usually not so obvious, since they are imbedded deeply within the congregation's design. So the leaders work with the obvious, rather than understanding the not-so-obvious forces that are operating in the organization's belief system. This is what is known as treating symptoms rather than treating the real problems.

The question we raise is this: What is more important in dealing with the problems facing your congregation today—to work on structures or to change the belief systems that drive the structures? We think the answer is becoming more obvious all the time.

> An organization can only produce what it was designed to produce. In order to get different results, its structures and belief systems will need to be modified. To attempt change without modifications to the structures and belief systems will only cause the system to "feed back." That is to say that for every attempted change there will be a compensating negative reaction intended to get things back on balance (or to achieve homeostasis).[6]

Virtually all problems in our congregations stem from faulty, inadequate organizational designs (structures and belief systems). Good people achieve poor results in organizations with faulty designs. A well-structured administrative committee, whose belief system holds that its job is to maintain what is already there, will perform poorly in a situation that requires new approaches and some risk taking. In management you "get what you design for, not what you hope for."[7] An airplane that is designed to carry one hundred passengers, five thousand gallons of fuel, and ten thousand pounds of cargo will not be able to fly with two hundred passengers, ten thousand gallons of fuel, and twenty thousand pounds of cargo—no matter how much the pilot revs the engines or how long the runway—because the engines will not be able to develop enough thrust to move the plane down the runway, and the wings will not provide enough lift to allow the laws of aerodynamics to suck the plane up into the air. If the plane is to achieve results outside of its design characteristics, it will need to undergo some significant design alterations. Good intentions on the part of the pilot and crew simply will not suffice.

Likewise, a ship that is designed to turn 45 degrees in five miles will not turn 45 degrees in three miles, no matter how hard the pilot pulls on the wheel. Before the ship will ever be able to turn 45 degrees in three miles, some significant modifications will need to be made to the design of its rudder and trim tabs.

We use these simple engineering design illustrations to emphasize a most important principle regarding efforts aimed at achieving better performance and results from our structures and programs: you can change the structures all you wish; however, unless the belief systems that determine relationships, the distribution of power, informal communication patterns, mutual expectations, and decision making are also changed, the results will remain the same and eventually they even get worse.

Change efforts in religious organizations almost always focus only on the structures of the organization. Almost never do they address the changes that are needed in the organization's belief systems. Several denominations are currently engaged in attempts to stem membership declines, to narrow the gap between shrinking contributions and increasing budgets, and to stem the tide of dissatisfaction and disillusionment that is growing among members at the grass roots level. However, few if any of the change efforts deal with systemic design conditions. Most of the change efforts carried out by denominations to date focus only on structural concerns; such efforts only make matters worse. But denominations are notoriously slow learners, and so we continue to make the same mistakes, over and over again.

Some of the most popular ineffective change efforts utilized by denominations are:

1. **Merger.** (Can you think of any denominational merger in the past thirty years that has reversed the membership and financial declines of the merging bodies, or have the declines continued unabated?)
2. **Relocation of national offices** from the East into the American heartland in order to be in closer touch with the constituents. (Can you think of any denomination that has relocated its offices whose constituents now feel more in touch and cared for?)
3. **Restructure.** (Can you think of a denomination that is better off because it has restructured its national and judicatory agencies, some over and over again?)
4. **Downsizing national staffs.** (Can you think of a denomination

that has stemmed its declines and gained more goodwill by reducing its number of national staff ?)

We think that the answer to all of these questions is no. Why then do denominations continue doing these things? Because we are all products of our histories and, since the time of the industrial revolution, managers have always believed that if you can create the perfect structure, all of your problems will go away. By now, however, the Church should be aware that for all of our structural changes we continue getting smaller and leaner. We have done so for thirty years, but our problems still persist.

Changing structures without installing new belief systems will change nothing—except, perhaps, further weaken the Church by outplacing many of our best leaders and thinkers. If we cannot solve our problems with the leaders and staff people we have, how will we solve them when we have less experience and brainpower working on them? The problems confronting our denominations and congregations today are structural—but they are also more than this. We also have deeply embedded belief systems that must be addressed. We might illustrate this principle as follows:

Figure 8.2

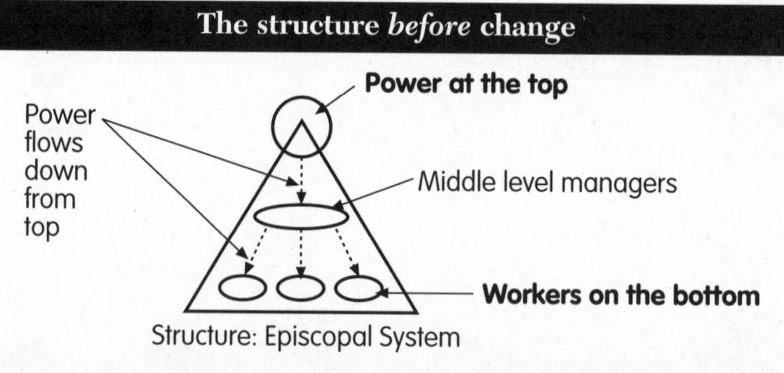

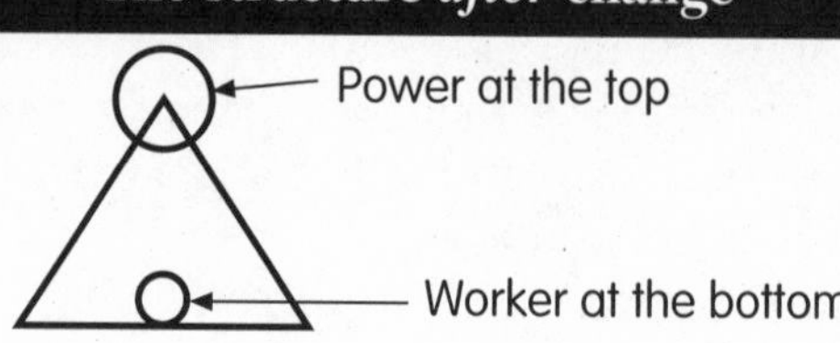

The Structure After Change

The belief systems in both structures hold that:

1. There always has to be someone on the top, who holds all the power.
2. The one on the top shares power downward, as he wishes.
3. Those in the middle and on the bottom have no power, except that which the boss on top chooses to give them.
4. The person on the top is supposed to take care of those in the middle and on the bottom.
5. In return for being cared for, those in the middle and on the bottom will comply with the wishes of the one on the top.
6. All problems can be solved by changing the structure (not the belief system).

The sketch on page 146 illustrates the popular idea of downsizing, rightsizing, or losing unnecessary organizational fat—but you will notice that the belief system was not changed at all (see chapter 9). It is still the same structure except with fewer layers of management and with less workers.

Virtually every congregation with which we work attempts to solve its problems by making adjustments to the structures of the congregation-as-system (e.g., get a new pastor, have a better finance campaign, pray for a revival) without addressing the deeper issues of the congregation's belief systems.

How can one test the appropriateness of the congregation's organizational design? The test is simple. Honestly answer one question: "Are we getting the results we want?" If not, then the structure is channeling the many energies of the congregation into results you don't want—or the structures are blocking the flow of energy from moving toward the results you do want. Appropriate structures will allow energy to flow freely throughout the entire system—and toward the results for which you are looking.

QUESTIONS FOR REFLECTION UPON YOUR CONGREGATION'S ORGANIZATIONAL DESIGN

1. Clearly define the organizational belief system that imbues your church's structure. Are you satisfied with this belief system?
2. Do you create structures that do not allow leaders and members to live up to your belief system? If so, how can you facilitate change in the situation?
3. Are you getting the results that you want? If not, are you open to metanoia in regard to your organizational belief systems and structures?
4. Are there symptomatic conditions within the congregation that you have been mistaking as problems? How can you reframe the situation in order to pinpoint the problem?

Organizational Alignment

The congregation-as-system is aligned when all of its structures and resources function in unanimity in accomplishing the corporate vision. An important role of its feedback system is to help the congregation come into alignment. A congregation is nonaligned when two or more of its entities work at cross-purposes. The primary characteristic of a nonaligned congregation, or team, is wasted energy. By contrast, when a commonality of direction is achieved, then individual and organizational energies are harmonized. Even very diverse elements can have focused energy in a design that creates and sustains common vision. Common spirit and synergy develop from an aligned team or joint effort.

In one church in which we served as consultants, the structure never allowed for pastoral staff members to meet with the church board. The board would make decisions pertaining to the ministries without having any conversation with the pastors whatsoever. The result was confusion and endless hours of wrangling. The belief system that caused this structural distance between the board and the staff was that the congregation would not trust decisions that were made with the staff pastor's involvement.

All of this wasted energy occurred not because they were bad people, but because of a poorly designed organization.

As outsiders we spotted this problem immediately, and pointed it out to the board and the staff. Everyone agreed it was a major problem. However, it took nearly three years before this flaw in the organization's design was finally corrected. Old habits die hard.

Sketch A in Figure 8.3 illustrates how some structures are not in alignment toward corporate vision; in fact the design works against the vision. Sketch B, however, illustrates that all structures are in alignment and moving together toward the corporate vision. The structure and belief system that did not provide for formal meetings between the board and pastoral staff, in the illustration above, thwarted the alignment of the persons who were involved, and wasted much energy in untangling confusion and endless hours of conflict. Simply having formal meetings with the involved parties, however, does not guarantee alignment, for there is also a structure to the meetings that determines how energies, ideas, and feelings are channeled or thwarted.

Figure 8.3

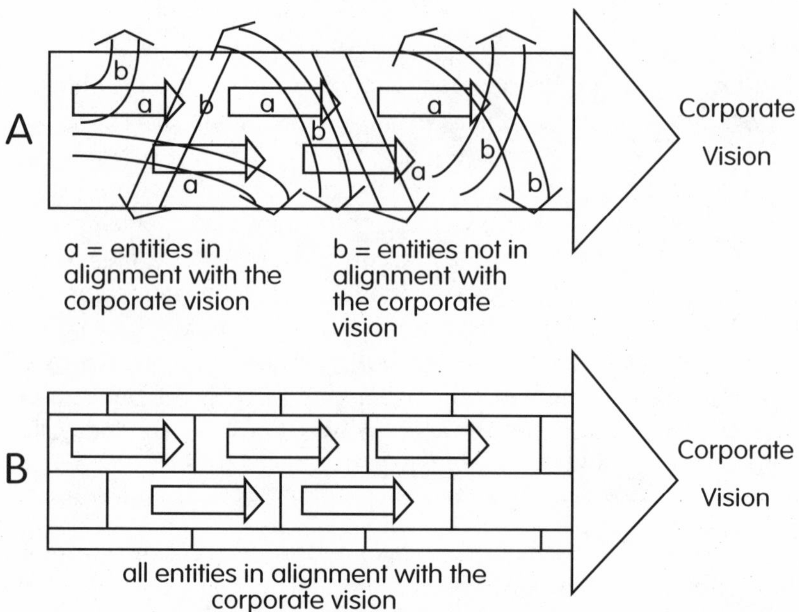

Results in diagram A -- 'a' programs, persons, and ministries are aligned with the corporate vision and move along together, but are constantly smashing up against the 'b' entities that are not aligned with the corporate vision.

Results in diagram B -- all programs, persons, ministries, etc. are aligned with the corporate vision and move along together with no wasted energy.

Organization Designs Channel or Block the Energy Flow

The congregation's design channels, or blocks, the energy of its interacting entities in such a way that it helps to achieve, or hinder, the vision and ministry of the organization.[8]

> Mission and ministry consume energy; spirituality and vision produce energy; organizational designs channel or thwart energy.

Examples of such channels are communication networks, decision-making processes, formal and informal meetings, assessment, and planning. The energy required to achieve the congregation's mission or goal must pass through these channels. If the channels are clear and supportive, the mission or desired goal will be achieved. But if the channels are blocked, or designed to accomplish something else, the desired results will not be realized.

A prime example of an organizational structure which can easily block the flow of energy in a congregation is the pyramid (top down) structure of an organization. David Watson, an Anglican priest, illustrates how a narrow passageway through one person can block the congregation's energy and well-being (See Figure 8.4).

> The vicar or minister is usually the bottleneck, if not the cork, of his church: nothing can go in or out except through him. No meetings can take place unless he is the leader or chairman. No decisions can be made without his counsel and approval. I know of some parishes where the laity cannot meet even for Bible study and prayer unless the vicar is present. . . . This concept of the church makes growth and maturity virtually impossible. Members are unable to develop into the God-given ministry they could well experience because, in structure and practice, there is room for only one minister.[9]

Figure 8.4

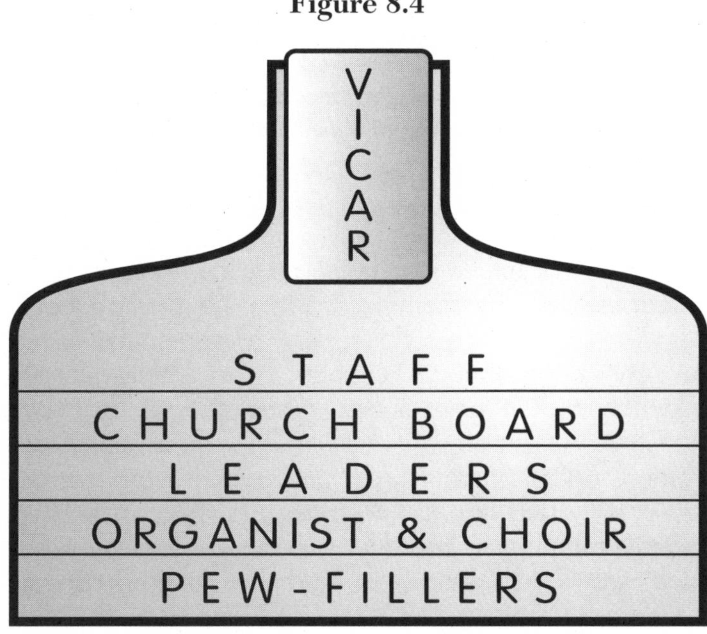

Watson suggests that such a structure builds up pressure in the bottle, resulting in the bottle exploding into numerous house fellowships and house churches where there is room for the sharing of ministry among the laity. Without new wineskins (structures), the explosion is almost inevitable.[10] While the explosion may take some time in happening, there are signs that point to its inevitability, or to the congregation's declining health. When the paid and volunteer leaders spend more and more hours in meetings with administrative committees, or fill their own staff meetings with administrative details rather than forward ministry planning, the church is in trouble, because the structures are channeling energies into organizational habits of diminishing returns. The more time spent in administration, the less time spent with those who actually do the work—those who deliver the ministries directly. When the pastor's evenings are virtually consumed by meetings with administrative committees, the church is in big trouble. Endless administrative committee meetings consume the pastor's energy, foster resentment among spouse and children, and ultimately condition the pastor to view her entire ministry as one big committee meeting.

We know a pastor who in the mid-1980s was appointed to a large congregation. In his first walk through the building he discovered that a leak in the roof of the Christian Education building had brought down pieces of the ceilings on three floors of the building. Students and teachers walked over the fallen plaster each week as they entered their rooms. When he inquired of the trustees regarding this condition most of them said they knew nothing of it. When he then inquired how they could be trustees and not know about the leak in the roof, they were silent. Then he asked them one-by-one how long it had been since they had done a walk through the building. They all agreed that they had never done a walk through. Furthermore, none of them attended Sunday school or taught a Sunday school class, so they had no reason to be in that part of the building.

Perhaps not so parenthetically, this trustee board met incessantly and insisted that the pastor attend every meeting. The president of the trustee board was an automatic member of the congregation's administrative board, but he flatly refused to attend because he was so busy with the trustees that he had no time to attend the administrative board meetings. Consequently communications between these two important groups were nonexistent.

The pastor decided that attending every meeting of the trustees was not a good use of his energies. He informed the trustee president of this decision and asked that the president give him a copy of the agenda for meetings a week in advance, so that he might decide whether he wanted to attend. The president did not take this as good news. In fact, he took it as a direct affront. He felt that the pastor did not appreciate his faithful labors. He got word around the congregation that the pastor was ignoring the most important committee in the entire church, and began a letter writing campaign to the bishop to discipline or remove the pastor immediately. Meanwhile, a concerned layperson, who held no administrative position in the church, efficiently organized a program to raise the necessary $20,000 to repair the roof and arranged for workers to do the job.

Who is to blame for the less than satisfactory dynamics in this situation? The truth is, no one. The problem lies in the organization's design. A bureaucratic committee cannot quickly respond to an emergency situation. Its structure does not allow energy to change course quickly. There are too many meetings to attend, too many layers of policy to adhere to, too many levels of approval to be secured, or too many other administrative concerns clamoring for attention. Thus, any well-meaning group of good and caring individuals coming together in a bureaucratic structure will soon act like bureaucrats. These same persons placed in different structures with different belief systems, however, will often not act this way at all.

How could this man change his behavior so dramatically? It certainly was not because he had a change of heart regarding the pastor. The answer is that structures greatly influence a person's attitudes and behaviors. Different structures channel the flow of energy in different directions. A bureaucratic structure channels energy into survival behaviors (the purpose of a bureaucracy is to survive) by insulating itself from instability and when it does so it is meeting its intended purpose. Such structures are not meant for growth or change. Should there be such desires, the structures compensate with resistance.

> When the trustee president's term expired he lobbied the pastor to appoint him to another influential committee—the staff parish relations committee. When his efforts to politic his way onto this committee failed, he then made a run for a seat on the congregation's nominating committee—another highly influential committee. This effort also failed. Then the pastor arranged a visit with the disappointed nonplaced bureaucrat. In the course of conversation the exasperated man said, "All right then, I'll take any job you want me to take, only don't put me on the TV ministry." The television ministry was experiencing great difficulties.
>
> The pastor subsequently created a special task force to solve the many problems in this troubled ministry, and appointed the man to serve as task force leader. The pastor instructed the committee to turn this ministry around within six months. He also informed them that at that time the task force would cease to exist. If they could not complete the task, then another task force would be created to take on where they would leave off at the end of six months. Throughout the six months the man continued his letter writing campaign to the bishop—but he also organized the task force in a most effective manner. Six months later the TV ministry had been taken apart and put back together again, stronger than ever.

In order to assess how the organization's design may channel or hinder energy, Linda S. Ackerman offers three crucial questions for which the manager must get the answers:

1. What channels will help the organization achieve its mission and intended results? What decisions must be reached, what needs to be communicated and with whom, what is the right timing, and so on.
2. What existing channels are contrary to the organization's mission

and intended results? This question must include the political realities in your organization as well.

3. What channels yet need to be designed or created to help the organization achieve its mission and intended results?[11]

The Path of Least Resistance

Energy always follows the path of least resistance. For example, the path of least resistance in a traditional administrative committee is to maintain what exists, to change nothing, and to resist any outside attempts to induce change. People will use their energies to resist change because the path of no change is least resisted in traditional or bureaucratic structures. Administrators and administrative committee members are not necessarily being obnoxious when they resist new ideas or changes—they are simply doing their job—maintaining what already is.

Three major blockages that divert energy from the more important concerns into paths of least resistance are: bottlenecks, limiting factors in the congregation's design, and a lack of clear mission or purpose. We examine each of these energy "diverters":

Bottlenecks: We stated earlier that bottlenecks are usually persons or groups. The president of the trustee board, discussed above, functioned as a bottleneck. His lust for power, his resistance to the pastor's attempts to make the board more effective, and the campaign he launched to get the pastor removed from the parish all diverted his own energy from correcting the problems that had developed in the building's maintenance; and these also diverted the board's energy from doing its job. The board was stymied as its members became torn between doing their job as trustees and coming to terms with the conflict that had erupted between the trustee president and the pastor.

Limiting factors: Limiting factors can be described as systemic or organizational bottlenecks. Limiting factors refer to inadequacies in the design of the congregation or in one of the congregation's subsystems. A congregation's energy is blocked or diverted when it confronts a problem that blocks its forward progress. Whether persons act as bottlenecks or limiting structures, the results are the same. The energy of the congregation is diverted or blocked until the limiting factor is identified and removed. For example, placing persons as heads of committees, without providing them the training they need to know how to lead committees, or failing to give them the resources they need to do their job well, will eventually prove to be a limiting factor to all of the efforts and ministries of the entire church-as-system. How can a committee work well when it doesn't have the foggiest idea of what it is supposed to produce? It can't. So, its energy will be blocked, or worse, will be diverted into endless wrangling and nonproductive meetings.

The staff of a denomination's missionary agency was particularly frustrated. The missionary effort of this denomination has a long history of being one of the best in the world. Yet, over two decades the denomination's missionary effort experienced a growing lack of financial and moral support from its congregations. The staff and board assumed that this was due to a growing lack of interest in missions on the part of its local constituents.

The staff contracted a consulting firm to conduct a listening process involving all of its congregations. The consultants and staff began by conducting focus groups of clergy leaders, local missionary program leaders, and members of the congregations. They gained some powerful feedback. First, it became apparent that the members of the denomination did not want less missionary endeavor—but more. Second, they heard that the local missionary volunteer leaders were frustrated and discouraged by the fact that the staff continually invited requests for help which they then did not provide, and urged the local leaders to write letters telling the staff what resources they needed to carry out their local missions programs—letters which never received a response from the mission's staff.

The pattern of asking local leaders to request help that was never provided and to write letters that were not answered was a limiting factor to their missionary efforts around the world. Hence, congregations lost their once intimate and immediate touch with the national staff, and the local missions leaders felt increasingly neglected and unappreciated. The energies of the local missions units were diverted into feelings of frustration resulting from being appointed to a task about which they greatly cared, but being left alone to fend for themselves when they didn't know what they were supposed to be doing.[12]

Lack of a clear mission or purpose: The lack of clear mission or purpose is a primary reason for blocked or diverted energies in local congregations. Hundreds of thousands of volunteer leaders, teams, and committees flounder aimlessly for lack of knowing what they are supposed to accomplish. They may have some idea of what they are supposed to do, but no idea of the end result for all of their effort. As a result, the volunteers divert their energies into "make work" activities with no focus or lasting benefit, or they just shut down; they become lethargic or reactionary. The lack of a compelling mission or a clearly defined end result becomes a severely limiting factor in channeling the energies of volunteer leaders and workers.

The Influence of Habits

Organizational behaviors and processes—practiced long enough—eventually become habits. Habits are repeated cycles of behaviors that eventually become fixed as the only proper way to do things. Good habits allow the congregation to accomplish a great deal without spending much mental or emotional energy. We don't have to think about our habits, we just do them—and sometimes our habits "do" us.

Most of our personal habits are benign, because they are of such little consequence; for example, brushing your teeth with your right or left hand. However, some habits are highly consequential. The health or illness of a congregation can be strongly influenced by one or two organizational habits. Therefore, it is vital to identify and understand what the habits are that govern the congregation's behaviors, so that they might be changed if necessary. On the other hand, the church may develop some highly beneficial habits, such as spiritual disciplines that replenish the energy supply. These, too, need to be identified so that they might be protected.

The religious manager must work to align all areas of the congregation—its mission, structures, intrapersonal and interpersonal relationships, organizational design, and spirituality—in ways that will support the corporate vision and bring about needed change efforts. Identifying the congregation's habits, and understanding their effects, deserves the manager's utmost attention because the organization's habits exert tremendous influence upon how and where energy flows throughout the congregation.

Changing the Energy Flow in the Congregation

To change the flow of energy in the congregation, the positive and negative patterns of energy flow must be identified, and their effects understood. Once the patterns are understood, decisions can be made regarding how to change negative flows of energy. There are a number of things the manager can do to change the flow of energy in a congregation:

1. Be clear with yourself and with everyone else about the corporate mission, your customers, the services you offer, the desired results, and constraints.[13] Once negotiated, understood, and committed to, they become the givens regarding where the congregation's energies will be directed.
2. Help people to recognize their own habits, and to understand the results of the habits. Do these patterns accomplish the mission, serve the customers, and bring desired results? If not, what are the obvious and not so obvious results of these efforts?
3. Create mirrors for individuals and groups to see how their habitual patterns of behavior divert the congregation's energies, causing them to flow into unwanted results. Sometimes this is the only thing that is necessary to motivate persons and groups to change their habits.
4. Build in feedback at all levels of the organization. Obtaining valid and useful information is necessary to help a group determine the quality of its work. For example, taking time at the end of a meeting to talk about how people feel about the meeting, the ways decisions were made, and so on, are ways to help a group take a look at themselves.
5. Break up destructive patterns. Remove those persons who consistently block the group's efforts. Make it a habit to give responsibility to those people who have already proven responsible—in their family settings, on their jobs, in working on community based service projects, in local politics, or in former assignments in the church. If persons do well on their jobs, in their families, and in community projects, they will most likely do well in the position to which you are planning to recruit them. If they do poorly in all of their other relationships, they will likely do poorly in the church—wherever you appoint them.

6. Intensify or overload a nonproductive habitual pattern so that it will end. If two staff members are having minor disagreements but fail to address them, give them an important project to force them to work together and to look at their issues. If an individual, or a group, is a bottleneck, give them something substantially more to do, so that they have to "clear the channels" between them. Sometimes things have to become more intensified before they get better—they may even have to explode or break down before they can be fixed.[14]

Enhancing the Energy Flow in the Congregation

Do you know where the energy flow is in your congregation? What turns people on, what their passions are, what they get excited about? Most importantly, do you know the flow of energy that is inside yourself? What excites your passions and gets all of your "juices" flowing? Once you know the answers to these questions, there are a number of things you can do to strengthen the flow of energy throughout the congregation:

1. Again, be clear yourself and with everyone else about the corporate mission, your customers, the services being offered, desired results, and constraints.[15] Unless you are ever vigilant in this, individuals, groups, and perhaps the entire congregation will little by little divert energies into lesser pursuits. Left to itself, an organization tends always to drift into less important activities. It almost never will drift into more productive ministries.
2. Be a storyteller. One responsibility that seems always to gravitate to the pastor is to be the steward of the congregation's story. Every congregation has its own unique story. This story is more than "facts"; it also includes myths, mottos, or slogans which over the years have taken on a life of their own, and which now serve to empower or weaken the congregation's vision of its current capabilities.
3. Elicit the stories of the people in the congregation. Beyond the congregation's story, each person within the organization has his or her own story. Early in revivalist church traditions, a time was

given each week for "testimonies"—accounts of how God had "saved" or had been with them in recent days. The desired effect of the testimony time was to cause the individual to reflect on the movements of God in his life—that very week. Furthermore, the testimony of one was meant to encourage the faith of others. Through the sharing of their stories, energy was channeled into matters of everyday living. Indeed, a vision for the congregation often emerges from these narratives about God's grace.

Unfortunately, over the years the stories told in most testimony meetings became predictable and filled with repetitious, parrot-like platitudes. So the testimony meeting went by the board. However, there is still a place for testimonies in the church today. For a modern example of the power of testimonies, watch the weekly television broadcast sponsored by Robert Schuller and the Crystal Cathedral. Each week you will see and hear the testimony of a guest, who tells the story of how God is active in his or her life—every day. Robert Schuller does not need to repeat the mission of Crystal Cathedral over and over again. Every week the people are reminded of the Crystal Cathedral's mission in real life—through the telling of someone's story.

Few people present the need for a recovery in storytelling better than Richard A. Jensen. He writes,

> The future of Christianity [or congregations] does not depend on the necessity of literate discourse. The biblical faith was handed on for many centuries with very little recourse to literate discourse. It was done by telling stories! Storytelling has been a far more central component in the handing on of the faith than has literate discourse! We must not forget that.[16]

Perhaps if we would put as much work into knowing and telling the congregation's story as we put into a month of sermons, we would have something with which persons could connect their own personal dreams and passions.

Storytelling can be a powerful yet entertaining way to engage people. Each class, each ministry, has a story—a narrative of its events, characters, trials, and tribulations. Dramatic intrigue may include risks and vulnerabilities, needed courage, humorous events, and the conflicting subplots and principal characters.[17]

Again, each person has a story that can be seen in relation to the story of a particular project within the congregation. Taking enough time to listen to another person's story may be all that is necessary to keep the energy flow "coursing" through that person.

The parrot-like banality of testimony can be avoided. Some congregations assign a staff person to select individuals to tell their brief stories of God's grace during the worship service. The staff person assists the teller by helping him or her to write out or organize the narrative, which they edit together. This filtering process improves the quality of the testimony, and it also encourages a compact, timely witness.

4. Assist leaders and members to get in touch with and share their vision for the church. Each person has a vision. The personal stories of people are connected to personal visions. Energy can fast dissipate if people are not clear how their work and vision connects with the congregation's larger work and vision. When a person feels that her personal vision is taken seriously, new energies flow through her. A prepackaged vision handed "down" to her may mean nothing to her.

QUESTIONS FOR REFLECTION UPON YOUR ROLE IN ORGANIZATIONAL ALIGNMENT

1. In what ways have you generated people and programs that you have "designed for," but that are not what you "hoped for"?
2. Are any of the blockages discussed previously at work within the congregation (e.g., bottlenecks, limiting factors, or lack of a clear mission and purpose)? If so, how can you "unclog" these channels to help the church achieve its mission and ministry?
3. What energy patterns are flowing in the congregation that are detrimental in the long run? How can you change those energy patterns to influence corporate vision and spirit?
4. In what practical ways can you enhance the virtuous energy that is currently flowing in your congregation?

How You Can Facilitate Organizational Alignment

- After recognizing improper alignment in some area of the congregation, ask your leaders: "What open channels will help the church achieve its mission and ministry? What existing, blocked channels are contrary to the church's mission and ministry?"
- Be clear about the church's vision and mission. Without a clear understanding of where you want to go, you will never get there!
- Create unique mirrors for individuals and groups to see their bad habits that are causing energy to be diverted within the congregation!
- Break up destructive patterns!
- Provide honest confrontation for those who continue to block the group's mission.
- If their actions continue to block the mission, overload or intensify the habitual pattern until it is destroyed.

The Essence of the Congregation's Design

1. Organizations carry out tasks in the way in which they have been designed.
   - You generate the people and product you design for, not what you hope for.
2. In order to change the results of your efforts, both the structures and belief systems must be altered.
   - Without change in both of these spheres, the congregation-as-system will negatively compensate to bring things back to "normal" (homeostasis—the way things were before any modification was made).
3. If only structural changes are made, the system may become leaner, but the results will remain the same.
   - The belief system of an organization holds the power behind the structures and programs; therefore, they must also be altered for lasting change to take place.
4. Mission and ministry consume energy; spirituality and vision produce energy; organizational design thwarts or channels energy.
   - If the channels are clear and trustworthy, the energy will flow in the direction of the desired mission or goal.
   - If the channels are blocked, the energy will dissipate, and the desired results will not be accomplished.

In this chapter we have introduced the subject of organization design. We have also considered the importance of alignment and energy flow throughout the congregation's structures. We will now turn our attention to bureaucracy—the organizational design that has dominated the scene in modern times, including the Church.

9

Bureaucracy and Paternalism: Vestiges of a Dying Order

Now hear this
Now hear this
This is the captain speaking
This is the captain speaking
That is all
That is all[1]

Old Navy proverb

One definition of a bureaucracy is a business, or any other institution, that exists to carry out an organization.[2] The American Protestant church, as it developed, adopted a number of different organizational structures—Episcopal, Presbyterial, Congregational, and various combinations of these three. With the industrial revolution in the late-nineteenth century, a new and sweeping design for organizations came into being—bureaucracy. Bureaucracy proved so powerful that its influence spread across the entire Western world; exerting an especial effect upon all types of organizations and institutions in the United States, which was the birthplace of bureaucracy.

Whether Episcopal, Presbyterial, or Congregational, virtually all American denominations today operate out of an organizational design that is a bureaucratic structure, coupled with a paternalistic belief system.

> American denominations and congregations tend to be designed around bureaucratic structures and paternalistic belief systems.

Presently there are signs pointing to a new design of American organizations. The new design is *partnership* that is infused with a strong belief system of *stewardship*. For purposes of our discussion, it is vital to understand the present effects of bureaucracy upon congregations, and to understand the structure and belief system of partnership, which is already showing signs of replacing bureaucracy in American secular institutions and which we believe will also displace bureaucracy in the American churches (See chapter 10).

Bureaucracy

Bureaucracy—born as a late-nineteenth century adaptation of patriarchy—grew up quickly in response to the organizational concerns spawned by the Industrial Revolution and the invention of the assembly line: how to organize and coordinate the work of hundreds of people to produce one product; how to organize workers around small, repetitive tasks; and how to assure the compliance of hundreds of people to management policies. These were concerns never before confronted by management, except perhaps by the managers who oversaw the construction of the pyramids in ancient Egypt. They faced these same questions, but left few, if any, live persons to document the answers. They killed the slaves who built the structures, and the managers kept scant notes.

Bureaucracy was once considered innovative because of its greater efficiency through the division of labor, its development of management as a profession in a hierarchical chain of command, its promotion of scientific studies and predictability, and its provision of a uniform set of rules and procedures. Each emphasis encouraged the coordination of many different specialists who worked toward a common end. Far too often, however, the different specialists never saw the common end. This mechanistic approach to intepreting reality in the world and universe, developed in the 1600s to the middle 1800s, analyzed individual parts at the expense of the larger interaction among the parts. Stanley M. Davis describes this worldview. "In the mechanistic science and technology . . . the heavens were a mechanism and the world was a huge machine. If you understood how the heavenly machine functioned you could design your own, more practical versions. These theories became the engines of the Industrial Revolution."[3]

Since World War Two, however, the social and industrial environments have changed drastically, and bureaucracy's inability to effectively respond to these changes has displaced American industry as the indomitable giant in the world—precisely because bureaucracy resists any change to its structure and because the American worker is becoming increasingly dissatisfied with bureaucracy's belief system. So, in recent years corporate America has been shedding its bureaucratic plethora and, since it is almost impossible to change the bureaucratic structures, American institutions have set about to destroy them by cutting out layer after layer of management structures.

This challenge to bureaucracy is not limited to the United States. Most bureaucratic institutions worldwide are facing formidable challenges. Those once totalitarian governments, operating under the assumption that ordinary people are not capable of looking out for their own interests and the interests of the common good, have collapsed with dispatch and categorical resoluteness (consider, for example, the almost overnight collapse of the mighty Soviet Union).

A late-nineteenth-century sociologist, Max Weber, became famous as the primary architect of bureaucracy. Weber respected and assisted bureaucracy; yet he also dreaded the changes he foresaw it would bring to the social fabric of the industrialized countries. He wrote regarding the near impossibility of changing the bureaucratic machine: "Once it is fully established, bureaucracy is among those social structures which are the hardest to destroy. . . . bureaucracy has been and is a power instrument of the first order—for the one who controls the bureaucratic apparatus."[4]

The Structure of Bureaucracy

Weber identified the structural components of bureaucracy as: (1) A hierarchical chain of command; (2) specialization by function; (3) uniform policies covering rights and duties; (4) standardized procedures for each job; (5) a career based on promotion for technical competence; and (6) impersonal relations.[5] Bureaucracy, according to Weber, needed a structure that would assure control, consistency, predictability, and compliance. Guilford and Elizabeth Pinchot describe the structure of bureaucracy, its successes, its failures, and what they see replacing it (see Figure 9.1).[6]

Figure 9.1

What Bureaucracy Is	Why It Once Triumphed	Why It Fails Now	What Replaces It
Hierarchical chain of command	Brought simple large-scale order Bosses brought order by dominating subordinates	Cannot handle complexity Domination not best way to get organization intelligence	Vision and values Teams (self-managing) Lateral coordination Informal networks
			Choice
			Free enterprise
Specialization *Organization by function* *Uniform rules*	Produced efficiency through division of labor Focused intelligence Created a sense of fairness Clearly established power of bosses	Does not provide intensive cross-functional communication and continual peer-level coordination Still need rules, but need different rules	Multiskilling specialists and entrepreneuring Organization in market-mediated networks Guaranteed rights Institutions of freedom and community
Standard procedures	Provided crude organizational memory	Able to use unskilled workers	Overcame old ways
Responds slowly to change	Does not deal well with complexity	Does not foster interconnection	Self-direction and self-management
Force of the market and ethical community	A career of advancing up the ladder	Bought loyalty	Furnished continuity of elite class of managers and professionals
Few managers needed and more educated workforce expects promotions; therefore, not enough room for advancement	A career of growing competence Impersonal relations	A growing network to get more done Reduced force of nepotism	More pay for more capabilities Helped leaders enforce tough discipline and make tough decisions
Information-intensive jobs require in-depth relationships	Strong whole-person relationships	Options and alternatives	Strong drive for results
Coordination from above	Provided direction for unskilled workers	Furnished strong supervision required by rapid turnover in boring jobs	Educated employees are ready for self-management
Self-managing teams		Lateral communications and collaboration	

A hallmark of bureaucracy is, of course, hierarchy. Hierarchy is similar to patriarchy in that both hold that there must be—and can only be—one person or collective at the top. The idea of an essential hierarchy coupled with paternalism constitute the cardinal assumptions of a bureaucratic belief system. Paternalism as a belief system can operate even when the organization is not structured as a bureaucracy. For example, local churches in congregational-based systems are often operated as a hierarchy even though they are not organized as a bureaucracy—with the pastor or the council controlling from the "top," and everything else happening "beneath" their control.

QUESTIONS FOR REFLECTION UPON BUREAUCRACY

1. Does your organizational design depict hierarchy as described in the left column of Figure 9.1? When was the last time your pastoral staff and lay leadership discussed your organizational structure?
2. Is your organizational design working for you now? Is it because of the reasons portrayed in column 2?
3. Is your organizational design showing signs of pressure points as depicted in column 3?
4. Do any of the ideas in column 4 appeal to you?

Bureaucracy has been the favored organizational structure in American corporations and institutions for over a hundred years. More recently, however, bureaucracy has been shunted aside (especially in business) because it has become the perfect prescription for nothing getting done.[7] What happened to cause this shift of bureaucracy toward ineffectiveness? The major shift has to do with relationships and trust in the workplace and in our governments—and with the type of changes that are experienced by everyone in the modern environment.

The Loss of Trust in Bureaucratic Systems

Americans no longer believe they can trust their leaders, and are demanding greater accountability on the part of all leaders, from presidents to pastors. The "throw the bums out" attitude that invaded the national election booths in November 1994 was not a little party to break the gray monotony of an impending fall season; it was a statement: "Bureaucrats, beware!"

This distrust in bureaucratic systems has been growing in the American consciousness since the trauma of the Civil Rights era, the endless Vietnam War and a president who deliberately lied about it, followed by another president who criminalized himself in an attempt to ensure his reelection, and the bureaucrats running the big three automobile industries (and other industries) whose greed and arrogance cost America hundreds of thousands of jobs, cost the American economy billions of dollars, and set the nation on course for its largest trade deficit in history.

The suspicion of bureaucrats is now endemic in the American culture; they are distrusted until proven trustworthy. This is true for religious bureaucrats as well as others.

Changes Affecting All People

The single most unsettling change in the world today is all that goes along with moving from the industrial age into the information computer age. We now have a totally new kind of instability to confront; one which the bureaucratic patriarchs cannot control. For decades the bureaucrats in the highest political, industrial, and religious offices convinced us that they had everything under control and, if we simply trusted them, they would make everything all right. Who believes this today? Certainly not the rank and file, perhaps not even the bureaucrats themselves. Bureaucracies, however, are designed to resist change and, if change cannot be resisted, they try to squelch it. Either way the bureaucrats remain at the top, and in control.

The changes brought about by the information computer age, however, are beyond the control of everyone. No one can stop the advance of information now that computers, satellites, the Internet, and the World Wide Web are here. Only a few years ago the world was agog with the speed of jet travel. Then came space travel and lunar explorations—greater distances, greater speeds. What could possibly happen next? The computer information age was what happened next.

Change in one new development or area of the world seems to have an interactive influence on speeding things up in many other areas: e.g., Neil Armstrong's stroll on the moon; the invention of the personal computer; the collapse of the Berlin Wall in 1989; the collapse of the once mighty Soviet Union in 1991.

Actually, these changes are no more astounding than the changes that Americans have encountered in previous generations. The invention of the radio must have been just as astonishing as the invention of the computer; the invention of the lightbulb as amazing as the first laser surgery; the invention of the airplane as surprising as space travel. What is different about the changes of today, however, is that the events that are changing the world presently are out of the control of even the most powerful bureaucrats in the world. For the first time in American history, at least, things are happening that our leaders and their bureaucratic machinery cannot predict, nor control.

It's enough to give us a headache. Perhaps it has. The sale of aspirin-type products has increased by 50 percent since Neil Armstrong took his one step—giant leap for humankind.[8]

What is required of organizations and their managers today? When the environment experiences a great deal of change, the organization must change its structures, belief systems, products, and programs as well. Significant change in the environment puts the organization back to zero.[9] Past success counts for nothing when the environment undergoes sweeping change. In the face of great changes, the organization must structure itself to be lean, flexible, courageous, and quick, or else it will take on the characteristics of a twenty-ton Tyrannosaurus Rex tiptoeing blindfolded through a field of land mines. Why, then, is there so little change in the ways in which industrial, governmental, and religious institutions conduct their business and relate to their constituents? The answer is simple: bureaucratic structures exert greater influence upon the behavior of leaders, managers, and workers than the people do upon the bureaucracies.

Tom Peters, a noted consultant to America's larger organizations, doesn't hold much hope for the future of bureaucracy, or organizations that cling to traditional structures. He says that we live in crazy times and crazy times call for crazy organizations. Bureaucracy is not a crazy organization. It is thoroughly rational, highly structured, and tightly controlled—from the top all the way to the bottom. All the way down it's all the same. No Change![10]

Bureaucratic structures tend to become so entrenched over time that they cannot be changed in an orderly manner. Tom Peters suggests that when structures cannot be changed, the only hope is to destroy them. However, there was a time when bureaucracy served a great purpose—it propelled its masters into the forefront of the industrial revolution. In their excellent book *The End of Bureaucracy & The Rise of the Intelligent Organization,* Gifford and Elizabeth Pinchot state:

> Given that bureaucracy is in such ill repute today, it is hard to remember that it once was considered a great organizational innovation. By organizing the division of labor, by making management and decision making a profession, and by providing an order and a set of rules that allowed many different kinds of specialists to work in coordination toward a common end, bureaucracy greatly extended the breadth and depth of intelligence that organizations could achieve.
>
> Bureaucracy created a system capable of effectively managing the massive investments, division of labor, and large-scale mechanized production of capitalism. Its organizational power drove the initial rapid growth of steel, chemical, and automobile industries.
>
> Despite all these successes, respect for bureaucracy is declining. As in so many other areas of life, what brought great success in the past has become the limitation of the present. Suddenly everyone knows that bureaucracy is slowing us down and keeping our organizations internally focused and uncreative. It is time to question bureaucracy.[11]

The Belief System of Bureaucracy: Paternalism (Parenting).

At its inception, much about bureaucracy was impersonal and inhumane. Those at the top equated the three elements of the assembly line to be of equal value: rubber, steel, and human workers. Bureaucracy's belief system included the idea that if a belt wears out you throw it away and put in a new one; if a bearing wears out you throw it away and put in a new one; if a worker wears out or breaks down, you remove him and put in a new one. This belief system left no room for thought of workers' concerns such as pension plans and insurance programs. However, as time passed workers organized themselves into unions and, in this form of collective power and resistance, forced the bureaucracy to become more humane.

Bureaucracy's refined and more humane belief system is described as *paternalism.* Paternalism is characterized by: (1) benevolent dictatorship: "We own you but don't worry, we will take care of you"; (2) dependence: "We expect you to take care of us"; (3) dominance:

"Even though the people at the top dominate us, they will do so in a humane manner"; (4) control: "Someone has to be in charge"; (5) compliance: "If you keep quiet and do your job, you will get along OK here"; and (6) manipulation: "So what if you don't like your job; this job is better than no job." Peter Block describes paternalism as:

> "The traditional role of line management was to be in charge of patriarchy, their primitive statement to employees being, 'We own you.' To balance this, human resources [divisions have] been put in charge of paternalism. Their primitive statement to employees, 'Don't worry so much about the fact that they own you, because we will take care of you.' This combination creates the golden handcuffs that make living in a world of dominance and dependency so tolerable. As subordinates, we yield sovereignty with the expectation that those in charge of us will care for us in a reasonable and compassionate way. . . . Leadership does not question its own desire for dominance, it asks only that the dominance be implemented humanely. [In paternalism] the handcuffs of control become golden when they are fitted with the promise of protection and satisfaction.[12]

The Persuasiveness of Bureaucracy and Paternalism

Paternalism at the top persuades those in the middle and bottom to become dependent and passive. In a paternal belief system, people come to believe that those at the top should take care of them and, strange as it may seem, many people want to be parented. It may not be articulated as such, but in practice there are many who shrug off all responsibility for the well-being and direction of the organization in which they are employed, or the church to which they belong, and leave it up to those in charge.

How do the leaders of bureaucratic religious institutions feel about all of the dependency, compliance, and passivity on the part of their paid and volunteer workers, and the members? They love it. Though they spend many hours every day complaining about the lazy workers and the indolent members, the religious leaders will never try to change their behavior because a bureaucratic structure and a paternalistic belief system need these conditions in order to survive. The problem with bureaucracy and parenting is that "it steals accountability from the middle and the bottom of the organization."[13]

QUESTIONS FOR REFLECTION UPON ORGANIZATIONAL STRUCTURE AND BELIEF SYSTEMS

1. Does the present belief system and corresponding structure within your church adequately compensate for a changing environment?
2. What are your present ideas to organize yourselves in order to be most effective in your own context?
3. What are the signs of paternalism in your congregation? What are its effects upon the attitudes of members?

Bureaucracy, Paternalism, and American Religious Institutions

All mainstream denominations—and most of the younger, evangelical, American-born denominations—are patterned after bureaucratic structures. Increasing bureaucracy in the growth stages of a denomination seems to be a step forward in reducing the chaos and confusion that come with growth. However, when order and stability becomes the primary goal, they also become a major barrier to growth and renewal.

In spite of all the changes that have occurred in the last half of the twentieth century, most denominations have made no compensating changes in their structures or belief systems. There have been many mergers of denominations, but the changes made to structures and operating belief systems as a result of these mergers have basically consisted of changing some "boiler plates" and "sweeping the deck." The bureaucratic or patriarchal structures have remained almost totally unaffected. Even after dislocating scores of judicatory personnel—as the Presbyterians have done over the past twenty-five years—the bureaucratic structures remain essentially intact. Unless there is a dramatic change in the belief systems that define relationships and governance processes, new people and programs will soon be squeezed into old molds.

The important consideration for our discussion is that the congregations are patterned upon the structures of their respective denominations. Paternalism in the congregation is never healthy, and can sometimes lead to a complete systems breakdown. We were called to help a district superintendent in a medium-sized, evangelical denomination work through a tragic example of what can happen when a congregation depends upon its pastor to take care of them.

The congregation had less than two hundred members. The pastor was greatly concerned that they did not have a Christian school to guard their children from the evils of public education. He coerced the congregation to build a school facility offering kindergarten through eighth grade classes for the community. The church board had many doubts about the congregation's ability to fund such an undertaking.

After several months of the pastor's pushing and the board's resisting, the pastor presented a set of drawings for a new school and declared that he had been working with a local builder who, because it was for a church, had agreed to build the facility for forty dollars a square foot, an amount greatly lower than the usual cost of construction in that area. The pastor also stated that he had recruited the necessary administrators and teachers, who had all agreed to donate their time, or to work for very low wages. With this news the board agreed to launch the project.

The board never took care to speak with the builder regarding how he could build the building for this low amount, nor did they ask for the names of the workers in order that they might get written contracts from each one stating that they would volunteer their time or work for substandard wages. (Do you see how the board was expecting the pastor to take care of them, so that they need not take the necessary time and effort to take care of their own responsibilities?)

The board presented the plan to the small congregation, who, upon the word of the pastor and board, approved the school project. Shortly after construction started the board discovered that the builder's quote was merely a verbal estimate. In fact, the actual building cost was several times higher than the estimate. In order to finance the project, the members of the congregation were called upon to give all they could—and ultimately to mortgage personal and business properties to help pay the costs. This effort, though highly sacrificial, was insufficient to pay the mounting obligations. Consequently, the church floated junk bonds, and the members were called upon to sell them to family and friends across the country. Through such mortgages and junk bonds the board succeeded in obtaining a loan of nearly a half million dollars from a local bank. (Do you see how the congregation got itself into this situation by expecting the board and pastor to take care of them?) Not one member asked to see written contracts before the project was approved. And then, when they found themselves in dire circumstances, they counted on the pastor to take care of them, who kept saying, "This is God's will for us, and the Lord will provide. God is just testing our faith."

But apparently the Lord was not in the mood to favor the paternal pastor. The building was completed. Then the board discovered that only a small number of teachers and administrators had agreed to volunteer their time, and only until the school was up and running. The rest expected at least minimum wages from the start.

After some months of operation the congregation defaulted on its bank payment. The bank notified the denomination's judicatory official. In order to save its reputation, and to spare unsuspecting people from financial ruin, the denomination paid the bank note. The school collapsed. The congregation was totally dispirited. Many left. At about this same time, the pastor felt a call to another ministry, and he, too, left.

Paternalism fosters the hiding of information that "is just too complex to be understood by those people." "We do this only because we care about them. Like children, they are unable to process the intricacies and complexities of the information; therefore, we must avoid giving them the hard truth." All of this is done with the best of intentions—a sincere desire to take care of others. The final result is, of course, deception, betrayal, chaos, and eventual destruction.

Even as we write these words, a news article comes across our fax machine. It makes clear that paternalism is no longer an acceptable belief system for religious organizations:

> Judgment Day has arrived for the organization that oversees Assemblies of God churches in Washington and northern Idaho—not with

> fire and brimstone, but with the cold click of an accountant's calculator. . . . Regulators said the organization's accounting system had overstated the district's net worth by $17.7 million.
>
> In a worst-case scenario, according to a mailing to noteholders . . . , the district's loan fund could have to file for Chapter 11 bankruptcy protection and investors would lose some of their money. . . . But the securities agency found that the organization's top leadership had resisted coming to terms with the problem for nearly two years.
>
> By the time the district's finances were untangled by an outside accounting firm, the superintendent had retired, the business manager had resigned, other staff members were laid off, and the district's Kirkland administrative building and Falls Creek Conference Center in Snohomish County were up for sale.
>
> As a result of the state's findings, church officials had to admit in the "recission" letter mailed . . . to thousands of investors, they had misled the note-holders about the solvency of the organization. . . . What prospective purchasers of the notes were not told was that money from the revolving fund was also used to mask huge annual deficits in the Northwest District's operational budget. . . . Even now, few among the district's members are aware of the extent of the crisis.[14]

We do not believe that these church officials were acting out of malicious intent. They were not lining their own pockets. They were, however, acting in a true paternalistic manner to shield their congregations and investors from the hard truth—they desired only to take care of them. How could a situation like this go on over a period of years without being detected? The answer is simple: the congregations and investors wanted the church officials to take care of them, or they did not have the courage to confront them. Hundreds of investors chose to take no notice of early warning distress signals, to trust the word of their leaders uncritically rather than care for themselves by taking the time and effort to assure this was a financially solid and a fully honest investment offer.

Organizational structures and belief systems of this type are living on borrowed time. Such behavior will no longer be tolerated in secular and religious organizations.

The experience of the denominational district office, recounted above, is but the tip of a huge iceberg that is becoming more obvious in denominational structures. The leaders of religious organizations may do all they can within their power to resist it, but some of them will meet the "wolf on the other side of the door." Loren Mead describes the pressure in *The Once and Future Church: Reinventing the Congregation for a New Mission Frontier:*

> The funding shortfalls in judicatory after judicatory . . . have been getting worse for three decades. Although imaginative marketing, vigorous capital fund campaigns, staff reductions, and re-organizations can paper over the problem temporarily, the real concern is only postponed. People of the church will support what they understand to be mission. What they see coming from their denominational offices does not look like mission to them anymore. No number of bishops and executives will convince them that it is a duck if it keeps barking. The church's people hear quacking in other places and want help from the judicatory. They are not particularly interested in supporting systems that do not seem to help them very much with what they want to be working at—the mission.
>
> I believe that the church of the new age or paradigm is going to need strong effective leadership and skill from the judicatories. But judicatories designed for Christendom will not be sufficient for the new church.
>
> I believe that the ministry role crisis, which has been so painful for clergy and confusing to laity over the past half-century, will, in the next generation, make the work of the denominational executive or bishop extraordinarily difficult. Some judicatory systems may not survive. Some national systems are already in serious trouble. A wise friend states the case more dramatically than I do: "It seems to me," he says, "that what God is doing right now is dismantling the denominational systems as fast as possible."[15]

When you stop to think about it, paternalism is hardly the best structure, whether at the general, judicatory, or local level. Why then are so many religious organizations built on this model? The answer is simple: we all want someone to take care of us.

QUESTIONS FOR REFLECTION UPON PATERNALISM

1. Does it ring true in your congregation that people want to be taken care of? What are the signs that lead you to your conclusion?
2. Where did you gain your own belief systems about organizational structure? How do your belief systems compare with other church leaders and managers?

The Denomination's Role as Regulatory Agency: An Example of Worn-Out Wineskins

Lyle Schaller describes "The Changing Role of Denominations" in *21 Bridges to the 21st Century.*[16] In it he describes two exceptionally influential patterns of institutional structure and behavior of American Protestantism. One pattern is the erosion of power and influence of leaders and agencies within denominations. The second pattern, both a cause and product of the first pattern, is the creation of many single-purpose networks outside of denominational structures. These networks have focused on mission and ministry, and not on the elaborate institutional apparatus too often inherent within denominational structures.[17] For example, the Churches Uniting in Global Mission (CUGM), created in 1991, is a coalition whose members include pastors from various denominations, including the United Methodist, Presbyterian, Lutheran, Episcopal, Southern Baptist, United Church of Christ, Reformed, and American Baptist, as well as Charismatic, Holiness, Christian, Assemblies of God, independent, and other traditions. Other recent networks include: the Leadership Network that began in the 1980s to assist senior pastors of large churches and the Willow Creek Association, which was created in 1990 to provide resources for congregations whose mission and ministry was to reach the unchurched.[18] These networks come into existence, according to Schaller, because of the needs of pastors and congregational leaders that are not being met by the traditional structures in American Protestantism, including the denominations, seminaries, church-related colleges, and older parachurch organizations. Schaller says that with the increasing effectiveness of these coalitions and networks and the erosion of the traditional power structures, roles, and functions of denominations, the very future of denominations is in question.

How do denominations respond to these changes? They deny and ignore them as long as possible—and perhaps to the very end. Denominations have evolved into "regulatory agencies." The certain sign of this trend to function as a regulatory agency is when "[The denomination] adopts rules and regulations that must be followed by individuals, congregations, and regional agencies as well as national agencies."[19] One may presume that as the regulatory authority and practice of denominations increase, so will the number of congregations who decide to secede from those denominations (or at least they would if they could).[20]

Schaller continues, "The most significant implication of this new role of denominations as regulatory agencies centers on one word: *trust*."[21] He then goes on to draw a most surprising conclusion: "The obvious implication of this growing emphasis on regulation by distant denominational agencies is that the *volunteer leaders and the ministers in the local situation cannot be trusted*"(*italics added*).[22]

When the faceless denominational agencies act as unilateral makers and enforcers of denominational policies on any and every subject, they lose the trust of their members and the general populace. However, this lack of trust is expressed and felt most strongly at the level of the local congregations. The people equate the denomination's regulations and "statements" with their local lay and clergy leaders—and they no longer trust them. For Schaller this explains in part why younger ministers and laity are moving toward the independent and nondenominational congregations.

QUESTIONS FOR REFLECTION UPON YOUR EXPERIENCE OF BUREAUCRACY AND PATERNALISM

1. In what specific ways have you been empowered by bureaucracy and paternalism within your congregation? In what ways have you been obstructed by this belief system and structure?
2. How has paternalism affected relationships within your congregation?
3. Is paternalism an operating factor in the roles of the church staff? Does it enable or incapacitate them?
4. What interventions might you make to move toward a more effective belief system and structure?

Is there an alternative to bureaucracy and paternalism? Yes. And like it or not, many denominations and local congregations are already inching toward it—not because they want to, but because of increasingly unsatisfactory results. The alternative is partnership with the concept of stewardship as its governing principle. We will proceed now to look at the organization that is coming, one that is already mounting a frontal attack on all bureaucracies and paternalism. This attack is slower in coming to the denominations, but coming it is nonetheless.

> The last of a dying civilization is that somebody will be writing a procedure.[23]
>
> John Gardner

The Essence of Stewardship

The Essence of Understanding Traditional Organizational Structures and Belief Systems

1. A changing environment demands a changing organizational structure.
    - Bureaucracy was invented to organize work within a stable environment while continuing to remain paternal.
2. Bureaucracy is embedded within the belief system of paternalism.
    - The expectation is that those at the top will take care of those at the bottom.
    - Without dependency and compliance, paternalism will not work.
3. Significant change in the environment will put all organizations back to "zero."
    - Past success counts for nothing when the level of technology, thinking, quality, and so on has gone through significant change.
4. This significant change has caused old ways of organizing (bureaucracy and paternalism) to become outdated and irrelevant.
    - There must be a creative and unique means by which congregations can be structured in order to accommodate rapid and drastic change.

How You Can Evaluate Your Own Structures and Belief Systems

1. Develop an awareness of the belief systems and structures that are exerting influence upon you and the leaders in the church.
    - Are they enabling or restricting?
2. Organize "teams" of people to be a part of the leadership structure.
    - "Teams" provide a decentralized leadership base that enhances the ability of a congregation to compensate for change.
3. Be intentional in your creation of "rules and regulations" in your organization.
    - If these principles (written or unwritten) are not empowering people toward creative mission and ministry, why are the rules in place?
4. Foster the relationships of the church's leadership!
    - Can outsiders be included as insiders as well?
    - What level of cooperation is at work?
5. TRUST! Create it. Develop it. Earn it. Nurture it. Talk about it.

And no one puts new wine into old wineskins; otherwise the new wine will burst the skins and will be spilled, and the skins will be destroyed. But new wine must be put into fresh wineskins. And no one after drinking old wine desires new wine, but says, "The old is good" (Luke 5:37-39). or "The old is good enough" (NASB).

10

Partnership: A New Era in Organization Design

Figure 10.1

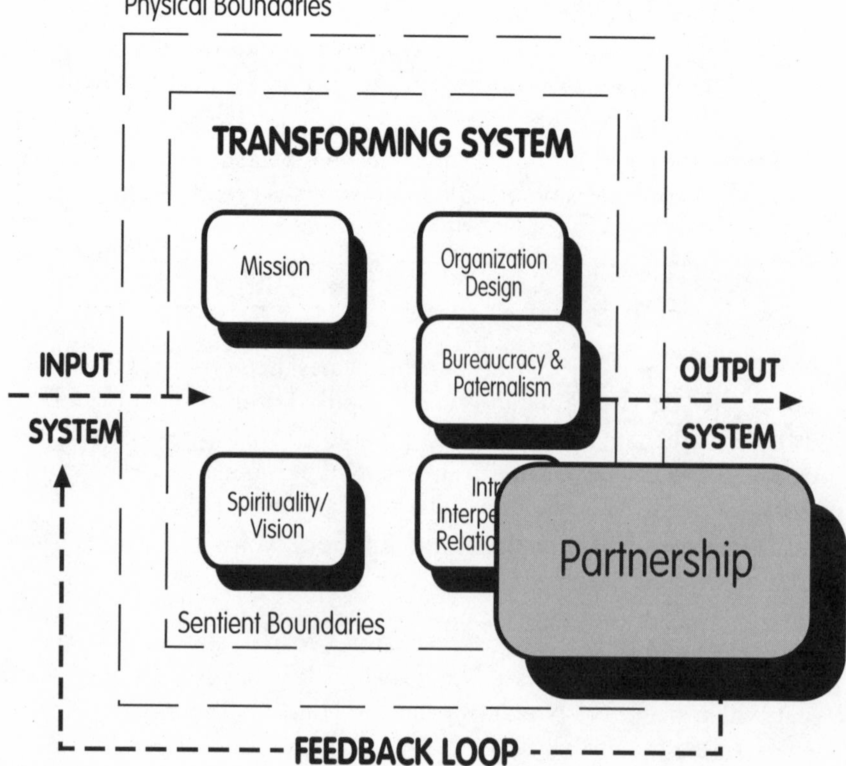

I do not call you servants any longer, because the servant does not know what the master is doing (John 15:15a).

Advances in management theory over the past three decades are spawning breakthroughs into new understandings of relationships between corporations and stockholders, managers and workers, owners and stakeholders, religious managers and congregations. There is a coming together of theory and practice around the idea that many of the old images and understandings—such as leader and follower, manager and worker, top and bottom—no longer define the new realities or serve a useful purpose.

In this chapter we discuss a new design for organizations that is coming upon the scene of secular and religious institutions. This new understanding of management is called *partnership.* The belief system for partnership is called *stewardship* by some and *servanthood* by others.[1] Peter Block defines stewardship as follows:

> Stewardship is the set of principles and practices which have the potential to make dramatic changes in our governance system. It is concerned with creating a way of governing ourselves that creates a strong sense of ownership and responsibility for outcomes [not only at the top but also] at the bottom of the organization. It means giving control to customers [the congregation and its workers] and creating self-reliance on the part of all who are touched by the institution. This is what will get us closer to our marketplace. It is the connection with our marketplace. That is the answer to our concerns about [our results and future].[2]

Stewardship must be the governing principle of a partnership structure, or partnership will not work.

The Demise of Christendom and the Search for a New Organization Paradigm

Loren Mead, in *The Once and Future Church,* states that the old Christendom paradigm is passing away, and that we do not know what will replace it.[3] However, many recent developments suggest that partnership, in whatever form or adaptation, will be the next paradigm for religious organization design. Partnership models will replace many of the present structures and beliefs that give form to our denominational agencies and congregations. But this will not happen without a great deal of trauma and pain. John Wesley was converted at Aldersgate, but he went "most unwillingly."

Like Wesley, few religious managers or congregations change their ways willingly. They change only when they are handed a convincing wake-up call, when they are forced to change in response to shrinking memberships and budgets or overwhelming conflicts. The wake-up call is sounding and has been sounding for more than fifteen years, as our congregations and denominations bleed red ink in their membership, attendance, and contribution figures.

There are, we think, three primary reasons for the reluctance of denominations and of congregations to heed the call: (1) Bureaucracies are almost impossible to change, and those that do change usually must come near to the brink of death before doing so; (2) Bureaucratic leaders love their position on the top, and will exert every effort to stay there; and (3) The pastors and members at the local level, executives at the judicatory level, and officials at the national level are accustomed to their position in the structure; old habits die hard.

The Hallmarks of Partnership

The hallmarks of partnership are: (1) absolute honesty; (2) straight talk; (3) the right to say no; (4) joint accountability, a balance of power; (5) no promises of security; (6) the elimination of status symbols and perks; and (7) the exchange of purpose.[4] We will discuss each of these in the context of partnership as an organization design.

Absolute Honesty

Partnership requires absolute honesty in all conversation and reporting, because all partners have equal right to all information. Absolute honesty also involves complete disclosure. Withholding information pertinent to one's work or membership falls under the category of the manager's sins of omission.

Peter Block suggests two questions managers need to ask in order to help them decide how to relate with their partners in any consequential circumstance: (1) "How would partners handle this?" and (2) "What policy or structure would we create if this were a partnership?"[5] Answering these questions with honesty will always move us closer to partnership, even if we are organized in a bureaucratic structure.

Straight Talk

Tom Melohn describes straight talk, or plain talk, as something "different from honesty. Obviously you must first be honest. But then you've got to tell it straight—no embellishments, no qualifiers. Straight ahead. Plain vanilla."[6] Straight talk is more than words. It also includes actions, kept promises, openness, and transparency. For example, a congregation cannot engage in straight talk if it is not working hard to achieve a record of outstanding quality in all of its ministries and if the service record of all the workers cannot stand up well to critical review. Actions and quality of this kind may be the plainest talk possible. "What you do rings so loudly in my ears that I cannot hear a word you are saying." The baby boomer generation decides quality not upon tradition but upon the delivery of services and honesty. So, we must "walk our talk."

Without doubt one reason why many churches have trouble holding the commitment of members is that the leaders fail the test of straight talk regarding what the church wants and expects from them. They attempt to make the cost of membership appear to be a "bargain basement transaction" when, in fact, they hope the member will become a "top floor" commodity. Plain talk with prospective members includes the values and expectations of membership: tithing, doing ministry, faithful attendance, and continual learning. For example, the prospective member might be told, "The standard of giving for our members is the tithe. Your tithe will go toward producing the worship services you attend, the ministry in which you are engaged, the maintenance of our facilities, and the care we will extend to you and your family. In return we will give you quality—and if we fail in our commitment to quality, please tell us so—plainly and immediately."

The Right to Say No

In partnership, participants have a right to say no. Saying no is how we differentiate ourselves, but it does not mean that we always get what we want. Without permission to say no, saying yes has little meaning. And while there may be situations when the supervisor may have the final authority because of her position, everyone still has a right to say no. Therefore, everyone has a voice.[7]

Joint Accountability

In a partnership there is joint accountability. No one is to blame—because each person is fully responsible for the results and the bottom line. Leaders are no longer parents who are responsible for group morale and taking care of subordinates. Each person is responsible for one's self and for cooperation and the outcomes of the organization. That is, the freedom of partnership must also include the accountability of each person for the success or failure of the congregation's purpose and goals.

No Promises of Security

Security comes in many different forms: emotional security, job security (for paid workers), and a sense that the church is headed in the right direction; it will not fail me—ever. In *Management and the Activity Trap,* George Odiorne speaks of organizations and leaders who are people shrinkers.[8] In relating to such an organization, a person always goes away feeling sapped of energy, a little less self-confident, or less than what one was before the encounter. In people-shrinking congregations there is no emotional security but a growing sense of being ever more dependent upon the pastor and leaders.

Security for paid workers entails providing a sense that the church is headed in the right direction, that it will continue to need the worker's services, and that the church will continue to be a place where the worker can grow. Security means that we will treat our workers with the same care and commitment to long-term relationships as we would the members of our own family.

Security for the members of the congregation involves a sense that the church is headed in the right direction, that it will continue to meet the spiritual needs of the people, and provide opportunities for the members to grow and be involved in ministry that matters. In a congregation persons have a legitimate right to expect emotional and job security, and they have a right to know for certain that the church is headed in the right direction. However, in a partnership design these rights come at a price—for each one of the members and workers bears a responsibility and is accountable to work toward these ends. There are no passive observers, no Monday morning quarterbacks in a partnership.

In a partnership congregation, when one person, or several, demand rights and privileges for themselves that they will not fully accord to all the others, or if they are not carrying their fair share of work and responsibility, or if they refuse to be accountable for the quality of their participation, then straight talk is needed to set the record straight regarding the fact that they cannot expect security, service, or recognition without working for it.

The Elimination of Status Symbols and Perks

Status symbols and perks are the language of power in hierarchical structures. Many status symbols and perks are very obvious; for example, whose name appears in the top box on the organizational chart or on the reserved parking spaces; or who has the office with the plush furniture? Others are not so readily apparent to the eye. For example, we worked with a church in which the pastors call the board members by their first names, yet the pastors insist upon being addressed by their titles (Reverend, Pastor, or Doctor) and their last names. In some congregations when leaders attempt to do away with such trappings, their efforts are resisted by subordinates who don't want the balance to shift, in case they should attain the pinnacle and deserve similar perks and honor.

The Exchange of Purpose

In the exchange of purpose, partnership means that every person at every level of the organization has a right to know the truth, and has a responsibility to help to define the vision.[9] Work and planning processes should include enough time for the purpose to become defined and refined through dialogue with all partners included. Those who do not participate when invited to do so are choosing some kind of compliance or dependency. They are choosing not to be partners.

For some, partnership may sound too ideal; for others it makes no sense, or it simply is not the organizational structure they prefer. To make partnership work well requires certain prerequisites.

How Does Your Church Measure Up To the Partnership Hallmarks?

1. Are you open and honest in your communication to the congregation and leaders?
2. Do you "walk" what you "talk" within the context of leadership?
3. Do members and workers have a right to say "no" in your congregation? If they do not, who is forcing people to say "yes"?
4. Is your congregation involved in joint accountability? Or do persons tend to blame others?
5. Does your congregation provide a sense of false security?
6. To what degree is your church involved in bestowing status symbols and perks?
7. Are you hesitant to suggest these prerequisites for partnership to the staff and lay leaders? Why?
8. What are you afraid of having to give up if your church were to adopt a partnership design? Why?

The Essential Prerequisite for Partnership

Selecting the Right People

There is an inviolate precondition for creating a congregation based upon partnership: you must begin by selecting the right people. If you cannot begin anew then you must begin by building "pockets of partnership" wherever you can—by enlisting the right people in the appropriate programs or ministries whenever you have the opportunity to do so.

In partnership you are looking for a different breed of staff workers and volunteers—persons who are trustworthy, who have passion for the mission and the future of the church, who are self-starters, who take great pride in their work and are quality driven, who are able to work well with others, and who possess a healthy self-esteem.

Without such people, all partnership efforts will lead to frustration and failure. You cannot force people to bear the burden of responsibility that partnership will place upon them. You cannot force them to share the vision. Moreover, many people will resist self-accountability because they want to be cared for, and to be excused for poor quality performance. For partnership to succeed, it will require that these persons are not placed in positions of leadership or responsibility. Partnership rises or falls on your ability to select the right people and to put them in the right places.

Partnership requires turning nearly all of our old notions about management upside down—literally. For example, there are myths that set limits to the number of persons for whom the manager can offer direct supervision (earlier called span of control). Some say five to eight is about right; others assert fifteen is too many. Limiting the number to these levels makes sense when the purpose of management is to control. Partnership, however, places no limits to the number of persons a manager can supervise, because every partner is expected to manage himself or herself as though he or she were the boss—for each is responsible for the welfare of the entire congregation.

There will always be someone with greater responsibilities than others—a pastor, a partner-in-charge. Of this Block says, "Partnership does not do away with hierarchy and we still need bosses. People at higher levels do have a specialized responsibility, but it is not so much for control as it is for clarity. Clarity of requirements. Clarity about value-added ways of attending to [the people we serve and the ministries we offer]."[10]

The Major Impediments to Finding the Right People for Partnership

Partnership in the congregation faces some unique barriers, which makes the local church one of the most difficult of all organizations in which to install partnership structures and stewardship/servanthood belief systems. What are some of these barriers?

The Nominating Process

Virtually all denominations have long established norms and processes for filling volunteer positions in the congregation. First, many denominations specify the committees and other positions that must be filled. Second, the guidelines often specify that these positions are to be filled by a nominating committee that is comprised of members in the congregation. This sounds very democratic. The truth is, however, that the process as followed in a vast majority of congregations simply sells important lay leadership and ministry positions to the lowest bidders.

In many instances the pastors feel strapped by the process because they have long since learned that there are few secrets kept by the nominating committee. Therefore, when persons are named to positions whom the pastor feels are unqualified, he feels restrained to voice his objections. He fears the word will get back to the nominee, and hard feelings will ensue. As a result, many key positions are filled by persons who will not perform.

This condition is often exacerbated in congregations that vote on the pastor's tenure, because the rejected nominee has family and friends in the church—all who remember these things when the time comes to vote on the pastor. Since the pastor didn't want so-and-so to be the chairperson of a particular committee, we don't want him as our pastor.

Asking Volunteers to Name the Job They Want in the Church

There is a systems law that says, "If you don't want the answer, don't ask the question." The law fits well in this discussion because if you ask and then say "no," you have almost certainly disappointed or disenfranchised the would-be volunteer. To do this once is a mistake. To do it a second time is stupid.

The remedy is simple: don't ask for volunteers. Ask for partners, or ask for ministers. The word *volunteer* is fraught with problems because it creates images in the minds of many that are unhealthy. Too many persons feel that if they can volunteer to do a job, they can also volunteer to do it poorly. Recruit the workers one-by-one and face-to-face, following agreed upon recruitment process and standards for all workers.[11] In many of the successful congregations, we hear a common theme in our interviews: there are no volunteers here, all are ministers. For example, pastor Rick Warren at Saddleback Valley Community Church tells us that the church has one thousand ministers. A few are ordained; the rest are members of the congregation who are selected from those who progress through the church's spiritual growth process.[12]

Supervision and Assessment in Partnership Structures

Supervision and work assessment are always problematical in congregations. First, scores of lay boards feel that the pastor's work should be evaluated, but blanch at the thought that the work of the volunteer workers and the committees should also be evaluated, using the same standard used to evaluate the pastor.

QUESTIONS FOR REFLECTION UPON SELECTING THE RIGHT PEOPLE

1. Where are the potential "pockets of partnership" in your congregation?
2. How would you characterize your staff workers in terms of being trustworthy, passionate for the church's mission and future, self-starters, quality driven, able to work well with others, and possessing a healthy dose of self-esteem?
3. Do you have a plan to train your staff workers in these areas?
4. Are there patterns in the frustrations of your staff workers? Can you explain this?
5. Are you pleased with the ways in which lay leaders and volunteers become trustworthy workers in your congregation?

In a hierarchical structure the authority resides with the people up on top. They never expect to be evaluated. After all, who beneath them could possibly understand their jobs well enough to evaluate them? In partnership, however, the authority lies wherever a partner is. Therefore, all partners must be open to evaluation by the other partners. At a minimum, partnership will require a change in the ground rules of supervision and of assessment.

More radical than this, however, is what a true partnership calls for by way of the performance appraisal process. Partnership turns the hierarchical, top-down theories of performance appraisal on their heads. In partnership, annual performance reviews, for example, would begin at the bottom of the line and work upward from there. And why not? Have you ever felt satisfied by the assessment of your performance made by some "omniscient authority" above you? Not often, if ever. As Peter Block says, "It's not easy to play God, so why not stop trying? Let each person be responsible for conducting two appraisals: his or her own and the person he or she works for."[13] In partnership, performance assessment is not top-down; it is bottom-up. As an associate pastor, for example, I would assess my own performance in reaching my goals and also assess how well the senior pastor (if this is to whom I report) supports me in reaching my goals. I would also assess how well she did in achieving her own work goals. This arrangement for performance assessment expresses a common interest in each other's success.

Such assessment comes far closer to stewardship than top-down models. Stewardship is holding something in trust for another; it is as

Peter Block points out, "the willingness to be accountable for the well-being of the larger organization by operating in service, rather than in control, of those around us. Stated simply, it is accountability without control or compliance."[14] Bottom-up assessment accomplishes this.

This type of bottom-up assessment again points us to the necessity of beginning with the right people. Who cares to be evaluated by persons who eschew self-responsibility for quality in their own work assignments? Not many. Rather, if one is to be assessed by others, one hopes that they at least understand what good work looks like—and that they can be trusted to do so in their own ministry areas.

The issue here, however, is more than the structure of the supervisory relationship. It is crucial to enlist the right people for the needed assignment. No amount of structural adjustment can completely correct the damage done by the enlistment of the wrong people for the job.

QUESTIONS FOR REFLECTION UPON SUPERVISION AND ASSESSMENT

1. How are you presently assessing your own performance? Are others involved in the process?
2. How can the organizational climate and individual resistances be changed so that everyone wants to learn how to improve and be more effective in ministry?
3. Is it possible for your staff to evaluate "upward"? Do you see any benefits in this?

Partnership in Action

Current Examples of Partnership

Here is an example of one congregation that has designed its structure upon a partnership model with a belief system of servanthood and stewardship. The story was told to us by David Trotter, a graduate student who is working in the church.

I have been at Calvary Church Newport-Mesa for six months. Tim Celek is the pastor, and I serve as a small group leader.

The first thing I noticed about the church was the quality of the services and facilities. Each service usually starts with a high-powered, emotive secular song that sets the tone for the meeting. After a "welcoming" from the pastor, another song is performed (either secular or Christian). At this point a drama is presented, which directly relates to the topic that the pastor will teach. No matter what the church presents on a particular Sunday, the core message is always that people matter to God. The actual mission is: "Helping people who say no, say yes—yes to God!"

After six months, I am developing several relationships within the leadership structure (particularly with the Associate Pastor of Small Groups, Small Group Interns, and Small Group Coach).

Although not presented in the main service, the idea of being a "servant" is seen to be crucial to the church. This concept is most clearly presented in the Leadership Seminar and the Small Groups Orientation. The entire concept of service centers around the image of three pyramids or "hierarchical triangle."

The church operates on the principle of three triangles placed side-by-side. Each of these triangles stands for a different part of their approach to leadership. The inverted triangle is a form of leadership that emphasizes "more responsibility, less rights," and which is based upon an exegesis of 1 Corinthians 9.

The right triangle undergirds the leadership with "support and encouragement," which is based upon an understanding of Hebrews 10:19ff. The left triangle also supports the inverted triangle with the "power of God," which is described in Galatians 2:20 and Ephesians 3:20.

The three triangles demonstrate that the more power the leaders claim for themselves, the less the people will be willing and able to support them. The rectangle that provides a basis for all three triangles is the "Foundation of Christ."

The role of a leader at Calvary is to be a true servant to everyone, but particularly to the unchurched. The phrase "descend into leadership" is continuously stressed. One must become a servant in order to lead, because perks and applause should not be the reward of a leader.

I have never seen a group of leaders so committed to serving the people of a congregation and people who don't know

Figure 10.2

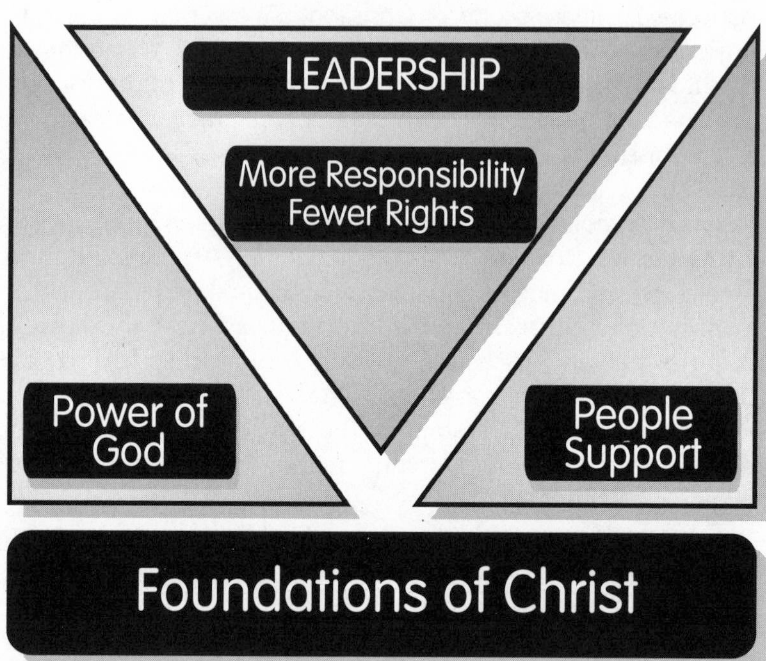

Christ. These leaders are constantly doing whatever it takes to get a job done in a high quality manner.

One of the main characteristics of leaders at the church is that they do not draw attention to themselves or expect attention to be given to them. The unchurched come to an event or service, and they see a *group* of genuine leaders who are there to lead by serving them.

This attitude quickly eliminates any ideas that the church is merely just there for more contributions, or that the pastor wants to be the "star."

David further told us that in virtually every staff meeting the pastor draws the three triangles on the white board and then, pointing to the bottom of the inverted triangle, says, "I want to remind you that it is our privilege to be here, and to be the servants of all the people who are in our congregation from this position, the position of the servant of God's people." The church was founded in 1988, and its weekend services average an attendance of 1,300 adults and children.

The elements of this story that tell us this church is based on a partnership model are:

1. A clear stewardship belief system that informs their actions and provides them a measure for monitoring their ministries and relationships.
2. A decentralized power structure with leadership growing "up" from within the congregation.
3. The elimination of perks or status symbols that set "important" people apart from the rank and file. Pastors and all other leaders must give up their perks. However, even when the pastors want to do this, others will resist.

Pastor Bob Ona and the pastoral staff of the Brookfield Assembly of God Church in Brookfield, Wisconsin, are attempting to take some steps toward a partnership model. The pastors recently gave up their designated parking spaces, which are the closest ones to the front door of the church. This would allow the space to be reserved for persons with handicapping conditions. Many members immediately resisted, complaining that they would no longer be able to know whether the pastors were in the building if they didn't park in their designated spaces.

Bishop Mary Ann Swenson of the United Methodist Church experienced a similar reaction when she started parking away from designated slots at the conference center in Colorado. The staff apparently wanted to know if she was in or out that day, and watching her parking spot was one way of knowing.

Steps Toward Partnership

1. Start with the right people. It cannot be overemphasized that in all partnership efforts you are looking for a different type of paid and volunteer worker, persons who are self-starters, team players, and proud of doing good work, those who search for quality in all important areas of their lives. Such persons are passionate about working in a partnership design. They are trustworthy; they will carry out their responsibilities with a minimum of top-down regulation. Moreover, they are capable of maintaining open and honest communications and relationships.

The difference between bureaucratic and partnership personalities might be diagrammed as follows:

Figure 10.3

The Bureaucratic Personality	**The Partnership Personality**
Compliant	Trustworthy self-starter
Careful to go "by the book"	Passion for results
Immersed in activities	Works toward results
Good is good enough	Pride in high quality performance
Dull and predictable	Constantly surprising you with something good
Manageable and predictable	Assumes responsibility to manage his or her self and work

Apart from having the right people involved in partnership, the most valiant efforts of the pastor will fail.

When you discover that you have selected someone who does not meet these criteria, you must have "straight talk" conversations with him. If after working with this person for a reasonable time and being careful to explain your expectations of him in plain talk, he still does not assume self-responsibility, you will have to remove him—or else the entire partnership design will be weakened.

In saying this, we mean nothing derogatory about persons who cannot serve in a partnership structure. They are not the mistake; the mistake is always on our part. We select and recruit them, but we do not take sufficient care to make adequate predictions of their behavior in a partnership context. The following is an example shared with us by a United Methodist pastor:

> In this church a fifty-year-old member was elected to serve as one of the lay leaders of the congregation. Within a few months it was apparent that he was not suited to this most important job. However, the pastors did not want to hurt him, and so they avoided plain talk and honesty.
>
> Rather, they reasoned that he was quite evangelical, he could talk a mile a minute, he always complained that the evangelism committee wasn't doing a good job. So they decided to appoint him to be the chairperson of the evangelism committee.
>
> It took him about three months to throw the evangelism ministry into complete chaos and conflict. The hard work of other people to build the outreach ministry was lost.
>
> Now there was no alternative. Plain talk was mandatory. The worker was removed from the evangelism committee; whereupon he did exactly what the staff worried about when they struggled over removing him as lay leader. He left the church. But in the meantime he had destroyed a good and worthwhile ministry.

Where the mistake lies in this story is obvious. The unqualified man was not the problem. The pastors who moved him from one failed position into another position, without engaging in plain talk and honest feedback, actually did an injustice to him, and ultimately did great damage to the church's ministry. In partnership, low quality and untrustworthy performance cannot be protected or rewarded.

2. Move ministry decisions out of the administrative committees and into the hands of those who are actually doing the ministry. In partnership those who do the work manage the work. This simple change eliminates all the levels of organization that talk about ministry and programs but don't do hands-on ministry.

3. Organize around constituencies—elementary children, junior highs, senior highs, singles by choice, divorced, and so on. Stop organizing around functions: Christian Education, Stewardship, Missions, and so on. In organizations whose products are people, it is virtually impossible to create partnership models by organizing around functions, because the people who are delivering the services of the church are not delivering them to functions, but to people.

For example, consider the Junior High youth (constituency) and Sunday school (which is a function of Christian Education). When you call a meeting of the Christian Education committee (a committee or function), who shows up? The Christian Education committee members, the Christian Education Director, and perhaps a pastor. In this meeting the Junior High youth are not represented.

When you call a meeting of the Sunday school workers, who shows up? The Sunday school Superintendent, the teachers, a representative from the Christian Education Committee, and the nursery workers. In this meeting the Junior High youth are represented by their teacher. But no one else in this group has any hands-on contact with the youth. Now we are in position to ask the partnership question: "How can the Junior High youth teachers forge a partnership ministry in this setting?" They cannot.

What happens if the entire Christian Education program is organized around constituencies (instead of functions), and we call a meeting of the Junior High youth ministry team? Who shows up? The Junior High Sunday school teacher, the Boy and Girl Scout leaders, the day camp director, the soccer coach, the youth pastor, and the director of the acolytes (since in our scenario the Junior High youth serve as acolytes). Now let's ask the question, "How can the Junior High Sunday school teacher forge a partnership ministry in this setting?" Easy. When we focus on the Junior High youth as a constituent group, then we bring together all of the people who work with them. Now we can plan a comprehensive ministry model that encompasses every contact the church has with the youth, and plans can be made to work in partnership to transform their lives by working in harmony and not in isolation from one another.

What we have said regarding the Junior High youth can be said of every constituent group in the congregation. Organizing around functions makes partnerships virtually impossible, while organizing around constituents makes partnerships meaningful and rewarding.

In our illustration we designed a *structure* for the Junior High youth ministry that will make partnership possible. We did not design a *belief system* for the youth ministry. Creating the appropriate structure is important, but it is not enough. Unless the new structure is imbued with a clear and compelling belief system about relating to and ministering to these youth, the only thing that will change is the structure.

Is it possible to project a belief system of partnership, stewardship, and servanthood upon a hierarchical structure? Though it may be inconsistent with what we have said earlier, we think it is possible to moderate the belief system of a hierarchical design. You may begin talking about partnership and servanthood with your leaders by turning the bureaucratic pyramid upside down and asking them, "If we were to view our structure from this angle, what would it suggest about our roles and examples as leaders? What would it suggest regarding the expectations we would have for all the workers?" We take our cue from Calvary Church in Newport Beach, California, whose partnership model we considered earlier in this chapter.

You might begin moving the leaders and workers toward partnership by putting such a diagram before them and saying, "Here is where we are—at the bottom of the power and position triangle. It is our privilege to serve these people, beginning with the least, and those still outside our congregation." Then teach them how to plan and do ministry from the bottom up instead of the top down.

Another way to conceptualize a partnership structure is to view the partnership structure as a circle, with the "Partner-in-charge" positioned at the edge of the circle, not at the top of the pyramid.

In this model we have placed the leader at the edge of the circle. The leader is managing from the edge. Richard Bondi says it is easier for ministers to respond truthfully if they think of themselves as living at the edge of their communities, rather than at the center—where all the power is.[15] Joel Barker, in his video *The Business of Paradigms,* says that all new paradigms are written at the edge. This is because the power people in the center have too much to preserve by guarding their place at the center.[16]

Figure 10.4

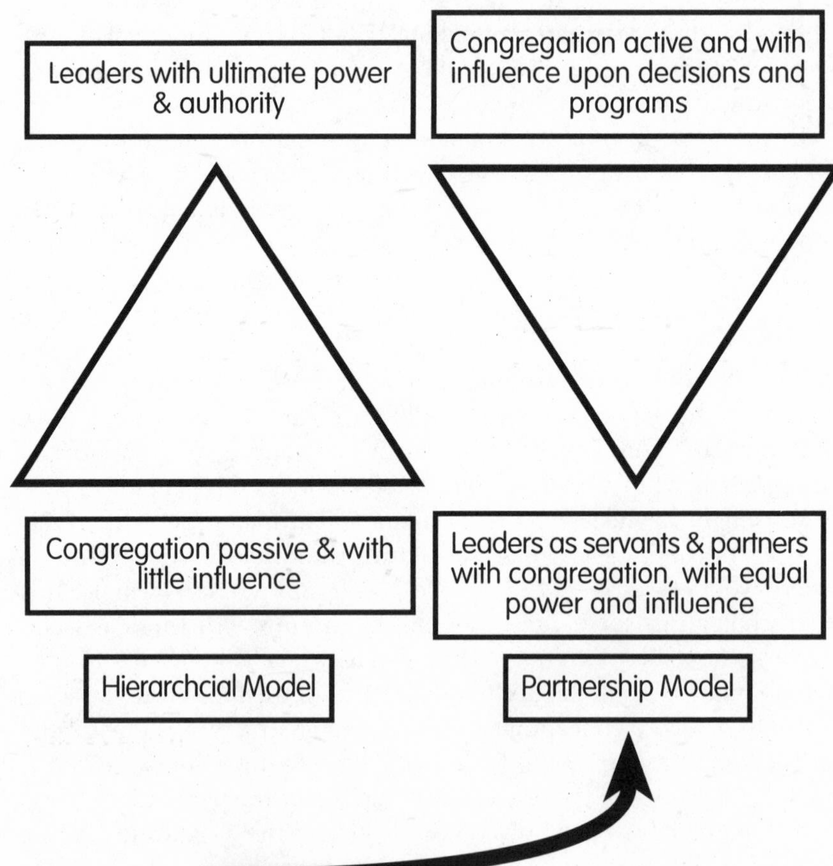
Leaders with ultimate power & authority
Congregation active and with influence upon decisions and programs
Congregation passive & with little influence
Leaders as servants & partners with congregation, with equal power and influence
Hierarchcial Model
Partnership Model

Figure 10.5

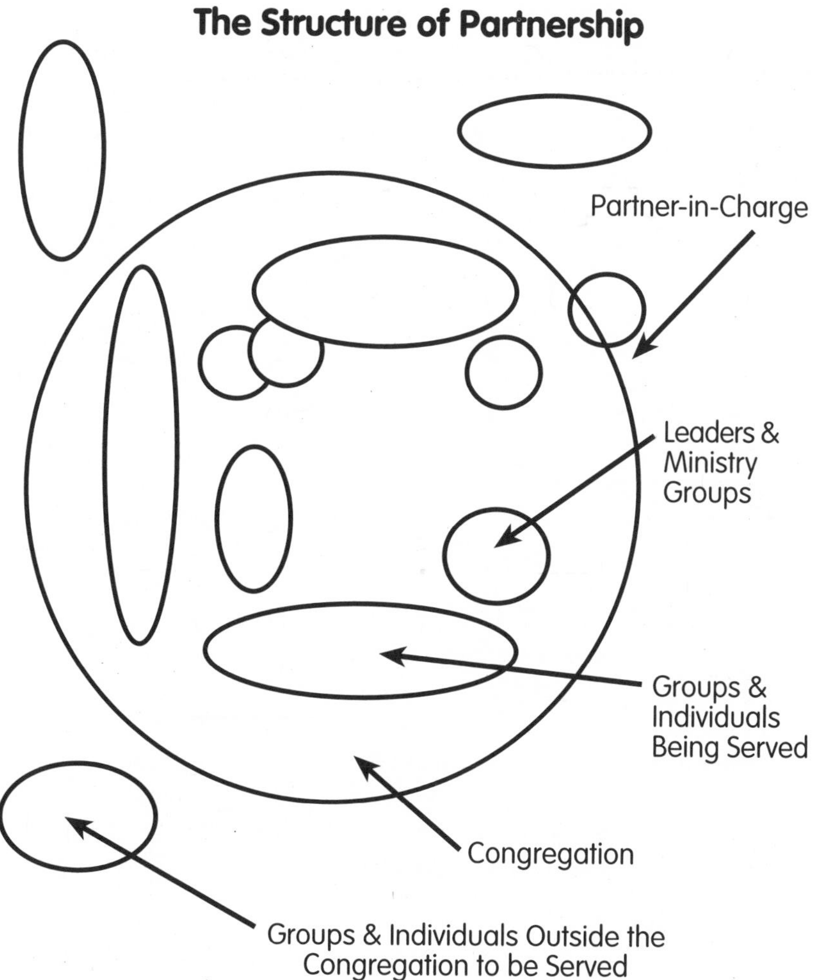
The Structure of Partnership
Partner-in-Charge
Leaders & Ministry Groups
Groups & Individuals Being Served
Congregation
Groups & Individuals Outside the Congregation to be Served

Operating Principles for Partnership

1. Partnership ultimately depends upon recruiting the right people. If you recruit the right people, you have gone the greater distance toward realizing your goals in partnership. Age, education, or experience and not the most important criteria for selecting the right people.
2. Everyone is of great value, but not everyone wants to be a partner. Not everyone is self-responsible, trustworthy, or passionate, and some want primarily to be cared for.
3. Learning together is the mind set for partnership teams.[17]
4. The principle of "no surprises" only makes sense in bureaucracies. In partnership you begin with the right people and then say to them, "Go ahead—surprise us with something good."
5. Most religious leaders don't want equality, comradeship, or partnership. Look at the trappings they (we) continue to support: reserved parking spaces, larger offices with furniture made out of real wood, large windows, special garb, and extra technology perks.
6. Jesus wanted partners, not subordinates or clones. He selected twelve and mentored them. Then he selected seventy and immediately sent them out to minister. How could he trust them so soon? Because he recruited the right people. However, he did make one "mistake" in his recruiting, which contributed significantly to his later problems.
7. Treat the entire congregation as partners. Practice straight talk, absolute honesty (never lie, ever), joint accountability, elimination of status symbols, no promises of security (for nonpaid workers this means mediocre performance is not excused or rewarded), the right to say no, and exchange of purpose.[18]

Stewardship is not a panacea. There may always be situations in which hierarchical structures are appropriate and facilitating. These situations, however, are no longer universal. The religious manager must learn to read the situation with open eyes and make reasoned judgments as to what type of design will be most beneficial in each important situation.

QUESTIONS FOR REFLECTION UPON PARTNERSHIP

1. In what practical ways could you shift decision-making power into the hands of lay workers, while still assuring quality decisions?
2. How can you help the congregation move beyond thinking in triangles? Should you turn the triangle upside down? Or, should you begin to think in circles?
3. Do the present leaders characterize bureaucratic personalities or partnership personalities? If you were to implement a form of partnership, would leaders need to change?

The Essence of Partnership

1. The hallmarks of partnership include:
    - Absolute honesty.
    - Straight talk.
    - Joint accountability.
    - No promises of security.
    - The elimination of status symbols and perks.
    - The exchange of purpose.
2. The prerequisite of ultimate importance for organizing work around partnership is that you must begin by selecting the right people.
    - People who are trustworthy, quality-oriented, self-starters, and flexible.
    - When mistakes are made in recruiting the right people, "plain talk" is in order.
    - When plan talk doesn't solve the problem, the problem person must be relieved.
3. Partnership does not do away with hierarchy completely!
    - Partners at higher levels with specialized responsibilities are there for clarity, not control.
4. Partnership will be resisted, because many people desire to be reliant and dependent. That's what they've been taught!

How You Can Implement Partnership

1. Recruit the right people to the right positions! Don't ask for volunteers.
    - These people must be trustworthy, quality-oriented, self-starters, and flexible.
2. Recognize the bad habits of persons and groups that work against partnership.
    - When a belief system or structure violates partnership, it must be changed or eliminated.
3. Within any consequential circumstance, leaders need to ask:
    - "How would partners handle this?"
    - "What policy or structure would we create if this were a partnership?"
4. Don't just turn your hierarchy upside down! Begin to think in circles.
5. Treat the entire congregation as a partnership.

PART FIVE

The Congregation's Relationships

Introduction

We have a mystery on our hands . . . it is the mystery of how we, weak and limited persons that we are, can look all the uncertainty of life full in the face and say, I will make one thing certain: my presence in the life of another person.[1]

Lewis B. Smedes

Are you and your coworkers filled with excitement about being with others in the church to participate in the church's life and ministry—or do you and others look for excuses not to be a part of the church's ministry? Is there laughter in the hallways because people are actually enjoying conversations with one another—or do people hurry in and out of the church, stopping only for perfunctory conversations? Do the workers feel they are part of a team, or do they "keep to themselves," isolated, and ministering out of "guilt filled" duty? Can people be honest with each other—expressing even their fears, anger, and sadness?

There are some churches whose narthex, sanctuary, hallways, and parking lots are filled with a spirit of genuine community among its workers and attendees. But there are far too many churches that are filled with a spirit of "uptightness," anger, passive-aggressive energy, and outright judgments. This all has to do with the congregation's energy source expressed in its relationships. People give expression to the goodwill, energy, and fruit of the spirit (or lack thereof) in congregations. One person's attitude can change things in significant ways.

It is the religious manager's task to provide a climate that enables people to work freely, responsibly, effectively, and joyfully with others. This is one of the greatest gifts a manager offers to a congregation.

Managers view relationships from a unique perspective. Preachers, for example, define relationships out of the spoken Word and its encounter with the listener; pastoral caregivers define relationships out of accompanying others on their journey and the eventual healing of hurt, pain, or problems; but managers define relationships out of working with others for their own empowerment and capacity to serve. Stephen Covey explains:

> When you fully empower people, your paradigm of yourself changes. You become a servant. You no longer control others; they control themselves. You become a source of help to them. If you want to influence and empower people, first recognize that they are resourceful and have vast untapped capability and potential. Understand their purpose, point of view, language, concerns. . . . Be loyal. Don't do other things that undermine the emotional ties. Maintain credibility. By empowering people, you increase your span of control, reduce overhead, and get out of unnecessary bureaucracy.[2]

In Part Five, "The Congregation's Relationships," we address the community life of working relationships within the congregation, including how organizational mission and structures have an impact on relationships (chapter 11); the manager's use of power as currency, our aversion to power, our source of power (chapter 12); understanding the complexities of conflict and how to manage such differences (chapter 13); a family systems view of congregational dysfunction (chapter 14) and the manager's intervention (chapters 15).

11

The Congregation's Working Relationships

True love is found in the affirmation of another person's identity and stewardship, in seeking his or her growth and good, not in interpreting all the other person's responses in terms of one's own needs, hungers, or desires.[1]

Stephen R. Covey

Figure 11.1

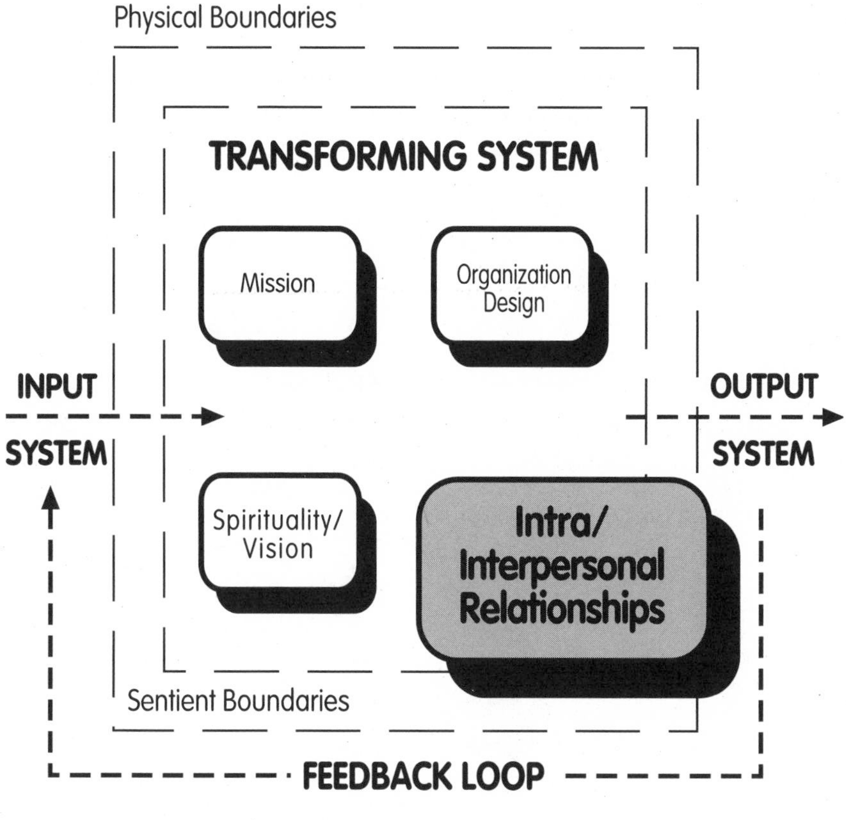

The Effects of Mission and Organizational Design upon Relationships Within the Congregation

In a congregation the quality of intrapersonal and interpersonal relationships is largely a result of three interacting conditions:

1. The degree to which the congregation's mission is framed and communicated in a clear and compelling manner so that the mission inspires the passions and commitments of the people.
2. The degree to which the mission is relevant to the needs and opportunities that are present in the local community and in larger environments.
3. The match between the mission and the ministry programs, policies, and services that are intended to achieve the mission.

The congregation's mission and its organizational design (structures and belief systems) have an interdependent relationship with each other. Mission is achieved through the organization's design, its structures, and belief systems. Deciding the best design depends upon the mission that the design and structures intend to support.

The appropriateness and effectiveness of the mission and the organizational design affect the ways people feel about themselves, about one another, and about the church. Mission and organizational design are the cause; relationships are the effect. This is a reality largely ignored by the leaders of congregations. In fact, most people believe just the opposite. They believe that if the members were more loving, got along better, and were willing to work together—then the programs would flourish and the church would more ably impact its community.

The truth is that people generally want to get along; they want to give themselves to the ministry of the church. But healthy relationships do not develop in a vacuum; they are conditioned by the success of the congregation's ministries, the appropriateness of its missional understanding, and organizational design. When, for all their efforts, they see little or no results, people become frustrated,

> Healthy relationships do not develop in a vacuum. They are conditioned by the congregation's mission and ministry effectiveness.

disappointed, anxious, and begin to look for someone to blame. Soon the quality of life in the community erodes, and relationships between people shrink both intrapersonally and interpersonally.

The mission's relevance to the environment and the effectiveness of the congregation's programs and ministries have a robust effect upon the quality of human relationships in the congregation. In systems thinking the quality of intrapersonal and interpersonal relationships in a congregation is an important part of the information which is fed back into the system. The congregation feeds back its satisfaction, frustration, or disgust regarding the leadership, management, programs, and results through the quality of its human relationships.

Eroding human relationships are not the cause of problems, but they are the results of inappropriate and ineffective relationships between the congregation's mission, environment, design, and spirituality.

Intervening in order to improve intrapersonal and interpersonal relationships in the congregation should not be done in isolation from thinking through the other components of the system's transforming process: the mission, organizational design, and spirituality. Making direct intervention into relationships will have no lasting effect if the other components are not addressed. As a matter of fact, interventions into relationships may be most effective when they are directed toward the other components of the transforming system: mission, organizational design, and spirituality. Usually the real cause of conflict and relationship breakdown is embedded in these components.

The Historical Development of Relational Belief Systems

From the late 1800s American institutions have experimented with three different organizational designs, each with its own relational belief system that determined how the organization attempted to structure its human relationships (see Figure 11.1). The historical timing of the organizational designs and their resulting human relationships do not parallel perfectly. We can, however, give a rough approximation:

Figure 11.2

Date	Organization Structure	Relational Belief System
1870–1946	*Bureaucracy*	*Theory X*
1946–1963	*A More Humane Bureaucracy*	*Human Relations*
1963–1990	*An Awakening Bureaucracy*	*Theory Y*
1985–	*Systems*	*Partnership*

Relational Belief Systems Defined

Theory X

In 1960, Douglas McGregor codified the beliefs that bureaucratic managers traditionally hold of their workers. He called this belief system Theory X, which is characterized by the following assumptions:

1. Work is inherently distasteful to most people.
2. Most people are not ambitious, have little desire for responsibility, and prefer to be directed.
3. Most people have little capacity for creativity in solving organizational problems.
4. Motivation occurs only at the physiological and safety levels (people are only motivated around their own survival and safety needs).
5. Most people must be closely controlled and often coerced to achieve organizational objectives.[2]

The Theory X belief system grew up with the invention of the assembly line and bureaucracy, as for the first time in history large groups of people were brought together to work in specialized and impersonal jobs to produce a product. From the beginning of the industrial revolution, workers were viewed as having the same value as rubber and steel.

As a belief system, Theory X was responsible for the rise and strength of the labor unions in America, because the workers eventually realized the need to have a way of defending themselves against the capricious attitudes of bureaucratic management.

Theory X experienced its first strong challenge after World War Two, as young men and women who had witnessed the wanton destruction of human flesh by forces on both sides of the war (e.g., Auschwitz, the atomic bomb) returned home and headed to college. There they had time to reflect and evaluate the results of Theory X carried to illogical extremes. Nonetheless, the vestiges of Theory X still exist in the thinking and behavior of many American institutions. It is perhaps safe to say that Theory X remains as a belief system in religious systems as much or possibly more in other American institutions.

Human Relations

As young men and women streamed into the halls of American universities in the late 1940s and 1950s, a new belief system for relationships was envisioned. It was termed human relations or the human organization.

One phenomenon of the human relations belief system was that all persons in the organization were seen as equals. This gave rise to the infamous leaderless group meeting where no one had the courage to plan an agenda. So, people would come to the meeting and the so-called leader would begin by saying, "Well, now that we are all here, what do we want to talk about?" The elements of the human relations movement are listed below:

1. Decisions are made by the group through informal, intimate, and fluid relationships.
2. The leader's style is to be sensitive and nondirective. The leader's role is to create an atmosphere conducive to expression and participation.
3. Persons learn to seek and accept responsibility when properly motivated.
4. Communications flow in all directions, as the leader encourages individual participation and contribution in all areas of planning and decision making.
5. The goals of the organization are subjective rather than objective, as the purposes of the group emerge from open discussion.

Human relations never reached the point of acceptance where it was incorporated as the belief system for structuring relationships in American industries and businesses. It did, however, find a ready acceptance in many religious organizations, social service institutions, creativity teams, and psychotherapy programs. Its most significant contributions were found in the classrooms of colleges and universities where it was taught to thousands of persons who would later manage small companies and huge organizations. Human relations had a strong influence upon weakening Theory X attitudes across the board in American institutions.

The human relations movement reached its zenith in the mid-1960s and 1970s. We have no proof of any correlation, but the human relations movement reached its zenith in religious organizations at the same time that the mainline churches turned into their deep and protracted declines.

The first strong challenges to human relations as a belief system for large institutions came with the Black Revolution and students' unrest which resulted in upheavals (e.g., inner-city and university riots, not the least of which was the riot in Chicago surrounding the 1968 Democratic Convention). The challenge to human relations was delivered by such eloquent African American preachers as Jessie Jackson and Martin Luther King, Jr., who pointed out that talking about all Americans being coequals was a far cry from delivering the goods. From this time, human relations as a belief system waned. The important insight to be gained is that talking about love, acceptance, and equality in a congregation is one thing; actually living in relationship with another is quite another.

> Love in the congregation is not limited to an emotion—it is comprised of intentions and actions that bring persons closer together in transparent honesty, mutual goodwill, and equality.

Theory Y

At the same time he codified Theory X, Douglas McGregor also codified a more mature and humane relational belief system which he termed Theory Y. McGregor's focus was upon what he called "the human side of enterprise," in which he asserted the assumptions by which leaders and managers determine how the followers or workers will relate to the organization.[3] Again we are reminded that the quality of relationships in a congregation are the result, and not the cause, of the congregation's organizational design and effectiveness in ministry. The following are McGregor's elements of a Theory Y belief system:

1. Work is as natural as play, if the conditions are tolerable.
2. Self-control is often indispensable in achieving organizational goals.
3. The capacity for creativity in solving organizational problems is widely distributed in the population.
4. Motivation occurs at the social, esteem, and self-actualization levels, as well as at the physiological and security levels.
5. People can be self-directed and creative at work if properly motivated.[4]

As a belief system, Theory Y has exerted tremendous influence upon the advances in thinking about organizational structures and belief systems since the 1970s—especially systems thinking and partnership. This is not to say that all organizations and institutions adopted this belief system. Far from it. It is perhaps safe to say that relationships in most congregations today are still more influenced by Theory X than by Theory Y. It is also safe to say that America's secular institutions are far ahead of their religious counterparts in moving beyond Theory Y to Partnership (discussed in chapter 10).

QUESTIONS FOR REFLECTION UPON YOUR OWN RELATIONAL BELIEF SYSTEMS

1. Which of these belief systems most nearly describes your personal beliefs about how persons and committees should be viewed and managed?
2. Which of these belief systems most nearly describes the congregation's belief system?
3. What changes should you and/or the congregation be making in your/their belief system? How will you get this done?

We now turn our attention to a discussion of how persons in any organization may move from surface relationships into deeper, more authentic relationships.

Stages of Community Development

M. Scott Peck, in his book *The Different Drum,* describes the different stages (or natural order) that groups go through in becoming a true community. They are: pseudocommunity, chaos, emptiness, and community.[5] Groups, like individuals, have their own identity, yet there are common elements to group formation wherever it occurs:

Pseudocommunity

When starting a new group or team, most people pretend or make-believe that they have created an instant community. The members are pleasant, avoid embarrassing others, and shy away from saying or doing anything that might upset the acceptance they are pretending to have for one another. This, says Peck, is pseudocommunity. It is the first step toward achieving true community.[6]

Instant community is too good to be true. True community requires time and effort to build the mutual trust that is necessary for persons to "give" themselves to one another. It is hard work to be honest with others in a group, especially when there are forces that call for your conformity and support. When a leader, or other group members, ignore or minimize individual differences, the group is in pseudocommunity—they are pretending that they are a true community. The denial of individual differences is the central "pretense of community," according to Peck.

In this first stage of group life, we wonder if others are like us, if our ideas will be accepted, and whether we will be able to make a difference. We also wonder what others are like. What are their expectations? What do they think of me? When persons do not honestly disclose what is going on inside of them and when people do not actively listen to each other, then people remain at an emotional and spiritual distance from one another.

It is only when individual differences are not only allowed but valued that the group will move into the second stage of group or team development: chaos.

Chaos

The second stage of group development is chaos. Chaos is awkward and confusing; it has no rhythm and no grace. It is a time in the development of a group when people will preach at one another in an attempt to fix or convert others. Unlike conflict in a mature group, chaos is noisy, selfish, counter creative, and not constructive. People talk down to each other with their own ears plugged, and they display no sensitivity to one another's feelings. In chaos, the individuals feel trapped and wonder how to get out of the misunderstanding. How did we get to this place? Now, who can rescue us? Such are the internal questions of individuals in chaos.

In chaos, many leaders will try to rescue the group—only to push it back again into pseudocommunity instead of accompanying it through the chaos. Chaos is uncomfortable, and the "strong" leader regains control of her own tensions by establishing tight controls of law and order. Under law and order tactics, the people swallow their frustrations—for fear that the chaos might erupt again. So they finally conclude that they need Robert's Rules of Order to assure that this kind of thing won't happen again. But Robert's Rules of Order were never intended to build community. Robert's Rules of Order were meant to establish order—and this is just what is not needed. The group must move through chaos in order to arrive at the third stage of community development: emptiness.[7]

Emptiness

Emptiness is the realization that the group is not a well-knit team after all. It is the realization that they have a long way to go before they will be an authentic community, and that the "community" they claimed when they first got together was a lie.

Nevertheless, when the group arrives at emptiness they are much wiser. Now they understand the true condition of their life together. Notwithstanding the discomfort of emptiness, it is the most crucial stage of the group's journey. Because now everything hangs in the balance. Some will be tempted to bail out, to cut their losses and run. In this climate many will press for getting back to the way things used to be, which, of course, will only lead them back into pseudocommunity. Many groups do this very thing—and stay stuck in perpetual pseudocommunity.

The group that decides not to go back, but to move into and through the emptiness stage must empty themselves of everything that was not working well in chaos. This is not easy, for the members now find it most difficult to communicate or to trust one another. Nonetheless, the members must empty themselves of their need to try to fix others, or to control the group and its agenda.

What is most needed in the stage of emptiness is the commitment of every person as much as possible to share inner fears, sorrows, defeats, and failures. People cannot love a person until they know the person. So, emptying requires a sacrifice that "hurts because it is a kind of death, the kind of death that is necessary for rebirth."[8] In disclosing oneself, persons move from "rugged" to "soft" individualism.[9] Persons become more aware of what is inside themselves and, at the same time, more sensitive to what is happening inside others.

It is through getting to know each other at the inner core that the group passes through emptiness and into the final stage of group development: community.

Community

Community is that stage of development in which the whole group is greater than the sum of its individual parts. The synergy from the group is greater than each individual need or perspective. There is a whole new level of acceptance, trust, and insight. Tilden Edwards points out, "Proliferation of such friendships perhaps can help shape, deepen and stabilize the shallow spiritual infrastructure of the Church, aiding in its renewal and unique service to society."[10]

QUESTIONS FOR REFLECTION
UPON YOUR OWN PARTICIPATION IN A GROUP

1. What interpersonal skills do you possess or lack that are necessary to move others from pseudocommunity into true community?
2. Are you willing and able to be transparent and open to the discomforts and risks involved in living within community—or do you distance yourself from community? If you cannot fully participate in the demands of authentic community, what are the chances of the congregation, the board, etc., ever becoming an authentic community?
3. Where is the congregation, this particular ministry team, the board, etc. located in Peck's taxonomy of the stages of group development? What should you be doing now to assist them to move toward becoming a true community?

The leaders of a group must examine their personal motives for wanting to create communities in the congregation. Never attempt to start community experiences for others in order to "fix" them, until you are willing to be in such community yourself and for yourself. Otherwise the people will know your motive in a minute. The following story of Jerry Seiden, pastor of Harbor Christian Fellowship in Costa Mesa, California, illustrates this point. These are his words.

Brian's Community

I thought the excitement and change of a new church and city might cure the burnout and disappointment I experienced in my first pastorate. During the first six months in my new church, my own pride and fear prevented me from asking for help. In the past when I had been honest with members of my congregation, I always regretted it. Things shared in confidence somehow became public knowledge. Even elders and leaders used my confessed weaknesses to gain advantage.

I didn't feel I could go to other ministers for support. Each time I met with them, they seemed to never get beyond the old "nickels and noses" conversation. "How many did you have last Sunday?" one preacher would begin. Another would answer, "Well, we packed them in again as usual!" I always found my most base and aggressive tendencies arising at ministers' fellowships. I wanted to get angry and growl, "Damn it, don't any of you ever feel overwhelmed with panic? Don't any of you ever hate people and want to quit? Don't any of you ever lose members and take it personally? Am I the only one scared to death?"

My District Superintendent referred me to a Christian counselor who worked with a number of pastors. This ex-pastor-turned-counselor told me to get an elderly friend, eat a good diet, walk daily, and pray more. I didn't get a chance to say much in the two $150 sessions. He claimed that he knew what was wrong with me before I opened my mouth.

I did get support from my physicians. In fact, I got so much support that I always had enough for pills to relax my muscles, calm me down, kill the pain, help my depression, and put me to sleep. I used a host of drugs including narcotic painkillers for eight years, but of course, I was never addicted. . . . I just couldn't stop. The doctors had a pill for everything but peace.

The change I so desperately needed began on the Sunday morning I met Brian, who came past me as I shook hands at the back door. He introduced himself and added that he was a recovering alcoholic who needed to learn more about his "higher power." When I asked about his higher power, he described a two-thousand-year-old tree in New Mexico.

Over the next three weeks, I spent time sharing my personal faith in Christ with Brian. After dealing with some past wounds inflicted by overzealous Christians, Brian finally received Christ as Savior. I was committed to disciple Brian, and I continued to meet with him. But as I shared the basic principles of the Christian faith with him such as surrender, trust, confession, repentance, I found that he already had a depth of understanding and maturity. He didn't just possess head knowledge; he had a deep spirituality that controlled his daily actions and attitude. What's more, he manifested qualities and fruits of the Spirit that I had long taught but never experienced. He had peace—a peace born from childlike trust that God was in charge, that God's will was best, that God would take care of him.

When I asked Brian how he could possibly have this maturity, he responded that for seven years he had been working the 12 Steps of Alcoholics Anonymous and had been in community with people just like him—people who had hit bottom and admitted their need for God. Brian's spiritual bounty shamed me. I cut off the relationship. I don't even remember the excuse now. All I remember is the way Brian reached out to me and invited me to attend "a meeting" with him.

The meeting was a 12-Step "speakers meeting," and Brian was the speaker. Brian left me at a seat in the back row. I hadn't brought a thing to read so I spent my energy twirling my wedding ring and watching "the alcoholics." Half of the crowd of eighty or so talked and drank coffee inside and the other half talked and smoked outside. It didn't take me long to figure out that I was overdressed. I felt as out of place as Bubba and Sissy at a debutante ball. Everyone seemed to stumble over me and ask if this was my first time. I wanted to make it clear that I was not one of them, so I responded, "Just a guest, thank you." Finally a word from the podium brought everyone to their seat.

That night they celebrated sobriety birthdays. The strangest creature awarded tokens, and the same birthday cake, over and over. He was an overweight middle-aged man with hairy legs and two day's growth of beard on his face; he was dressed like a woman complete with dress, pumps, earrings, lipstick, and wig. Everybody seemed to know him and think nothing of his appearance. Every time someone stood up to be recognized for months or years of sobriety, the crowd clapped, cheered, and congratulated. This strangely dressed man offered hugs and awarded tokens.

I wanted to be critical, self-righteous, even mockish, but I couldn't. These people had something I didn't. They had unwavering acceptance for one another within a context of honesty. All I had was church.

After that meeting, my relationship with Brian changed. I surrendered my role as his discipler and Brian assumed a role as my sponsor. He taught me how to know and trust God and how to hunger for God's will only. That was hard because I had too long been expecting God to make "my will be done."

In time, I found that I didn't need the medicine. The God who had been waiting on the edge of my life was suddenly invited in to be the master. He didn't take the pain. He helped me face it, feel it, learn from it, and grow beyond it. God opened my eyes to see how old survival techniques had become character defects that blocked my faith and created my pain. And God gave me the courage to surrender these old and familiar habits and replace them with trust.

Brian also introduced me to a new community. A community that probably resembled Jesus' early group of followers more than did my fellowship. I began to meet with people who all freely confessed their need for God and their inability to live life without God's constant presence and direction. These people heard my pain and didn't try to fix it. They shared their experience, strength, and hope, not their advice. They gave me a place where I could be real and safe and loved without the fear of condemnation. They extended to me the kind of acceptance I needed to finally find healing. Now it's my greatest joy to pass it on. I feel more genuinely Christian today than I ever have.

Relationships in the Congregation

To this point we have discussed relationships as they are conditioned and experienced in all types of organizations. We will now turn our attention to some items that are more (but not exclusively) apropos to relationships in religious communities, more specifically the congregation. Few institutions value community so much as do congregations. Congregations naturally understand that, for them, relationships are lived out within the context of a faith community. The persons who comprise the congregation have a sense that they are something more than a group or an organization. They see themselves as a community of persons who have been brought together in a common quest to be in relationship not only with one another, but also with God.

Intimacy in Relationships

The actions of Jesus as he began his public ministry demonstrate that he felt the need for an intimate community. Accordingly, he invited persons not only to work with him, but to live out their lives together in intimate closeness with him. So intimate did the relationships of this small group become that one would lean his head upon Jesus' breast without shame. Jesus' extended community included men and women. He was unashamed to allow a woman to touch him, to kiss his feet, and to rub his feet with her hair. When someone complained of this display of intimacy, Jesus defended her actions—taking no initiatives to stop her (Luke 7:6ff).

It is striking that Jesus chose to share his experiences of highest ecstasy (Mark 9:1ff) and of deepest agony (Mark 13:34ff) with a small group of comrades. Many people try to sanitize Jesus' deeply felt needs to be in intimate relationships with others by saying that his intent in all of these relationships was only to disciple the people. However, even a cursory reading of the Scriptures cited above will convince the discerning reader that there was much more going on here than discipleship. Jesus cultivated intimate and enduring relationship for the sheer love of being in fellowship. He dearly loved to sit at the table with his friends. These relationships renewed his energies. He was able to disciple others because he was close to them. Discipleship is better caught than it is taught. However excellent the tutoring, discipleship will hardly be caught in a stiff, one-up-one-down relationship.

It is important, therefore, that the pastor does whatever internal work that is necessary to relate to persons with appropriate degrees of distance and intimacy. The quality of the pastor's intrapersonal and interpersonal relationships will set the tone for relationships in the congregation. If the congregation cannot sustain close and healthy relationships with one another, it is unlikely that the people will be able to sustain intimacy with God.

The Sacrament of Human Relationships in Christian Community

Thomas Hart, in *The Art of Christian Listening,* describes how something as concrete as listening in the context of Christian community is a channel of God's grace.[11] When God's people enter into serious conversation, Christ is present as each becomes for the other the incarnate Christ. Why do the dying poor and sick become uplifted in the presence of Mother Teresa and her sisters? Because these servants of Christ incarnate the love and presence of Christ among the company of the afflicted. Why do people often experience Christ's presence over dinner in a serious conversation with friends fully as much as in a Sunday morning worship service? Because God's presence is not limited to the sanctuary. God yearns to be present in our everyday relationships as much as in the cathedral. As Hart poignantly asks, "Is there any more compelling bearer of the holy than the human person made in God's image and likeness in the first place, and, as a Christian, striving to put on Christ? This is the root of the church's sacraments."[12]

Behaviors That Limit the Sacrament of Community[13]

1. To take responsibility for another person's life. The manager who attempts to take responsibility for others does not help them, but imprisons them in self-defeating dependence and immaturity. These complimentary attitudes of patronage and dependency may work for a while, but in the long run such relationships will not contribute to community or to individual growth. When the pastor assumes responsibility for many people, she soon becomes an anxious and harried presence in the midst of the others' anxiety. She becomes a part of the problem and not a part of the solution.

2. To prematurely fix another's problem or carry their pain. Some managers, feeling uncomfortable with another's pain, cope with their own discomfort by trying to fix it for the other and themselves by using theology or platitudes to pacify their own feelings.

How, then, should the pastor respond to a parishioner's pain? Tom Chappell, founder and president of Tom's of Maine, explains, "One major difference between a [congregation] and a well-oiled machine is that one of the [congregation's] 'parts' had a fight with his wife this morning; another wants her daughter to go to college but can't seem to save enough money for the tuition; another has had a death in the family."[13] Workers in the church community have problems that sometimes require long-suffering hospitality and a commitment of long-lasting accompaniment, not cheap solutions that are more for the benefit of the "fixer" than anyone else.

> Roger's father was an interim pastor in a small congregation in Wisconsin. In the congregation, a young husband and father left his wife and family for several years, then contracted AIDS. After reestablishing contact with his wife, she invited him back. She and the small congregation nurtured him until his death.

The church among all institutions views a person as an uncommon individual with unique feelings and experiences. It is during one's own journey through pain, loss, fear, success, and joy that we experience God's presence despite God seeming absent. When the manager attempts to remove another's problem and pain, he cuts them off from the grace of God that is sufficient to accompany and sustain them in all of life's experiences, however good or bad.

3. To offer one's experience, wisdom, and holiness to another, thus making it unnecessary for them to explore and learn for themselves. Working in the ministries of the church affords tangible opportunities for persons to explore and develop their own capabilities in the presence of God. This is mediated through relationships with others as they plan and work together. To give an answer for every question is to short-circuit another person's own quest for knowledge and disallows them the privilege of working through their own issues and of learning how to be more effective in their ministry. It does a person no favor to constrict her to experience her own journey through the "greater" experience of another.

4. To attempt to make the other into a different person. Pastors and all members of a congregation must come to grips with their insatiable desires to change other persons into images of their own making. The manager can facilitate experiences that occasion the potential for growth, and he can help others to identify their charisma. But attempts to change them or to make them as objects in one's own image does violence to their uniqueness and freedom.

The above illustrations are only a few of the ways in which one's relationship with the pastor or involvement in the congregation can inhibit God's presence and stunt the growth of the individual. How, therefore, can one manage in ways that make the community a sacrament for God's presence?

Behaviors That Contribute to the Sacrament of Community[15]

1. To listen. Listening demands being fully alive and present, setting aside one's own needs in place of the other's needs. When listening to expressions of sorrow and other deeply held emotions, when exposing deep concerns, when hearing the same story repeated again and again, listening can be hard work and very demanding. Nonetheless, to give one's full attention and time to listen to another's story and to celebrate its ordinariness, pathos, or joys is to share together in the sacrament of God's presence in the life of the other. A guiding principle for all of us might be to listen more and talk less.

2. To be a companion. As a companion, the manager does not promise to be a savior, to fix everything, to provide for every need, or to take the pain away. She does, however, promise to be there, to accompany but not direct, to be available but not be intrusive. The companion is very different from the traffic cop who may give clear signals but never accompanies the lost traveler to his destination. The companion says, "Come, we will go there together."

3. To love. While love is in the church's vocabulary, it is not always apparent in its behavior. But when it is, nothing comes closer to God's presence on earth. Christian love transcends program ministries, personalities, and differences; it is what makes the difference in relationships within the congregation. Karl Menninger, after decades of work in psychiatry and psychotherapy, concluded this simple truth: unlove makes people unwell, and love alone can make them well again.[16] Love is both a gift and a choice; it is such actions in which God dwells. Loving God is not an emotion; it is an intention so strongly held that it changes our motives and our behaviors. Likewise in the congregation, love is not limited to warm feelings. It is an attitude- and behavior-altering intention to live in harmony with everyone in the church family. A guiding principle for all of us might be to never give verbal expressions of love unless we genuinely feel love for the other person. The word *love* is probably the most used and least meant word in the church. What a pity.

4. To be oneself. God's presence is more likely found in congregations of leaders and members who are truly themselves, who do not hide behind status or role, but who are transparent and humble. Of such persons Jesus said "Here is one who has no guile." In the final analysis, just about the only gift you have to share is the gift of yourself, warts and all. When one gives oneself, she is truly strengthening the sacrament of community.

As a manager within a congregation, whether you like it or not, you are a highly public icon of the quality of community within the congregation. On one hand, creating a sense of community is difficult, requiring specific skills and established principles for structuring relationships. On the other hand, however, community is striving to happen all of the time. What is required of you is to give it permission to happen, and to participate in it.

QUESTIONS FOR REFLECTION UPON YOUR CONTRIBUTIONS TO THE COMMUNITY'S LIFE TOGETHER

1. Which of the behaviors that limit community life do you too often employ in your relationships with people? What are the long-term results of this behavior upon your ministry? Upon others?
2. Which of the behaviors that contribute to community life do you not utilize enough in your relationships with people? What are the long-term results of this behavior upon your ministry effectiveness? Upon others?
3. What concrete steps could you take even now to improve the quality of community in the congregation, the official board, a group, etc.?
4. Are there persons in the congregation whose interpersonal skills and habits are such that their participation undermines community? How will you work with them to get them the help they need, or at least to reduce their negative effects upon the life and the ministry of the congregation?

We are all more or less blind to our behaviors, habits, and theories that weaken community and cause persons to shrink rather than grow. It is difficult to mirror ourselves to ourselves in interpersonal matters. Further, our interpersonal behaviors are strongly influenced by our intrapersonal realities. What we experience on the inside is reflected in the mirror of our public image. Few of us are skilled enough to be one person on the inside, and another on the outside.

As consultants and teachers, we work with many pastors whose interior lives are deeply troubled, and whose interpersonal skills are seriously lacking. Yet most are totally oblivious to this. Therefore, for some, responding to the above questions alone is not sufficient. You may need to ask several persons in your house, and in the congregation, who will be fully honest, to help you decide your correct answers to the questions. Beyond this assistance, however, is the possibility of counseling and psychotherapy. If you need it—get it. We each can profit from some form of psychotherapy once in a while.

Above and beyond all that we have discussed heretofore is the possibility for the congregation to move into covenant living—the blessed sacrament of life together with God. We will now proceed to discuss how we may, indeed, experience life together with God at the heart of our fellowship.

Relationships Lived Out in Covenant Communities

> We have worked with a church board that is in covenant to begin its meetings in silence. In addition, the board members daily read the same Psalm, and each keeps a spiritual journal. They begin each board meeting with a time of sharing what God is saying to them through their daily prayer times. The pastor reports that he is still waiting for the other (old) shoe to drop, when meetings were laborious, long, and often cantankerous. There is still disagreement, but disagreements are no longer fueled by hidden agendas and one-upmanship. Relationships are now characterized by mutual concern for one another, truthfulness, and caring.

Max DePree, chair and CEO of Herman Miller, Inc., the furniture maker that was named one of *Fortune* magazine's ten best managed and most innovative companies, writes, "My goal for Herman Miller is that when people both inside the company and outside the company look at all of us, not as a corporation but as a group of people working intimately within a covenant relationship, they'll say, 'Those folks are a gift to the spirit.' "[17]

Any group can live in healthy relationships, but living as a covenant community adds a new and vital dimension. However, actually living in explicit covenant with one another remains in the church one of those things that, like the weather, "everybody's talkin' about but nobody's doin' nothin' 'bout."

Covenant living, like discipleship, is best learned by example. Every pastor should model covenant living by being in a covenant community himself and second, by giving public witness to the benefits that the covenant and the covenant community bring into his private life and public ministry. Finally, the pastor should consistently invite and encourage each member to do likewise.

Jesus' Model for Establishing a Healthy Relationship

In the Gospels we see that Jesus fashioned a style for managing his intrapersonal and interpersonal relationships; this included the three movements of affirmation, challenge, and separation.[18] By this style he managed his relationships with people, and thus managed to find time daily to be alone with God.

He affirmed people through actions and words of encouragement, healing, and teachings. Jesus also challenged persons to become something more than they were. And, after the affirmation and challenge, he sent the person or the crowd away, or he left them there. This he did in order to make persons free and responsible to decide how to respond to the challenge or invitation Jesus had given them. Jesus never assumed responsibility for the other person's decisions or actions. This is separation.

Jesus practiced another type of separation that is important for us to consider for our own life and work. He separated himself from people and activity in order to restore his energy and spiritual reserves through solitary communion with God. Again and again the Gospel writers remind us that he sent them away while he, himself, went alone to pray. We see that he had his favorite prayer places—outdoor oratories where God met him. Jesus practiced these separations for the sheer joy of being with God, and in order that he might return to the crowds with new energy and effectiveness.

The religious manager's relationship with the people must include these same ingredients—affirmation, challenge, and separation.[19] And if this relational system does not suit your uniqueness, then you must develop another set of interpersonal disciplines to inform and guide you in managing the relationships within the congregation.

Regardless of your relational management system you must learn separation in order to care for yourself. Even a small congregation will often include enough needy persons who are always wanting to restore their energies by sapping the pastor's inner resources. Whenever a pastor's life suffers shipwreck, one of the causes is almost certain to be that he could not separate himself from his friends, or that he allowed "energy sappers" to be too close to him for too long. Either way his spiritual reserves are soon depleted, and his ministry stalls.

The example set for us by Jesus demonstrates need to build a rhythm of daily brief retreats in our lives. An hour a day in silence and prayer will generally renew the pastor's spiritual reserves. When the demands of ministry are unusually heavy, the pastor will need to separate herself for a longer period of time; an eight-day retreat each year and a thirty-day retreat every six years, or so, will add immensely to one's spiritual and emotional reserves. So if you feel the need to drop out of sight for a while—do it! There are monasteries and convents all over the world that will welcome you, provide you with a spiritual director, and care for you. You will return to active ministry with fresh insight and a renewed commitment to the task that God has assigned to you.

For the daily retreat, in addition to saying, "just do it," we add that, for most of us, it isn't easy. There are times when our inner resistance is stronger than our inner resolve. For all our good intentions, we fail to keep the daily retreat. So we say, "start again." When you miss a day or more, don't be tough on yourself and, above all, don't allow yourself to feel guilty. If you feel guilty, it is almost certain that you are doing the discipline for the wrong reasons.

The daily retreat is for spiritual nourishment, just as the meal is for our physical nourishment. When we miss a meal or two, we may feel hungry or even a bit weak. Eventually, we just get ourselves back to where the food is, and we eat. So it should be with our spiritual nourishment. When we feel spiritually weak, we get ourselves back to where the spiritual food is and eat, allowing ourselves no remorse for the many meals we may have missed.

QUESTIONS FOR REFLECTION UPON PRIVATE AND PUBLIC DISCIPLINES REGARDING YOUR RELATIONSHIPS WITH OTHERS, AND WITH GOD

1. Do you have a management style, a set of management principles that inform your relationships with people, and help you to manage your time in order to care for your own needs?
2. How would you describe your management style to someone else?
3. Do you have a well-kept discipline for daily retreat time to nourish your spiritual and mental needs? Have you a discipline for longer retreats? What are the circumstances that most consistently cause you to surrender your intentions in order to respond to some "urgent" but less important item?
4. Do you have a covenant community to whom you are voluntarily accountable for your spiritual and professional life? If not, what hinders you from this?
5. Do you teach and support work groups and ad hoc groups living in covenant with one another; i.e., official board, teachers, informal groups?

The Essence of Understanding the Congregation's Working Relationships

1. The quality of the relationships in a congregation is the result of the organizational design and ministry effectiveness.
2. Relational belief systems have emerged from particular organizational structures.
   - Bureaucracy produced specialized, yet impersonal job relationships (Theory X).
   - Human relations emerged as a response to bureaucracy (Theory Y).
   - Stewardship emerges as a response to partnership.
3. Love in a congregation is not just an emotion.
   - It is comprised of the intentions and actions that bring people closer together in vulnerable communication and mutual loving kindness.
4. Community does not evolve overnight.
   - Developing relationships requires an intentional effort from both parties.
   - Intimacy is nurtured through stages of growth and development.
5. Intentional efforts to proceed toward community include listening, being a companion, loving, and being oneself.

How You Can Enhance the Congregation's Relationships

1. Clearly define and communicate a relevant, community-oriented mission.
    - Healthy relationships in a congregation are the result of an appropriate and effective mission and structure.
2. Understand your relational belief system.
    - Does this belief system energize or encumber the congregation's relationships?
    - What changes might be made in the belief system?
3. Recognize at what stage the congregation and particular ministry teams are located in terms of Peck's stages of group development.
    - If you do not know at what stage a group is located, how will you be able to help them?
    - What practical steps can you take in order to facilitate the group's relational growth?
4. Actively seek opportunities in which you can promote behavior that contributes to the "sacrament of community"!
5. Teach and model Jesus' example of establishing healthy relationships.
    - Affirmation
    - Challenge
    - Separation

12

The Use of Power in Ministry and Management

Great temptations keep company with great powers. The little man fighting his little battles wishes that he were the great man so that the more easily he might overcome them; but when he understands the great man he sees that storms circle around his higher altitudes that make the petty battles of the lower level seem insignificant. The acorn seedling may be impeded by a few dead leaves, but it never will shake in the angry grip of the tempest until it becomes an oak. The analogy of our experience at once suggests that our Lord was tempted not less but more than we are. Haggard and hungry in the wilderness, as Tintoretto painted him, he was facing temptations that our puny powers can hardly imagine. "If thou art the Son of God, command that these stones become bread"; "If thou art the Son of God, cast thyself down"; "All the kingdoms of the world . . . if thou wilt worship me." His masterful powers were met by masterful temptations.

Harry Emerson Fosdick

Power tends to corrupt and absolute power corrupts absolutely.

Lord Acton

Human life is a strange tale of securing power, having power, and losing power. The reality, risk, seduction, and cruciality of power outrun our capacity to understand or explicate it.[1]

Walter Brueggemann

Figure 12.1

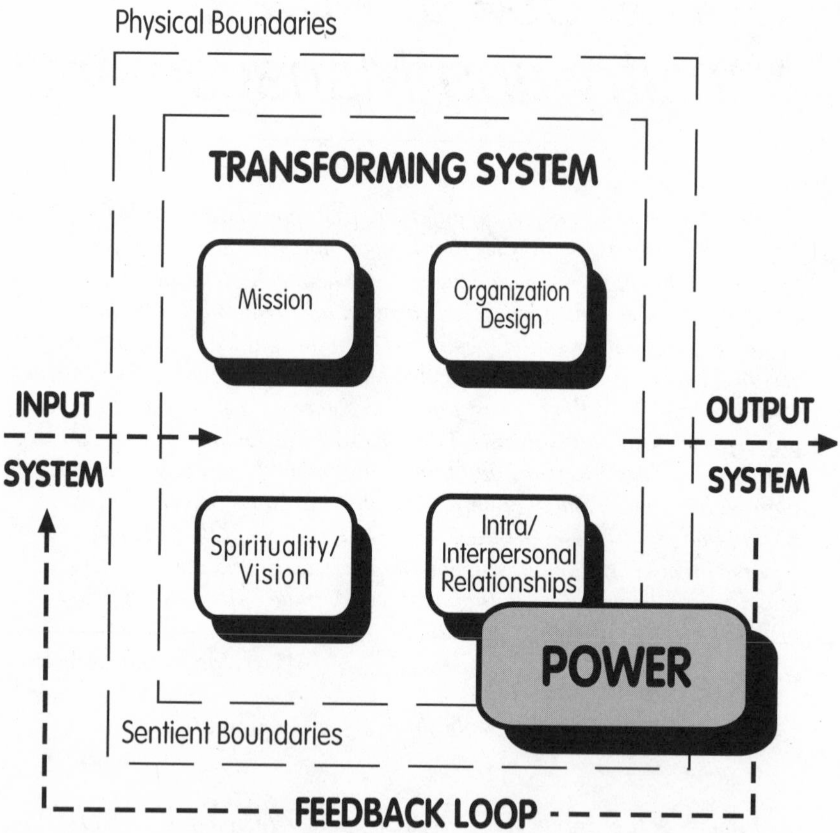

We want leaders and managers who can make a difference; yet we seek to "cage" or "tame" them.[2] Why this preoccupation with power? James MacGregor Burns explains:

> [We are preoccupied with power] in part because we in this century cannot escape the horror of it. Stalin controlled an apparatus that, year after year and in prison after prison, quietly put to death millions of persons. . . . Between teatime and dinner Adolf Hitler could decide whether to release a holocaust of terror and death in an easterly or westerly direction.[3]

We are potentially both agents and victims of power. The two essentials of power are motive and resources, both of which are interrelated.[4] When resources decline, motive can only lie idle, and when motive is lacking, resources soon diminish. We may have the power, for example, to terminate an employee, but we are not so motivated. Or, we may have the motive to give thousands of dollars to balance the budget, but lack the personal resources. Power does not exist without motive and resources, but it relates to the relationship and purposes of the power holder and the power recipients.

Building upon these concepts, Burns defines power as "not property or entity or possession but as a relationship in which two or more persons tap into motivational bases in one another and bring varying resources to bear in the process."[5] Power exists whether or not it is sought for. It may benefit or destroy people and organizations. Any discussion of management must include a consideration of the use of power.

Power: The Currency of Management

Management is a special kind of power. Stated another way, power goes with the territory of management. In congregations managers possess a kind of "raw" power by reason that they exert tremendous control and influence over the utilization of all of the congregation's human and physical resources. The managers sit "in the seats of power," and the pastor-as-manager's seat is the most powerful of all. Yet many pastors are oblivious to the power they possess as managers.

Power, and how persons use it, has more influence upon human relationships in organizations than any other factor in the organizational setting. George Odiorne imaginatively describes two types of managers, people growers and people shrinkers.[6] Managers can exert control over persons at several levels of relationships, all the way from forcing persons into inactivity or into pursuing meaningless or unattainable goals (the people shrinker), to structuring the organization to call forth the best of persons' abilities to work for themselves and the organization (the people grower).

The religious manager is given power from two sources: first, God gives power; and second, people give power. It is often amazing to observe how willing a congregation is to hand over power to the pastor.

Even when the pastor is twenty-five years old, just out of seminary, and newly ordained, a church board of older, more experienced and wiser men and women hand over to the pastor huge amounts of power from the day she arrives. This trust should never be abused, but often is. Power is heady stuff. The temptation is always to believe that one deserves all the power that the congregation hands over, and that he is fully equipped to wield it unilaterally. In our years of work as conflict managers we have seen many congregations and pastors completely destroyed because the pastor gave in to the temptation of believing that because he had been given the power, he obviously knew how to use it.

On the other hand, we have also observed pastors who feel totally powerless, and therefore abdicate their role as leader and manager. This, too, destroys congregations and pastors, though usually not so dramatically as in the former case. Our work in congregations has led us to believe that pastors in the "congregational" systems of government are more tempted to usurp and abuse power, whereas pastors in denominations with centralized bureaucracies are generally more tempted to abdicate their power, for fear of rocking the boat and gaining the attention of judicatory officials.

Aversion to the Use of Power[7]

Many managers in religious organizations express an aversion to the use of power. These persons generally support their position by raising such arguments as follows:

1. The rule of noncoercion: people should not be forced to do what others want them to do, but should be free to refuse.
2. The rule of explanation: people should not be seduced into compliance but should be told what is wanted of them.
3. The rule of self-direction: people should be free to decide for themselves how they want to guide their lives.

These three "rules" sound so Christian. Herein lies the difficulty in opposing such rules in the church. It is true that persons should not be forced. They should not be seduced. And they should be free to decide for themselves. But in managing paid and volunteer workers, these rules may lead to anarchy or, more commonly, systems paralysis.

On the other hand, persons are not to be treated as androids. Any organization that succeeds must have managers who understand and use power to free persons to be fully responsible for themselves, and to work with others toward desired and worthy ends.

Four Types of Power and Their Results

There are at least four types of power commonly used by religious managers. They are exploitative power, coercive power, utility power, and principle-centered power. We will discuss each of these in an ascending order of effectiveness.

Exploitative Power

Exploitative power is manipulating others and is motivated by a desire to destroy. Lord Acton concluded that this kind of power "corrupts absolutely." Those who stand in the way become "things" or "objects"; they are not seen as persons. This is the most destructive expression of power, since it uses some form of violence to achieve its desired end. When firearms are used or death threats are made, this is a form of exploitative power. In our experience as conflict managers, we have observed the threatened use of weapons and death threats in various congregations. A more common use of exploitative power in the church, however, is when the pastor or some layperson does violence to persons' minds and spirits by willfully contrived behaviors meant to destroy persons, whether spiritually, physically, socially, or communally. Unfortunately, this type of exploitative power is altogether too common in congregations. The results of exploitative power are that persons are often scarred forever.

History proves that the use of exploitative power is delimited by time. Sooner or later those who are still "alive" will rebel—and win. Aleksandr Solzhenitsyn observed: "You will have power over people as long as you don't take everything away from them. But when you've robbed a man of everything, he's no longer in your power—he's free again."

Coercive or Manipulative Power

Coercive power is based upon a desire to intimidate or deceive. The intent of coercive power is to get people to follow without question or resistance. The "con" artist is an example of one who uses coercion to get his or her way. Coercive power is based on a fear that if the manager doesn't have his way, things will fall apart.

Coercive power or manipulation may create an initial illusion of effectiveness, but over time persons shrink under negative manipulation, and there is an accruing effect of distrust and "stuckness" throughout the congregation.

Utility or Nutrient Power

This kind of power is power directed toward other. Nutrient power grows out of a concern for the welfare of the other person or group. Much of what happens in the normal operation of congregations is fueled by such utility power. It is based on a sense of equity and fairness. The results of utility or nutrient power are that the managers are trusted, respected, and honored. People follow them, because they know the manager cares for them; thus, they want to believe in her. This is not blind faith, but informed commitment. Eventually, however, changing demographics, conditions, and relationships will erode the confidence that the people once had in the utilitarian manager.

Principle-Centered or Integrative Power

This kind of power is exercised with others, rather than over others. The principle-centered manager believes that his power, used wisely, will cause others in the congregation to have more power, and their greater power will cause him to have more power.

Integrative power is principle-based. This is to say that the manager does not manage capriciously or by whim. Rather, she follows a set of effective and clearly communicated principles in carrying out her managerial duties.[8] This is the type of "management" that students often experience in a relationship with a highly respected and beloved teacher.

The results of principle-centered power are that mutual commitment and respect for one another grow continuously, and eventually the congregation will be marked by quality, distinction, and excellence in all relationships and programs.

Whenever a management problem or opportunity arises that requires the involvement of people, the manager must make a choice—whether to adopt an exploitative, coercive, utilitarian, or principle-centered management power orientation. Steven Covey suggests ten "power tools" to assure that one is using one's power legitimately. We list them below:

Steven Covey's Ten Power Tools for Management

1. **Persuasion,** which includes sharing reasons and rationale, making a strong case for your position, while maintaining genuine respect for followers' ideas and perspective. Tell *why* as well as *what.* Commit to stay in the communication process until mutually beneficial and satisfying outcomes are reached.
2. **Patience,** with the process and the person. In spite of the failings, shortcomings, and inconveniences created by workers and members, and your own impatience for achieving your goals, maintain a long-term perspective and stay committed to your goals in the face of obstacles and resistance.
3. **Gentleness,** not harshness, hardness, or forcefulness, when dealing with the vulnerabilities, disclosures, and feelings people might express.
4. **Teachableness,** which means operating with the assumption that you do not have all the answers or all the insights, while valuing the different viewpoints, judgments, and experiences of others.
5. **Acceptance,** withholding judgment, giving the benefit of the doubt, requiring no evidence or specific performance as a condition for being accepted by you.
6. **Kindness,** sensitive, caring, thoughtful, remembering to do the little things that often so important to a relationship.
7. **Openness,** acquiring accurate information and perspectives about persons, holding each one in high regard, regardless of what they own, control, or do. Giving full consideration to others' intentions, desires, values, and goals rather than focusing exclusively on your own.
8. **Compassionate confrontation,** acknowledging error, mistakes, and the need for persons and groups to make "course corrections" in a context of genuine care, concern, and warmth, making it safe for them to risk.
9. **Consistency.** Guard against using your leadership as a manip-

ulative tool when you don't get your way or are feeling trapped. Rather, constantly act out of a set of values, a personal code, that strengthens your character and reflects who you are and what you are commited to.

10. **Integrity,** honestly matching words and feelings with thoughts and actions, with no desire other than for the good of others, without malice or desire to deceive, take advantage, manipulate, or control; constantly reviewing your intent as you strive for congruence.[9]

QUESTIONS FOR REFLECTION UPON YOUR OWN USE OF POWER

1. Are you a people grower or a people shrinker? In what specific ways do you exemplify this characteristic?
2. Do you tend to seize or abdicate power? How does this tendency affect the life of the congregation?
3. Which type of power do you tend to utilize?

The Source of the Manager's Power

God Is the Source of All Power

Once God has spoken;
twice have I heard this:
that power belongs to God (Ps. 62:11).

In [Christ] all things in heaven and on earth were created, things visible and invisible, whether thrones or dominions or rulers or powers—all things have been created through him and for him (Col. 1:16).

The Scriptures provide surprising insights into power and its use. God is all powerful, more powerful than all other sources of power. God is *omni-potent* (see Deut. 8:17; 1 Cor. 15:24; Matt. 6:13; Rev. 5:13).

> God greatly desires to share God's power with those who respond to the call—but we often deny or resist it.

Even a cursory study leads us to the realization of the power that is resident in God, and God's sincere desire to share that power with us, in extravagant proportions. Why, then, are our ministries so lackluster and our results so banal?

There are some foundational causes for this: first, we are tempted to "put ourselves down." We belittle the magnanimous promises of God regarding the results which may accrue to our labors, because we simply believe they are too good to be true—for us and our ministry. This was the condition of Zechariah in Luke 1. Here was God offering him all the power and the exact results he most wanted; and there was Zechariah saying, "No, no, it can't happen through me. I am too old, and my wife is not suitable."

Second, we stubbornly refuse to give ourselves to the spiritual disciplines which, alone, open us up to receive the power that is always flowing toward us from the Source. The transfiguration story (Mark 9:1-29) teaches a plain lesson that many of us ignore to the expense of our own effectiveness. The lesson is this: Jesus was only able to do what he did in the valley because he conversed with heaven on the mountain. When the day ended and the crowds had left, the disciples asked, "How is it that you could heal the lad, and we could not?" The teaching session concluded, "Some things only happen through prayer." In Jesus' ministry, and in ours, the mountain and the valley incidents are not isolated conditions.

Third, we tend to judge our power by our status in the denomination's structures and by the size of the congregations we serve. It is difficult to learn that the way to have power is to give it away. And so we cling to power as do others in our society—by using the bargaining chips of position and promotion, status, perks, titles, rewards, and punishment.

Two years ago we had opportunity to spend some days with a group of missionaries from another continent. The missionaries were discouraged and disheartened. As we listened we discovered that they were not discouraged because of failure—but because they had experienced great success, igniting a season of tremendous growth in the national church. Now the work was carried on entirely by national leaders, and the missionaries had lost their sense of importance.

The Power of Your Personal Example

Your greatest demonstration of power is by the power of the influence of your own example—and this is wholly dependent upon your courage and your integrity. This power no one can take from you. It can only be sacrificed upon an altar of your own choosing.

In the Second World War there were four military chaplains who, as the ship they were aboard was sinking, gave their life jackets, and their lives, away to keep four recruits from drowning. This was a powerful act, far greater than the arsenal aboard the sinking ship. This power did not come from their ordination or their status as military officers, but from the annointing God gave them at the time of their call and from the strength of their own faith. The power of the influence of their example survives to this day, inspiring military officers and troops alike. This is true power.

An event in every United Methodist congregation is the charge conference, which is the annual business meeting of the congregation, usually attended by the district superintendent. It was charge conference time in the district, and the DS was out night after night attending conferences. Times are tough in many UMC congregations as they cope with declining memberships, escalating costs, and so on. Congregations place much blame upon the district superintendent, who arrives occasionally as the representative of the denomination. This DS had gone through a number of less than pleasant meetings; his anxiety was rising, and he had a number of conferences yet to go.

One morning his wife reminded him that this was his birthday, and that the kids were having a little party for him that evening—and he better not forget! Well, he had forgotten and had scheduled a charge conference with a small congregation for that evening. He would just have to be home for dinner, cut the celebration short and still make it to the charge conference.

It was a delightful little party. His teenage son gave him a pair of Superman shorts, and everyone wanted him to model them. So he put on the Superman shorts and modeled them for his family. Time got away before he remembered the charge conference! He rushed into the bedroom to dress. No time to take off the Superman shorts. Suit on, tie on, and run!

It was not a nice meeting. The people complained about the apportionments, the conference, the state of the church, and other things. He tried to interject a little humor. Big mistake! The folk were not in the mood for humor. They just complained all the more.

Before long he was sweating and getting angry and thinking to himself, "How did I ever get into this job? I don't need this harassment. Tomorrow I'm going to tell the bishop I've had enough."

Then he thought, "I don't need to put up with this stuff from these people; they can't hurt me—I've got on my Superman shorts!" He sat down—and then he thought, "Hey! Not only do I have on my Superman shorts, I've been baptized. I belong to God. I am not here alone." With that he relaxed and listened and smiled at the people. Soon the complaints trailed off and the people mellowed. The conversation turned to fruitful topics. It was a good meeting.

When the going gets tough, don't forget to wear your Superman shorts, and remember from whence your power originates. You belong to God.

The Temptations That Come with Power

Are you tempted? Then you have the capacity and capability to do something good and worthwhile for God, and the people. Are you tempted greatly? Then you have great capacity and capability to delight the heart of God, and to serve in the work of God with distinction. The chances are, however, that if you are not tempted, you are out of touch with your capabilities, your power. Whatever the temptations, one thing is certain—there is a way out, for no temptation has come to you that others have not experienced and overcome. God will not allow you to be tempted beyond your capacity to resist; instead, with the temptation, God will provide you a way out so that you may be able to overcome it (see 1 Cor. 10:13). This good news doesn't make resisting the temptations any easier. It does, however, add a note of hope and nobility to our resistance.

When it comes to power, religious managers are confronted with two very different temptations. The first is the temptation to feel and act as though one has no power, to experience a pervading sense of powerlessness—and thus to be tempted to deny continuously the gifts and power that God has given for ministry. This is the temptation Satan offered to Jesus in his time of great trial, when Satan showed him the pinnacle of the temple and said, "If you really are who you say you are, then cast yourself down and you will see whether the angels will protect you."

"Cast yourself down," or put yourself down—make yourself little, low, and insignificant. This is the temptation of the manager who feels that he is powerless, and who believes that the promises of Christ regarding power for ministry are simply too good to be true—for him (see Mark 3:13-15; 6:7-13; 16:15-18).

The second temptation that confronts the religious manager in the use of power is just the opposite from self-deprecation. It is the temptation to be spectacular, to be glitzy. This is the temptation Satan offered Jesus when he said to him, "Worship me and all the kingdoms of the world, and all its glory, can be yours."[10]

The third temptation that confronts the religious manager is the temptation to be relevant, to be able to meet pressing human need by his or her own effort. This is the temptation Satan presented to Jesus when he said, "If you are really so great, then turn these stones into bread." Turning stones into bread, the desire to be relevant, seems like a legitimate aspiration since every one needs bread. Even Jesus, at that moment, was famished and in need of bread. To be relevant, what an insidious temptation. Henri J.M. Nouwen describes his former life of acclaim in academic appointments as "a tightrope artist trying to walk on a high, thin cable from one tower to the other, always waiting for the applause when I had not fallen off and broken my leg."[11]

The lesson Jesus teaches us by his temptations is clear: in all circumstances neither deny nor misuse the power given to you by God for the doing of your ministry. Power has the ability to hurt as well as to heal. Each one of us must guard with care the deposit of power God has placed into our stewardship.

QUESTIONS FOR REFLECTION UPON YOUR SOURCE OF POWER

1. How do you understand the source of power in your ministry? Where does this power originate?
2. How can you harness the power of your personal example more effectively in your management responsibilities?
3. What pseudo-symbols of true power do you cling to?
4. Are you tempted to "put yourself down" or to "be spectacular" or to "be relevant"? How do you deal with these temptations?

The Essence of Understanding the Use of Power in Ministry and Management

1. Power emerges from two different sources.
   - God gives you power to reach a goal.
   - Your role in a congregation also gives you considerable power.
2. The manager has the option of using four types of power: exploitative, coercive, utility, or principle-centered.
3. Power should go beyond transactional relationships; it is the energy by which a leader is concerned for others.
4. Temptations are a natural by-product of power.
   - Temptations appear in the form of denying or misusing power.

How You Can Effectively Use Your Power

1. Become a people grower!
   - Learn to empower people with your influence.
2. Diminish your use of exploitative, coercive, and utility power.
   - Begin implementing principle-centered power that is based on mutual commitment, respect, and trust.
3. Develop the ten "power tools" in your leadership repertoire.
4. Begin looking for practical ways to use these "power tools" in your everyday life.
5. Tap into the true Power Source through the practice of spiritual disciplines.

I claim to be no more than an average man with less than average ability. I am not a visionary. I claim to be a practical idealist. Nor can I claim any special merit for what I have been able to achieve with laborious research. I have not the shadow of a doubt that any man or woman can achieve what I have, if he or she would make the same effort and cultivate the same hope and faith.

Mahatma Gandhi

13

Conflict Management

How do you keep going? When you are nurtured in solitude, strengthened in conflict, and proven in hopelessness.

Bill Wilson, a pastor in Brooklyn

Men [and women] do not shoot because targets exist, but they set up targets in order that throwing and shooting may be more effective and significant.

John Dewey

Figure 13.1

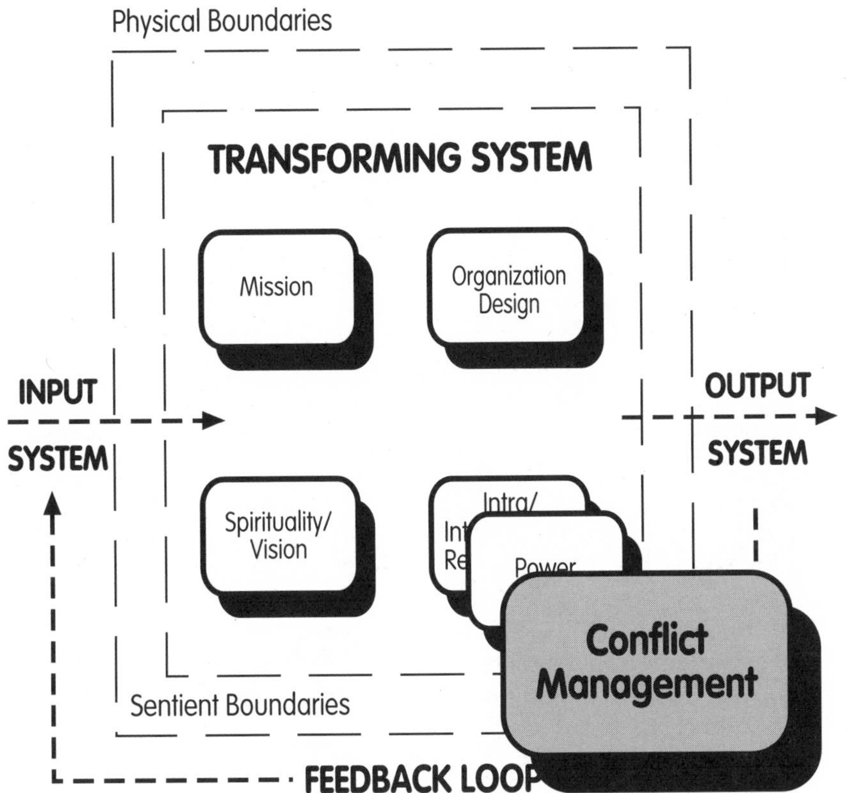

In the management of human relationships within congregations, conflict and conflict management are essential topics. Christians are human, and sometimes it appears that Christians are more prone to conflict than others. Conflict in the church that goes on and on toward no beneficial end is like pouring sand into the bearings of a machine. Unmanaged conflict frays nerves and wears down persons' patience until finally, all the ministries of the church grind to a halt. Some persons fight to the finish; others break their ties with the congregation and go elsewhere.

Church Conflict: All Too Familiar

The following article appeared in the *Chicago Sun-Times,* November 2, 1991:

Strife-Torn Peoria Church to Vote on Keeping Pastor

An election at a fractious Peoria church will decide the fate of its pastor and settle a conflict that has prompted violence, vandalism, and lawsuits.

Judge Robert Cashen of Peoria County ruled this week that the Rev. Cleveland Thomas, Sr., must stand for election if he is to remain pastor of New Morning Star Missionary Baptist Church. The feud became violent after about 250 church members voted to remove Thomas in October 1990. A Peoria judge later declared the vote invalid.

In recent months, Thomas has been unable to preach at services. When he takes the pulpit, opponents sing and shout him down.

Thomas's opponents object to what they call his aloofness, strict adherence to fundamental Bible law, and failure as a charismatic preacher. Others support Thomas and are angered by repeated interference during services. They want protesters arrested.

Judge Cashen appointed Arthur Greenberg, president-elect of the Peoria Bar Association, to oversee the balloting.

Violence has escalated after Thomas padlocked the church and opponents cut the chains. Police then imposed a curfew. Police have been summoned to the church almost weekly as the confrontations escalated into fistfights around the pulpit.

The factions have separate board chairmen, church attorneys, and bank accounts. Two offerings are taken each Sunday.

> So foul a sky clears not without a storm.
>
> Shakespeare's King John

This case is not as extraordinary as it may seem. For those who work as consultants and mediators in church conflict the story is common, even mild.[1] On any given day there are conflicts just as volatile raging in congregations along with thousands of others that are wounding good people and weakening good ministries.

In June 1993, the pastor of the Assemblies of God church in Kittitas, Washington, set about to remove several people from the congregation. The persons who were to be removed from the congregation claim that they were never informed of the reasons for their dismissal. The action severely divided the congregation and in November 1994, a melee erupted in one of the church services, which was reported in a local newspaper. The following is an abbreviated account of the incident:

Church Squabble Erupted into Altercation at Sunday Service

A five-month-long church dispute spilled into the public arena when City of Kittitas police were called to the Assembly of God Church shortly before noon on Nov. 14. The visit was in response to a fight reported during the Sunday morning worship service.

As a follow-up to that incident, two city officers were instructed to stand by at the city police station last Sunday in case there was another disturbance. . . .

[Officer Rosa] said he was later contacted by the church's pastor, Gary Jeffery, who told him he had been assaulted and threatened, but wanted to check with his attorney before deciding whether to pursue assault charges. After speaking with an attorney for the region's Assembly of God churches, Jeffery decided not to pursue charges.

"I'm into peace and restoring people," Jeffery said, "I want peace and harmony in the church. It's too bad that some people created an environment of fear and violence."

But others believe it's the pastor and board's past action that is the root of the problem. . . . [L]etters had been sent by Jeffery and church board members to former board member Jerry Marchel and his wife, Phyllis. They state that their church membership had been revoked by the board due to their disagreement with church leadership.[2]

It appears, however, that the pastor did not pursue peace and harmony very long. A January 8, 1994, newspaper article gives an account of a court hearing in which the pastor charged that he had been harassed by a group of the church members during one of the church services. He further claimed that his life had been threatened:

Kittitas Church Dispute Continues at Court Hearing

[A group] of disgruntled churchgoers in Kittitas [is accused] of bypassing the local church's authority in bringing allegations of improper behavior against the church's pastor. . . . But other testimony, brought out under questioning by the group's attorney, painted a picture of former church members and nonmembers as being denied a fair hearing before the congregation, and being ignored by district and state Assemblies of God officials. . . . The anti-harassment orders being sought [by Pastor Jeffery] would bar 12 people from having any contact with Jeffery or his family, or from coming near the church.[3]

The following account was carried in the Ellensburg newspaper on January 11, 1994:

Judge Rejects All but One Harassment Claim by Pastor

Judge Thomas Haven yesterday dismissed all but one of the 12 anti-harassment orders sought by a Kittitas . . . pastor against former congregation members. Haven said Pastor Gary Jeffery failed to prove [that] group members threatened him.

An anti-harassment order was approved against Jim. . . . Haven said that . . . Boswell assaulted Jeffery by touching his chin. . . .

Haven said Jeffery and his attorney, Richard Bueschel, failed to prove threats were made against the pastor's life, failed to show that the group stormed the church stage during the Nov. 14 incident, and failed to show that the pastor was trapped by the group in his church office after the scuffle.[4]

After the initial dispute in June 1993, the pastor of a nearby church in the same denomination attempted to befriend the excommunicated members and the members who sided with them. Allegedly, as a result of this, the pastor of the nearby church was counseled by two board members to resign from the church, though there were no charges against him. Later, it is alleged, a district official visited with the pastor and his wife, stating that there were no charges against them. Nonetheless, the deacons were allegedly told by the district officials to circulate a petition against the pastor. However, not all of the church members were allowed to see the petition. The deacons were told not to show the petition to the pastor or his wife. The pastor resigned on Father's Day, 1994.

The pastor of the Kittitas congregation resigned and left town in early 1995. There were about 100 people attending the church in June 1993, when the incident began. Reportedly, the Sunday congregation now numbers about 13 to 16 people.

As startling as this story is, we suspect that every reader knows of conflict situations in local congregations that are just as deplorable. We acknowledge that the above case is somewhat anomalous, but it does serve to illustrate some realities which we observe in our work with conflicted congregations:

1. Often (perhaps 90 percent of the time) when a congregation is engaged in highly destructive conflict, the pastor is either the perpetrator or is deeply involved as one of the conflict parties.
2. In highly destructive church fights the involvement of judicatory officials usually makes matters worse because they do not understand conflict management, and they come with their own agendas to preserve the denominational interests.[5]
3. Church conflicts often become habitual and escalate in ever tightening cycles of destructive behavior.

Conflict can actually be good for a congregation; it stirs things up and gets energies flowing, perhaps allowing for necessary change. It helps to clarify goals and differences of opinion. However, when church people fight dirty, when members want only to assail one another hoping to do each other harm, there comes a time when evil has its way in wreaking havoc. Such conflict inflicts open wounds upon human psyches, shatters relationships, and blurs the focus of mission and ministry.

Congregations leaders may err in two directions, either by identifying a conflict as sinful when it is actually normal and healthy, or by not calling a sinful conflict for what it really is—evil and destructive, reflecting the dark side of human nature.

Whatever sociological spin we care to put on destructive conflict in the church, the Scriptures take a dim view of it, claiming there are many conflict behaviors that keep persons outside of the reign of God. Paul names these behaviors as: enmities, strife, jealousy, malice, quarrels, dissension, factions, and envy. He says those who engage in such behavior "will not inherit the kingdom of God" (see Gal. 5:19-21). Paul admonishes Christians to avoid those Christians who engage in "profane chatter" as well as those who "cause dissensions" (see 2 Tim. 2:16-17; Rom. 16:17).

A Simple Definition of Conflict

One way to define conflict is to say that conflict (1) begins when someone takes an action that (2) is perceived as a threat to someone else's territory (physical, social, power, position) and (3) the threatened person launches a reaction aimed at protecting the territory. Another definition might be: conflict is what happens when two objects (ideas, people, nations, etc.) try to occupy the same space at the same time; for example, two airplanes attempting to occupy the same air space at the same time.

Major Sources of Conflict in the Church

There are, of course, a myriad of reasons why members of a congregation fight with one another. We will limit our discussion to a small list of conflict sources that seem most common and unique to religious organizations. John M. Miller has identi-

Lyle Schaller observes that more church conflicts happen over music than any other thing. Vernon McGee adds that when Satan fell out of heaven he fell into the choir loft.

fied five major factors within the church that explain the continual bombardment of its own "internecine battles," the sources of conflict in the church:

1. In the church, people sometimes do battle with one another because they feel strongly about certain things. The key word here is *feel.* Feelings and emotions often are much more powerful than thought or reason in ecclesiastical disputes. We might wish it were otherwise, but it is not.
2. Another explanation for church battles is that with astonishing regularity Christians encounter legitimate differences among themselves. It is not merely a case of feelings running high; but there are two or more valid positions which can be taken with respect to any one question.
3. Even when there are not many basic differences among Christians, there is a whole rainbow of shades of color among us regarding everything. Christians come in all sizes and shapes. This is true of minds and spirits as well as bodies. You find ebullient Christians and indolent Christians, optimistic and pessimistic Christians, ultra eager, excited, enthusiastic, incisive, cool-thinking, placid, cautious, somewhat skeptical, and downright stick-in-the-mud Christians.
4. Emotions, differences of opinion, and shading of personalities and issues create conflict in the church. Add misunderstanding to the list.
5. As though the previous four factors were not enough to stimulate ecclesiastical warfare, there is another, less excusable source. This is unvarnished human cussedness, sinful cantankerousness. What cruel treachery Christians visit upon one another.[6]

Conflicts Arising from Faith Commitments

There is one source of conflict that is almost totally unique to religious organizations: the conflict of faith commitments. At first blush it might appear that this type of conflict would not be located in a local congregation, since all the people there have a common commitment to the congregation and some commitment to the denomination of which they are a part. However, just the opposite is more likely the norm. People conflict with one another in the congregation because they share the same faith, but they disagree about the practical implications of this commitment.

The followers of Jesus were continually surprised at the sometimes painful cost of commitment and fidelity to the mission of Jesus. Their faith commitments made demands upon them that they were not able to keep, however honorable their intentions. Peter promised Jesus, "Lord, I am ready to go with you to prison and to death!" (Luke 22:33*b*), only to be reminded of the emptiness of his claim a few hours later as he was recognized as one of Jesus' friends by a servant girl. Among the many expressions of the interior, spiritual struggle of a faith commitment, perhaps none is more explicit than Paul's, "I do not understand my own actions. . . . I can will what is right, but I cannot do it. For I do not do the good I want, but the evil I do not want is what I do" (Romans 7:15*a*, 18*b*-19).

Our personal struggles with our faith commitments spill over into our relationships within the community of faith. We feel strongly about the implications of faith commitments. Paul strongly confronted Peter for ostracizing himself from the Gentiles because of pressure by the Judaizers, "But when I saw that they were not acting consistently with the truth of the gospel, I said to Cephas before them all, 'If you, though a Jew, live like a Gentile and not like a Jew, how can you compel the Gentiles to live like Jews?' " (see Gal. 2:14). Paul is saying that he rebuked Peter in front of everyone who was there.

Paul gives us insight into another conflict in the early church when he writes to the church in Corinth: "It has been reported to me by Chloe's people that there are quarrels among you . . . What I mean is that each of you says, 'I belong to Paul,' or 'I belong to Appollos,' or 'I belong to Cephas,' or 'I belong to Christ.' Has Christ been divided?" (1 Cor. 1:11-13*a*).

If the pioneers of the Christian faith had struggles with their understandings and commitments of the faith, we should not be too surprised by our own conflicts around such matters. According to Hugh F. Halverstadt, the "parties' core identities are at risk in church conflicts. Spiritual commitments and faith understandings are highly inflammable because they are central to one's psychological identity. . . . [Christians] may question or even condemn one another's spirituality or character."[7]

Ineffective Organizational Structures or Ministries

Roy W. Pneuman has described several ways that ineffective organizational designs can contribute to conflict in the church. We will list four of Pneuman's premises:[8]

1. *Structural ambiguity*. Such churches have no clear guidelines about the expectations and responsibilities of individual ministry positions (clergy and laity) as well as committees/boards. No one knows who is supposed to be doing what and, therefore, any idea or attempt to do something is up for grabs. There can be continual bickering about the agenda and/or actions of any person or committee.
2. *Confusion regarding the pastoral roles.* With the sum total of all the expectations that are placed on the pastor, including those within himself, it is no wonder that the pastor's role and responsibilities are always fertile ground for conflict.
3. *The pastor's leadership style.* Closely related to the pastor's roles and responsibilities is her leadership style. Most congregations in conflict will sooner or later get around to blaming the pastor's leadership style as a major cause of the conflict. "If only she gave more direction; we need to know what she expects of us." "We need more affirmation and caregiving from our pastor." "She's such an autocrat—it's obvious that she cares more about budgets and buildings than people."
4. *The changing size of a congregation.* The growth or decline of a congregation can be a source of pain and pressure. In times of decline, the congregation often attempts to structure itself the way it was structured in its glory years with all the same committees and offices. Much energy is put into keeping all the structure together intact and unchanged, rather than searching for new structures that will better serve the present realities. Now there are not enough good people to fill all the slots, so inept and uncommitted persons are put into crucial leadership positions. They fail at their tasks and the situation worsens. Frustration builds and people lose heart.[8]

Conversely, as congregations grow, they require additional structures to integrate the additional people and the expanding ministries.

Peter F. Drucker proposes that whenever a congregation grows or declines by 20 percent it is a signal that the entire structure of the church should be reviewed and revised as necessary to more effectively contain and coordinate the new circumstances.

Intercultural Differences

The changing demographics portend a great increase of intercultural differences in many congregations. In the 1980s some 7 to 9 million (legal and illegal) immigrants streamed into the United States, largely from Asia, Latin America, and the Caribbean. These immigrants represented about 40 percent of the total U.S. population increase in the 1980s. Similar trends are evident in the migration patterns across Europe and the former Soviet states.

The nations of the world will continue to become more heterogeneous. Yet virtually all of the churches are comprised of homogeneous groups. The increasing heterogeneity of the nations will open up tremendous opportunities for evangelism. Successful evangelistic efforts can destroy the homogeneity of the congregation, causing increased tension and conflict, as persons of various cultures come together around matters of their common faith—but uncommon traditions.

Solving Problems and Managing Conflicts Across Cultures

Distinctly different cultures are becoming a natural, albeit difficult, phenomenon in communities with growing and shifting populations. Increasing numbers of churches are experimenting with this growth by sharing facilities and, sometimes, by merging congregations. These become a seedbed for conflict within churches. Philip R. Harris and Robert T. Moran have identified a five-step process for solving problems across cultures:

1. Describe the problem as understood by both cultures.
2. Analyze the problem from two cultural perspectives.
3. Identify the basis for the problem from both viewpoints.
4. Solve the problem through synergistic strategies.
5. Determine if the solution is working multiculturally.[9]

Less obvious, perhaps, is culture as a source of conflict in fairly monolithic settings. For example, Edgar H. Schein discusses how persons use different coping styles in their capacity to express their aggressive feelings as well as their tender, loving feelings (this was based on earlier work done by Wallen and Horney):

1. The **"sturdy battler"** type is tuned toward locating in other members those who are strong and who are weak, those who can be controlled and who will be controlling, those who have authority and therefore need to be fought or watched, and those who are winning and those who are losing. Sturdy battlers are threatened by too much affection, and by the possibility that they will lose their ability to fight. They will, therefore, always attempt to create a group world in which one can test oneself against others and gradually determine a workable "pecking order."
2. The **"friendly helper"** type is tuned toward locating in other members those who are warm and who are cold, those who are helpful and who are not, those who are supportive and those who are threatening. Friendly helpers are threatened by too much aggression, by the possibility that they will not be accepted or liked or will be overwhelmed by feelings of hostility. They will, therefore, attempt to create a group world in which people can work closely together, be supportive, and like each other.
3. The **"logical thinker"** type is tuned toward locating in other members those who think clearly and those who are fuzzy, those who are accurate and who are inaccurate, those who are structured and who are not, and those who are oriented toward procedures and those who are not. Logical thinkers are threatened by any degree of emotionality in the group setting because they are afraid that they will be overwhelmed by their own feelings of aggression or love. They will, therefore, try to create a group world in which logic, structure, and procedure dominate, in which feelings are irrelevant and can be legislated off the agenda.[10]

These styles, learned in earlier cultural settings, are then brought into new situations where initially they are likely to cause communication problems and to slow down group formation because each type, in the effort to create the perfect group world, will threaten each of the other types.

In our work with conflicted cross-cultural congregations we have observed a few common characteristics:

1. Regardless of how the congregation becomes intercultural, if it succeeds in making the transition, the different groups come together with good intentions and high hopes of a more prosperous future than any group could realize alone.
2. When problems grow into conflicts it is usually because the Anglo pastor speaks only one language (English) while the ethnic pastor speaks both English and the language of the ethnic group. Thus, the Anglo pastor can converse with only one side of the equation, while the ethnic pastor can communicate with both sides. Over time the Anglo pastor comes to resent his shrinking lack of information and alternately begins to distrust the ethnic pastor—often fearing that the ethnic pastor is conniving to have him removed.
3. When conflict erupts between the two pastors, it is only a matter of time before similar tensions grow between the two groups. Again, the dynamics are the same. In a congregation meeting, for example, the Anglos can only understand the part of the conversation that is spoken in English, while the ethnic group understands all of the conversation, whether spoken in English or the ethnic language. This weakens and threatens the English-speaking people. Unnecessary conflicts result.

These observations have led us to believe that the best way to manage intercultural conflict is to anticipate the problems at the time the congregation is moving to welcome another ethnic or cultural group, and to deal with the anticipated problems in the course of putting the new church or the new programs together. In addition, there are certain things a pastor fundamentally should do if she plans to minister in cross-cultural situations. For example:

1. The pastor or both pastors should learn the languages of both groups so that everyone in the congregation can converse with both (or all) of the pastors. Then both pastors can also offer priestly care to everyone in the congregation.

2. Anglo lay leaders should also study the language of the other group, as should the leaders of the other group study English, if they do not already speak it. Unfortunately, many ethnic lay leaders will speak both languages, while none (or only a few) of the Anglo lay leaders will speak the other language.
3. The members of the host church (in case of mergers, sharing the same facilities, etc.) should be educated in the customs, foods, and religious practices of the "guest" group that is coming into the church. To know another culture is almost always to appreciate or even to enjoy the other culture. To not know the other culture is to disapprove of it, or even to fear it.

Except for isolated rural areas of our country, those pastors and congregations who wish to expand their ministries now or in the future will have to learn how to engage in successful intercultural ministries and relationships. This will come as bad news to many pastors and congregations, as their communities transist from being purely one culture to being multicultural and multiethnic. For one thing they will find their homogeneous pool drying up and will be confronted with the realities of either becoming a multicultural congregation, or continuing the slow decline to extinction.

QUESTIONS FOR REFLECTION UPON CONFLICT MANAGEMENT

1. When have you experienced church conflict in the past? Which of John Miller's five major factors were at work in the situation?
2. Does the organizational structure of the congregation tend to contribute to conflict? What modifications could be made to release the pressure point?
3. Do you tend to operate as a sturdy battler, a friendly helper, or a logical thinker? How does this tendency help or hinder your efforts in intercultural situations?

Three Dimensions of Conflict

Whatever the source of the conflict, if it is not managed, it will soon take root in one of three dimensions: values and traditions, purpose and goals, or programs and methods.[11]

Conflict over Values and Traditions

Value conflicts are, of course, the most difficult to resolve because persons (by definition) place more significance on values than they do on goals or methods. The good news is that there are not many value conflicts in local congregations. Persons involved in congregations decided to belong to a particular one because their values were similar to those of the congregation.

The bad news is that in successful congregations, conflicts over values and traditions will likely escalate as the congregation turns its attention toward reaching and serving new oncoming generations, for example, Generation X. Each new generation enters the church with new and different experiences and values. Generation X, for example, abhors old traditions but values authentic relationships much more than do most older generations.

Of course the congregation may choose to just skip over problem generations like Generation X, and wait for the next generation to come along. However, the congregation that misses Generation X will likely not survive beyond 2025. Thus present-day pastors and congregations will likely face more conflicts over values and traditions as we move into the twenty-first century.

There is little hope in reaching compromise in value conflicts, because if you compromise on a value, then it is no longer (for you) a value. The conflict management strategy, therefore, must be to engage all of the parties in a search for a higher value that can unite them. Then the lesser values are no longer so divisive.

A secondary strategy is to have each conflict party "put on" or "wear" the values of the other party, to live with them a while, to see how things look and feel from the other party's perspective. Sometimes a party will discover that they can live with the others' values quite well.

Conflict over Purpose and Goals

The second most difficult conflicts are conflicts over purpose and goals. Goals are desired future conditions that grow out of our sense of values and our mission, which are highly influenced by our traditions and boundaries.

Goals add measurable substance to the congregation's values and to its sense of mission. Whenever there is a conflict of goals it is probably due to one or both of the following conditions:

1. There is no clear sense of mission, so that there is no benchmark for deciding the desirability of one goal against another.
2. There is an antagonist, or an antagonistic group, who insists that the congregation pursue the goals as she defines them (more will be said about antagonists in the church in the following chapter).[12]

Conflict over Methods

Methods are the actions that the congregation takes to achieve its goals. As such, conflicts over methods tend to be the least volatile—because "there is more than one way to Rome." To resolve most conflicts over methods, the manager must seek an arena for creativity in planning the congregation's programs and services.

Nonetheless, even conflicts over methods can be serious enough. Consider, for example, the following case in which the entire congregation agreed upon the vision for the future of the church and upon the major goals. However, two methodological conflicts arose simultaneously. One was a conflict among the professional staff regarding how the senior pastor managed the professional and the support staffs. The second was a conflict among the longtime members and the lay leaders regarding the programs that the staff put together to accomplish the goals.

> The congregation had about 1,500 longtime members and 1,000 new belongers. The new belongers fully supported the methods of the staff, while the longtime members did not. The conflict became highly volatile and dangerous, and involved virtually all of the 2,500 people.
>
> Board members received death threats, as did the pastor. The police suggested that the board only meet with the congregation behind bulletproof glass. The board decided against this, but they did allow the public conflict sessions (usually about 1,000 people) to be sprinkled with plainclothes police, just in case violence should erupt. There was no physical violence in the public meetings, but the sessions were charged with hostility, demands, and threats.

When differences in any dimension (values, goals, methods) become severe enough, persons feel that their own self is being nevertheless threatened, and when persons feel personally threatened, they counter with threats against others—or they leave the church.

The conflict discussed above illustrates that even a conflict over methods can become volatile and dangerous, depending upon the levels of trust persons have for one another, their ability to communicate effectively with one another, and the overall cohesiveness of the group.

Levels of Conflict

Conflicts in each of the three dimensions may be carried on at various levels of intensity. The level of intensity is conditioned by how high the stakes are for winning, by trust for one another, by the extent to which persons are willing and able to communicate openly and honestly, and by the extent to which persons are willing to suspend personal judgment and desires in order to search for common ground. These interpersonal realities can be scaled to depict a hierarchy of levels of conflict. The levels of conflict are identified and described as follows:[13]

Level one conflicts are problems to be solved. There is no blaming as people work toward specific, temporal solutions.

Level two conflicts are disagreements. At this level of conflict, persons are positioning themselves out of self-protection, wanting to come out looking good. The focus shifts from specifics to becoming more generalizing. Trust declines. While persons are not hostile, they are cautious and tend to withhold information.

In **level three** conflicts, the objective shifts from self-protection to winning. People take sides, forming into clusters around specific issues. The language that is used becomes distorted in magnification, dichotomization, and overgeneralizing.

In **level four** conflicts the objective changes from wanting to win to wanting to hurt or get rid of the opposing party. Each party believes that the other side is all bad or won't change. Principles of justice and truth become personalized causes, and parties are cold, unforgiving, and often self-righteous.

Figure 13.2

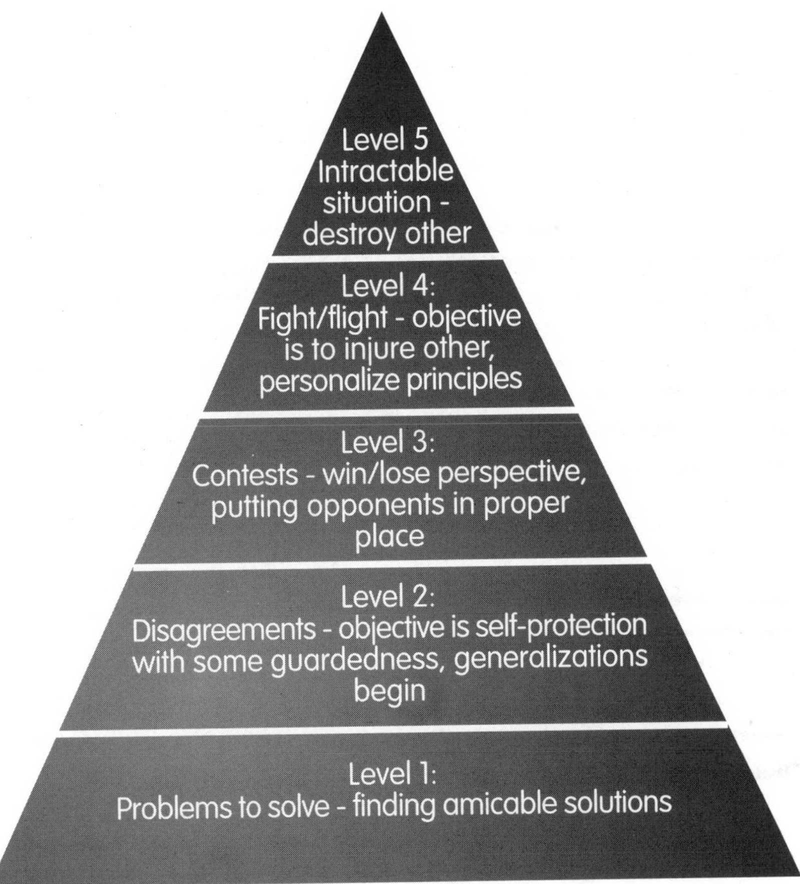

Level five conflicts are intractable, unmanageable situations where the objective is to destroy the other party, making certain that they will never again be able to obtain another position of influence or value in the congregation.[14]

Intervening into Conflict

Assumptions in Intervention Work

In the care and nurture of intrapersonal, interpersonal, and intergroup relationships within the congregation, every pastor must learn the basic skills of conflict management and teach them to the lay leaders. The pastor could lead new workers and committee members through a conflict management training process,[15] or offer periodic classes on conflict management and family systems theory.

Avoiding conflict because of wanting to be liked by everyone, or due to some inner fear, is no excuse for allowing unresolved and destructive conflict to go on in the church. We acknowledge that intervening in conflict situations is risky and sometimes filled with hurt and frustration. Nonetheless, intervention is necessary if the promise of shalom and effective ministry is to continue within the congregation.

The purpose of any intervention is to create more healthy persons, relationships, and/or organizations. Conflict management is a specific intervention, aimed toward turning self-defeating behavior into habits of self-enhancing behavior. Specific goals in conflict intervention are to resolve the broken relationships and manage, not necessarily resolve, the differences.

Social science models are descriptive and may help us understand what is taking place, but these models do not deal with guilt, scars, or brokenness—as resources in the Christian faith do. The use of Scripture, listening to God, and fasting are means of grace that help to turn destructive patterns into constructive patterns. However, they must be used with discernment. For example, while individual prayer is crucial, public prayers at inappropriate times can make conflict much worse. There are no shortcuts when the scars are deep and the history of conflict is long-lasting. We can't pretend that it will go away.

A group or religious organization may suffer for a long time if conflict was ignored or poorly managed. Should an individual or group leave the congregation, others may act like the conflict is over. But unresolved conflict becomes part of the individual and corporate psyche. Persons will go for many years with unresolved pain and guilt.

Persons and/or groups must have a certain level of trust and willingness in order to communicate. If trust is not there, then the first step in intervention is to establish a trusting environment. The following are specific steps, while not necessarily in this order, that can be taken: (1) Give people permission to disagree over issues; (2) Listen to the different parties in order to empower them (the goal is for each party to be able to state his/her case with strength and effectiveness); and (3) Provide a safe place for individuals so they aren't irreparably hurt, and so that they do not irreparably hurt others.

Various Intervention Models

There are three different models of intervention:

1. **The expert model.** The expert model assumes that the expert (the interventionist) knows everything about the peoples' problems and what is necessary to correct the situation. The people who are in the conflict know little or nothing about correcting the matter. Therefore the expert makes the diagnosis, decides on the prescription, and carries it out without the advice or involvement of the conflict parties.
2. **The doctor-patient model.** The physician model assumes that the "doctor" and the patient both know something about the symptoms of the condition. Therefore the patient (those in conflict) is actively involved in deciding the diagnosis. The doctor, however, is the only one who knows the appropriate prescription.

   In this model, therefore, the interventionist (the doctor) involves the conflict parties in developing an accurate description of the situation. The parties also separate what are symptoms and what are the real problems. Then the doctor alone decides and prescribes the cure. The conflict parties then carry out the prescription.
3. **The process consultation model.** The process consultation intervention assumes that the conflict parties "own" the conflict, and therefore they are the only ones who can describe the problem and its symptoms. Further, they are the only ones who can decide and administer the cure.

   The fact that they have been unable to do this alone is a clear indication that they cannot create a process that will allow them to do so. Therefore, they need someone who can decide on an appropriate process and lead them through it—so that they may solve their own problem.

   Both the process consultant and client conduct the diagnosis, the client decides on the "get well" plan and carries it out, with the process consultant coaching the processes.[16]

We believe the latter model to be most effective in conflict intervention because the participants are involved in the process and, therefore, are more likely to support the outcomes. People in conflict situations often know what they need, but they do not know how to do it. Since conflicts are primarily problems of human interactions and processes, process consultation is the most effective way of dealing with these complex issues. As a matter of fact, the process consultation model, in volunteer organizations such as the congregation, is generally the only intervention that works.

Intervention Designs for Groups and/or Organizations

Destructive conflict tends to be cyclical and habitual in nature, carrying on self-defeating habits. Once these habits are ingrained into the participants' consciousness, they become automatic, and persons become unaware of their own destructive behavior. Those who intervene in conflict situations must break the cycles of destructive, self-defeating habits and turn the patterns into habits of constructive, self-enhancing, intentional behavior.

To help break these destructive cycles and turn them into constructive ones, there are three major issues which must be addressed: (1) generate valid and useful information; (2) allow free and informed choice; and (3) motivate internal commitment to the agreements reached.[17]

1. Generate valid and useful information. Separate truth from error; explore assumptions and interests of parties; purge rumors and charges. The primary leadership skills needed in this phase are active listening, empathic understanding, care-giving, analysis/evaluation, and discernment.

• *STEP ONE: Initiate the process—talk to leaders and to key players.*

If interpersonal of trust and communication are high, meet with all conflict parties as a group. If not, meet with leaders or representatives of conflict parties separately.

The purpose of this step is to find out initial perceptions, the quality of relationships among conflict parties and their wants and interests.[18] Determine whether they want the conflict resolved, or if they have already made up their minds and are unwilling to negotiate any kind of change.

• *STEP TWO: Gather the data.*

After the initial meeting, with what valid and useful information do you still need in order to understand what is going on in the conflict situation? Decide if you need additional interviews, questionnaires, focus groups, instruments, delphi technique, etc.

• *STEP THREE: Assimilate and analyze the data. Give feed back to the conflict parties.*

Look for patterns and differences among the parties in their perceptions of the issues, the quality of their relationships, and what they want to see happen.

2. **Allow free and informed choice.** Conflict parties must feel safe enough to be honest about their own feelings concerning the conflict issues and relationships. They must also develop a clear road map of what they wish to do. In order to preserve the internal commitment to the agreements reached, and in order to allow parties to assume responsibility for their own destiny, it is important that the conflict parties be part of the decision-making process and outcomes that will affect their life and work together.

During phases two and three, it is important to monitor continually the status of relationships among the conflict parties and their commitment to involvement in the plan as it is being created.

• *STEP ONE: Set up meetings where parties (or their representatives) can talk to each other.*

Separate the relational issues from the matters of substance. In conflict that is deeply embedded, emotions may be more important than the issues. When parties feel threatened, for example, anger can generate fear. And fear-filled persons will react to preserve themselves and their opinions. Recognize your own emotions as well as those of the conflict parties. Be aware that your own issues may be triggered—stay separate. Can you empathize with all parties? Help others express their feelings. It may be that you merely allow people to "let off steam." Active listening will help you understand and empower persons to be clearer in what they feel and perceive.

Review ways that parties can "sin" in conflict situations: aggression, manipulation, avoidance. If needed, provide an opportunity for persons to ask for forgiveness, remembering that parties need time to heal and develop the courage to forgive.[19]

Look for areas of agreement regarding the issues. Determine if there is sufficient agreement between parties to enable them to collaborate in reaching resolutions and decisions. The intervention skills that are needed during this phase include: providing support to areas of agreement, helping participants personalize the benefits of alternative solutions, and summarizing/structuring the agreements.

Look for areas of disagreement and determine whether there is openness to negotiate these areas. The intervention skills needed include affirming the right to disagree and knowing how to manage the timing of intervention processes so that people do not feel pressured, or that conflict swept under the carpet.

• *STEP TWO: Appeal to a higher principle around which the controversy is centered.*

Is there a standard of fairness to which you can appeal—Scripture, policy, principle?

• *STEP THREE: Generate as many options as you are able to and see if one emerges that is satisfactory for all parties.*

If not, test for change consensus, and/or a willingness to live together in spite of nonnegotiable differences or disagreement.

The areas of disagreement are made explicit with both parties, and collaborative decisions are made as to how the parties will live and work together in spite of their differences. Intervention skills needed are generating options and helping the group identify possible compromises with the personal benefits of their compromises.

3. Motivate internal commitment to the plan or agreements that are reached. This means that the choice of action has been internalized by each member so that he experiences a high degree of ownership and accepts responsibility for the choice and its implications. The choice fulfills his own needs and sense of responsibility as well as those of the organization.

Commitment to the conflict management plan is also enhanced by putting the plan in writing, which includes the agreements that have been reached, "checkup dates" and a method for identifying the "pinches" (someone begins to feel tension regarding how well the plan is working out).

A covenant pledging future relationships should also be written, signed, and celebrated by all parties. The covenant includes translating the agreements reached into individual promises of support and accountability, which is then presented by the group to God—as their faith commitment to lay down the fight and to live in trust and harmony.

The Pain of Forgiving

Forgiveness is a crucial matter in conflict among Christians, and it cannot be entered into lightly. Lewis B. Smedes, author of *Forgive & Forget: Healing the Hurts We Don't Deserve,* describes the difficult, long-suffering process needed by people as they work through the stages of forgiveness: hurting, hating, healing, and beginning again.[20]

The first stage of forgiveness, according to Smedes, is *hurt*. During this phase one may feel completely assailed by pain, be numb to it, or be minimally aware of it. Whatever the case, it is vital to explore the places where pain may be dwelling and experience it.

Hate is the second stage, marked by feelings of rage; it is during this phase that we continue to wish that the person(s) who harmed us would suffer at least as much as we are suffering. It is important not to rush through or minimize these two stages, but to allow time and space for a complete catharsis.

The third stage is *healing*. Healing happens naturally if grieving and anger run their course. The following are characteristics of this stage: a genuine ability to wish the best for the one(s) who sinned against us, taking responsibility for our part in the conflict, and gaining deeper insight into God's forgiveness of us.

Beginning again is the final stage, marked by a readiness to come together again with the one(s) who offended us and finding a new freedom to move on. We finally come to agree with John Patton when he writes:

> Human forgiveness is not an act but a discovery that I am more like those who have hurt me than different from them; that I am capable of also hurting others very deeply. I am able to forgive when I discover that I am in no position to forgive. Although the experience of God's

> forgiveness may involve confession, and the sense of being forgiven for specific sins; at its heart it is the recognition of my reception into the community of sinners—those affirmed by God as his children.[21]

Forgiveness is much more than forgetting, or excusing, or pretending there is no conflict.[22] Sweeping the hurt under the carpet will only pile up, so much so that every time there is even the slightest movement on the carpet, the dust will scatter and get into the eyes, nose, and throat. Then, the eventual spring cleaning job of sweeping it all away will only get harder, especially when anger turns into malice. Smedes writes, "Malice, unrelieved, will gradually choke you. But anger can goad you to prevent the wrong from happening again. Malice keeps the pain alive and raw inside your feelings, anger pushes you with hope toward a better future. . . . Malice is misery that needs healing. Anger is energy that needs direction."[23]

QUESTIONS FOR REFLECTION UPON YOUR ROLE IN CONFLICT INTERVENTION

1. What model of intervention do you tend to migrate toward in the event of conflict? Why do you tend to move toward this particular model?
2. Are you inclined to avoid conflict in order to be liked by everyone? How can you foster a paradigm shift toward a more healthy view of conflict?
3. How can you become a more effective conflict manager in your situation?
    - Acquiring more information about conflict management.
    - Dealing with my own shadow side.
    - Developing an awareness of my emotions in conflict situations.
4. In what specific areas of the congregation does forgiveness need to transpire? In what areas of your own life?

The Essence of Understanding Conflict Management

1. Conflict begins when someone takes an action that is perceived as a threat to someone else's territory (physical, emotional, social, etc.), whereby the threatened person launches a reaction aimed at protecting the territory.
2. The implications of faith commitments are a breeding ground for conflict.
    - Because one's psychological identity is at risk, people resort to questioning one another's spirituality.
3. More effective structures can be a crucial key to dealing with conflicts in a congregation.
4. Whatever the source of conflict in a congregation, it is found in one of three spheres:
    - Values and traditions.
    - Purpose and goals.
    - Programs and methods.
5. Forgiveness plays a dynamic role in the life of the Christian community.

How You Can Become an Effective Conflict Manager

1. Identify ineffective organizational structures that contribute to habitual conflict.
2. Develop an awareness of your own manner of dealing with conflict.
    - Sturdy battler, friendly helper, or logical thinker?
3. Help others to develop healthy communication patterns.
    - Give people permission to disagree over issues.
    - Listen to the different parties in order to empower them.
    - Provide safety for individuals so they are not irreparably hurt, and so they do not irreparably hurt others.
4. Implement the three phases of breaking destructive cycles.
    - Generate valid and useful information.
    - Allow free and informed choice.
    - Motivate internal commitment to the agreements reached. Clearly define and communicate a relevant, community-oriented mission.

In this chapter we have discussed conflicts that involve more or less healthy persons who are able to communicate and relate to others in helpful ways, even though this may require the assistance of a third-party conflict interventionist. Unfortunately, the congregation will sometimes have persons who cannot function at this level. The following chapter will discuss conflicts when this is the case. We will proceed now to a consideration of conflicts that involve persons who are dysfunctional in one or more areas of their lives.

> And the peace of God, which surpasses all understanding, will guard your hearts and your minds in Christ Jesus . . . and the God of peace will be with you.
>
> —Paul's letter to the Philippians (4:7, 9*b*)

14

Family Systems Theory Applied to Religious Organizations

Figure 14.1

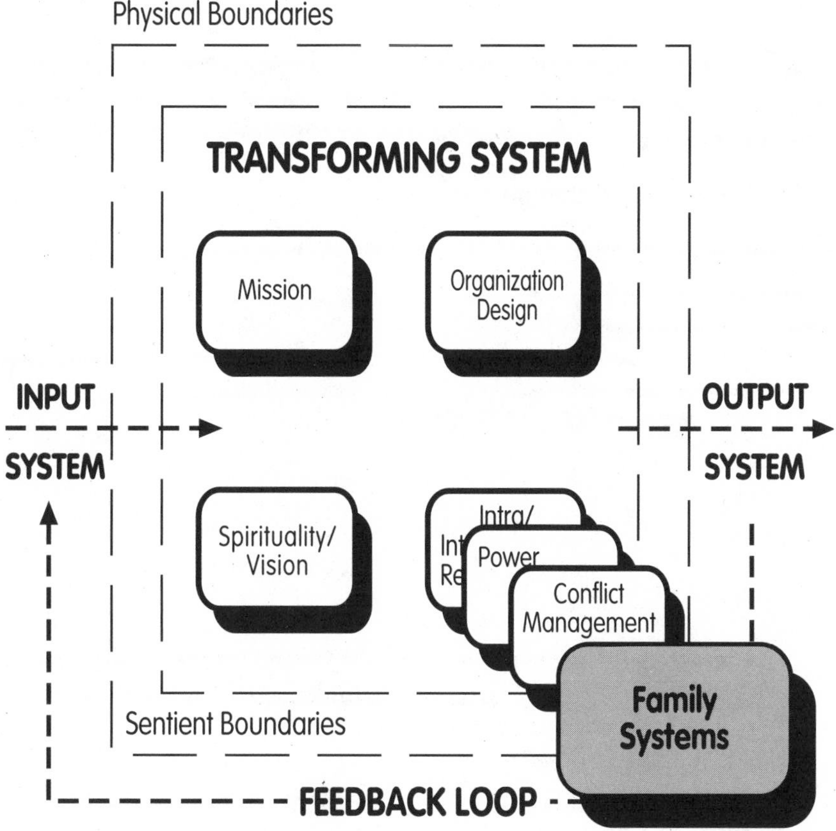

The original inspiration behind the Franciscan movement came from words addressed to Francis from the cross at San Damiano in Assisi: "Francis, go rebuild my house which is falling into ruins."[1]

Thomas of Celano

When the congregation is a healthy system, individual members thrive because of the empowering influence of the life of the body. When the congregation is unhealthy, our efforts to equip a few motivated individuals are usually doomed.[2]

R. Paul Stevens and Phil Collins

In the previous chapter we described conflicts involving persons who are able to function more or less effectively in all of the important areas of their lives: home, work, social groups, and community. Even though they may have serious disagreements and some outright fights, they are, nonetheless, socially and psychologically well-adapted people. Most church conflicts presuppose reasonably healthy and functional persons who get themselves into conflicts, some of which will require planned interventions to help persons work through their differences.

Dysfunctional Congregations

From time to time persons not so socially or psychologically well-adapted become members of congregations and they bring their maladjustments with them. If they are not healed in the church, sooner or later they will almost certainly become a source of conflict that reflects their own internal disappointments with life, and which is evidenced in a consuming brokenness. This type of worldview is termed "dysfunctional." In these situations an entirely new body of theory and interventions are needed—because dysfunctional people engage the congregation by an entirely different set of rules when they are in conflict. As you move through the next two chapters, please keep the following principles in mind:

1. **Persons who are competent with certain skills may also be dysfunctional in their relationships within the church,** because the church is a unique system that takes on many characteristics of a family.
2. **Often a relatively small group is dysfunctional in a church, with the rest of the people being competent.** It is not often that everyone in the congregation is dysfunctional.

3. **An entire congregation can become dysfunctional.** This is more often the case in smaller congregations, but it also happens in fairly large congregations. Obviously, not all of these people are dysfunctional in all other areas of their lives, but as members of the church family system they all engage in dysfunctional behavior.

Family systems theory is a relatively new body of knowledge and processes for treating a dysfunctional family that, when applied within proper limits, can give us valuable insight into the behaviors of dysfunctional congregations, and how to intervene into their dysfunction.[3] Dysfunctional persons make entrance into a congregation through a number of avenues, such as:

1. The congregation hires a new pastor who is dysfunctional.
2. Persons who are dysfunctional become new members.
3. Over time, members experience a series of events which can move them toward dysfunction: for example, a divorce, substance addiction, losing one job after another, child abuse in the home. Somewhere along the way a once healthy person moves toward dysfunction.

An underlying characteristic of virtually all dysfunctional persons is that in earlier generations there has been a history of dysfunction: addictions, co-dependencies, divorce, a pattern of losing, and so on. This means that dysfunction is most often a family affair that usually spans generations. For this reason, the body of theory which addresses dysfunction in persons' lives is appropriately termed family systems theory.

It is usually the case that dysfunction in a congregation has been passed on from one generation to the next, perhaps becoming dormant for several years, only to reappear at a later time.

Several years ago we interviewed the father of two young daughters, who sat as a board chairperson of the congregation that he and his family attended for several years. He sought us out for counsel when he learned that a year previous an older member of the congregation had sexually molested the pastor's young daughter. The pastor, however, had decided "for the sake of the ministry" not to disclose the incident and had instructed his daughter to tell no one.

After one year, the pastor's daughter told her friend, the board member's daughter, who then told her father. The board member talked to the pastor, but the pastor begged him to tell no one, stating that if the incident became public, it would ruin the church.

The board member was distraught and went to the only psychologist in the area for help in deciding what to do. The psychologist, a longtime therapist in the community, told him that over the past thirty years she had heard of many such incidents in the congregation. She had spoken to several pastors over the years who, upon learning of the incidents, had chosen to leave the congregation without making the situation public.

Now the board member was filled with fear that the same thing might happen to his own daughters, but he did not want to make the incident public, since the pastor begged him not to do so.

We brought the board member together with his district superintendent and had the board member tell what he knew to the district superintendent. The superintendent, who knew nothing of the situation, told the board member that he must go public, with his (the superintendent's) support.

This tragic story illustrates how dysfunction in a congregation can span generations and yet never become known. A dysfunctional congregation will do almost anything to keep from disclosing "the family secret."

In this congregation the illness had been passed on from one perpetrator to another—persons who were addicted to child molestation. The highly dysfunctional behavior was able to continue because there was always someone in the congregation who was willing to play the co-dependent role that is necessary to keep the dysfunction hidden, or at least excused. The co-dependents in this case included the pastors who left without disclosing the dysfunction and other members who undoubtedly knew, but kept the "secret."

This suggests a most interesting phenomenon, which we repeatedly observe in our work with dysfunctional congregations: Dysfunctional congregations have a most uncanny ability to locate and hire dysfunctional pastors. There is something mystical about the ability of dysfunctional congregations and pastors to find each other. Over thousands of miles, working only with applications, job descriptions, and a few phone calls, they come to know that they are "kin."

The previous case describes a severely dysfunctional congregation in which various members filled crucial, necessary roles that allowed the dysfunction to continue over generations. Not all dysfunctional congregations are so dysfunctional. Dysfunction comes in degrees. Some congregations are highly competent; others are highly dysfunctional, while yet others fall somewhere in between. Figure 14.1 is a matrix depicting family/congregation relationships on a continuum of function to dysfunction:[4]

Figure 14.2

Capable negotiation, warmth, intimacy, humor	Ambivalence not recognized, warm relations then control struggles, negotiation pain, neurotic	Conflict is hidden not obvious, committed to rels but no closeness, Warmth in rels ranges from High-low	Chaotic, tyrannical control, rigid, depressed, outbursts of rage, obsessive	Confused communications, lack of shared Focus, despair, cynicisim, schizophrenic
Highly Competent	Competent but pained	Complementary dominant-submissive	Conflicted	Severely dysfuntional

We will now describe the basic building blocks of family systems theory. To one who is unfamiliar with family systems theory, it may at first appear to be complex. It is. But if you take the time to study this material, it may bring you helpful insight into some confusing and discouraging dynamics in a congregation you once served—or one you may have observed from a distance.

Family Systems Theory

When a family is under stress or not meeting the needs of its members, the anxiety does not occur solely because of one person. Such problems have more to do with how people relate to each other. Stress and anxiety are a family affair. Therefore, in order to understand the behaviors of individual family members, it is important to see how persons function in their family contexts. What is their family life? How do members communicate? What are the family rules? What are their beliefs? How are individual needs met? Who keeps the family secrets? The answers to these questions are patterns that give clues to understanding the behaviors and attitudes of individual members. David S. Freeman defines certain assumptions of family systems theory:

Assumption One: The family as a whole is greater than the sum of its parts. When family members are together, they respond according to the emotional dynamics going on at that time in the group. When taken out of the family context, an individual may behave differently.

Assumption Two: If you change one part of the family system, you change the whole family. A change in one part of the family system will affect all other parts. The family has to adjust to the change one member may bring, for example, when that person refuses to play old games or relate to other members the same way.

Assumption Three: Family systems become more complex and organized over time. Each day brings new problems, information, and opportunities to a family. As such, it is dynamic and changing as it grows more complex over time. The family must grow, adapt, and adjust if it is to survive with the changes in the environment as well as those internal changes.

Assumption Four: The family is open, changing, goal directive, and adaptive. The family does have resources within its own ranks to deal with internal needs as well as external threats and opportunities. It also has potential for coming up with its own strategy to meet its challenges.

Assumption Five: Individual dysfunction is a reflection of an active emotional system. Conflict and anxiety do not occur solely because of the personal struggles of one person or group. Problems have more to do with relational networks and how individuals function within those networks. When a certain member's role is dysfunctional, it serves as a role for other members in a reciprocal process. These reciprocal roles are established over time and become normative and predictable among the members. As a matter of fact, these dynamics may contribute toward an inability of a group or congregation to move toward relational, spiritual healing and effectiveness. They become stuck in their dysfunctional patterns. What are these patterns and how can one understand them?[5]

Those who espouse systems theory stress that, instead of concentrating on isolated, individual parts, one must view and consider the interrelatedness of things as a whole.[6] How do individual parts influence other parts, and what are the patterns of their influence? The pattern of behaviors is sustained by the particular function of each individual's part in the family relationship. That is, each family member has a role to play in the family system. And if a member does not play his or her assigned role, then the family pattern will be upset—and in a dysfunctional family to upset the family pattern is seen as catastrophic.[7] Family systems theory views the entire family as a single emotional unit.[8] Since one must look at the entire system as a total entity in order to see the dynamics and influences of individuals and groups upon the entire system.

So it is in the church. A new pastor, for example, learns quickly what is expected of him in order for the congregation to function as it always has, regardless of what was lauded as the desire for change and the need for "a new leadership" during the initial interviews with the pastoral selection committee.

In a dysfunctional system not only does the system let each person know what is expected of him, the system also seeks to force a person into a role that will help ensure that the dysfunction will continue. This is one reason why family systems theory stresses that in a dysfunctional family, treating the symptoms of one person, while failing to treat all of the interrelated parts, will only perpetuate the family dysfunction. Others will try to compensate for the change in the one person. Therefore, in order to treat the dysfunction of any one member, the entire family should be treated simultaneously. When this is not possible, the person must be enabled to understand the "generation to generation" influences that his family has had upon him and to lay down the guilt and shame of the family dysfunction.

Making Application to the Congregation

In a congregation, these emotional processes distinguish the congregation's relational subsystem from its other subsystems such as mission, organizational structures, and spirituality. The emotional patterns of a relationship system are complex and difficult to ascertain; there are at least two reasons for this:

1. Each person, including the leader/manager, is a part of the system and thereby is influenced by the system, just as she influences the system. A pastor or consultant who thinks she is a change agent without also being changed by the relationship is naive.
2. In addition to the relationships within the system, each person brings his own intrapersonal dimensions from life's experiences, family of origin, spirituality, and values. Unresolved, unconscious issues from one's family of origin will be projected onto relationships within the congregation. To make these realities conscious is sometimes painful, but it is necessary for our own growth and the growth of the congregation, as M. Scott Peck reminds us:

> Remember in the story of the Garden of Eden, we became conscious when we ate the apple from the Tree of the Knowledge of Good and Evil. Consciousness then became for us both the cause of our pain and the cause of our salvation, . . . Consciousness is the cause of our pain because, of course, were we not conscious, we would not feel pain. . . . But while consciousness is the whole cause of pain, it is also the cause of salvation, because salvation is the process of becoming increasingly conscious.[9]

QUESTIONS FOR REFLECTION UPON FAMILY SYSTEMS

1. What, if any, dysfunction have been passed down over time within your congregation?
2. In what ways do you exert influence upon others and receive influence from others in your current congregational system?
3. What intrapersonal dimensions (experiences, family origin, etc.) are you bringing into the system? In what specific ways do these dimensions help or hinder others?

As we sort through the complexities of emotional processes in the congregation's relationships, there are several key concepts from family systems theory that can help us make sense of the emotional patterns within the congregation that can make the unconscious patterns a part of our consciousness. These include anxiety, boundaries, emotions, triangling, symptom bearer, and homeostasis. Understanding each of these patterns and how they relate to one another in a dysfunctional family (or congregation) system helps us to understand how to intervene into the dysfunctional behaviors, or how to treat the family disease. These patterns may be viewed on a set of continua to help determine the relational health and extent of dysfunction in a family or congregation. This is illustrated in Figure 14.3, below.

Figure 14.3

Patterns of Relational Health and Dysfunction of Organizations and Systems

Functional Behaviors	**RELATIONAL HEALTH:**	**Dysfunctional Behaviors**
Brought to light and addressed.	ANXIETY	Denied, or habitual and . . . . chronic
Balance between self and others	BOUNDARIES	Rigid and distant, or . .enmeshed,/co-dependent
Expressed in responsible ways	EMOTIONS	Supressed or . . . . .out of control
People own up to own feelings; appropriate self-disclosure	TRIANGLING	People gossip and triangle others to alleviate tension or . . . . to collect injustices
Individuals/group take responsibility for themselves	SYMPTOM BEARER	Blame is internalized in self-righteousness or externalized in rage against . . . . others(s)
Interdependence and proper balance	HOMEOSTASIS	Viscious cycles of self- . . . . defeating behavior

Anxiety

In every relationship system, people eventually become anxious. This anxiety, acting as an alarm system, lets people know that something is not right, that there is a potential crisis. But anxiety also presents the opportunity for the relationship to change and grow. Therefore, anxiety can be the demise or the lifeline of our relationships. Different triggering events set anxiety off in different organizational settings. For example, a major change or loss that takes people by surprise can trigger anxiety. A petition circulated to expunge the pastor, a church leader who suffers a moral crisis, or a key family leaving the church may be the triggering event that raises the anxiety level within a congregation.

> So do not worry about tomorrow, for tomorrow will bring worries of its own. Today's trouble is enough for today. (Matt. 6:34).

Making Application to the Congregation

Anxiety in a congregation is most often released in a free-floating manner and finally "lodges" in persons who are most vulnerable or responsible. This is especially true for those who cannot tolerate contrariety, or those who do not learn how to manage differences. Anxiety has no focus; therefore, its free-floating, erratic influence weakens the group's objectivity and creativity. Options are restricted with automatic, reflexive responses. At the same time, however, anxiety can be the motivation that is, in fact, our extrication when it is brought to light and addressed. Peter L. Steinke explains. "Anxiety provokes change. It prods and pushes us toward innovation or transformation. If, however, it reaches a certain intensity, it prevents the very change it provokes. What is stimulus becomes restraint. We 'lose our head' or 'cool,' as we say, essentially our awareness and composure; we are too reactive to be responsive."[10]

Anxiety is a warning signal to the congregation that there is some threat, some need that must be addressed. This is acute anxiety that is situational and "time-based."[11] The healthy congregation will acknowledge the situation and address it so that, in due time, the anxiety is abated. Chronic anxiety, however, is a habitual condition that never ends.[12] No longer a warning signal, chronic anxiety embeds itself in the very fabric of the relationship, becoming a part of the nature of the system itself. What seems trivial to someone from the outside triggers the anxious behavior on the inside.

Chronically anxious members will act out their anxiety in an attempt to get relief, all of which is highly dysfunctional to the relationships and to the organization (e.g., spreading rumors, making accusations, and exaggerating events). Even if the conditions were changed or the issue resolved, dysfunctional persons will find another reason to feed their anxiety, and they will attempt to displace their anxiety on others. When others take up their anxiety and begin to "act out," the dysfunctional persons relax. Now they don't have to be anxious because the pastor, board, or some other group is carrying the anxiety. This becomes a vicious cycle of (1) be anxious; (2) make others anxious; (3) rest a while; and (4) be anxious again.

Another indicator of extreme dysfunction, illustrated in Figure 14.2, is the denial that any anxiety even exists. Now instead of being overly concerned in their anxiety, the people deny any reality of anxiety. They claim everyone is together in a kind of perpetual love-in: "We are all one happy family. Everyone loves one another. Everything is just fine. What a close group we are!"

Such claims demonstrate warning signals, or at least they signal a fear to admit what is actually happening. Denial of such reality produces a blindness to the true condition, so the persons are no longer able to recognize their unconscious destructive patterns. They are totally oblivious to the fact that they are acting in a dysfunctional manner. If they are to be healed, they will need a guide or counselor who understands family systems theory and cares enough about them to accompany them back to health. This is not easy.

Boundaries

Boundaries help us to know ourselves and to know others. In human relationships we need to be alone and separate, and we need to be close and together. No one defines this reality more poignantly than Dietrich Bonhoeffer, who became a martyr for the faith at the end of World War Two:

> [O]nly as we are in fellowship can we be alone, and only he that is alone can live in fellowship. . . . Each by itself has profound pitfalls and perils. One who wants fellowship without solitude plunges into the void of words and feelings, and one who seeks solitude without fellowship perishes in the abyss of vanity, self-infatuation, and despair.[13]

Boundaries let us know how close we want to be in relationship with others, whether we wish to be intimate with them or keep them at a greater distance. Likewise, boundaries also let us know how much we wish to be alone and to what extent we can sustain intimacy with ourselves.

Persons who have no boundaries for themselves will gravitate into one or more less-than-healthy types of relationships. They may withdraw from others, building barriers that are impossible for others to penetrate, or they may build boundaries against themselves, structuring their time so they need never "come home" to themselves. There are two expressions of dysfunctional boundaries: one is addiction to being close, too close—being stuck to others. The other is cutting oneself off from others, maintaining aloof distances from others and never self-disclosing one's feelings.

Making Application to the Congregation

In the church, persons who subvert their own interdependence because of their need to stick to others become "meeting freaks" or addictive volunteers; they never have time for solitary prayer or reflection, nor time to be silent before God. While cut off from true relationships with themselves and with others, even though they are physically present with others, they become perennial groupies who must always have a company around them. More than being together with others—they are stuck together with others, so that they have no thoughts other than the group's thoughts, no opinion other than the group's opinion.

Persons who become highly anxious about being alone become clinging vines, clutching at relationships. Eventually their boundaries become so enmeshed with other dysfunctional persons in the congregation that they become unable to think or feel without taking cues from those to whom they cling. Instead of touching others' lives, they clutch them.

The only persons who can endure relationships with this type of person are those who also have clinging needs, who become highly anxious when they are cut off from their relationships for even a short time. Such persons in the congregation eventually find one another and become stuck together. When any one moves in a certain direction, they all move in that direction. This is the series relationship pattern. People are stuck together because they draw their "energy" and "breath" from their dysfunctional, symbiotic relationships.

On the other side of the ledger are persons who are cut off from all relationships with others. They may become a "solitary" wanting only and always to be alone, and thus they are cut off from true relationships with others and with themselves. Being anxious about being close, these persons relate only from an emotional distance, cut off from feelings, isolated from others. Such persons function by covertly avoiding relationships or overtly battling them. The result is neither intimacy nor community, because all of their relationships are constantly being cut off.

This person becomes the perennial loner in the congregation and often exerts tremendous influence upon the church by reason of his refusal to self-disclose, so that everyone is left guessing about what he wants. He continually complains about the pastor or the board, but refuses to work to resolve matters or to solve problems. This person often wants a power position in the church, but wants to run the show all by himself. He wants power in order to insulate himself from the need of relationships in order to have his way in the church.

Peter L. Steinke illustrates the extreme dysfunction of separation and closeness as well as the dimensions of relational health in Figure 14.4.[14]

Figure 14.4

Cutting Off	Defining Self	Touching Others	Clutching Others
reactive	intentional	spontaneous	reactive
automatic	chosen	playful	automatic
emotionally driven	objectively aware	emotionally expressive	emotionally driven
dependent	responsible for self	responsive to others	dependent
aggressive or defensive about keeping distance unaware of own need for others	self-directed action aware of self	trusting exchange aware of others	aggressive or defensive about embeddedness unaware of own need for self
stiff, rigid boundaries	flexible boundaries (able to reinstate after loosening them)	boundaries lost in play, self-forgetfulness	soft, porous boundaries

Cutting Off	Defining Self	Touching Others	Clutching Others
overfunctioning to achieve self-sufficiency	functioning for self	allowing others to function for themselves	overfunctioning to achieve togetherness
minimal support, feedback, or encouragement from others	self-respect	respect for others, allows others to be themselves	forces others to be like self or allows others to force oneself to be like them
difference gained over against others	defines self from within	defines self to others	differences are unacceptable; relationship defined by sameness
narrow goals	clearly defined goals for self	clearly defined relationships goals	vague, nebulous goals

The two middle columns of Figure 14.4 list descriptors of a healthy balance between a "definition of self" and "touching others." The outside columns represent the extreme dysfunctions of "cutting off" and "clutching others."

Boundaries and Overfunctioning

As the leader of a large congregation, Moses once complained to God: "Where am I to get meat to give to all this people? For they come weeping to me and say, 'Give us meat to eat!' I am not able to carry all this people alone, for they are too heavy for me. If this is the way you are going to treat me, put me to death at once" (Num. 11:13-15*a*).

Especially prevalent in religious organizations is the boundary issue of overfunctioning. Overfunctioning is the condition of assuming an unhealthy responsibility for the way others function and for the quality of their relationships—and then becoming anxious when they still not act as we think they should. Taking on responsibility for certain members, groups, or the entire congregation is a setup that draws out the dark and lonely side of the leader—frustration, discouragement, anxiety, lack of spiritual vitality, and even suicide prayers, as seen in Moses' prayer, above.

Clergy who overfunction take on the responsibility for the feelings, thoughts, and spirituality of others, while giving to others the responsibility for their own feelings, thoughts, and spirituality. Overfunctioning is one way of managing anxiety and handling relationships under stress. For some it is a natural reaction in their attempt to lift another person's spirits or tell the person exactly what they need to do. Later, the person may recall that her advice was unsolicited, but such behavior helps the overfunctioner to deal with such stress.

While many leaders complain that a congregation's members are not being responsible enough, they will continue to reinforce the unresponsible pattern by taking the responsibility upon themselves. Often a relationship of unhealthy dependence is developed with leaders who exhibit slave- or martyr-type leader behaviors.[15] Overfunctioners and underfunctioners reinforce each other in a circular fashion, and it takes a strong decision by at least one of the players to stop the destructive pattern.

In his prayer, Moses finally came to a vulnerable state, expressing his honest feelings to God. This is hard for overfunctioners who have difficulty sharing their own vulnerability with others—they seem to always know what is best for others as much as for themselves, moving in quickly to advise and rescue others. They also have difficulty allowing others to struggle with their own problems. The spiritual effect of overfunctioning is portentous. In subtle yet profound ways, overfunctioning depletes the interior life of the leader. For the overfunctioner, everything hinges on controlling the other person. The challenge for the overfunctioning person is to learn how to take more responsibility for his or her own self and less responsibility for the thoughts, feelings, and behaviors of others.

Emotions

Peter L. Steinke points out, "The church is more than its emotional processes, but it is never less than these processes."[17] These emotional processes provide clues to determine how a church family governs its life together, help to explain why a particular congregation resists growth and change, and help to assess and intervene in conflict situations that are particularly confusing.

What makes your church unique and different from other churches in your community? The easy ways to define the differences between

> Tears are like blood in the wounds of the soul.[16]
>
> Gregory of Nyssa

congregations include: theology, history, size, architecture, and social practices of membership. A discerning visitor, however, will also recognize the emotional processes within each congregation—joy, caregiving, support, commitment, and excitement, as well as pain, hostility, rigidity, suspicion, apathy, or fear. Strangely enough this emotional life is less evident to those deeply involved in the congregation.

Many congregations will not permit, much less encourage, the expression of "negative" feelings of sadness, hurt, anger, or fear. In many congregations, such feelings are just plain wrong. It is not the Christian way. Or, the feelings are not to be trusted, since they are dangerous to explore and certainly not to be expressed.

While such unwanted feelings are suppressed in much of the contemporary church, examples of these emotional states are almost embarrassingly expressed in the Gospels. It is said, for example, of Jesus' followers that "An argument arose among them as to which one of them was the greatest" (Luke 9:46). Can you imagine this argument taking place within the board meeting of your church? Hardly! We have more sophisticated and oblique ways of expressing our true feelings. The writers of the Gospels give us glimpses of the emotional processes among the disciples and Jesus. Much to our chagrin, the presence of Christ did not do away with these realities. His presence actually seemed to exacerbate these feelings.

The boundaries we were taught from our family of origin have much to do with how we view and express our emotions in our current relationships. Persons who were violated when family members crossed over the line (or boundary) sexually, physically, or emotionally, are contrasted with those in families who built an emotional barrier (or boundary) around themselves. These two different types of families of origin result in two different kinds of emotional wounds.[18]

Children whose boundaries were violated tend to express emotions by exploding their anger or by imploding their anger inside themselves. The hurt and wounds from violent assaults suppressed their terror and rage, causing them to maintain secret hurts for their own survival. Children trade justifiable expressed anger for internal shame, believing that they themselves are responsible. In adult life, these individuals are afraid of getting too close, because such intimacy is associated with the loss of autonomy.

Children whose boundaries were "fortresslike" tend to experience adult life as emotionally empty. They become stuck in their attempts to placate others (commonly referred to as co-dependence). Growing up in isolation brings fear of rejection and of abandonment by those closest to them. It is very difficult to develop and maintain perfect boundaries. Therefore, most adults show some kind of combination of these behaviors. The importance of these extremes is that the normal feelings of sadness, hurt, anger, or fear are neither encouraged nor modeled very well in the family. What is encouraged, however, is that family members be happy, perfect, or stoic.

Making Application to the Congregation

In dysfunctional congregations, one emotional extreme in relationships is to suppress and build walls around one's feelings. Such people communicate only from the head with little or no affective behavior. The other extreme is where there are few or no boundaries and people are out of control with little rational discourse, predictably acting out their anger and "dumping" it on everyone else.

Add to all of this the teaching in many churches that feelings of sadness, hurt, anger, or fear should not be experienced by "good" or "strong" Christians, and the result is emotionally crippled adults not knowing how to "speak the truth in love," and leaders struggling with boundaries of separation and closeness, solitude and intimacy. We can learn much from the example of Jesus, who was honest with himself and others, and who valued and asked for the support of close friends:

> [Jesus] came out and went, as was his custom, to the Mount of Olives; and the disciples followed him. When he reached the place, he said to them, "Pray that you may not come into the time of trial." Then he withdrew from them about a stone's throw, knelt down, and prayed, "Father, if you are willing, remove this cup from me; yet, not my will but yours be done." Then an angel from heaven appeared to him and gave him strength. In his anguish he prayed more earnestly, and his sweat became like great drops of blood falling down on the ground. When he got up from prayer, he came to the disciples and found them sleeping because of grief. (Luke 22:39-45)

The Scriptures are filled with stories of people who penetrate and express the full range of human emotions. Indeed, the pages of the Psalter are wet with tears, crumpled in anger, held in fear, and lifted high with joy. Prophets caught in their aloneness prayed suicide prayers; families committed deceit and murder; disciples argued where each would sit in the kingdom; and ancient congregations experienced strife, jealousy, and contention.

Our journeys are unique and must be traveled with a commitment to growth and to the future. As M. Scott Peck writes: "We cannot go backward. We can only go forward. . . . through the desert of life, making our way painfully over parched and barren ground into increasingly deeper levels of consciousness. . . . what characterizes those relative few who are fully mature is that they regard it as their responsibility—even as an opportunity—to meet life's demands."[19]

Life is difficult—life is complex.[20] Constructive suffering is worth all of our efforts to make conscious our unconsciousness, to deal with the extremes of suppressed or "acting out" emotions with the hope of intimate, honest relationships.

The alternative to acting responsibly with our emotions, and to work on resolving individual issues, is to project our anxiety or "shift the burden" onto others in a series of emotional triangles.

Triangling

Perhaps the most common way of binding anxiety is through triangling. This is seen by many theorists as the basic building block of all emotional systems.[21] It takes three parties to triangle. Emotional triangles take on many forms. When two parties in a dysfunctional relationship become uncomfortable with one another, the most anxious of them will "triangle in" a third person as a way of stabilizing their own relationship. This focus on the third party works to lower the anxiety or take pressure off the two persons in the original relationship. The third party need not always be a person. Oftentimes the third party is a concern or issue that fills out the triangle.

A person is "triangled" in when she is caught in the middle as the focus of an unresolved issue. The person who finally ends up carrying all of the pent-up anxiety becomes the symptom bearer (see the following section in this chapter). The lower the anxiety, the safer it is to self-disclose and talk about oneself in a relationship. The higher the anxiety, the greater the likelihood that the anxious parties will attempt to triangle someone else or some other concern. The symptom bearer will then end up carrying the anxiety for the others, who are then free to go their own ways, feeling less anxious and less responsible for the situation that caused the anxiety in the first place.

Making Application to the Congregation

In a local congregation, gossip is a universal form of triangulation that focuses on the faults of another and, therefore, takes the focus off of the persons engaged in the gossip conversation. The higher the anxiety, the more likely people will be to triangle a third person whom they hope will take away their anxiety by being blamed for the problem. All of this is often carried out along a gossip trail or by "passing the buck," until a symptom bearer is discovered who cannot pass the buck any further, and so becomes the personification of the others' anxiety.

For example, the story of anxious Adam who, being confronted by God, triangled Eve into the relationship. Being brought into this triangle caused Eve a great deal of stress. So, in her anxious response, Eve blames the serpent. Now we see another triangle; God, Eve, and the serpent.

We have found that primary targets for becoming symptom bearers are the pastor and the pastor's spouse or family. Dysfunctional congregations have an uncanny ability to hire a pastor who is also struggling with personal dysfunction. In such cases, the pastor becomes a popular candidate to be the symptom bearer because he is, indeed, bearing symptoms of dysfunction.

The more enmeshed people are in their relationships within a congregation, the greater the number and intensity of triangles forming a triangle web, illustrated in Figure 14.5:[22]

Suppose the church leadership is dealing with declining attendance. The senior pastor expresses concern (anxiety) to the church council about the declining attendance trend (Triangle A). Several influential members of the church council, in turn, shift the burden of their anxiety to the senior pastor, blaming her for a lack of visionary leadership and planning (Triangle B). Shortly thereafter, several associate pastors hear about the church council's "attack" on the

Figure 14.5

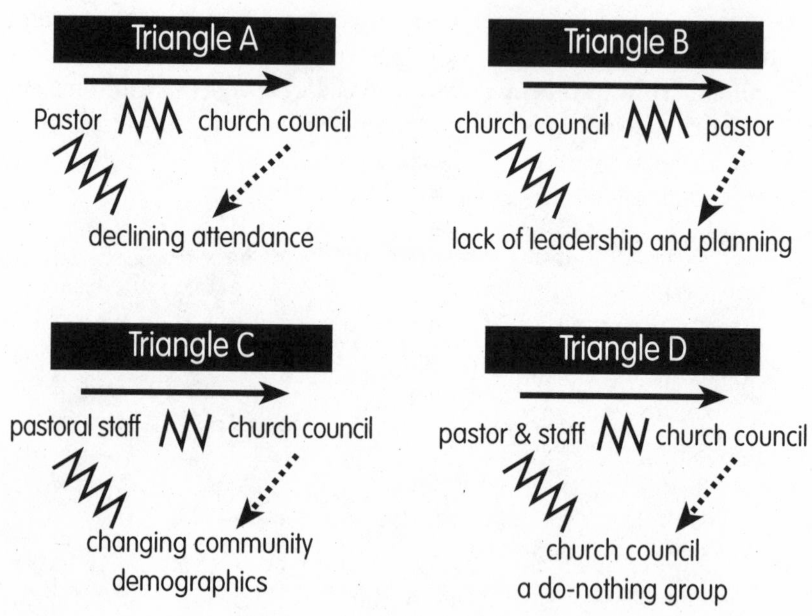

senior pastor and meet together informally, citing the changing demographics of the community as contributing to the declining attendance. After all, the senior pastor cannot control the entire economy and bar people from moving out of the area (Triangle C). When the senior pastor and pastoral staff get together, conversation focuses on the irresponsible council members who only want to make executive decisions and are not willing to "get their hands dirty" in actual ministry. If they would reach out and befriend the visitors who do come, the church could assimilate new members more effectively (Triangle D).

As long as these "emotionally stuck" persons perpetuate interlocking triangles and project the blame upon others, the congregation's leadership groups are captive to their own emotional processes. Passing the burden around is not the same as shared responsibility. The leadership is stuck! There is little hope for any constructive change without identifying and examining the emotional processes that are binding the leadership groups in their own paralysis.

Symptom Bearer

When anxiety in a congregation increases, people unconsciously attempt to "purify" themselves by locating the problem in the "problem" person(s) or condition; that person(s) becomes the "identified patient" or "symptom bearer" of the congregation. At closer look, however, the individual or group issues are the results of dysfunction within the congregation as a whole.[23]

When the people in the Old Testament sinned, the priest would ceremonially place the sins on a scapegoat and kill it as a means of purifying the people. In medieval times, a community in stress would identify someone as the "witch" and burn this person at the stake in order to purify the community. Today, the dysfunctional congregation identifies someone as the "patient," the symptom bearer, and blames that one person or group of persons for all the problems in the church.

However, the symptom bearer is not necessarily the "sick" member of the congregation. The congregation as a whole is the carrier of the illness. Congregations can easily get caught up in blaming someone for all their troubles. The rest of the people then take no responsibility for their own part in the condition. A beginning sign of health is when persons stop blaming others and begin to take responsibility for their own involvement in the situation that is producing the anxiety.

Therefore, in dealing with dysfunction it is often best not to deal with the symptom bearer. Rather, one should coach the person or group who has the capability to bring positive change to the condition. It is also worthwhile to help persons deal with unresolved issues in their own family or with their own jobs that may be projected onto the concerns in the church. In sum, the symptom bearer is not the problem but rather becomes the visible expression of problems more deeply enmeshed within the congregation.

What we have discussed up to this point in a family systems model—anxiety, emotions, boundaries, triangling, and symptom bearer—can be seen as part of the congregation's homeostasis.

Homeostasis

Homeostasis is "the tendency of a group to strive perpetually, in self-corrective ways, to preserve the organizing principles of its existence."[24]

We have experienced congregations whose emotional climates are highly volatile. It seemed that the congregation could "self-destruct" at any moment. But it didn't. People stay together in the midst of tremendous pressure and pain. Why? Because of the congregation's efforts to maintain homeostasis, those forces that keep things "on balance." This balancing process is made up of different forces, more often implicit than explicit. In complex organizations such as a congregation, it is often hard to identify the balancing processes. Nevertheless, the balance does adjust toward a "desired" level, toward homeostasis.

For example, it may be okay for the youth pastor to conduct an outreach into the community's schools and evangelize a few gang members. But soon there are comments such as, "If too many of 'those kind' come into our church, what will happen to our own youth?" "We've already seen some of our young people dress like them and, besides, we must not neglect Christian education at the expense of outreach." Such are the views and arguments of those members who feel the tension of change and seek to get things back on balance by acting in such a way as to retard a particular kind of growth.

The same forces that shape the feeling of family togetherness in a congregation are the same forces that hinder change when the congregation is "stuck together."[25] Dysfunctional congregations come to a point when they will "stick together" at all costs even to their own detriment, as Friedman points out:

> In work systems, the stabilizing effect of the identified patient [or symptom bearer] and the resistance from the togetherness at all costs help explain why even the most ruthless corporation (no less churches and synagogues) often will tolerate and adapt to trouble-making complainers and downright incompetents, whereas the creative thinker who disturbs the balance of things will be ignored, if not let go.[26]

Another example of this homeostatic condition is a thermostat which does not maintain the room temperature at a fixed point, but it keeps the temperature within a temperature range, say 68 to 72 degrees. We have observed the pastor "turn up the thermostat" when discussing a particular issue. And immediately or soon thereafter, a board member will "turn it down." You can count on it—with a new force (new idea or reinforcing cycle) there will be a balancing force (resistance, stability). Much of this is done as a rather "normal" resistance to new ideas or to change. But when such behavior becomes extreme and set in inflexible patterns, it is no longer healthy but dysfunctional.

Changes That Affect Homeostasis

According to Friedman, there are several major changes which may promote the "issues" that affect the homeostatic conditions of a system:

1. Changes in the family of the spiritual leader.
   a. Birth, death, illness, divorce, hospitalization, affair or other marital problem, psychotherapy . . . , child acting out or leaving home, aged parent's needs, a problem in the extended family of the minister or his or her spouse.
   b. Professional change in the life of the spiritual leader; for example, personal advancement, studying for or earning a new degree, dedicated involvement in community project, new responsibilities in extended faith system, extension of contract, granting of tenure, change in location of office.
2. Changes similar to 1a and 1b, above, in the personal or professional lives of key lay leaders or other members intensely involved in the issues that have arisen.
3. Changes in the long-term constituency of the parish: racial, professional, philosophical, average age, etc. In congregations that have long been run by a few families, a conflict in the congregation can, as in a family business, appear to be about new ideas or a change in philosophy, but the intensity may actually reflect personal issues in the families, particularly intergenerational problems.
4. Changes in the church family's professional leadership.
   a. Hiring, firing, or the resignation of a key professional person (especially the administrative secretary or choir director).
   b. Rise or elimination of interpersonal conflict between two professional leaders.
5. Changes in the extended family of the church hierarchy or the parish system.
   a. Death or retirement of a founder, builder, or charismatic organizer.

b. Restructuring of the reorganization of the regions or parish system (decentralizing, recentralizing, creating more or fewer subgroupings).
c. If a church or synagogue is part of an ethnic group, general anxiety in that "extended" system can escalate anxiety over specific issues in the various "nuclear" congregational groupings.[27]

While any one of these issues does not necessarily cause problems, the combination of these issues in homeostatic forces is able to contribute to intense congregational anxiety. This helps to explain how a particular issue may have certain consequences at one time and very different consequences another time.

QUESTIONS FOR REFLECTION UPON THE PATTERNS OF RELATIONAL HEALTH AND DYSFUNCTION

1. What dysfunctional levels of behavior are exhibited regularly within the congregation (anxiety, boundaries, emotions, triangling, symptom bearer, homeostasis)?
2. Are there specific people or groups of people who are causing these behaviors to be escalated to the point of being "stuck"?
3. If so, how can you facilitate a movement toward a healthier behavior?

Series Relationships Versus Parallel Relationships

Closely related to all of the elements of family systems theory that we have already discussed (especially those elements of emotional triangles, homeostasis, and overfunctioning) is the concept of series relationships versus parallel relationships. In reference to this concept, Friedman illustrates the range of possible relationship patterns in an organization by referring to the series and parallel currents in an electrical system.[28]

Series Relationships

When a set of electrical components is connected in series, all of the outlets are connected in such a way that the electricity runs through an outlet on its way to other outlets down the line. Therefore, if one outlet malfunctions or loses its power, all of the outlets down the line will also lose their power. You may have seen strings of Christmas lights in which when one light burned out, all the lights farther down the string received no electrical current and went out also; not because they had burned out, but because they had "run out" of energy. We can diagram this in Figure 14.6, below:

Figure 14.6

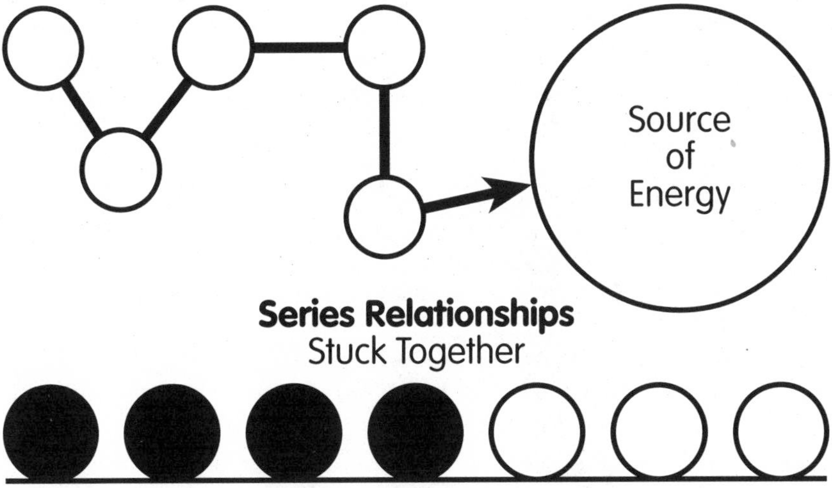

Source of Energy

Series Relationships
Stuck Together

Christmas Tree Lights in a Series Circuit

Making Application to the Congregation

In dysfunctional relationships, people are often "strung" together in a series relational pattern. They become stuck together because each one depends upon the others who are in the relationship line "ahead" of them to provide the "energy" in their dysfunctional relationship. If any one decides to get well or to step out of the line, all of the others connected farther down the line will eventually run out of energy.

This analogy may sound contrived but it is very real. In a severely dysfunctional congregation, or group, there is tremendous effort to keep everyone playing their assigned roles. In the dysfunctional pattern this seems like a matter of life or death. If one person decides to step out of his assigned role and get well, everyone else will feel that they have run out of oxygen. And just like a fish that flops around violently on the riverbank as it senses that oxygen is running out, so people in a dysfunctional situation will become extremely agitated, overfunction, disrupt, and become violent when they feel their energy source being cut off.

Series relationships are not intimate, authentic relationships. The people are not *together* as much as they are *stuck together* in ways that paralyze and maintain the dysfunction of the relationship. Predominantly, series relationships result in enmeshed feelings that do more than guide—they control the system, resulting in distortion and fantasy. Missing during a crisis is the circuit breaker, which can help relieve some of the burden of a tension overload. As stated earlier, the same dynamics that bring emotional closeness to relationships can also prevent growth and change from taking place. The patterns are habitual.

Parallel Relationships

When a set of electrical components are connected in a parallel pattern, each outlet has its own independent connection to the main source of energy (see Figure 14.7). Therefore, each outlet is far less dependent upon the other outlets in the same line for its energy. In a parallel circuit, one or more outlets may malfunction and lose energy, but this will not cut any of the other outlets away from the energy source.

Making Application to the Congregation

Parallel relationships are relationships in which each member has a healthy sense of self-differentiation and, therefore, maintains an independent connection to the main source of energy. During times of stress, while parallel relationships may appear to be less connected, they are capable of handling more anxiety. One person's source of energy and response to a situation does not depend upon being stuck together with others, responding to every situation as the group responds. Rather, the person can listen to others' points of view, but then think through the issues for himself; this becomes a process that may take time, depending upon the complexity of the issues.

Figure 14.7

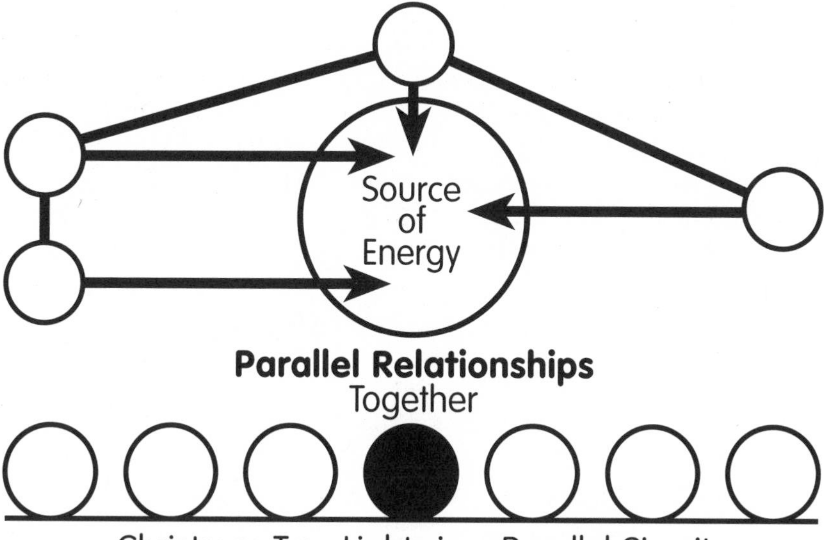

Christmas Tree Lights in a Parallel Circuit

Those in parallel relationships are less anxious about change, and they do not overreact when others dysfunction. Parallel relationships are more resilient in and after crisis. Therefore, the parallel interdependence offers greater potential for healing to take place within the congregation because of the openness to change and growth.

In this chapter we introduced family systems theory, as it might be applied to healthy and dysfunctional situations in the church. We discussed the major building blocks of family systems theory: how

QUESTIONS FOR REFLECTION UPON THE SERIES RELATIONSHIPS WITHIN THE CONGREGATION

1. What "series relationships" are at work in your leadership staff? In your congregation?
2. Are you involved in any "series relationships" at the present time? From what "parallel relationships" in your life can you continue to learn?
3. In what specific ways can you help to facilitate "parallel relationships" in the congregation?

anxiety is handled by members of the congregation; how members and the group determine their boundaries in interpersonal relationships; how members express or suppress their emotions; the degree to which triangling takes place; how blame is internalized or placed on the symptom bearers; and how all of these forces determine the homeostasis of the congregation's emotional processes.

When there is dysfunction within the congregation, all the rules for intervention in such congregations change. The next chapter addresses the ways to intervene in dysfunctional congregations.

The Essence of Understanding Family Systems Theory Applied to the Congregation

1. Dysfunction in the church often reflects a person's own brokenness and internal disappointments with life.
2. Family systems theory focuses on the interrelatedness of things as a whole.
   - Each person in the system brings his or her own life experiences into the life of the group.
   - If one thing is changed in the system, the rest of the system is affected.
3. Unconscious patterns of behavior can become a part of one's consciousness through the identification of several key concepts: anxiety, boundaries, emotions, triangling, symptom bearer, and homeostasis.
4. Series group relationships are found when people are stuck together.
5. Parallel group relationships are characterized by a healthy sense of self-differentiation.

How You Can Apply to the Congregation Family Systems Theory

1. Understand your own intrapersonal dimensions that you bring to the congregational system.
   - How do your life experiences contribute to the health of the congregation?
   - How do they contribute to the dysfunction of the congregation?

2. Identify people and groups of people who are involved in dysfunctional behaviors that affect the life of the church.
   - Refer to Figure 14.2 to help determine the relational health and extent of dysfunction in the congregation.

3. Recognize series and parallel relationships within the leadership staff and the congregation.
   - Are any of these relationships causing a widespread "short-circuiting" on a regular basis?
   - If so, how can you become a consultant in the situation?

15

Intervening in Dysfunctional Systems:

A Family Systems Approach

Leadership and management have inherent power because effecting a change in relationship systems is facilitated more fundamentally by how leaders function within their families than by the quantity of their expertise. . . . There is an intrinsic relationship between our capacity to put families together and our ability to put ourselves together.[1]

Edwin H. Friedman

Family systems theory is a way of describing the character and behaviors of groups in a church, or the entire congregation, that have become dysfunctional in areas of life and work. When dealing with congregational dysfunction, as compared to normal conflict, all the rules change. The theories and processes that work well in normal conflict situations do not work in dysfunctional settings. Dysfunction calls for a different approach. In this chapter we consider how one might intervene into dysfunctional group or individual behavior; in doing so we describe the interventionist's major tools and models.[2]

How Organizations Become Dysfunctional

Compulsive/Addictive Behaviors and Co-Dependency

When organizations "dysfunction," there are usually relationships that can be characterized by addiction and co-dependency. The addictive culture is one lens of understanding complexities in human relationships. While the list of activities, substances, and types of relationships might vary, addictive cultures cut across denominational and theological lines. Don Williams writes about this tragedy from his own experience as a pastor:

> Later I would come to understand that I was unconsciously using my tumultuous life to fill an emptiness in my soul that only God could heal. But at the same time I stuffed my ministry—little by little—into the void instead. The more I stuffed addictive behaviors into this painful void, the bigger it grew. It would not be filled. As my frantic activity consumed me, I became powerless over it. I was addicted to the point of complete physical and emotional exhaustion. To compound my condition, the Church fed my problem because it became an addictive organization in its own right. . . . The addicted world is grinding up the Church, leaving little that is distinctive of her life.[3]

The Church has begun to open the doors of its closets, encouraging more of its adherents, clergy and laity, to step out and to be honest about their struggles. According to Williams, "Professional ministers often fall into substance abuse in order to lift, even for a moment, the burdens of their parishioners which they have chosen to carry alone to fill their personal emptiness."[4] Compulsive/addictive behaviors in the Church include, but certainly are not limited to, chemical dependency. (i.e., drugs, alcohol, nicotine, caffeine, sugar); they may also be process addictions (i.e., sex, money, work, conflict, gambling). Anne Wilson Schaef and Dianne Fassel define addiction as *any process or substance that begins to have control over us in such a way that we feel we must be dishonest with ourselves or others about it.* Addictions lead us into increasing compulsiveness in our behavior.[5]

The important point is that process addictions provide the same function as a chemical or substance addiction. Both types of addictions provide a barrier that stops people from being in touch with and exploring more fully themselves, their spirituality, and their real world. What the addiction does for the individual or group is alter their moods in order to escape the unwanted feelings. Gerald May describes this struggle:

> The longing at the center of our hearts repeatedly disappears from our awareness, and its energy is usurped by forces that are not at all loving. Our desires are captured, and we give ourselves over to things that, in our deepest honesty, we really do not want. . . . Theologically, sin is what turns us away from love—away from love for ourselves, away from love for one another, and away from love for God. When I look at this problem, psychologically, I see two forces that are responsible:

> repression and addiction. We all suffer from both repression and addiction. Of the two, repression is by far the milder one. . . . While repression stifles desire, addiction attaches desire, bonds and enslaves the energy of desire to certain specific behaviors, things, or people. These objects of attachment then become preoccupations and obsessions; they come to rule our lives.[6]

Addiction involves a cycle, beginning with a need to act out for pleasure or to alleviate pain. A person's reality base is distorted in this self-defeating habit as a mood change takes place. Fearing the lessening of pleasure or a deeper awareness of pain, the person resolves the dilemma by repeating the cycle. And increasing attachment builds with the repeating cycles until the addictive chemical or process itself becomes a normal way to function.

Addiction, however, is more than the individual and its destructive cycle. Addictive relationships must have at least two parties to play out the dysfunction: addicts and co-dependents. While the addict uses a substance or process to escape from his or her unwanted feelings, the co-dependent stabilizes the situation so it doesn't collapse, thus preventing the addict from feeling the full consequence of his or her behaviors. Addictive behavior has much to do with the enmeshed roles played by members of a family or organization. Both the addict and co-dependent suffer from surrendering the inner life as Virginia Hoffman further describes:

> Co-dependents will "cut out their center"—that core of self that can think, feel, decide, and act—and hand that center over to someone else, either to another person, or to the family, or to some institution or system. The co-dependent then acts by "remote control," taking cues not from the inside, but from that other source. . . . They will cling to this substitute-center even when the thoughts, feelings, and actions it dictates begin to destroy their lives. They will hold on as if survival depended on it, as if they had no other choice.[7]

The attention of the addict is on the substance or process, and the attention of the co-dependent is on keeping everything in order. Addictive relationships are about self-alienation and the loss of self. The focus outside the self insulates persons from real feelings and issues, and since both parties are not honest in taking responsibility, the blame is often placed on someone or something else. As Crosby explains, "Both addiction and codependency are part of the addictive process, the codependent expression supports the addictive dimension at all levels and, in turn, codependents are rewarded by the addictive system for their loyal support."[8]

The dysfunctional persons, therefore, reenact their own pain on those around them in different ways, including control, aggression, crisis orientation, self-centeredness, unresolved issues that go on for years, judgmentalism, rigidity, gossip, unreliability, and perfectionism. In an addictive system, co-dependency is normative and even a sign of loyalty among its members—honor and shame are focused on conformity and nonconformity of individuals within the organization.[9]

What many people discover in their own dysfunction is a three-step definition of addiction that describes their own experiences, especially in the Church: (1) Please others in order to increase pleasure and escape pain; (2) Develop a habit of reinforcing experiences out of fear of losing pleasure; and (3) Shut down emotionally, which results in a person not being able to experience the full range of human feelings.[10]

Levels of Addiction in the Church

More often than we care to admit, the addictive process can also be seen in religious organizations. Ann Wilson Schaef proposes four levels of organizational addiction within afflicted organizations that increase with complexity at the higher levels:[11]

1. A first-level addiction in an organization is one in which a key person is an addict. In the church this may be the pastor, a key lay leader, or a highly influential member. While some may be substance abusers, more often than not, the addiction is work, sex, romance, self-abuse, power, or money. The members relate to the addicted leader feeling uneasy and guilty, and no matter what they do or how hard they try, it is never enough. Shaef illustrates this pattern through the words of a pastor's adult daughter who since her father's death came to terms with his addiction:

> His work was the most important thing in our family. If any of us complained about never seeing him, he always had the excuse that he was doing "the Lord's work" and working himself to death was justified. . . .

> Although he was always working on the run, his actual productivity decreased. He recycled old sermons more and more often. He died in his late 40s and no one ever knew him. I feel like I had a nonrecovering alcoholic for a father. He did not really serve Christ or the church. I now know he served his disease.[12]

Especially in the church, workaholism is one of the more socially accepted addictions. Yet workaholics may actually be less productive than others, and the entire organization suffers from their preoccupation with control, judgmentalism, perfectionism, and self-centeredness. Even with a congregational church polity, the power addict in the church may manipulate or withhold information to get his way, while being viewed by peers as a skilled leader. The addiction to power may reside in an individual, group, or the entire church structure, and the appetite of such people is as intense as for the alcoholic or drug addict.

Schaef lists a few more addictions at this level. The romance addicts, the ones who believe the end justifies the means, are addicted to an illusionary world where even dishonesty seems necessary. Self-abuse seems to underlie many other addictions. Taking care of ourselves, for example, with a good diet, exercise, and free time is hardly permissible for the highly valued "Type A" personality in the church. The demands of ministry—that stretch the clergy and their families into a thin rubber band of tension ready to break—are often in the very structural fabric of the church (e.g., low salaries, unpaid clergy spouses and families, and long hours are often inadequate for the clergy trying to make ends meet).

2. *A second level of addiction is when individuals join the organization and bring their dysfunction with them.* This may be the person who joins the congregation as a result of a church split. In addition, the church (or program ministry) functions as the enabler or co-dependent that actually supports the addict in his or her addiction. When persons suffer from a poor sense of self, they may seek validation by "taking care of" others. Anger and other "negative feelings" are unchristian—therefore, the only choice is to repress them, and the result is mixed, nondirect messages. For example, how many church boards put teeth into their confrontation of their workaholic pastor?

Instead, the co-dependent boards choose to pretend that workaholism is not a problem, even though the staff is going crazy and a great deal of activity is making more havoc than results.

While some workaholics appear to offer much benefit to a congregation because of their hard work, they prefer to work alone. Workaholics find it almost impossible to work well on a team, especially since no one can do a "perfect" job as well as she can. The truth is that some leaders have more turmoil inside themselves when the organization is free from turmoil. They become anxious, almost poised for the new crisis so they can exercise their "saving" leadership. The "sins" of such congregations enable these leaders to get away with and even cover up their dysfunction, and nothing will change as long as the church is a co-dependent with the addiction.

3. *The third level of addiction is when the congregation as a whole functions like an addictive substance; the congregation itself provides the "fix."* The church functions as an addictive substance when the members become hooked on the services and promises of the church—and ignore how the entire system is really operating, often overlooking the warning signs of dysfunction. Persons are addicted to the church in several ways—for some it is the work of the organization. An addiction to even a good cause, however worthy, is never a substitute for one's spiritual life, which includes tending the awareness of Christ's presence and the means of keeping that awareness alive and vital.[13]

For others the addiction may be the particular "promise" of the organization. For example, any person who is trying to substitute the congregation for the family he or she never had will soon be disillusioned. The disillusionment may be the setup of the congregation by the parishioner to meet unfulfilled expectations of the past. Or it may be the congregation who promises to provide the "family" never experienced by the parishioner. Such promises are never fulfilled as people go from church to church trying to find their substitute family.

4. *The fourth level of addiction is when the congregation itself becomes an addict.* In this instance the dysfunction of several members finally invades the behavior of the entire congregation. Communications is indirect, not open or honest. Emotional triangles continu-

ally spring up. Gossip runs rampant. The programs and leaders become skilled in incompetence, and finally all the systems cease to function in a healthy or effective manner.

It is important to note that these four levels of addiction can occur simultaneously or by themselves, although as Schaef points out that it is hard for level four to take place without the first two levels. In level four the entire congregation searches for a "fix" that eases its pain and alters its reality. This dysfunction often manifests itself as an incongruity between what the church says and what it does. The following are examples of inconsistencies: Insisting on honesty and openness while covering hidden salary benefits, trumpeting Christian community virtues while treating staff personnel like second-class human computers, and pretending that everyone is involved in making decisions when everything is done to keep people out of the loop—all of these are examples of how congregations split off the reality of how they behave from what they espouse their mission to be.[14]

Church history has its share of clerics who were so corrupted in their ambition for power and appetite for money that we wonder how it could get so bad. The clergy were part of the intellectual and moral decline of the Frankish empire, 850–950:

> Higher offices in the church often had huge benefices attached to them and this led to the practice of simony—the buying and selling of church offices. The initial investment might be high, but then one was assured of a regular income for life. Needless to say, this practice inflicted a number of bishops in the church who had no interest in living the gospel and whose lives were indistinguishable from those of other members of nobility.[15]

One can only wonder what will be said of the current period in church history. While watching a television evangelist confidently proclaim Christ's return in his lifetime in front of an audience whose waving arms are in agreement, we wonder how many of his assets he is liquidating now so that his gospel can be advanced with urgency.

We know from experience that entire congregations can become addicted to the same things that foster addiction in individuals, such as power, sex, popularity, money, religion, and control. Organizational addiction can be seen concretely in personnel practices, control issues, or how the congregation interprets power, and how it over-functions for people. The organization becomes the "infrastructure" that organizes people and resources dysfunctionally and perpetuates the future of those institutions through its ideology.[16] This type of organizational culture is one that promotes and sustains addictive behavior and dysfunction. Obsessive patterns in relationships—denial, dishonesty, frozen or anxious feelings, anger, controlling behaviors—are cultivated at unconscious levels in addictive organizations. As Thomas Merton points out,

> There is no greater disaster in the spiritual life than to be immersed in unreality, for life is maintained and nourished in us by our vital relation with realities outside and above us. When our life feeds on unreality, it must starve. It must therefore die. There is no greater misery than to mistake this fruitless death for the true, fruitful and sacrificial "death" by which we enter life. The death by which we enter into life is not an escape from reality but a complete gift of ourselves which involves a total commitment to reality. It begins by renouncing the illusory reality which created things acquire when they are seen only in their relation to our own selfish interests.[17]

The Twelve-Step Recovery Program

The most effective process for intervening into dysfunctional congregations, or groups within the congregation, is the twelve-step recovery plan, developed and used first by Alcoholics Anonymous (AA).[18] Cofounded in 1935 by William Griffith Wilson and Robert Holbrook Smith, AA's program was influenced by the Oxford Group renewal movement during the 1920s and 1930s in England. The Oxford Group, declaring itself an organism, not an organization, met in hotels and homes sharing participants' spiritual life over meals. This movement based its teachings on six assumptions: (1) human beings are sinners; (2) persons can change; (3) confession is a prerequisite to change; (4) the changed soul has direct access to God; (5) the age of miracles has returned; and (6) those who have been changed are to help change others.[19]

Alcoholics Anonymous cofounder William Wilson incorporated the Oxford Group's five procedures into AA's philosophy. They included: (1) giving to God; (2) listening to God's direction; (3) checking guidance; (4) restitution; and (5) sharing, both confession and witness.[20] When Wilson and Smith attended Oxford Group meetings in New York during the years 1935–37, they met Episcopal clergyperson Samuel Moor Shoemaker, Jr., who, along with other leaders in the Oxford Group, articulated the heart of AA and its assumptions about self-examination, acknowledgment of character defects, and restitution for harm done.

Today this journey is utilized by many addicted and co-dependent persons, such as workaholics, overeaters, adult children of alcoholics, overspenders, and sex addicts. For persons in recovery peace is the thematic goal for persons in the first three steps is peace with God; steps 4–7 is peace with ourselves; steps 8–10 is peace with others; and steps 11-12 is keeping the peace.[21]

The twelve steps are most appropriate for use with a congregation or church group that has become addictive from dysfunction in its behaviors and relationships. The orientation of the twelve steps is "God-ward," and the processes are familiar to every Christian; repentance, confession, prayer, restitution, metanoia, commitment, a trust in God to provide the strength needed day by day, and evangelism.

One advantage of using the twelve steps with congregations is that there are many persons in every community who are familiar, skilled, and experienced in the processes for utilizing the twelve steps with groups. These persons may become your consultants and trainers in working with dysfunctional families or groups. These are the leaders of twelve-step groups who have a good reputation for their effectiveness.

QUESTIONS FOR REFLECTION UPON DYSFUNCTIONAL ORGANIZATIONS

1. Are there any key leaders within your church who have "addictive" tendencies?
2. Are there any groups of people who tend to relate in a dysfunctional or addictive manner?
3. Does your organization as a whole function as an addictive substance that "hooks" your attenders?
4. Has your congregation become an addict? Specifically, how has this dysfunction manifested itself (communication, behavior, etc.)?
5. How can the twelve steps help you to intervene in dysfunctional situations in your congregation?

To say that all dysfunctional behavior in the church results from addiction may seem to be extreme. In those situations where the analogy does not apply, there is, however, another way to look at intervention into dysfunction. We will discuss the method below, suggesting that this approach may be seen as the meta-model, and the twelve steps as a single process within the larger model.

Rules for Working in a Dysfunctional Organization

1. Be a non-anxious presence. In a dysfunctional setting anxiety passes around from person to person, group to group, as persons engage in their destructive behaviors: addiction, co-dependency, gossip, whining, complaining, blaming. When these conditions prevail long enough, it is possible even for the healthy members and leaders to be caught up in the anxiety.

However, when one gets caught up in the system's anxiety, then he becomes a bearer of the illness and is no longer able to bring health and healing. To remain non-anxious in the presence of free-floating anxiety is easier said than done. Nonetheless, the interventionist must remain outside of the anxiety. The capacity of leaders and managers to contain their own anxiety regarding church conflict—the conflict that is not related to them as well as that conflict in which they are a major player—may be the most significant capability in their arsenal for conflict management.[22]

What dysfunctional members want you to do is to get anxious, lose control, act out—and then they will point to you and say, "See how sick she is, how unable to control herself. She is the cause of all of our problems." Once they succeed in tagging you as the identified patient, your usefulness in helping the sickness is over.

2. Coach the healthy members of the congregation. Don't give too much attention to the dysfunctional members. By this we do not imply that you should ignore them as their priest, but don't get caught up in their complaints and gossip; don't try to assuage their hurts; and don't let them determine how you spend your time or what you do.

> Your role is to coach the healthy while working to make the entire system aware of its sickness.

Do give attention to those who are most healthy in the congregation; coaching them to not get caught up in the anxiety and emotional triangles, showing them how to deal with the dysfunction, and encouraging them to stay out of the trap of overfunctioning. As Friedman points out, "Overfunctioning is . . . the mode by which clergy inadvertently teach [others] to be obssessed with the salvation of others rather than their own."[23] In dysfunctional settings only the family can heal the family, and only the healthy members of the congregation can heal the congregation's dysfunction. This is almost universally true.

3. Stay out of the emotional triangles. In a dysfunctional system, emotional triangles multiply like rabbits. Two things are required of you. First, stay out of all emotional triangles. And when you discover that you are caught in one, immediately bring the two parties together and tell them that you are "triangled" into their problem, and that you are stepping out *now*.

Second, coach the healthy members to guard against getting brought into emotional triangles. Teach them how triangles get started, how to spot a triangle, and how to stay out of them.

Emotional triangles are insidious. Many triangles will entrap you before you know it because many of them seem so innocent. One of the most common types of triangles occurs in a board meeting when the board discusses a problem between two persons or groups—and then suggests that you should go to one of the parties and tell them thus-and-such. It all seems so innocent. The board is concerned and wants the pastor to use his influence to settle the matter. But as soon as you go to one of the parties, you are caught in a triangle between the two opposing groups.

Rather than do this, suggest that the board call the two parties together with the board to discuss the matter, or suggest that the board chairperson go to both parties. Then you have avoided the triangle, and you are in position to help both parties and the board, should the opportunity present itself.

4. Withdraw support from series relationships and support parallel relationships. Coach the healthy members to recognize series relationships, and to understand their negative effects upon persons who are in the series relationships and upon the life and work of the congregation.

When you see persons who are trying to step out of a series relationship, coach them and support their efforts to break the relationship. Whenever a person tries to step out of a series relationship, all the others who are connected to the relationship will exert great pressure to keep the person with them. They will go to every extreme to keep the person in—because it feels to them that their life depends upon the person staying in the relationship. And to some extent this is true, because when one person breaks the series chain, it cuts several other persons off from the energy source that is feeding the series relationship.

5. Relate to everyone openly and honestly. Don't try to cut secret deals with anyone. It never works. Such efforts will backfire and you will wind up being seen as the identified patient—the one who is causing the problems.

Being anything less than fully transparent is dysfunctional and, above all else, you must continue to function effectively before everyone. Two dysfunctional parties in conflict will suddenly join forces to entrap anyone whom they assume might be trying to break their emotional triangles, or otherwise stop their "game."

6. Create an awareness of what dysfunction is, what it looks like, and what its results are in the life of a congregation. Teach the board and other persons in the theory and principles of family systems theory, and coach the healthy ones who are closest to the dysfunctional parties.

7. Get professional counsel. Working with conflicted or severely dysfunctional situations requires skill and confidence. Beyond your personal study and preparation, seek professional tutoring and counseling when you realize you are unable to handle the situation alone.[24]

8. Tend to your inner life. Serving a dysfunctional congregation will test your psychological, mental, and spiritual mettle. Your first line of defense is to tend to your own self. Remain rested and healthy. Establish a firm routine for daily prayer and reflection. Take a day or two every month as a time of spiritual retreat. It is said that if you draw near to the Lord, the Lord will draw near to you. We always need this nearness. When serving dysfunctional congregations, however, we need it more than ever. Therefore, you must do whatever is necessary to care for yourself.

QUESTIONS FOR REFLECTION UPON WORKING IN A DYSFUNCTIONAL ORGANIZATION

1. In what specific ways do you need to be a non-anxious presence in your church?
2. What person or groups can you "coach" into an awareness of the congregation's dysfunction?
3. In what emotional triangles are you presently involved? How can you effectively step out of the situation?
4. From what series relationships do you need to withdraw your support? What person or groups can you "coach" into parallel relationships?
5. How can you creatively produce an awareness of dysfunction within the congregation?
6. In what ways are you intentionally nurturing your inner life in light of your participation in a dysfunctional organization?

In this chapter we briefly presented the essentials of intervening into dysfunctional congregations. The body of knowledge regarding dysfunctional families and organizations is expanding rapidly. We encourage you to continue your learning in this field. The helps are available in libraries, universities, and from private sources. We would wish you might never need to intervene into the lives of dysfunctional persons, families, or congregations. However, we live in a society that exhibits many signs of dysfunction among our citizens. The chances are high that you will eventually work in a congregation that exhibits these same signs. When you do, immediately find the help you need and intervene to bring the congregation to greater degrees of health.

> Even such as ask amiss may sometimes have their prayers answered. The Father will never give the child a stone that asks for bread; but I am not sure that He will never give the child a stone that asks for a stone. If the Father says, "My child, that is a stone; it is no bread," and the child answers, "I am sure that it is bread; I want it," may it not be well that he should try his "bread"?[25]
>
> George MacDonald

The Essence of Understanding Family Systems Theory Intervention

1. When dealing with congregational dysfunction, as compared to normal conflict, all the rules change.
    - Dysfunctional situations call for a different approach to intervention.
2. One of the most effective processes by which intervention can take place is through the twelve-step recovery plan.
    - Although the pattern of activities, substances, and relationships may be different, addictive organizations are found in all categories (churches, businesses, public services, etc.).
3. Being a non-anxious presence will allow the interventionist to remain outside the addictive cycle.
    - If you do not function as a non-anxious presence, you may be recognized as the identified patient.
4. Your main role is to coach the healthy members of the congregation while working to make the entire system aware of its sickness.

How You Can Intervene in Dysfunctional Systems

1. Identify people and groups who are promoting addictive behavior and communication in the congregation.
- Are these people aware of their dysfunctional tendencies within the congregation?
- Can you facilitate their growth through the use of the twelve steps?

2. Develop an awareness of your own dysfunctional tendencies so that you can remain outside of the situation as much as possible.
- Improve your ability to be a non-anxious presence in the dysfunctional circumstance.

3. Nurture healthy coaching relationships with the more healthy members in the congregation.

4. Creatively disclose the effects of dysfunction within the congregation so that unhealthy communication and behavior can be recognized by members.

5. Facilitate an environment of open and honest communication.
- Your ability to model healthy relationships plays a crucial role in the intervention process.

PART SIX

The Learning Congregation

Introduction

[W]e learn to execute such complex performances as crawling, walking, juggling, or riding a bicycle without being able to give a verbal description even roughly adequate to our actual performance. . . . When people who know how to ride a bicycle are asked . . . how to keep from falling when the bicycle begins to tilt to their left, some of them say that they regain their balance by turning the wheel to the right. If they actually did so, they would be likely to fail.[1]

Donald A. Schön

> The core learning dilemma of organizations: "We learn best from experience but we never directly experience the consequences of many of our most important decisions."[2]

Most of us believe that the most effective learning comes from direct experience. Should we be tilting to the left on our bicycle and turning the front tire to the right (to avoid losing our balance) but fall anyway, we hopefully will try another alternative, such as turning to the left. A bad consequence of one action leads most of us to consider another option. But this is not always so—sometimes we get into a vicious cycle that keeps repeating itself. Like other bad habits, we repress into our subconsciousness the reality of the situation (believing everything is okay), or we keep our secrets to ourselves (telling others everything is okay). Such churches fall short and get bruised, but they keep turning the front tire of the bicycle toward the right when they are leaning—because they "know this to be the right thing to do."

Many churches have discovered the cycles of growth that give their members vitality and a sense of accomplishment. Eventually, however, the growth levels off and perhaps even declines, and our temptation is to stay in the "rut of success" believing that if only we stay there, it will return us to the path of success. Sometimes we try harder to be successful by staying in the rut.

In pushing the bicycle metaphor further, we observe too many congregations who do not even attempt to "ride a bicycle on an adventure trail." They would just as soon stay in the sandbox and play it safe, where sand and toys are predictable, and where they can remain in control of the environment (a closed system).

All of these examples represent real churches who may not survive the future for obvious reasons—all have learning disabilities. Congregations who want to survive and have vital ministry in the future are those who are able to sufficiently reflect upon their own actions and learn from them.

In Part Six we complete the systems model for managing the congregation; these chapters address how congregations learn. In order to survive in today's environment, churches must learn how to learn.

16

The Learning Congregation

Feedback, Reinforcing, Balancing, and Limits to Growth

Pain is a signal of disease, not the disease itself. Indeed, it is primarily a disease-preventing mechanism. Without it we would all quickly become crippled. So . . . we need to experience pain for our healing and health. . . . A corporation that is blind to its own problems cannot be healthy.[1]

M. Scott Peck

The most powerful learning comes from direct experiences . . . through taking an action and seeing the consequences of that action; then taking a new and different action. But what happens when we can no longer observe [or ignore] the consequences of our actions?[2]

Peter M. Senge

Learning Organizations

Congregations who do not learn from the consequences of their own actions or from the observation of their own experiences disprove the adage, "Experience is the best teacher." For them experience teaches them nothing. Most organizations don't last as long as a person's life and, though they should have been able to see the problems coming, they didn't. Perhaps some individuals understood what was happening, but their warnings were not enough to make the entire organization understand and do something about the forces that eventually contributed to their demise.[3]

Organizations, according to Peter M. Senge, are actually poor learners. He writes, "Learning disabilities are tragic in children, especially when they go undetected. They are no less tragic in organizations where they also go largely undetected."[4] In this chapter we will identify ways for the manager to learn about the consequences of a congregation's actions, its outputs and feedback processes.

Figure 16.1

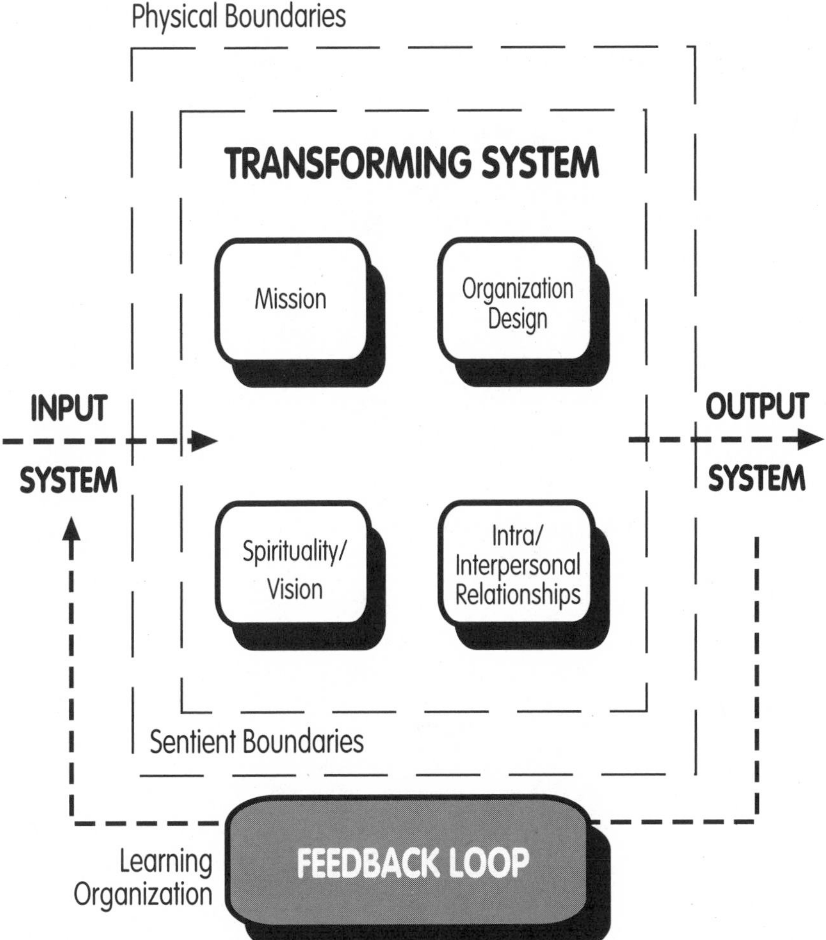

Like all organizations, the congregations-as-system imports needed resources from their environment into a "through-put" or transformation process, converting resources into energy. Much of this energy is used to keep the system alive and functioning.

The energy that is left over is exported back into the church's environment. These "out-puts" are of two types. One type is exported "waste": unwanted, and perhaps toxic, conditions that are no longer useful to the church (e.g., highly troublesome members who are excommunicated or physical facilities that are worn out). The other output type comprises valuable resources that the church exports to make the environment more reflective of the church's own values (e.g., missionaries, members given to help start a new congregation across town, new ideas or more effective approaches to ministry that are shared with other congregations—through seminars, writings, etc.).

The Feedback Loop

Crucial to an understanding of all systems is the feedback loop, which is one of the most important learning tools of the organization. The feedback (or renewed input) completes the cycle and includes all the information that the system generates that indicates the health of the organization, and the reactions of the members, users, and the environment to the congregation's actions and attitudes.

Feedback information is generated by the mere fact that the system is operating, but it is generally cast off and lost because the system pays no attention to it. Nevertheless, the congregation's feedback signals important trends and results of the congregation's activities. Feedback information signals the projected future of the church. For example, attendance and participation in the services of the church project whether the church will be alive and healthy in the future, or whether it will wither and die.

Gaining Feedback Information

Some types of feedback information the congregation is constantly generating are demographic trends of the congregation, financial patterns, growth patterns, current attendance figures compared to earlier statistics, staff and membership morale, average length of worker tenure, the number of social ministries, the percentage of first-time visitors who visit a second time, and the congregational tone and tenor.

If the congregation does not give careful consideration to its feedback information, two realities will occur: First, the congregation will miss many opportunities to strengthen its processes that promote success. Second, the system will not be cognizant of warning signs of conditions that, left uncorrected, may eventually destroy the church.

For example, earlier we spoke of the American automobile industry's inability to see that the American buyer wanted quality as much as power and style. Likewise, the industry ignored the negligible percentage of the market that turned to Japanese imports—until that percentage suddenly exploded into a huge proportion of sales. By then it was too late. The automobile industry chose to ignore its feedback information—a mistake that sent negative vibrations throughout the thread and fiber of American society. To this day this oversight is reflected in such things as loss of American jobs, the imbalance of payments, dramatically fluctuating American dollars, and a lower standard of living.

Just like the automobile industry, the church from prelates to pew warmers chose to ignore its feedback information that began sounding warning signals in the mid-1960s. When the church could ignore this feedback information no longer, the mainline church responded by fleeing the Interchurch Center at 475 Riverside Drive, New York City, initiating endless cycles of reorganization and otherwise putting Band-Aids on gaping wounds. The smaller denominations responded with myriad growth campaigns that were intended to double the membership in a decade, or double the number of congregations in a decade, or to make the people more spiritual. None of these well-intentioned efforts were intended to honestly confess and deal with the feedback information but to find a way around it. But failing to understand and deal with negative feedback information never works. Matters only get worse.

QUESTIONS FOR REFLECTION UPON FEEDBACK PROCESSES IN YOUR CHURCH

1. What formal and informal processes do you use to gain information about your programs and ministries?
2. What feedback are you denying or ignoring?
3. About what programs should you be getting feedback?
4. Who utilizes feedback information in your church? How do they use it?
5. How will you engage the church board and program leaders in a discussion of feedback processes?

Quality as a Type of Feedback Information

Gaining feedback is what the quality movement is all about. W. Edwards Deming was 41 years old when the Japanese bombed

Pearl Harbor; Deming was 50 years old when Japan with a destroyed economy asked this foreigner to help them turn their economy around; and Deming was 80 years old when NBC featured him in a broadcast, "If Japan Can . . . Why Can't We?"[5] More than any other person, Deming was credited with the radical turnaround of Japanese industry, which was based on a single premise, *quality*. It wasn't until his 80s that his ideas were received by his home country, the United States.

By occupation Deming was a statistician interested in sampling, quality control, and research. In 1980, when he was asked about the attitudinal difference between the United States and Japan, he replied, "[The Japanese] are using statistical methods. They have not only learned them, they have absorbed them. . . . They are giving back to the world (outputs) the products of statistical control of quality in a form that the world never saw before."[6] Obviously, statistics are not the desired end, but they are powerful tools to get the information needed about the system. While the term "statistics" can scare many people and turn many others off, some simple concepts in statistics can be the tools needed to at least organize and visually display data in understandable terms (the level of mathematics needed, according to Deming, is at the seventh or eighth grade level).

It is not our intent to write a course in quality or statistics in this section, but to introduce some of the tools that Deming used to help organizations continuously improve their effectiveness. Some religious managers have an innate resistance to analogies between machines and the functions or processes that are at work in congregations. For a review of this resistance to quality, we refer you to *Benchmarks of Quality in the Church.*[7] In systems language these tools help the system understand its feedback information. Deming's tools and training of thousands of Japanese engineers and managers were built on the foundational work of Walter Shewhart, a pioneering statistician who developed the Shewhart Cycle and eventually statistical process control (SPC).

Observing the manufacturing process, Shewhart was interested in any kind of variation in the system's feedback, believing that excessive variation had something to do with quality control. The "common causes" of variation, Shewhart and Deming believed, had something to do with such things as machinery, material, and machine operators. The "special" causes of variation might relate to such things as machine maladjustment, worn or broken tools, or an untrained operator. Deming came to understand that special causes of variation also included such things as fear, lack of commitment, and resistance to change. Figure 17.2 illustrates what happens when output variations go outside the control limits of an output.[8] Once output patterns are established, then the variations can be studied to determine their causes. "Special" causes are identified and addressed, and "common" causes are worked on to reduce them.

Figure 16.2

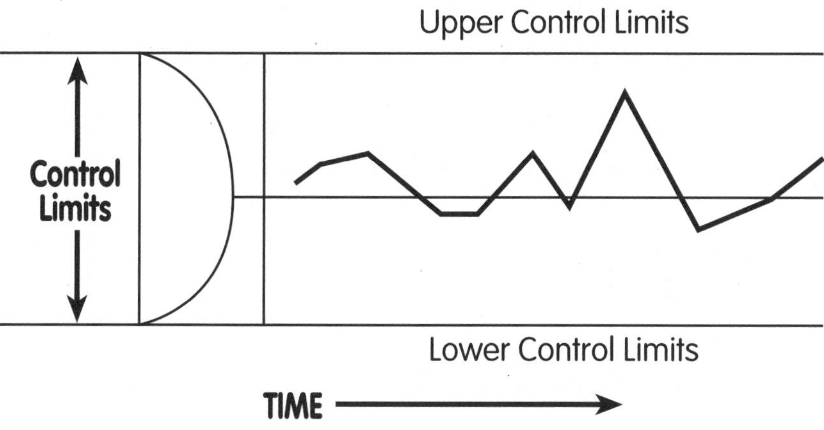

For example, when quality initiatives finally caught on in American companies, Motorola dramatically improved its defects from six thousand per million components in 1987 to forty per million in 1992.[9]

This discipline of understanding and dealing with feedback, illustrated in Figure 17.2, became known as The Shewhart Cycle. Later the Japanese termed it *kaisen* or *continuous improvement.*

A continuous cycle of improvement is made up of the following steps: managers plan a test or change that would hopefully improve the effectiveness of an organization or unit, then do the test, check the results, and act to improve the entire process based on what was learned.[10]

In sum, the feedback loop is the means by which the congregation "gathers up" this information and feeds it back into the system as an input. In fact, feedback information may be the most beneficial input that the congregation's leaders can receive. If this information is so important and so obviously easy to collect, why do most congregations ignore it completely? The best answer probably is because feedback information is so clear that it cannot be argued, and sometimes so painful that it cannot be denied.

Figure 16.3

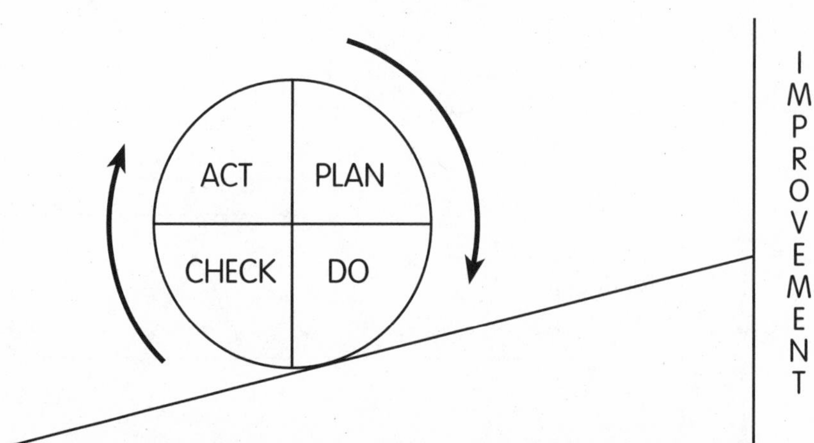

QUESTONS FOR REFLECTION UPON THE QUALITY OF YOUR CHURCH PROGRAMS AND MINISTRIES

1. What are you doing to emphasize quality to the church workers, and to the congregation?
2. Where do you see quality in your programs? How might you leverage these examples of quality to influence those programs where quality is lacking?
3. Where is quality lacking in your church? Is it okay for these programs to be poor quality?
4. In what programs is quality most important in order for you to become more effective in your outreach efforts? In your total church program?
5. Why do you ignore or excuse poor quality when you see it? Why do the other church leaders? Why does the congregation?
6. How might you leverage the programs which have quality to influence those which do not?
7. How might you engage the church board and program leaders in a discussion of the importance of quality for your outreach ministries? For other ministries?

There are two different types of feedback information: reinforcing (or amplifying) information and balancing information. We will discuss the two types in turn.

Reinforcing Feedback

Reinforcing feedback is information or a new condition that sets or reinforces actions that lead to growth, expansion, and greater satisfaction.[11] For example, when church members are satisfied (with the worship service, programs for children, youth, and so on), then energy renewal comes from the system itself. Or, the church's outputs (e.g., day camps for children and youth) may influence the community in a positive sense as the children and their parents tell their friends and neighbors who may then enroll their children in the church's youth programs.

> One associate pastor told us that 251 visitors from the community attended Sunday services during the first six months of 1994. They had a total of 387 visitors throughout the year. Less than 2% came because of the yellow pages, and over 80% visited the church because of personal referrals from their friends and acquaintances who were pleased with the church's ministry to their children and youth.

The church "listened" to this feedback by carefully tracking attendance and visitor statistics, and by utilizing a feedback process that enabled them to learn why each of these visitors chose to attend the services in 1994.

The feedback loop completes a cycle that forms a pattern, enabling us to see the interrelationships of things rather than individual "snapshots." Using the above illustration, Figure 16.4 demonstrates a set of conditions combining to constitute a feedback loop.

What makes a particular program grow? According to systems thinking, there is no one "cause," but rather a combination of "forces" in relationship to each other. Wherever you step into the cycle, you can look at different ways to see the relational dynamics and patterns. Some-

Figure 16.4

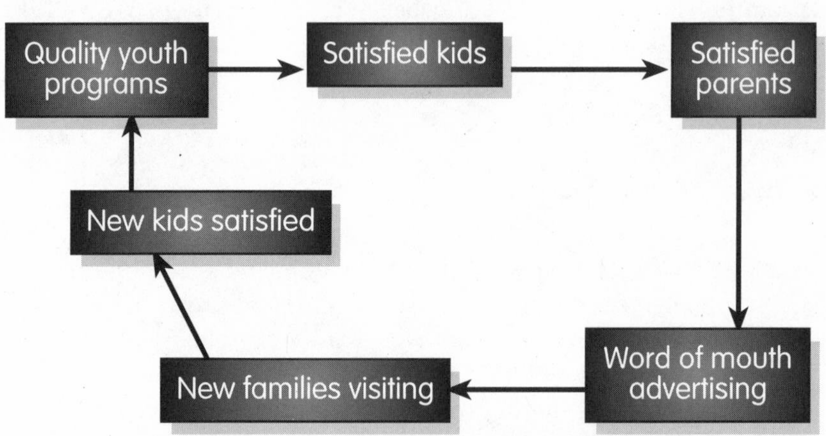

> A systems view goes beyond a linear cause- and-effect way of looking at things to identifying the patterns in feedback cycles.

times the relationships are clear and at other times more subtle. When we talked with the associate pastor regarding the dynamics in Figure 16.4, he told us that the growth in the youth programs led to increased quality in the children and youth programs. This was because the finance committee and the church board designated more money for these programs—due to their reputation and growth. With more resources the child ministries and youth ministries were able to launch new programs which in turn attracted more kids.

Reinforcing Positive Behaviors and Results

When the church is growing in any ministry, a reinforcing feedback cycle is at work. Positive reinforcing feedback cycles are the engines behind growth. They are habits of ministry enhancing behaviors of the congregation. Often the reinforcing cycle begins with small changes, but these small changes when linked systemically can grow into something much larger than the sum of the individual parts.[12]

Continuous improvement (or Kaisen) can build on itself, even if it is only a fraction each day so that perceptions are changed, the vision becomes clearer, and the entire organization is put on solid course. Tom Melohn, a CEO whose ideas on partnership were featured in *Harvard*

Business Review, describes how consistent behaviors of honesty grew into healthy patterns and eventually turned a failing company around:

> It took time—a lot of time—probably about two years. But our fellow employees slowly realized that we tried to be honest, bone honest, in everything we did.
>
> There are a couple of key elements at work here. First, all the pronouncements, all the [pontificating], they just don't work anymore—if they ever did. We've all heard too many words, empty words.
>
> Only actions count: consistent actions, every day, every night, every shift, every time. Then we'll believe again—slowly, ever so slowly . . . the little things really do mean a lot. It's like an Impressionist painting: a bunch of seemingly unconnected dabs or strokes, until you step back and view the completed painting. Then the pattern becomes clear. But remember, the pattern has to start with you. "Do as I say, not as I do" just doesn't work anymore.[13]

We have discussed those reinforcing cycles that promote health, growth, and positive change. These cycles are also termed *amplifying feedback* or what Senge identifies as *virtuous cycles.*

Figure 16.5

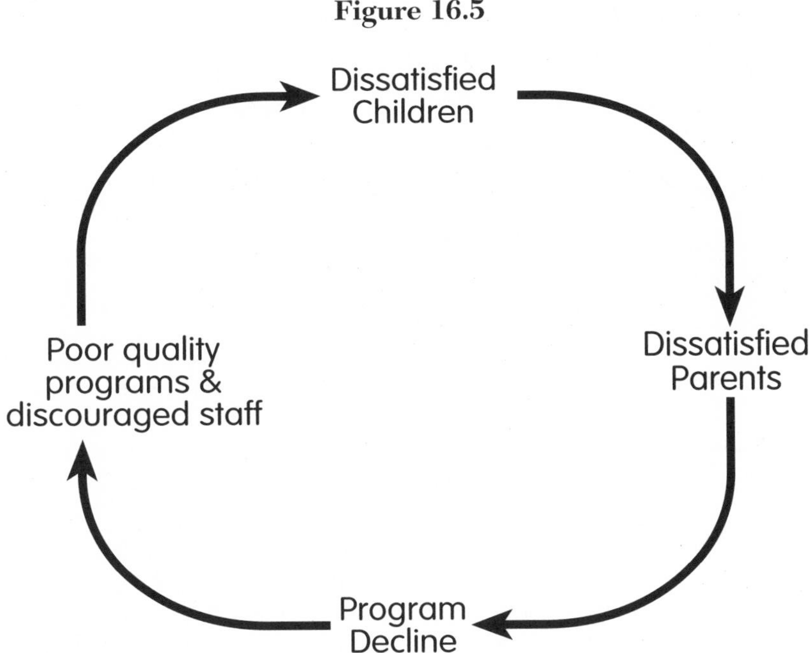

Reinforcing Negative Behaviors and Results

Reinforcing cycles can also be vicious cycles of accelerating decline. For example, consider the opposite of the above illustration: poor quality children's programs lead to dissatisfied kids, dissatisfied parents, and program decline. This cycle will eventually lead to degeneration, decline, and the death of a program or even a congregation (see Figure 16.5).

As small negative conditions build upon themselves, they become like a snowball rolling down the hill. The more it rolls down the hill the larger it becomes, and the more the momentum builds. Once the spiral of downward momentum begins feeding itself, there is almost no certain way to stop it. When negative behaviors or conditions join together they influence each other in an observable, reinforcing pattern. Time after time the situation repeats itself, making things worse. Another way to illustrate this vicious, reinforcing cycle is as follows (see Figure 16.6).

Figure 16.6

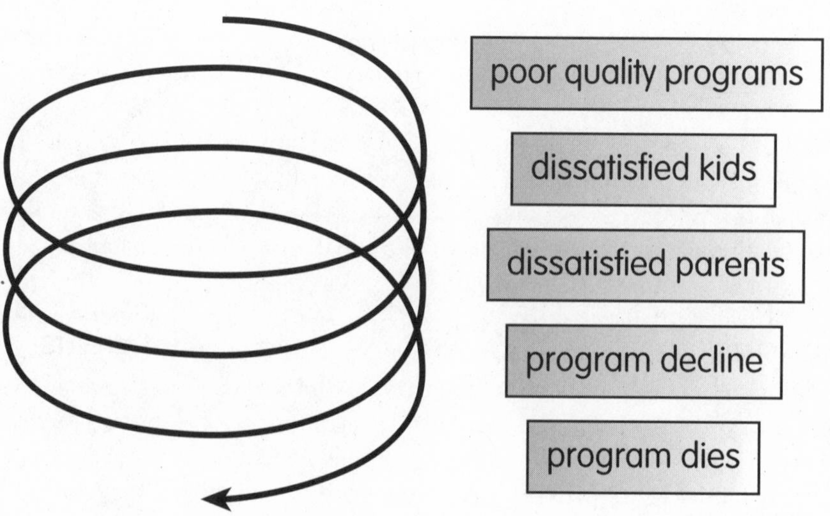

QUESTIONS FOR REFLECTION UPON REINFORCING PROCESSES IN YOUR CHURCH

1. Where do you see reinforcing cycles occurring in your church?
2. How might you strengthen these processes?
3. How might you leverage these reinforcing processes into other programs in the church?
4. Where do you see opportunity to initiate reinforcing processes in your programs? How might you go about this?

Balancing Feedback

Homeostasis

All living systems seek to exist in a condition of stability in which nothing happens out of the ordinary. The human propensity is to develop habits and, once the habits are fixed, to resist anything that might threaten to weaken or destroy the habit. Anyone who has tried to lose weight or to stop smoking knows firsthand the stabilizing feedback that is set in motion as soon as the habit is threatened. Immediately the mind kicks into gear with all sorts of arguments against the sought new condition. The mind says to the overeater, "It's no use starting a diet now. The Christmas holidays are only a month away. You know you have to eat at all the parties. Why not start on January 1st? The parties will be over." The mind says to the smoker, "Yes, you really should quit. But you just bought a new carton of cigarettes. You can't just throw them out. Why not finish the carton and then quit?" All such mind games are stabilizing feedback messages designed to protect the habit, to keep things on balance. Stabilizing feedback is a part of the balancing feedback loop.

Congregations, like individuals, develop habits. When the habit is threatened, the entire system will seek to balance the new efforts through resistance. We have observed many congregations pray for a certain change such as growth, and when growth occurs the congregation erupts into behaviors designed to stop the growth as soon as possible. Why? Because the congregation is accustomed (a well-developed habit) to its present size. New growth challenges that habit of size, and the congregation, like an individual, will find its "mind" raising all sorts of objections that are designed to stop the growth, and to shrink the congregation back down to the size it was, or smaller.

An evangelical congregation numbered less than fifty in Sunday attendance. For years these well-intentioned people prayed for revival. They conjoled the pastor because he could not spark growth.

Then the congregation suddenly grew to 150. The old congregation erupted into conflicts with the pastor; and confronted the newcomers, telling them to stay away. They voted the pastor out. When the dust finally settled the congregation numbered less than fifty. The congregation has not grown above fifty since.

How could this happen? The congregation was in the habit of having approximately fifty participants in its Sunday services, and they were also in the habit of praying for growth. But they were not in the habit of growing. So when growth occurred, the congregation-as-system fed into the system several actions and attitudes designed to get things back on balance as soon as possible, of having fifty in Sunday attendance. Every congregation wants to know that things are on balance, that nothing too much out of the ordinary will catch them unaware. Old habits are terribly hard to break.

Another common example of balancing feedback in congregations is their resistance to quality in their services and ministries. Most pastors, for example, who have attempted to improve the quality of any program in the church have experienced firsthand the balancing feedback that occurs—especially if it happens to have anything to do with the music program.

Balancing feedback is not a one-time correction but rather a constant dynamic that tries to maintain some homeostatic condition. Senge points out:

> Balancing feedback processes are everywhere. They underlie all goal-oriented behavior. Complex organisms such as the human body contain thousands of balancing feedback processes that maintain temperature and balance, heal our wounds, adjust our eyesight to the amount of light, and alert us to threat. . . . Balancing feedback prompts us to eat when we need food, and to sleep when we need rest, or . . . to put on a sweater when we are cold.[14]

A pastor recently told us that he desired to deepen the spirituality of his congregation. Persons in the congregation were experiencing all kinds of problems, but not expressing a practical or vibrant faith. So he decided to teach the spiritual disciplines for fifteen weeks on Sunday nights (e.g., how to pray, fast, and journal). People were initially excited by the teaching, especially several lay leaders and associate pastors. The pastors and lay leaders began to practice the disciplines.

But the rest of the congregation soon lost interest in the idea of practicing spiritual disciples. Within a year, members of the congregation were complaining about the same conditions in their lives and exhibited little or no interest in spiritual matters. Things had returned to about the way they were before the pastor conducted the fifteen-week emphasis on the spiritual life, and in some cases matters were worse.

The pastor then decided to be more intentional about spirituality and community life with the pastoral staff and church board. He conducted retreats for this group, and lengthened their business session in order to have time for sharing their spiritual journeys with one another. This had little effect upon the interests of the congregation.

Figure 16.7 illustrates a balancing feedback cycle. Thinking that the Sunday night teaching series would address the "gap" (see Figure 16.7, Intervention Number 1), the pastor introduced a reinforcing factor into the congregation, the fifteen week teaching series. At first there were some signs of change, yet a year later things were back to "normal," the way things were before he initiated the change process.

Figure 16.7

Intervention Number 1: Training Leaders in the Spiritual Disciplines

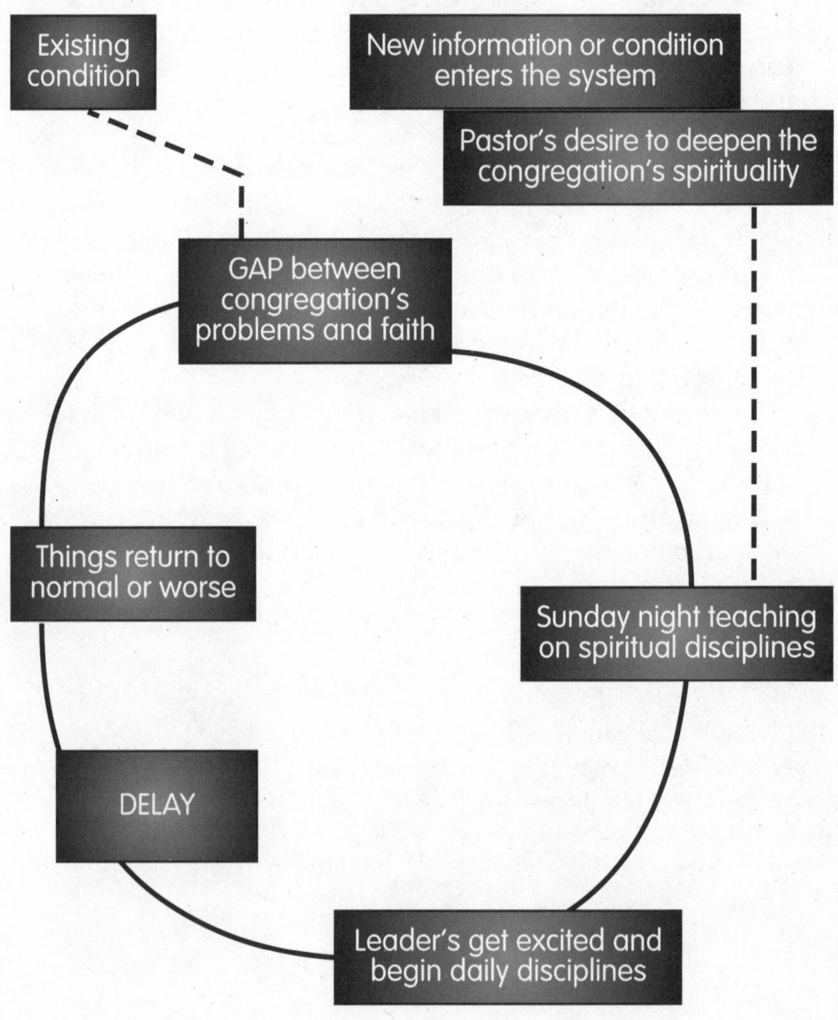

Another way of diagramming this intervention effort would be as follows in Figure 16.8:

Figure 16.8

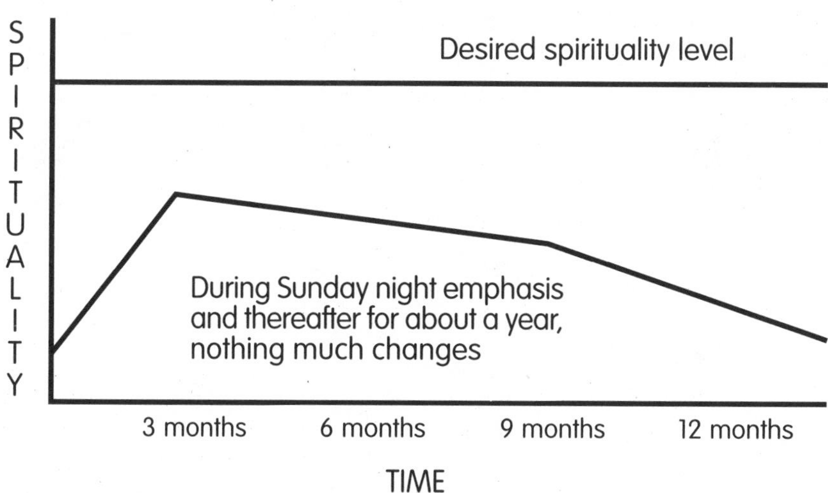

The intervention that was chosen by the pastor was primarily in the congregation's structure, the Sunday night service. The pastor intervened into the processes of the Sunday evening services by introducing an emphasis on the spiritual life and spiritual disciplines. However, this intervention was not sufficient to counteract the balancing processes that were set in motion to get things back on balance, where the congregation's spiritual condition was before the intervention was made. Apparently, the emphasis on spirituality did momentarily effect the homeostasis of the leaders. However, even this new condition was not sufficient to effect a lasting change.

QUESTIONS FOR REFLECTION UPON BALANCING PROCESSES IN YOUR CHURCH

1. Where are balancing processes inhibiting growth or working against positive change efforts in your church?
2. How would you identify the hidden, unobvious balancing processes?
3. How could you reduce the effects of balancing processes?
4. How might you engage the church board and leaders in a discussion of reinforcing and balancing processes in your church? The congregation?

A Serendipitous Reinforcing Cycle

Another kind of reinforcing feedback is present in the same congregation illustrated above. This time, however, we will illustrate a reinforcing cycle of spiritual growth that occurred shortly after the failed yearlong effort had ended. A tragedy entered the pastor's life that severely disrupted his own faith journey, plunging him into the dark night of faith experience; now a second cycle of "amplifying and balancing" conditions were introduced into his life, and the life of the congregation.

> The pastor's eighteen-year-old son suffered an accident while in a high school diving competition meet. The young diver survived, but became a quadriplegic.
>
> The personal tragedy plunged the pastor into the most severe faith crisis he had ever experienced. He discovered that heretofore his faith and acceptance of God's grace had never been severely tested. Now he took up the spiritual disciplines, not for the good of the congregation, but for his own survival. Now his prayer, fasting, and journaling became the means by which he held on to his faith.
>
> He shared his faith crisis with the congregation, telling them that the disciplines were proving sufficient to support his faith one day at a time. The congregation observed their pastor's faith journey in the midst of crisis, and learned from it.
>
> After several months, a curiosity and desire for a more authentic spirituality spontaneously spread throughout the very fabric of the congregation.

Earlier we spoke of reinforcing (or amplifying) cycles as being set in motion by two factors: new information or a change in conditions. The intervention that the pastor set in motion with his fifteen-week emphasis on the spiritual life utilized "new information." He gave new information to the congregation about the spiritual life and the disciplines which support the spiritual life.

Then tragedy entered the pastor's life. This tragedy came crashing down upon his family as a "new condition" thrust upon them, albeit very unwanted. This new condition set off a reinforcing cycle in the pastor's faith experience, first as he entered in the dark night, and second as he discovered at a visceral level that the spiritual disciplines supported him in his faith struggle. The pastor for his own need shared his experiences with his congregation as he passed through the dark night. Without intending to do so, his witness to God's grace throughout this dark experience set in motion a reinforcing cycle in the congregation as they realized that what he was saying rang true with what they observed in his life. The living witness of their pastor set in motion a second reinforcing cycle in the congregation. We term this cycle Intervention Number 2, and we diagram its amplifying effects upon the congregation below.

Figure 16.9

Intervention Number 2: A Tragedy in the Pastor's Life

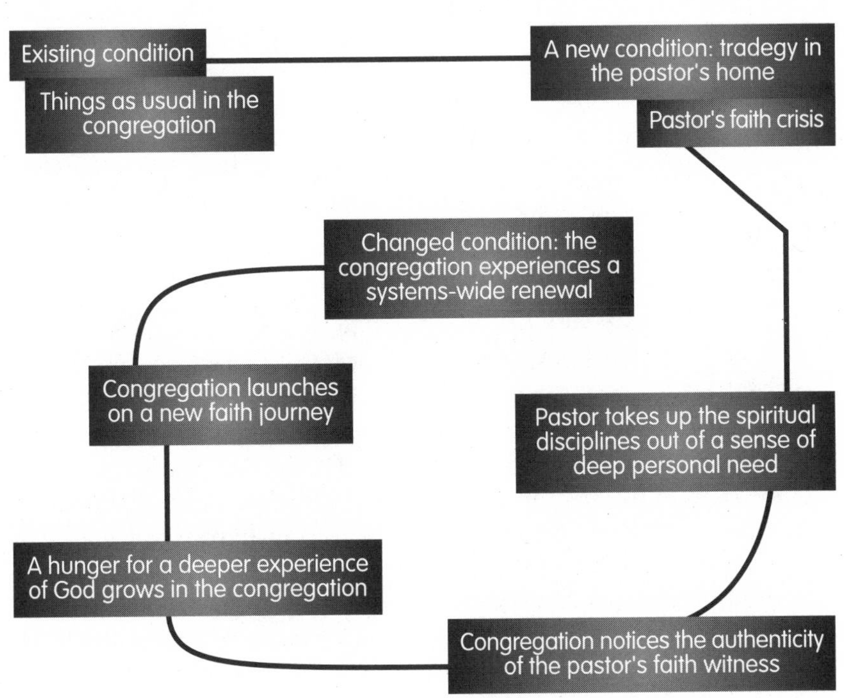

Balancing feedback processes, generally speaking, are much more difficult to identify than reinforcing cycles of feedback. In a condition of homeostasis, nothing new or different is happening. When there is the possibility of change, it is soon met with resistance that often seems to come out of nowhere, or else out of everywhere. Pushing the change effort harder will only make things worse unless the change effort addresses the implicit homeostatic assumptions that seek to keep the congregation immune from any change.

> We have seen many workaholic pastors who pronounce to the entire staff how they should take well-deserved time off for their own personal Sabbath and spend time with their families. Yet, few of them do. Why? Because the pastor has taught by his example that working seven days a week is to be valued above all else. There is an unwritten, well-established norm that people who overwork are admired. Hence, the unconscious resistance to pastor's pronouncement.

This important principle illustrated in the past several cases can be simply stated: If you push growth, you may grow for a while but then turn into decline. Senge describes this principle as *limits to growth.*[15]

Limits to Growth

Peter Senge proposes a systems theorem that states if you push growth you will decline.[16] Therefore, if you want your congregation to grow, you must focus on removing the barriers to growth that are built into your system. To focus upon growth puts the attention in the wrong place. Creating programs to stimulate growth causes us to put our focus on trying harder to reach the people "out there." When the denomination or congregation makes "trying harder" its focus of growth and development, it will likely grow for a while and then turn into decline. You may be trying harder to do the wrong things.

Sustained, systemic growth can only be achieved by putting the focus "in here on us." To set about removing the barriers to growth puts the attention where it belongs and where it will do the most good—"in here" on the quality of our ministries and the extent to which we succeed to meet the true needs of those whom we desire to reach.

Barriers to growth can be systems-wide as well as local. If the denomination has built-in barriers to growth, then these denominational barriers affect the growth efforts of every local congregation. This is not to say that the congregations cannot grow. All of them can. But it will require double or triple the effort to do so. Therefore, most congregations under such circumstances are not growing.

Barriers to growth within the denomination often exert great influence upon the growth of its congregations. This is what we mean when we say that barriers to growth are systems-wide. Barriers to growth in one part of the system infect every part of the system, from top to bottom and from bottom to top.

> In a recent conference on Church Growth and Development for Lutherans, Merv Thompson, one of the denomination's most successful growth pastors in the Evangelical Lutheran Church in America, stated that of all the Lutheran churches started in the last fifteen years, only 20 percent have grown beyond the number attending their first service.[17] Eighty percent have not grown beyond the number who attended the services on the first day. Most have declined.

What is happening in the new Lutheran congregations that causes 80 percent of them to stall, and possibly decline from the very first day of their inception? Certainly, the people who attend the first meeting and services for a while thereafter, fail to find the quality they are looking for in a church, and they fail to experience what they are looking for in their lives. They hoped to find these conditions in the new Lutheran church, but failing to do so they drift away.

What is the source of these barriers that make it difficult for the early attenders to continue attending the new church? Are all the barriers a result of the pastor and people who give themselves to the new missions effort? Not likely. It is more likely that many of the barriers are systemic to the ELCA, and are operative in the new church from the moment it opens its doors—or even before its first service.

One would think that the denomination would be shaken into a new sense of reality by such statistics, and would make every effort to discover the reason why only 20 percent of its new congregations grow. But most denominations do not enter into the deep soul searching that is required to discover and root out barriers to growth and quality in the system. It is less threatening to begin a new congregation once in a while—and hope that this time things will be different.

What shall we say then? Is there no hope for the Lutheran pastor and people who launch a new congregation? There is hope! The proof lies in the 20 percent of the new congregations that succeed in breaking through the barriers, whether systemic or local. They should know, however, that they may have to work twice as hard in order to achieve half of the results of another start-up congregation that begins with an "independent" posture, free of any denominational barriers to growth.

Whenever our efforts bump against limits, some of us just try harder, hoping we will outlast and outmuscle the resistance, the barriers to our efforts. But what if we identified the resistance and removed it? It seems too easy. And it often is. The first step is to admit what we already know about our explicit barriers to growth, and having confessed our obvious barriers to growth, to take decided steps to remove them. The second step is to do the necessary hard work that is needed to identify our more implicit, unobvious barriers to growth. This is hard work, but you will not achieve sustained growth or greater success in your outreach ministries until you do so.

A guiding principle here is: Beware of trying harder on those interventions or programs that may work for a while and then go awry, or of relying on those things that have worked for you in the past. Rather than putting all of our attention on the reinforcing cycle (e.g., a new growth effort), we would be wiser to try to understand the balancing processes that inhibit the success of our efforts.

Behind every growth program or quality improvement effort there are probably at least several "invisible" balancing processes. These limiting factors that contribute to the balancing processes may be within yourself (e.g., mental boundaries, paradigms, traditions, norms), within the congregation (e.g., paradigms, financial, human, technological), or in the environment (e.g., competition with other churches or organizations who are doing a quality job in the marketplace). With any of these limits, there are strategies that can make a difference, but they are not always obvious. They need to be searched out. More often than not, "our natural tendency is to look for what worked in the past and to redouble our efforts, instead of paying attention to the constraints."[18]

All organizations, including your congregation, will eventually run into underlying problems that demand your attention. Because of our own denial, or perhaps because we think the solution is too costly or too difficult, we "shift the burden" of the real, underlying problem to a much easier solution.

QUESTIONS FOR REFLECTION UPON THE LIMITS TO GROWTH IN YOUR CHURCH

1. Where do you see limits to growth in your church? How would you define them?
2. What can you do to remove these limits to growth?
3. Where might you find some leverage in the congregation to assist you in removing these limits?
4. How might you engage the church board, leaders, and the congregation in discussions about your limits to growth?

Shifting the Burden

Even if barriers to growth or quality can be identified, there is an inherent predisposure to shift the burden from weighty, systemic problems to dealing with symptoms of the problems.[19] "Shifting the burden" from real problems to symptomatic solutions is a vicious act. Senge warns against this:

> Beware of the symptomatic solution. Solutions that address only the symptoms of a problem, not fundamental causes, tend to have short-term benefits at best. In the long term, the problem resurfaces and there is increased pressure for symptomatic response. Meanwhile, the capability for fundamental solutions can atrophy.[20]

It's easy to desire "quick fixes." But a "quick fix" approach itself becomes an underlying problem in the system. We observe that pastors who take the "quick fix" approach appear to be in the know, believing that they are really addressing the problems. Many habitually deny the underlying problems and their reality, or they give up too easily when the congregation resists needed changes. Unfortunately, the real problems become more entrenched, even though the symptoms may disappear for a while. Making the necessary efforts to address a fundamental solution, as opposed to a symptomatic "solution," is the only thing that will bring lasting results.

Figure 16.10 identifies how "shifting the burden" works in the feedback processes.

Figure 16.10

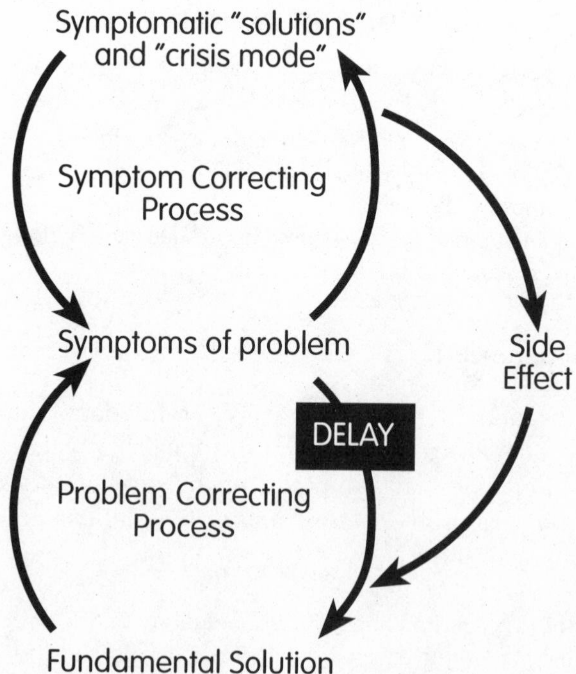

All congregations eventually run into balancing mechanisms that limit their growth. Organizations that survive a cycle of decline have learned to arrest entropy, a law of nature that assumes "all forms of organization move toward disorganization or death."[21] Open systems never rest or become static, they are always making the necessary adjustments in the transforming process (mission, relationships, structures, spirituality), and/or in the environment. These adjustments are crucial to the long-term growth and survival of the organization.[22] All efforts to maintain homeostasis are expressions of shifting the burden from problems to symptoms—in order to preserve destructive habits and attitudes in the congregation.

> A healthy organization—whether a marriage, a family, or a business corporation—is not one with an absence of problems, but one that is actively and effectively addressing or healing its problems.[23]
>
> M. Scott Peck

QUESTIONS FOR REFLECTION UPON SHIFTING THE BURDEN DYNAMICS IN YOUR CHURCH

1. Where are you seeking to deal with symptoms, and ignoring the real problems in your church programs and relationships?
2. How might you gain some leverage to help you address this issue with the church board, leaders, and the congregation?

The Essence of Understanding the Learning Congregation

1. The feedback loop is the "tutor" from which the learning organization must ascertain knowledge about itself and others.
    - This information indicates the health of the organization through the reactions of its members, users, and environment to the congregation's actions and attitudes.
2. Reinforcing feedback can be either virtuous or vicious in nature.
    - In virtuous cycles, a good situation becomes even better.
    - In vicious cycles, a bad situation becomes worse.
3. Balancing feedback seeks to prolong a condition of stability (homeostasis).
    - Congregations develop habits that counteract any change through resistance.
4. Limits to growth must be overcome through finding a leverage point, not by pushing harder.
5. Symptomatic "solutions" only preserve imbedded problems, not rectify them.

How You Can Facilitate the Growth of a Learning Congregation

1. Pay attention to feedback information.
   - This information enables you to see interrelationships, rather than individual "snapshots" of the situation.
2. Implement *kaisen* in your work environment.
   - Plan, Do, Check, and Act!
   - This is the means by which you gather feedback information and feed it back into the system as an input.
3. Become aware of reinforcing feedback cycles (negative and positive) and balancing processes.
   - There are invisible forces behind the cycles and processes that occur in your system.
   - Without identifying them, you become powerless within the situation.
4. Stop looking at the symptoms as the "real" problem.
   - As long as the fundamental cause goes without notice, the symptoms will eventually return.
5. When the symptoms return, there is an increased sense of pressure, and the capability for fundamental solutions dramatically decreases.

17

Quality and Continuous Improvement: The Ultimate Test of Management

The great barrier to Quality in the church is familiarity with poor quality. Having become accustomed to low quality, people do not want high quality—because, they say, "the old is good" (Luke 5:39).

In corporations "Benchmarking" is picking an institution that already does with excellence what you are trying to do better—then studying them to learn what they are doing, planning how you can get to that point, and measuring your progress against that Benchmark.

Norman Shawchuck

A defining spirit of thousands of congregations today is characterized by the desire to conserve and preserve what they have. The emphasis is to hold steady, play it safe, take no risks, be cautious, save some money to carry over into next year, reduce the expenses. It is projected these churches will no longer exist in the year 2050. The mortality tables already seal their fate—but they do not believe it.

We attended the Sunday worship services of a church in the eastern part of the country. There were 21 people in attendance. We judged the youngest person in the crowd to be at least fifty years of age. The liturgist pointed out several errors in the bulletin. The rest room was located through a door at the front, just to the left of the platform. Older people need to use the rest room quite often. The people were friendly and happy to have us in their church. After the service we asked some of the members whether there was a church nearby that had children. "Oh yes," they replied, "there is a new community church on the edge of town that has about 1,000 people, and several hundred children."

When visiting this kind of church, one gets a certain palpable feeling, a set of mixed emotions—uneasiness, sadness, ashamed to listen or to look. Whatever the emotion, we sense a certain spirit about the place and the services it offers. The people who attend there every Sunday, however, appear to be oblivious to the spirit or the fate that awaits them within the next 5 to 15 years.

There is lacking a spirit of vitality or a sense of urgency to do something—anything to attempt a renaissance. Another lack is a concern for quality in the things they are still able to do. Quality is never considered by such congregations. Conversations include the conservation of rapidly dwindling resources, or how awful and threatening the world has become. But in this situation to conserve is most certainly to lose, and to be poor quality is inviting the wolf to blow down the door.

The concept of quality warrants a discussion in this book on church management because it has become a central part of our cultural consciousness (particularly in the manufacturing and service sectors). Those organizations, including the church, who do not begin to take steps toward continuous improvement in quality will take a backseat to those who do.

W. Edwards Deming and Quality Go to Japan

Much of what we know about quality comes from Japan, for it was there, during the American restoration efforts of the Japanese economy, that the concept of quality management was first applied in a broad scale effort. But the Japanese did not invent the idea of quality. The founder and prophet of the quality movement in Japan was an American, W. Edwards Deming.

Following the war, General MacArthur's occupation forces were put in charge of putting a devastated Japanese economy back on its feet. Richard Luecke describes the conditions:

> The Japanese . . . lacked both practical engineering concepts as related to manufacturing and also fundamental management concepts and practices for effective control of business. The companies . . . were often housed in dirty, leaky sheds, and the quality of their manufactured goods was very poor.[1]

Deming was asked to help train the newly placed Japanese managers, engineers, and factory workers in producing high quality products with a minimum of material, and in less time. This he did and the Japanese listened and learned well. They were free to do this because they had lost everything. They had nothing to protect or preserve; no sacred cows to shelter, no egos invested in "but this is the way we have always done it."

In only fifteen years, by applying Deming's concepts of quality, the Japanese made great strides toward building a solid industrial base, and began exporting high quality automobiles to America. Within a decade the American buyer recognized that the Japanese automobile was far more reliable than its American counterparts. Expeditiously Japan carved out a huge market for their products in America, and the American automobile industry slid into a long and protracted decline.

Ultimately, industries all over the world lost multiple billions of dollars to Japanese industry; hundreds of thousands of jobs were lost, and the Japanese yen cut deeply into the value of the national currencies. For the Japanese, quality mattered. It mattered also to the manufacturers and the global economy, but it took decades before the industrialists recognized or admitted it.

The Churches and Quality

The same spirit that afflicted industry following the war also blighted the church and its leaders. They began to believe, "They will come because we are Methodist (or Presbyterian, or Lutheran, etc.). We don't need to evangelize; we have a good product. If people appreciate a good service they will come. We do good; we do no harm; we are educated; we have beautiful buildings, and we are well respected."

Denominations are greatly influenced by the behaviors and patterns of the secular institutions around them. So, in the 1950s the rich denominations went the way of the automobile manufacturers. One auto institution built bigger, more powerful, more costly cars; the church institution built bigger, more beautiful, more costly buildings.

For a decade and a half everything appeared to be going well with the automobile manufacturers and the denominations. Then, from 1964 to 1970 the denominations slid into decline. The dip was small at first, almost indistinguishable, but it was a sting that was certain.

It took the American people about fifteen years to decide that quality wasn't inside those old and magnificent, or in those new and glitzy, edifices—and two things happened: church attendance and membership declined as millions joined the ranks of the sidelined members. For example, from 1960 to 1984 the United Methodist Church membership figures dropped from 11 million to 9.2 million, and the figures have continued to drop at about 1 percent per year ever since.

Where did all those sideline members go? Many went nowhere. They joined the ranks of the Sunday morning couch potatoes. However, thousands more crossed over the bridge into those younger, high commitment churches who know that in today's competitive environment, "Good is not good enough. Only a commitment to total quality will do."

Why isn't "good" good enough? The answer lies in two realities, both of which are new since about 1975. The realities are *competition* and *choices.*

Competition. For centuries the churches knew nothing about competition. The local church was just about the only show in town. Denominations, especially the mainline churches, knew that they were without peer. Since 1975, however, the environment has become far more competitive in seeking to gain the attention and participation of the churched and unchurched alike.

With the advent of television, churches experienced their first real competition. Professional sports took huge bites out of the time people previously gave to the church. Then came resort areas, outdoor sports equipment, economical transportation. Before the church could mount an effective counterattack, millions of Americans were addicted to sports, weekend excursions, ski trips, and a host of other attractive choices that compete with the churches for people's time.

In 1975 a new competitor entered the arena—the high quality, nondenominational churches committed to a twin philosophy: (1) merely being good at what we do is not good enough; only excellence will do. And (2) we will do whatever it takes to reach the unchurched in our community. For the first time in their history, the denominational churches experienced a compelling competition from other congregations.

Choices. Since World War Two the entire American scene has gone wild in giving people—even the most common people—choices. The large grocery store may offer a choice of some fifty or sixty breakfast cereals. The large superstores may offer the shopper some 25,000 choices. Beyond the supermarket, on any given weekend, the family can take their choice—anywhere from a dozen events in rural communities to hundreds of possibilities in a large city. Now, choosing to attend church services on the weekend is a choice to be weighed along side a great variety of options. These phenomena are still new in American culture. Many churches have not yet awakened to their reality.

Today, the vast majority of denominations are caught in the habit of poor quality. Members resist change while the congregation declines. Even as the church stumbles, the congregation adopts a spirit of conservation, of "playing it safe."

Is there any hope for the church? Yes, there is. The hope for the church is seen today in the offices, plants, and mills around the globe. Finally, in the mid-1980s business leaders faced the facts; they had lost their way through the maze of world competition. *Total Quality Management (TQM)* suddenly became the buzzword. But TQM, by itself, is too little too late. Now industry and business are on a quest for a new spirit, and it is searching soul-deep.

Business leaders are learning that it is dreadfully difficult to turn an institution around. It may take another two decades to turn certain businesses around—if ever. But at least the large corporations are trying—some to unusual extremes:

In 1991 we had an opportunity to meet with the directors of human services for the General Electric plant in Cincinnati. There these people showed us a manual the Cincinnati group is using in bringing top managers and employees from across the board together to discuss the most important concerns of General Electric: visioning, leadership, team building, quality, continuous improvement.

The topics in the manual also focus upon the most important concerns of the individual General Electric employee. These include: our families, our relationships with God, our job security, our physical and emotional health.

When we queried as to why General Electric is giving company time for employees to come together to discuss such things as their family life, their physical and emotional health, and how they experience God, the GE personnel answered, "We give time to this because this is what GE people want to talk about, and we believe that concern for our families, for our health and future, and our relationship to God have influence upon the quality of our working relationships and the quality of our work."

We mused that GE might put us out of work, since we are clergy persons, and these topics sound a lot like church. The director of human services for GE in Cincinnati responded, "Well, we have to do this because the church is failing to do so."

Whenever we tell this story to our students and clients, the usual response is a complaint: "They aren't serious. They do it for devious reasons. They should leave the spirit to us. We are the Church." We also complain in similar fashion about the independent mega-churches, "They are just a social club. They are not faithful. They are just a big show. We are the faithful ones. We must be the faithful ones—after all we are getting smaller every year, and doesn't the Bible talk about the faithful remnant?" We pose a question, What will the Church be like when the faithful remnant no longer remains?

Clergy Training Institutions and Quality

When it comes to quality in ministry, seminaries and other clergy training institutions must be included in the conversation, since they have the first opportunity to form the opinions and practices of the clergy candidates. All later attempts to form the clergy aspirant will either be supported or frustrated by the earlier seminary experience. Among the rank and file there is the opinion that seminaries do not understand the new realities that currently confront congregations and their pastors. In *The Seven-Day-A-Week Church,* Lyle Schaller predicts that seminaries are training the last generation of pastors who have opted for a seminary education.[2] When looking for its leaders, Schaller says, churches are turning to the "service oriented" churches, the "seeker" or "user" minded churches, that are now training leaders to be quality conscious and to understand the contemporary environment in which the church must minister.

This leads to an important question: Why are many seminaries choosing to be unresponsive to the needs and interests of their clientele? There are three possible reasons:

1. They are interested in other things.
2. They lack the will or the resources to provide quality training.
3. They have intentionally decided to be unresponsive.[3]

The above list is often used to help understand unresponsive institutions in general. For the purposes of understanding unresponsiveness of seminaries in particular there is perhaps a fourth possibility:

4. The traditional, bureaucratic structures, around which most seminaries are organized, are not able to change curricula, teaching methods, and administrative procedures fast enough, or able to keep up with technology, in order to equip the student to effectively lead and manage in today's environment.

As teachers in clergy training institutions, we think the answer does not lie in possibility number two or three. Most seminaries possess sufficient resources, and their faculties see the need. We think the answer might lie in a combination of items number one and four: the priorities of some schools do lie elsewhere, such as training research scholars for the guild, and the bureaucratic structures of virtually all schools do not permit them to adapt curricula and classroom methods quickly enough to meet the current needs of the churches. It takes a seminary so long to move from point "A" to point "B," that making a timely response to the needs of their constituencies is always beyond their grasp.

There are exceptions—and we prefer to think that you attended an exception—to the prevailing denominations, seminaries, local congregations. We are aware that some denominations and seminaries are making concerted efforts to become responsive to the congregations that depend on them for well-trained pastors.

Rather than point the finger of blame when the system itself is in trouble, it is more appropriate for you to consider what you are doing to tend to the spirit of your congregation. For you, that is the major concern—perhaps the only necessary concern.

If you have been out of seminary for three years or more, you can no longer hold the school responsible for the quality of your ministries. At the very best the seminary can perhaps prepare a student to serve effectively for five or six years after graduation. By this time the social environments have undergone sufficient change so as to point the pastor-as-manager to obsolescence.

It is presently understood that the MBA graduate, the engineering graduate, and the physician graduating from residency, are entering work environments of such rapid change and advance in technology that, unless they keep up the pace of learning, their knowledge will be outdated in about three years. If they fail to continue learning after graduation, their jobs may be in jeopardy—as the employers go looking for new and more up-to-date graduates.

Thus, Peter Senge in his book *The Fifth Discipline* hammers home the point that to remain successful in our work we must give ourselves to Life Long Learning, and the organizations we manage must be transformed into Learning Organizations.[4] Such learning is of vital importance to the Church's future vitality and any local church's future existence.

QUESTIONS FOR REFLECTION UPON QUALITY AND CONTINUOUS IMPROVEMENT

1. In regard to quality, what spirit does your congregation nurture? Is this the spirit that you desire to share with the community?
2. In what ways has your church been affected by an attitude of arrogance in terms of an excuse for a lack of quality?
3. What are you doing to tend a spirit of quality within your congregation?
4. Are you involved in a lifestyle of Life Long Learning? Is your congregation?

The Three Keys to Quality and Kaizen

Learning and the will to give oneself to the necessary disciplines for lifelong learning, are a matter of spirit, pure and simple. There are no excuses to pardon our lack of learning, or of not creating learning organizations. But where does one begin to create an environment in which the church will learn continuously about quality in ministry? The founder of the quality concept, W. Edwards Deming, began by emphasizing "three keys" and one deceptively simple concept.[5] The three keys are:

1. Emphasize the involvement of all the volunteers in making quality improvements. Administrative committees by their efforts alone will never bring about a spirit of quality and kaizen.
2. Leaders and managers must take the lead in making quality happen.
3. Place ultimate attention on member/customer satisfaction.

The simple concept was first adopted by the Japanese as Deming worked with Japan to restore its industrial base after World War Two. The concept is *kaizen* or *continuous improvement*—continuously make improvements on what you are doing. Continuous small, incremental improvements will guarantee that quality will never be lost. The power of kaizen lies in its utter simplicity. For example, the Sunday school teacher might be encouraged and assisted to make small improvements in his teaching and relationships with his students. Or the director of the acolytes might be encouraged to search out how to make continuous improvements in the ministry of the acolytes. Think of it, if every Sunday school teacher, every youth worker, the workers in the nursery, the director of children's choirs, and so on would commit themselves to kaizen, the children's program in the church would be transformed—and would continuously be transformed without reaching an end.

Again we say that the three keys to quality and kaizen are adopted or rejected by managers and congregations as a matter of spirit. If an established congregation is ever to find the will and energy to take a journey toward quality, the pastor and leaders will need to care for the spirituality of the congregation. If the established congregation fails to generate a new spirit within itself, efforts for quality stand little chance of success.

We may feel that we do not know what quality and kaizen would look like in a church—but we all know what the programs of the church look like when quality and kaizen are not there:

A friend of ours, a pastor, was appointed to a church of more than 800 members. The church has declined in membership steadily since 1968. Almost immediately upon arriving she heard many complaints about the quality of the greeting and ushering programs. So bad was it that there had been several altercations between the ushers and members of the congregation who had tired of the ushers' unsatisfactory work. After observing the greeters and ushers for six months, during which time there was a quite physical argument between an usher and a member who had that day brought guests to the service only to be chagrined by the rudeness of the usher toward his guests, the pastor was convinced that something had to be done.

She called for a meeting of the ushers and the church board, in which she frankly told the ushers what she heard and observed. Well, the ushers did not take this as good news! Three usher families left the church. Many board members were incensed that she had driven these well-meaning ushers out of the congregation. Many members voiced their support of her actions privately, but none would speak openly with the board.

What this story doesn't tell us is how many dozens of families left the church over the years because of disappointment and embarrassment due to the ushers, the inferior sound system, and the poor quality music which to this day is still a steady diet in that place.

Old, destructive habits finally come to be accepted as divine right. They die hard. Nonetheless, a congregation that succumbs to low quality is a matter of spirit. By this the church enters into league with its adversaries—to discourage and offend countless numbers of souls as well as the thousands who never become active at all.

Reality has set in for managers of religious organizations. We know where we are. What is yet to be determined is where we will be at the year 2025. Possibly Bishop Richard Wilke of the United Methodist Church is right—that which will turn our deep declines around is a spiritual awakening, a repentance—a change of mind and of heart and of spirit.[6]

The key to this is not with our bishops or general agencies—but on the front lines with the pastors and lay leaders in every church. We can turn it around—one congregation at a time. To say we can't do it in "our" congregation will not stand up against the facts of recent history.

Consider the examples that emerged from the World War Two generations, whom we often criticize for being stuck in the past: When an army of untrained, unskilled women, girls, and the elderly streamed into the factories and shipyards to manufacture ammunition and machines, no one dreamed they could produce such high quality products—almost overnight. There is a lesson here for every religious manager; they were able to produce such achievements because they brought with them something more important than training and experience; they brought spirit. They dug down inside themselves and discovered soul.

Then after World War Two the Japanese had paltry resources with which to begin the arduous task of reconstructing an entire nation that had failed terribly. Hosts of their brightest and most capable citizens had died during the war; their factories and facilities had been destroyed. What they were left with were sheds, leaky buildings, and a terrific shortage of skilled workers. What they did have was the openness to learn and an indomitable desire to reconstruct their nation. However dispirited they were after their great defeat, they had not lost their national soul.

What have these examples to say to congregations? The war workers and the Japanese reconstruction effort both faced daunting circumstances in highly similar conditions: a lack of educated, skilled workers, a lack of experience, and a lack of resources. Yet, both groups were inspired by these less than ideal circumstances to a new collective spirit; they dug down deep and discovered soul.

Can the pastor of any church say that her circumstances are more dire than these? Probably not. What then shall we say? If quality is lacking, if the lusty desire for continuous improvement is lacking in the congregation—then what goes wanting in that place is spirit. And for some congregations there is an even deeper void—some have lost their soul. Like Dante's *Faust*, they have sold out to preservation, playing it safe in ailing traditions.

In such congregations, where must the manager begin in her

efforts to introduce quality and kaizen into the ministries of the church? Inspire a new "we can do it" spirit and build a sense of soulness. Until these are present it is not likely that other interventions will make a significant difference.

Examples of history teach clearly that resources and programs are secondary to spirit and soul. Someone once said that a person may own all the resources of the whole world and still lose his own soul. Contrariwise, if one is possessed of a life-giving spirit and in touch with soul-giving forces, then that person will succeed with all visible indicators to the contrary.

There is another lesson from history worth repeating here. The great movements and changes of human history are characterized by four conditions:

1. a small group of persons;
2. thoroughly devoted to a single cause;
3. with at least one powerful orator; and
4. an emotive slogan (sometimes also a banner) that excites, inspires, and energizes them to pursue the cause, at any cost.

The secrets revealed in this list are: that a small group of persons are more likely to make great accomplishments than a large group; that the true resource needed is a complete devotion to an inspiring mission (this realization sets the group apart from the larger populace); and that someone (or group) who can announce the cause in a passionate and compelling manner will energize the pursuit of the cause. Herein lies a lesson in change and improvement that every pastor should consider, lest he become discouraged by believing his congregation does not possess sufficient people or resources for doing what needs to be done.

Looking for Quality Closer to Home

In the final analysis it does the pastor and volunteer leaders little good to dwell upon the barriers to growth that are bequeathed upon them by attitudes and behaviors of the denomination's leaders and agencies. Far more beneficial to the local ministry is for the local leaders to commit themselves to the idea that "good is not good enough" and work to lead every ministry and volunteer into a continual quest for quality.

The congregation that does this will soon discover that high quality local ministries will more than compensate for the actions, behaviors, and statements of the denomination's regulatory agencies. Quality at the local level speaks for itself. Quality is something no one can give you, and no one can take away.

Growth and Quality in the Younger Denominations

In response to the vacuum of quality and spirit in the mainline churches, thousands of the unchurched and the inactive churched began attending the small, American born denominations (e.g., the Assemblies of God, Baptist denominations, the Church of the Nazarene) in increasing numbers. After 1980 the new, independent, community churches burst upon the scene and prospered in every large- and medium-sized community in America. Currently, many are doing equally as well in small population areas.

In the euphoria of this unprecedented growth, at least a few of the smaller, American born denominations let go of many of the things that had propelled their growth in the first place.

> The Assemblies of God, for example, stopped its consistent training of Sunday school teachers and workers, and soon began to cut back on its Sunday school and child evangelism efforts nationwide. At one time these were among the hallmarks of quality in the Assemblies of God denomination.
>
> Another change of renewal and growth came with the charismatic renewal that made its impact in local churches in the 1960s and 1970s. The quality and spirit of worship attracted thousands of persons to local assemblies.
>
> Results? After a period of rapid expansion the denomination began to stall. Several efforts were made to return to things as they used to be. In 1990 the denomination announced that the 90s were to be a "Decade of Harvest." The denomination's leaders decided to focus on growth. Amidst this was a call to "Return to Asuza Street."

Results? It appears that while there is unprecedented growth overseas, its Decade of Harvest may go down in history as a decade of decline in the United States. In 1994, for example, in the middle of the Decade of Harvest, there was a net increase of two churches on the North American soil in the United States. Over three hundred churches were planted; over three hundred churches were shut down.

If this is the final result for the Assemblies of God, we will all learn a lesson in feedback, in balancing systems. If you push growth, you will grow for a while and then decline. If you want to grow, you must not focus on growth, but on removing the barriers to growth.[7] To focus on growth puts the attention on trying harder. This may be worse for the organization until the question is answered, What is standing in the way of growth?

By the late 1980s and 1990s, decline was knocking on the door of the smaller denominations. Because they care more, or perhaps because they are less bureaucratically structured, several of these smaller denominations are responding with relative haste to reorient themselves to their internal and external markets. Several are undertaking efforts to restructure and renew themselves.

One can almost hear the apostle Paul saying to the churches, "You began so well; what caused you to stumble?" The answer will not be found in the church's environment. The answer lies much closer to home, at the very door of the church. The church's success following World War Two affected its spirit. Nothing weakens the church more than success. Success too often affects the congregation's spirit. The change of spirit has to do with a lessening of desire to reach the unchurched, and the lack of desire to do all things in a high quality manner—from greeting and ushering to meeting the most pressing social needs in the community.

QUESTIONS FOR REFLECTION UPON YOUR ROLE IN CONTINUOUS IMPROVEMENT

1. How can your congregation creatively implement the concept of kaizen (continuous improvement) on a daily basis?
2. Are you effectively emphasizing the involvement of all leaders and members in making continuous improvements?
3. Is your church concerned with customer satisfaction? If not, why not?
4. How is your church needlessly offending first-time visitors and regular attendees?
5. In what specific ways has your congregation "sold out" to preservation?

Quality is a matter of the right spirit. In achieving quality, the size of the congregation is not a significant factor. A house church of ten people can be a quality operation. But when spirit is lacking in any church, the relationships between persons are characterized by distance, distrust, and cool formality. If you walk into a church, for example, and the relationships you observe appear stiff, guarded, and "clammy," you likely have entered a place where spirit has been lost.

In this chapter we considered quality and its relation to the spirit and the soul of the congregation as a strategic component of the church's life, ministry, and results. The spirit of the organization breathes life into organizational structures. A structure without spirit, whether it be worship or the finance committee meeting, is a deadening structure. The harder persons work in such structures the more they die—inch by inch. It's all a matter of spirit.

However, you can turn a poor quality congregation around. It won't be easy, because many members are now stuck in the habit of poor quality. Attempts to move toward quality will set in motion balancing cycles of resistance. People, who do not want to "do quality" themselves, also tend to resist any and all quality improvement efforts initiated by others—as though ugly is beautiful, and garbage smells good. Such resistance to quality is of no divine Spirit, and of no earthly one either.

The Essence of Understanding Quality and Continuous Improvement

1. Nothing weakens the church more than success.
   - Many churches have adopted an attitude of superiority that has led to a decline in the quality of their services to the community.
2. Lifelong learning must be a part of the spirit of the congregation.
   - Without a sense of constant learning, the congregation will grow stagnant and lifeless.
3. Continuous improvement is often counteracted by balancing cycles of resistance.
   - Many of the members get stuck in a pattern of poor quality, because they are accustomed to it.
4. A lack of quality in one area of the church affects the entire church.

How You Can Implement Kaizen in the Congregation

1. Identify the strengths and weaknesses of the congregation in the area of quality.
   - In what specific areas does the congregation nurture a spirit of quality that is destructive to the mission of the church?
2. Implement kaizen in the life of the congregation.
   - What small improvements can be encouraged in the church's ministries on a weekly basis?
3. Emphasize the involvement of all leaders in the process of continuous improvement.
   - Without everyone's help, quality will quickly be resisted by the system's desire for homeostasis.
4. "Good is not good enough! Only a commitment to total quality will do!"

Postlude

We have chosen to end this text with a discussion of Quality in the church because producing a higher quality ministry is the focus of the entire book. The ultimate test of management is the quality of people and ministries it produces. In religious organizations, quality ministries depend upon high quality managers. We have written this book from this viewpoint: How can we, as authors, inform and inspire our readers to be high quality managers?

We now send this book abroad to its own affairs realizing that it is not easy to build high quality ministries, nor is it easy to bring ourselves to be high quality managers. Much work is needed at both levels. It is amazingly easy to become confused about personal and ministry priorities. We must be on guard all of the time.

We have had an opportunity to work with a group of laypersons and Jesuit priests whose ministry is to train Roman Catholic bishops in management. They work with bishops in many parts of the world, including the former Soviet Union bloc countries. In several of these countries the new governments are now returning to the Church the properties that were confiscated by the Communist regime.

For decades the bishops have had hardly two rubles to rub together; now they are receiving land, schools, hospitals, and so forth. Our friends tell us that when they ask bishops how they may help them, the bishops say, "We want a bank!" They have no money but they want a bank. They have absolutely no experience or training in managing fiscal affairs, yet they want a bank. What, we wonder, does a bank symbolize for these bishops: status, security, power?

How much we all want to believe that if we just had a "bank," if we just had more of (you fill in your word), then we would be more secure, effective, and satisfied in our ministries. Just like the bishops who want a bank, we seek a more effective and satisfying ministry along the path of Upward Mobility. It is not upward that we must now go, but downward—downward into the deep reserves that money cannot buy and status cannot proffer. Downward into that place with God where we might accept and relish in the fact that we are all paupers in need of God's reserves, beggars in need of God's bread.

Since we began our work on this text, we have observed many

changes in the church world that give us assurance in the future of the church. Even though some denominations and local congregations may not survive, the church will flourish. The surviving church, however, will not look anything like denominations and most congregations look today. It will be different.

Our limited resources are not sufficient to predict what the surviving church will look like. Of this we are assured, however: the church of the 21st century will be managed by a new breed of managers, both lay and clergy (if these distinctions survive). They will be men and women who are compelled by spirit, deep commitment, and courage. They will possess the courage and skill to smash worn-out traditions, to envision a better tomorrow, and to create the structures and belief systems to make it happen. Who could argue that this is not a "shaking out" time for religious organizations? Only those that are managed by capable, caring, entrepreneurial managers will survive.

To the extent that this text helps you to be one of those managers of the church in the 21st century, we will be gratified for our labors. We thank God that God has allowed us to frame the concepts that we herein commend to your consideration.

Notes

Scripture quotations in this publication, unless otherwise indicated, are from the New Revised Standard Version of the Bible, copyrighted © 1989 by the Division of Christian Education of the National Council of the Churches of Christ in the United States of America, and are used by permission.

Preface

1. Peter F. Drucker, *Management: Tasks, Responsibilities, Practices* (New York: Harper Colophon, 1974), pp. 11-12.

Introduction to Part One

1. Anthony de Mello, S.J., *Taking Flight: A Book of Story Meditations* (New York: Doubleday, 1988), pp. 83-84.
2. See Walter Brueggemann, *Living Toward a Vision* (New York: United Church Press, 1976, 1982), pp. 134-35.
3. Ibid., p. 137.

1. The Manager as Steward

1. M. Scott Peck, *A World Waiting To Be Born: Civility Rediscovered* (New York: Bantam Books, 1993), pp. 225, 227.
2. John A. Sanford, *Ministry Burnout* (Philadelphia: Westminster/John Knox Press, 1982), p. 9.
3. Roy M. Oswald, *Finding Leaders for Tomorrow's Churches* (Washington, D.C.: The Alban Institute, 1993).
4. Eugene Roehlkepartain, "Tomorrow's Leaders," in *The Christian Ministry*. May–June 1994, p. 10.
5. The desert fathers, and some mothers, were a large group of persons who fled the cities after Christianity was adopted as the state religion in the third century, and it was no longer dangerous to be a Christian. Seeing how this change of status brought new temptations in the lives of Christians and churches, the desert fathers and mothers fled to the desert in order to confront the powers of evil in the desert. Their warning was "swim for your life," and with this, they began a movement of men and women fleeing to the desert that lasted approximately 1,000 years. For additional reading, see *Philokalia* compiled by St. Nikodimos of the Holy Mountain and St. Makarios of Corinth (London: Faber and Faber, 1979).
6. Evelyn Underhill, *The Spiritual Life* (Harrisburg, Penn.: Morehouse Publishing, 1984), pp. 74-75.
7. Simon Tugwell, "Prayer," vol. 1, *Living With God* (Dublin, Ireland: Veritas Publications, 1974), p. 123.

8. Ibid., p. 124.
9. Walter Brueggemann, *Living Toward a Vision: Biblical Reflections on Shalom* (New York: United Church Press, 1976, 1982), p. 139.
10. Ibid., p. 139.

2. The Manager as a Person Before God

1. Adapted from John H. Westerhoff III and John D. Eusden, *The Spiritual Life: Learning East and West* (New York: The Seabury Press, 1982).
2. For an insightful discussion on these two paradigms of the church, see Loren B. Mead, *The Once and Future Church* (Washington, D.C.: Alban Institute Publications, 1992).
3. See Henri J.M. Nouwen, "The Selfless Way of Christ: Downward Mobility as Christian Vocation"; "Temptation: The Pull Toward Upward Mobility"; and "A Self-Emptied Heart: The Disciplines of Spiritual Formation," in *Sojourners* (June, July, August, 1981); and *In the Name of Jesus: Reflections on Christian Leadership* (New York: Crossroads, 1989).
4. Henri J.M. Nouwen, "The Selfless Way of Christ: Downward Mobility as Christian Vocation," in *Sojourners* (June, 1981), p. 14.
5. Ibid., p. 15.
6. Henri J.M. Nouwen, "Temptation: The Pull toward Upward Mobility," in *Sojourners* (July, 1981).
7. See M. Scott Peck, *A World Waiting to Be Born: Civility Rediscovered* (New York: Bantam Books, 1993), pp. 248-61.
8. Ibid., p. 249.
9. Ibid., p. 255.
10. Norman Shawchuck and Roger Heuser, *Leading the Congregation: Caring for Yourself While Caring for Others* (Nashville: Abingdon Press, 1993), pp. 45-57.
11. Compiled by Igumen Charition of Valamo, trans. E. Kadloubovsky and E.M. Palmer, *The Art of Prayer: An Orthodox Anthology* (Winchester, Mass.: Faber and Faber Limited, 1966), pp. 132, 137.
12. M. Scott Peck, *A World Waiting to Be Born: Civility Rediscovered* (New York: Bantam Books, 1993), p. 81.
13. John Wesley, *Standard Sermons* (London: Epworth, 1967), p. vi; as quoted by Steve Harper, *Devotional Life in the Wesleyan Tradition* (Nashville: The Upper Room, 1983), p. 29.
14. For help in knowing how to reflect upon the Word so that it speaks to you, see Rueben Job and Norman Shawchuck, *A Guide to Prayer for Ministers and Other Servants* (Nashville: The Upper Room, 1983), pp. 5-12. There you will find aids to make your prayer seasons rich encounters with God. You will also find help in developing a journaling discipline.
15. Warren Bennis, *On Becoming a Leader* (Reading, Mass.: Addison-Wesley, 1989), pp. 104-5.
16. Parker J. Palmer, "Leading from Within," in Jay A. Conger, ed. *Spirit at Work:*

Discovering the Spirituality in Leadership (San Francisco: Jossey-Bass Publishers, 1994), p. 24.

17. See chapter 7, "The Dark Side of Leadership," in Shawchuck and Heuser, *Leading the Congregation: Caring for Yourself While Serving the People* (Nashville: Abingdon Press, 1993).
18. Parker J. Palmer, "Leading from Within," in *Spirit at Work,* 32.
19. Ibid., pp. 32-37.
20. Ibid., p. 40.

3. What the Manager Manages: A Systems Approach to Management

1. Robert K. Greenleaf, *Servant Leadership: A Journey into the Nature of Legitimate Power and Greatness* (New York: Paulist Press, 1977), p. 54.
2. Peter F. Drucker, *The Practice of Management* (New York: Harper & Row, 1954), p. 50.
3. See Peter M. Senge, *The Fifth Discipline: The Art and Practice of the Learning Organization* (New York: Doubleday Currency, 1990).
4. Organizational systems theory was spawned with the advent of the space age, when for the first time in human history the problems at hand were too complex to be understood or addressed with a linear planning model. Systems planning was devised to help understand tremendous complexities in an uncertain and rapidly changing environment. With its commitment to working with the organization as a whole, rather than as a collection of separate entities, systems leadership is as much an art as a science. The artist views the whole scene in order to understand it, while the scientist breaks the specimen down into its smallest divisible parts in order to understand it. See Alvin J. Lindgren and Norman Shawchuck, *Management for Your Church* (Leith, N.D.: Spiritual Growth Resources, 1984), p. 32.
5. John A. Seiler, *Systems Analysis in Organizational Behavior* (Homewood, Ill.: Richard D. Irwin, Inc. and The Dorsey Press, 1967), p. 28.
6. M. Scott Peck, *A World Waiting To Be Born: Civility Rediscovered* (New York: Bantam Books, 1993), p. 339.
7. Ibid.
8. Ibid., p. 60.
9. Tom Chappell, *The Soul of a Business: Managing for Profit and the Common Good* (New York: Bantam Books, 1993), p. 57.

Introduction to Part Two

1. Richard Luecke, *Scuttle Your Ships Before Advancing: And Other Lessons from History on Leadership and Change for Today's Managers* (New York: Oxford University Press, 1994), p. 126.
2. See Amanda Bennet, "Many of Today's Top Corporate Officers Are the Right

People for the Wrong Time," in *The Wall Street Journal,* October 27, 1992, B1, B4.

3. Loren B. Mead, *Transforming Congregations for the Future* (Washington, D.C.: The Alban Institute, 1994), p. ix.
4. See Lyle Schaller, *The Seven-Day-A-Week-Church* (Nashville: Abingdon Press, 1992); Lyle Schaller, *21 Bridges to the 21st Century: The Future of Pastoral Ministry*; and *Innovations in Ministry: Models for the 21st Century* (especially pages 23-34); both of these books are published in the *Ministry for the Third Millennium* series published by Abingdon Press, 1994).
5. Loren B. Mead, *Transforming Congregations for the Future* (Washington, D.C.: The Alban Institute, 1994), p. x.
6. Lyle E. Schaller, *Innovations In Ministry: Models for the 21st-Century Church* (Nashville: Abingdon Press, 1994), p. 12.

4. The Congregation's Environment

1. Stephen W. Hawking, *A Brief History of Time: From the Big Bang to Black Holes* (New York: Bantam Books, 1988), p. 1.
2. See Lyle E. Schaller, *Innovations in Ministry: Models for the 21st-Century* (Nashville: Abingdon Press, 1994), p. 12.
3. Burt Nanus, *Visionary Leadership: Creating a Compelling Sense of Direction for Your Organization* (San Francisco: Jossey-Bass, 1992), p. 173.
4. Langdon Gilkey, *How the Church Can Minister to the World Without Losing Itself* (New York: Harper & Row, 1964), p. 1.
5. Ibid., p. 2.
6. Ibid., p. 3.
7. For an insightful discussion on this topic, see H. Richard Niebuhr, *Christ and Culture* (New York: Harper & Row, 1951).
8. For a more complete discussion of the different church-types see H. Richard Niebuhr, *The Social Sources of Denominationalism* (New York: A Meridian Book, 1929); and Loren B. Mead, *The Once and Future Church: Reinventing the Congregation for a New Mission Frontier* (Washington, D.C.: The Alban Institute, 1991).
9. Mead, *The Once and Future Church,* pp. 1, 12.
10. Gilkey, *How the Church Can Minister to the World,* p. 4.
11. Mead, *The Once and Future Church,* pp. 10, 14.
12. Ibid., p. 22.
13. Ibid., pp. 14-16.
14. One of the most important disciplines a congregation can learn is how to scan its environment, to really know its neighbors. We believe this is best done by personally experiencing the community through such efforts as taking the congregational leadership for a "walk through the community," distributing questionnaires, or conducting community focus groups to center on what would need to be happening in a church to attract their participation. When persons do a "walk through the community" they are instructed to pretend that they are looking at

the community for the very first time, or to pray that they might see the needs and ministry opportunities of the community as Christ sees them. When they come back together they talk about what they saw, heard, smelled, and felt. What impulses did they feel compelled to bring up for consideration regarding how the congregation might respond to its community?

Another more formalized way to scan the environment is to follow the steps as outlined by Carl S. Dudley:

Step One: Define Your Community. You can define your community from many perspectives, but we will focus on three: (a) chart the physical boundaries, (b) identify the anchor institutions, and (c) look for the gathering places.

Step Two: Identify the People. I suggest three perspectives: (a) observe populations and lifestyles, (b) note historical changes and current trends, and (c) review statistical summaries.

Once you gather the basic information that defines the community and describes the people, your committee should move to a second level of reflecting on the material and probing its implications. For many groups, the interesting—perhaps explosive—material comes through in their follow-up explorations. Steps three, four, and five are related: as you recognize invisible people you can begin to trace the intangible forces, and your sensitivity to both will be expanded by the people you interview.

Step Three: Find the "Invisible" People. Every community has people who are ignored, marginalized, or simply out of sight. By identifying these groups, your committee and the congregation become more sensitive to a range of conditions in your community.

Step Four: Analyze the Intangible Forces. Just as churches have always been concerned with spiritual forces, you should identify the social, economic, political, and religious forces operating in your community. The forces may be intangible, but they are real incentives and barriers in the lives of the people you are trying to reach and in the development of your ministry.

Step Five: Listen to Your Community. Based on this wealth of data and feelings, you can initiate conversations with a wide variety of people from every segment of community life.

The final level of analysis invites you to draw together the themes of your study and insights of your conversations to make a tentative choice for . . . ministry. Note that the same issues that you uncover in the community study are relevant, as your church seeks to reach out in a variety of ministries, from pastoral care to evangelism, from Vacation Bible School to stewardship of community resources. For each program you may shift the focus of your study, but basic questions remain: What are your natural, functional communities, and who are your marginalized peoples? What are the most evident human needs, and how effective is your community response? What does the gospel call you to do, and who might be allies in this ministry?

Step Six: Choose Your Focus of Ministry. Although a firm decision on the appropriate ministry depends on finding a comfortable fit between your social context and your congregational identity, we encourage you to bring your community analysis into focus by deciding on a possible ministry (or ministries). This preliminary inclination toward a particular ministry will greatly facilitate your later discussions.

See Carl S. Dudley, *Basic Steps Toward Community Ministry* (Washington, D.C.: The Alban Institute, 1991), pp. 1-3.

15. John A. Seiler, *Systems Analysis in Organizational Behavior* (Homewood, Ill.: Richard D. Irwin, Inc. and The Dorsey Press, 1967), p. 28.
16. George Parsons and Speed B. Leas, *Understanding Your Congregation as a System* (Washington D.C.: The Alban Institute, 1993), p. 1.
17. There are still hundreds or thousands of congregations in America that do not allow women to serve on the church board, to serve communion, or to serve as an usher. Such decisons are boundary issues—this part of the church is open to women, these are not.
18. See Norman Shawchuck and Roger Heuser, *Leading the Congregation: Caring for Yourself While Serving the People* (Nashville: Abingdon Press, 1993), p. 214. Attention to the environment, when taken to an extreme, has an implicit danger. The purpose of the mission of the church must not be so that it has, through its outputs, maximum influence on society, so that society reflects a congregation's values. That was an Enlightenment strategy which accomodated Christendom, as the Church tried to be a player in the creation of liberal, democratic nation states. (The intent of the nation state, governed by enlightened democrats and republicans, was to keep tribal factions from killing each other over religious issues.) Christendom is over. For postliberal observers it may be better to acknowledge that the attempt to influence societal values has failed, so that now we perceive how the congregation's outputs are intended to identify our enemies in society, those who are hostile to our mission. As Stanley Hauerwas puts it: no enemies, no Christianity. See *After Christendom?* (Abingdon Press, 1992).
19. Norman Shawchuck, Philip Kotler, Bruce Wrenn, Gustave Rath, *Marketing for Congregations: Choosing to Serve People More Effectively* (Nashville: Abingdon Press, 1992), p. 68.

5. The Congregation's Mission

1. Loren B. Mead, *Transforming Congregations for the Future* (Washington, D.C.: The Alban Institute, 1994), pp. 24-25.
2. Ibid., pp. 30-31.
3. Bob Slosser, *Miracles in Darien* (Plainfield, N.J.: Logos International, 1979), p. 7.
4. A paraphrase—written by Richard Wheatcroft, which appeared in "Letter to Laymen" May–June, 1962, 1—of Theodore O. Wedel, "Evangelism—The Mission of the Church to Those Outside Her Life," in *Ecumenical Review*, October, 1953, p. 24. See Howard Clinebell, *Basic Types of Pastoral Care and Counseling: Resources for the Ministry of Healing and Growth* (Nashville: Abingdon Press, 1966 and 1984), pp. 13-14.

5. Richard Luecke, *Scuttle Your Ships Before Advancing* (New York: Oxford University Press, 1994), pp. 59-60.
6. Lloyd Perry and Norman Shawchuck, *Revitalizing the 20th-Century Church* (Leith, N.D.: Spiritual Growth Resources Tel. 1-800-359-7363, 1982), p. 22.
7. Loren B. Mead, *Transforming Congregations for the Future* (Washington, D.C.: The Alban Institute, 1994), pp. 33-42, 121-25.
8. Mead, *Transforming Congregations,* p. 37.
9. Ibid.
10. Ibid., p. 36.
11. For a complete description of a mission statement process that has been used by hundreds of congregations, see Alvin Lindgren and Norman Shawchuck, *Management for Your Church: A Systems Approach* (Leith, N.D.: Spiritual Growth Resources, 1977).
12. Peter F. Drucker, *The Practice of Management* (New York: Harper & Row, 1954), p. 50.
13. Peter F. Drucker, *Managing the Nonprofit Organization: Principles and Practices* (New York: HarperCollins, 1990), p. 3.
14. Ray Bakke, *The Urban Christian: Effective Ministry in Today's Urban World* (Downers Grove, Ill.: InterVarsity Press, 1987), pp. 19-20.
15. See illustrations of Rick Warren and Bill Hybels, for example, in Norman Shawchuck, Philip Kotler, Bruce Wrenn, and Gustave Rath, *Marketing for Congregations: Choosing to Serve People More Effectively* (Nashville: Abingdon Press, 1992), pp. 34-37, 79-83.
16. Mead, *Transforming Congregations,* p. 41.
17. Drucker, *Managing the Nonprofit Organization,* pp. 45-46.
18. Victor E. Frankl, *Man's Search for Meaning* (New York: Washington Square Books, 1984), p. 17.

Introduction to Part Three

1. Henri J.M. Nouwen, *The Living Reminder: Service and Prayer in Memory of Jesus Christ* (New York: The Seabury Press, 1977), p. 11.
2. Peter Block, *Stewardship: Choosing Service over Self-Interest* (San Francisco: Berrett-Koehler Publishers, l993), p. 48.

6. The Congregation's Vision

1. John W. Gardner, *On Leadership* (New York: The Free Press, 1990), p. 131.
2. Norman Shawchuck and Roger Heuser. *Leading the Congregation: Caring for Yourself While Serving Others* (Nashville: Abingdon Press, 1993), chapters 5 and 10.
3. Some of these were taken from Ezra Earl Jones, *Quest for Quality in the Church: A New Paradigm* (Nashville: Discipleship Resources, 1993).
4. See Burt Nanus' excellent book on vision: *Visionary Leadership* (San Francisco: Jossey-Bass, 1992), p. 26.
5. For more information on Cardijn's visioning process see Norman Shawchuck and

Gustave Rath, *Benchmarks of Quality in the Church* (Nashville: Abingdon Press, 1994), pp. 47ff and Boniface Hanley, *Ten Christians* (Notre Dame: Ave Marie Press, 1979), pp. 217ff.

6. See David Bohm and Mark Edwards, *Thought, the Hidden Challenge to Humanity* (San Francisco: Harper and Row, 1990) in Peter M. Senge, *The Fifth Discipline: The Art and Practice of the Learning Organization* (New York: Doubleday Currency, 1990), p. 240.
7. Senge, *The Fifth Discipline,* p. 243.
8. Ibid., pp. 241-242.
9. See Shawchuck and Heuser, *Leading the Congregation: Caring for Yourself While Serving Others* (Nashville: Abingdon Press, 1993), p. 145.
10. Robert Fritz, "The Leader as Creator," in John Adams, ed., *Transforming Leadership: From Vision to Results* (Alexandria, Va.: Miles River Press, 1986), pp. 174-75.
11. Ibid., p. 175.
12. Ibid., pp. 175-76.
13. Our idea for this list came from Burt Nanus, *Visionary Leadership,* pp. 19-20.
14. Nanus, *Visionary Leadership,* p. 22.
15. See Senge, *The Fifth Discipline,* pp. 219-20.

7. The Spirit of the Congregation

1. Stanley M. Davis, *Future Perfect* (Reading, Mass.: Addison-Wesley, 1987), p. 190.
2. James A. Ritscher, "Spiritual Leadership," in John D. Adams, ed., *Transforming Leadership: From Vision to Results* (Alexandria, Va.: Miles River Press, 1986), p. 61.
3. Jay A. Conger, "Introduction: Our Search for Spiritual Community," in Jay Conger and Associates, *Spirit at Work: Discovering the Spirituality in Leadership* (San Francisco: Jossey-Bass Publishers, 1994), p. 2.
4. Joseph G. Donders, *Charged with the Spirit: Mission Is for Everyone* (Maryknoll, N.Y.: Orbis Books, 1993), pp. 1-4.
5. On the other hand, there are those congregations that seem to have no spirit whatsoever. It appears that a congregation may run out of energy altogether, and like an engine run out of fuel, display no sense of energy or spirit whatsoever. These congregations are flaccid, lackluster, insipid. They are willing prisoners to their external realities. Nothing much matters anymore as they limp along toward their eventual demise without a whimper. Or perhaps they sigh at the dim memories of yesteryear when they believed they could make a positive difference in the world. In *Marketing for Congregations* (the first book in the trilogy of which this book is the third), the authors say that many spirit-less congregations will not change until they decline to the point where they find themselves standing at the brink of death. Then as they stare into their open grave, some congregations decide to live—and in that moment of decision a new spirit is born among the people. The authors give the stories of many such congregations. The results of coming to a new spirit for these congregations are little short of miraculous.
6. Parker J. Palmer, "Leading from Within: Out of the Shadow, into the Light," in

Jay Conger and Associates, *Spirit at Work: Discovering the Spirituality in Leadership* (San Francisco: Jossey-Bass Publishers, 1994), p. 24.

7. Norman Shawchuck and Roger Heuser, *Leading the Congregation* (Nashville, Abingdon Press, 1993), chapter 7.
8. There is much more that can be said about the reformers Luther and Deming, and perhaps no one has yet said it better than Richard Luecke. For a more complete discussion of timing and ideas, see Richard Luecke, *Scuttle Your Ships Before Advancing* (New York: Oxford University Press, 1994).
9. Shawchuck and Heuser, *Leading the Congregation.*

Introduction to Part Four

1. Jay R. Galbrith, Edward E. Lawler III, and Associates, *Organizing for the Future* (San Francisco: Jossey-Bass Publishers, 1993), p. 87.

8. The Basic Components of Organization Design: Structures and Belief Systems

1. Peter M. Senge, *The Fifth Discipline: The Art and Practice of the Learning Organization* (New York: Doubleday Currency, 1990), pp. 235-36.
2. Henry Mintzberg, *Structures in Fives: Designing Effective Organizations* (Englewood Cliffs, N.J.: Prentice-Hall, 1983), p. 2.
3. For a discussion on organizational belief systems, see Charles Kiefer, "Leadership in Metanoic Organizations," in John D. Adams, ed., *Transforming Leadership: From Vision to Results* (Alexandria, Va.: Miles River Press, 1986), p. 193.
4. See Henry Mintzberg, *Mintzberg on Management* (New York: The Free Press, 1989), pp. 100-101; and Henry Mintzberg, *Designing Effective Organizations: Structure in Fives,* pp. 48-54.
5. Peter F. Drucker, *The New Realities* (New York: Harper and Row, 1989), pp. 260-61.
6. For the best discussion of this condition, see Peter M. Senge, *The Fifth Discipline.*
7. For a discussion of the ability of a denomination's structures to produce only that for which it was designed, see Ezra Earl Jones, *Quest for Quality* (Nashville: Discipleship Resources, 1994).
8. Every component of the congregation- as- system—the mission, relationships, spirituality/vision, input and output systems, boundaries, and feedback loop—has a structure.
9. David Watson, *I Believe in the Church* (Grand Rapids, Mich.: Eerdmans, 1978), p. 246.
10. Ibid.
11. Linda S. Ackerman, "Flow State Leadership in Action: Managing Organization Energy," in John Adams, ed., *Transforming Work* (Alexandra, Va.: Miles River Press, 1984), p. 247.
12. A consultation facilitated by Shawchuck & Associates, Ltd., a consulting firm ser-

vicing religious organizations worldwide, is located in Leith, North Dakota. Norman Shawchuck is president.

13. Reprinted with permission of the publisher. From *Stewardship: Choosing Service over Self-Interest*. Copyright © 1993 by Peter Block, Berrett-Koehler Publishers, Inc., San Francisco, CA. All rights reserved.
14. Ackerman, "Flow State Leadership in Action" in John Adams, ed., *Transforming Work,* pp. 249-53.
15. Block, *Stewardship,* p. 204.
16. Richard A. Jensen, *Thinking in Story: Preaching in a Post-Literate Age* (Lima, Oh.: C.S.S. Publishing Co., 1993), p. 65.
17. Ackerman, "Flow State Leadership in Action" in John Adams, ed., *Transforming Work,* p. 255.

9. Bureaucracy and Paternalism: Vestiges of a Dying Order

1. Peter Block, *The Empowered Manager: Positive Political Skills at Work* (San Francisco: Jossey-Bass, 1989), p. 46.
2. Stanley M. Davis, *Future Perfect* (Reading, Mass.: Addison-Wesley, 1987), p. 197.
3. Ibid., p. 198.
4. Max Weber, "Bureaucracy," in Joseph A. Litterer, ed., *Organizations: Structure and Behavior* (New York: John Wiley & Sons, 1969), p. 37.
5. R. H. Hall, "The Concept of Bureaucracy: An Empirical Assessment," *American Journal of Sociology* 69 (1963): 33.
6. Gifford and Elizabeth Pinchot, *The End of Bureaucracy and the Rise of the Intelligent Organization* (San Francisco: Berrett-Koehler, 1993), p. 37.
7. See, for example, Peter Block, *Stewardship: Choosing Service over Self-Interest* (San Francisco: Berrett-Koehler Publishers, 1993); Jay R. Galbraith, Edward E. Lawler III and Associates, *Organizing for the Future: The New Logic for Managing Complex Organizations* (San Francisco: Jossey-Bass, 1993); Richard Tanner Pascale, *Managing on the Edge* (New York: A Touchstone Book, 1990); Tom Peters, *The Tom Peters Seminar: Crazy Times Call for Crazy Organizations* (New York: Vintage Books, 1994); and Gifford and Elizabeth Pinchot, *The End of Bureaucracy.*
8. Kate Lewis estimates that in 1993 Americans used 30 billion aspirin; see Kate Lewis, "Maybe Don't Take Two Aspirin," in *Forbes,* May 23, 1994, pp. 222-23.
9. See Joel Arthur Barker, *Future Edge: Discovering the New Paradigms of Success* (New York: William Morrow and Company, 1992).
10. See Tom Peters, *The Tom Peters Seminar.*
11. Gifford and Elizabeth Pinchot, *The End of Bureaucracy,* pp. 21-22.
12. Reprinted with permission of the publisher. From *Stewardship: Choosing Service over Self-Interest*. Copyright © 1993 by Peter Block, Berrett-Koehler Publishers, Inc., San Francisco, CA. All rights reserved.
13. Ibid., p. 25.
14. See Dick Clever, "State Says Church Securities Issue Broke Anti-Fraud Laws," in *Seattle Post Intelligencer,* July 27, 1994, pp. 1, 8.
15. Loren B. Mead, *The Once and Future Church* (Washington D.C.: The Alban Institute, 1991), p. 39.

16. Lyle Schaller, *21 Bridges to the 21st Century* (Nashville: Abingdon Press, 1994), pp. 133-42.
17. Lyle Schaller, *21 Bridges to the 21st Century* (Nashville: Abingdon Press, 1994), pp. 135-37.
18. According to Schaller there are dozens of coalitions, networks, movements, and associations that have emerged in the closing years before the 21st century. See Lyle Schaller, *21 Bridges to the 21st Century,* p. 137.
19. Ibid., p. 139.
20. Ibid.
21. Ibid., p. 141.
22. Ibid., pp. 141-42.
23. John Gardner, quoted by George S. Odiorne, *Management and the Activity Trap: How to Avoid It and How to Get Out of It* (New York: Harper and Row, 1974), p. 37.

10. Partnership: A New Era in Organization Design

1. For a full discussion of these ideas, see Peter Block, *Stewardship: Choosing Service over Self-Interest* (San Francisco: Berrett-Koehler, 1993); and Robert K. Greenleaf, *Servant Leadership: A Journey into the Nature of Legitimate Power and Greatness* (New York: Paulist Press, 1977).
2. Block, *Stewardship,* p. 5.
3. Loren B. Mead, *The Once and Future Church* (Washington D.C.: The Alban Institute, 1991).
4. Block, *Stewardship,* pp. 29-31; and Tom Melohn, *The New Partnership: Profit by Bringing out the Best in Your People, Customers, and Yourself* (Essex Junction, Vt.: Oliver Wight Publications, 1993), pp. 31ff.
5. Reprinted with permission of the publisher. From *Stewardship: Choosing Service over Self-Interest*. Copyright © 1993 by Peter Block, Berrett-Koehler Publishers, Inc., San Francisco, CA. All rights reserved.
6. Melohn, *The New Partnership,* p. 31.
7. Peter Block qualifies, "There are, of course, limits on this. In any community there will always be different levels of authority. The boss will have 51 percent, the subordinate 49 percent. This means that when all is said and done, others will have the right to tell us what to do. This has no effect on our right to say no, even to say it loudly" in Block, *Stewardship,* p. 30.
8. George Odiorne, *Management and the Activity Trap* (New York: Harper and Row, 1974).
9. For a discussion on corporate vision in the local congregation, see chapter 10 of our earlier book *Leading the Congregation: Caring for Yourself While Serving the People* (Nashville: Abingdon Press, 1993).
10. Block, *Stewardship,* pp. 31-32.
11. For a good resource on inspiring persons to be committed to the jobs they take, see John Ed Mathison's book *Every Member in Ministry,* which outlines the every member commitment program of Frazer Memorial UMC in Montgomery, Alabama. The resource is distributed by Discipleship Resources, Nashville, TN.

12. See Norman Shawchuck, et al., *Marketing for Congregations: Choosing to Serve People More Effectively* (Nashville: Abingdon Press, 1992), pp. 79-80.
13. Peter Block, *The Empowered Manager: Positive Political Skills at Work* (San Francisco: Jossey-Bass, 1989), p. 70.
14. Block, *Stewardship,* p. xx.
15. Richard Bondi, *Leading God's People: Ethics for the Practice of Ministry* (Nashville: Abingdon Press, 1989), p. 14.
16. Joel Barker, *The Business of Paradigms: Discovering the Future* (Burnsville, Minn.: Charthouse Learning Corp., 1990).
17. Peter M. Senge, *The Fifth Discipline: The Art and Practice of the Learning Organization* (New York: Doubleday/Currency, 1990).
18. For a complete discussion of exchange of purpose, see Norman Shawchuck, et al., *Marketing for Congregations*

Introduction to Part Five

1. Lewis B. Smedes, *Caring and Commitment: Learning to Live the Love We Promise* (San Francisco: Harper and Row, 1988), p. 7.
2. Stephen R. Covey, *Principle-Centered Leadership* (New York: Summit Books, 1991), pp. 256-57.

11. The Congregation's Working Relationships

1. Stephen R. Covey, *The Divine Center: Why We Need a Life Centered on God and Christ and How We Attain It* (Salt Lake City, Ut.: Bookcraft, 1982).
2. Douglas McGregor, *The Human Side of Enterprise* (New York: McGraw-Hill, 1960).
3. Ibid.
4. Ibid.
5. M. Scott Peck, *The Different Drum: Community-Making and Peace* (New York: Simon and Schuster, 1987), see chapter five.
6. Ibid., pp. 87-88.
7. Ibid., p. 94.
8. Ibid., p. 100.
9. Ibid., pp. 95-103.
10. Tilden Edwards, *Spiritual Friend: Reclaiming the Gift of Spiritual Direction* (New York: Paulist Press, 1980), p. 101.
11. Thomas Hart, *The Heart of Christian Listening* (New York: Paulist Press, 1980).
12. Ibid., p. 7.
13. Ibid., pp. 21-25.
14. Tom Chappell, *The Soul of a Business: Managing for Profit and the Common Good* (New York: Bantam Books, 1993), p. 60.
15. See Thomas Hart, *The Heart of Christian Listening* (New York: Paulist Press, 1980), pp. 16-21.
16. Karl Menninger, *Whatever Became of Sin?* (New York: Hawthorn Books, 1973), p. 18; as quoted in Thomas Hart, *The Heart of Christian Listening.*

17. Max DePree, *Leadership Is an Art* (New York: Doubleday, 1989), p. 53.
18. See Norman Shawchuck, *What It Means to Be a Church Leader* (Leith, N.D.: Spiritual Growth Resources, 1984).
19. We've all been guilty of giving or have been the innocent guinea pig who has received a teacher's guide or quarterly the night before to start teaching a Sunday school. Before we could even come out with the words for a response, we hear the parting encouragement from the leader, "I know you'll do just fine. Please know I'll be praying for you, although you won't even need it."

12. The Use of Power in Ministry and Management

1. Walter Brueggemann, *Power, Providence, and Personality: Biblical Insight into Life and Ministry* (Louisville, Ky.: Westminster/John Knox Press, 1990), p. 49.
2. James MacGregor Burns, *Leadership* (New York: Harper Torchbooks, 1978), p. 9.
3. Ibid.
4. Ibid., p. 12.
5. Ibid., p. 15.
6. George Odiorne, *Management and the Activity Trap* (New York: Harper and Row, 1974), pp. 24ff.
7. In the discussion immediately following, we are indebted to Myron Chartier for a paper he wrote and shared with us titled "Power: The Currency of Leadership." Myron is Co-Minister of Christian Education and Family Life, The American Baptist Churches of Michigan.
8. For listings and discussion of principles for leadership and management see Steven Covey, *Principle-Centered Leadership* (New York: Simon and Schuster, 1990); and Tom Melohn, *The New Partnership* (Essex Junction, Vt.: Oliver Wight, 1994).
9. Covey, *Principle-Centered Leadership*, and Melohn, *The New Partnership*, pp. 107-8.
10. Nouwen, *In the Name of Jesus: Reflections on Christian Leadership* (New York: Crossroad, 1989), p. 59.
11. Ibid., p. 37.

13. Conflict Management

1. Such agencies include: Shawchuck & Associates, Ltd., Cannonball Trail, R.R. 1, Box 123, Leith, N.D., Tel. (701) 584-3002.
2. Mike Johnson, City Ed., *The Daily Record*, Ellensburg, Wash., Nov. 22, 1993.
3. Ibid., Jan 8, 1994.
4. Ibid., Jan. 11, 1994.
5. The involvement of judicatory officials can be highly efficacious when they understand conflict management, or when they work alongside a professional conflict manager.
6. John H. Miller, *The Contentious Community: Constructive Conflict in the Church* (Philadelphia: The Westminster Press, 1978), pp. 17-23.
7. Hugh F. Halverstadt, *Managing Church Conflict* (Louisville: Westminster/John Knox Press, 1992), p. 2.

8. See Roy W. Pneuman, "Nine Common Sources of Conflict in Churches" in *Action Information* (Washington, D.C.: The Alban Institute, March/April, 1992), pp. 1-5.
9. Philip R. Harris and Robert T. Moran, *Managing Cultural Differences* (Houston: Gulf Publishing Company, 1987), p. 257.
10. Edgar H. Schein, *Organizational Culture and Leadership* (San Francisco: Jossey-Bass Publishers, 1985), pp. 153-54.
11. See Norman Shawchuck, *How to Manage Conflict in the Church,* vol. I (Leith, ND: Spiritual Growth Resources, 1990, Tel. 1-800-359-7363), pp. 45-47.
12. Most congregations are what Chris Argyris terms a Model I organization, in which everyone covertly insists upon the right to define the goals, and then behaves in such a way to see that it happens. See Chris Argyris, *Intervention Theory and Method* (Reading, Mass.: Addison-Wesley, 1970).
13. See Speed Leas, *Moving Your Church Through Conflict* (Washington, D.C.: The Alban Institute, 1985).
14. Ibid.
15. Shawchuck, *How to Manage Conflict in the Church.*
16. See Edgar Schein, *Process Consultation,* vol. II (Reading, Mass.: Addison-Wesley, 1987), pp. 22ff.
17. The three major phases in this intervention are designed by Chris Argyris, *Intervention Theory and Method* (Reading, Mass.: Addison-Wesley, 1970), pp. 15ff.
18. Some of these steps within the three major phases by Chris Argyris were built upon those identified by Jerry W. Robinson, Jr., and Roy Clifford, *Conflict Management in Community Groups* (Champaign-Urbana: College of Agriculture, University of Illinois, 1974).
19. See Roger Fisher and William Ury, *Getting to Yes* (New York: Penguin Books, 1991). Their major steps in intervention are: separate people from the problem; focus on interests, not problems; invent options for mutual gain; and insist on using objective criteria.
20. Remember Smedes's four stages of forgiveness: hurt, hate, heal, and begin again. You know when you have forgiven when you can wish the other person well.
21. Lewis B. Smedes, *Forgive and Forget: Healing the Hurts We Don't Deserve* (San Francisco: Harper and Row, 1984).
22. John Patton, *Is Human Forgiveness Possible?* (Nashville: Abingdon Press, 1985), p. 16.
23. Smedes, *Forgive and Forget,* pp. 49, 109.
24. Ibid., pp. 109-10.

14. Family Systems Theory Applied to Religious Organizations

1. Michael H. Crosby, *The Dysfunctional Church: Addiction and Co-Dependency in the Family of Catholicism* (Notre Dame, Ind.: Ave Maria Press, 1991), p. 7.
2. R. Paul Stevens and Phil Collins, *The Equipping Pastor: A Systems Approach to Congregational Leadership* (Washington, D.C.: The Alban Institute, 1993), p. xv.
3. As we proceed with this discussion of family systems theory applied to congregations, we wish to inform the reader that some respected therapists caution that the dynamics of the nuclear family are sufficiently different from the dynamics within

institutions and organizations and, therefore, family systems theory should not be applied to any setting other than the nuclear family. There are also other respected therapists who are doing landmark work in demonstrating that family systems theory can be applied to groups other than the nuclear family. We believe if our readers will take the effort to study the theory and apply it with care, family systems theory can be a powerful resource for understanding the dynamics of dysfunctional congregations, and it will provide a framework for intervening into the dysfunction.

4. Adapted from Jerry Lewis, *The Birth of the Family* (New York: Brunner/Mazel, 1989), pp. 164-66.
5. David S. Freeman, *Techniques of Family Therapy* (New York: Jason Aronson, 1981), pp. 18-27.
6. Once learned, this single systems principle can almost immediately make you more proficient in understanding what is going on in a congregation or family—and what needs to be done in order to make it more functional.
7. Assigning the family roles is not a deliberate, rational process, rather it happens unconsciously as the family sytem moves each individual member into his or her role.
8. For selected examples of this literature, see David S. Freeman, *Techniques of Family Therapy* (New York: Jason Aronson, 1981); Virginia Satir, *Conjoint Family Therapy* (Palo Alto, Calif.: Science and Behavior Books, 1983); Michael E. Kerr and Murray Bowen, *Family Evaluation* (New York: W.W. Norton, 1988); Edwin Friedman, *Generation to Generation: Family Process in Church and Synogogue* (New York: Guilford Press, 1985); Peter L. Steinke, *How Your Church Family Works: Understanding Congregations as Emotional Systems* (Washington, D.C.: The Alban Institute, 1993).
9. M. Scott Peck, *Further Along the Road Less Traveled* (New York: Simon and Schuster, 1993), pp. 24-25.
10. Peter L. Steinke, *How Your Church Family Works: Understanding Congregations as Emotional Systems* (Washington, D.C.: The Alban Institute, 1993), p. 14.
11. Ibid., p. 20.
12. Ibid., pp. 20-22.
13. Dietrich Bonhoeffer, *Life Together: A Discussion of Christian Fellowship* (San Francisco: Harper and Row, 1954), pp. 77-78.
14. Steinke, *How Your Church Family Works*, p. 32.
15. The martyr leader attempts to maintain control over others by producing feelings of guilt and/or pity. The slave leader maintains a sense of worthlessness or guilt unless constantly occupied by some activity. The slave tries to assuage guilt; the martyr causes it. For more discussion of the slave and martyr leadership style in religious organizations, see Norman Shawchuck, *How to Be a More Effective Church Leader* (Leith, N.D.: Spiritual Growth Resources, 1990), Tel. 1-800-359-7363, pp. 26-27.
16. Richard J. Foster, *Prayer: Finding the Heart's True Home* (San Francisco: HarperCollins, 1992), p. 37.
17. Steinke, *How Your Church Family Works*, p. x.
18. See Donald R. Hands and Wayne L. Fehr, *Spiritual Wholeness for Clergy: A*

New Psychology of Intimacy with God, Self and Others (Washington, D.C.: The Alban Institute, 1993).

19. M. Scott Peck, *Further Along the Road Less Traveled: The Unending Journey Toward Spiritual Growth* (New York: Simon and Schuster, 1993), p. 23.
20. Peck, *Further Along the Road Less Traveled,* p. 13.
21. Murray Bowen, *Family Therapy in Clinical Practice* (New York: Jason Aronson, 1978).
22. Steinke, *How Your Church Family Works,* p. 51.
23. For example, an adolescent who is "acting out" may be a signal that the marriage is in trouble. A problem within a congregation may show up in the burnout of a lay leader or pastor.
24. Friedman, *Generation to Generation,* p. 23.
25. Ibid., p. 25.
26. Ibid.
27. Ibid., pp. 203-204.
28. Ibid., pp. 25-26.

15. Intervening in Dysfunctional Systems

1. Edwin H. Friedman, *Generation to Generation: Family Process in Church and Synagogue* (New York: The Guildford Press, 1985), pp. 2-3.
2. Not all conflict or inability to accomplish a task are signs of dysfunction. Dysfunction presupposes a complex of certain conditions which are discussed in chapter 14.
3. Don Williams, *Jesus and Addiction: A Prescription to Transform the Dysfunctional Church and Recover Authentic Christianity* (San Diego: Recovery Publications, 1993), p. 1.
4. Ibid., p. 15.
5. Anne Wilson Schaef and Diane Fassel, *The Addictive Organization* (San Francisco: Harper & Row, 1990), p. 58.
6. Gerald G. May, *Addiction and Grace* (San Francisco: Harper and Row, 1988), pp. 1-3.
7. Virginia Curran Hoffman, *The Co-Dependent Church* (New York: Crossroad, 1991), p. 23.
8. Michael H. Crosby, *The Dysfunctional Church: Addiction and Co-Dependency in the Family of Catholocism* (Notre Dame, Ind.: Ave Maria Press, 1991), p. 28.
9. Ibid.
10. Williams, *Jesus and Addiction,* p. 8.
11. Anne Wilson Shaef, "Is the Church an Addictive System?" *The Christian Century* (3-10) January 1990, pp. 18-21; also see Anne Wilson Schaef and Dianne Fassel, *The Addictive Organization* (San Francisco: Harper & Row, 1988).
12. Anne Wilson Shaef, "Is the Church an Addictive System?" pp. 18-19.
13. See "The Dark Side of Leadership," chapter 7, in Shawchuck and Heuser, *Leading the Congregation: Caring for Yourself While Serving Others* (Nashville: Abingdon Press, 1993).

14. See "Paradigms for Church Leadership," chapter 15, in Ibid., especially the concepts of espoused theories and theories in use, Model I and Model II organizations.
15. See John C. Dwyer, *Church History: Twenty Centuries of Catholic Christianity* (New York and Mahwah, New Jersey: Paulist Press, 1985), pp. 157-58.
16. See Crosby, *The Dysfunctional Church,* p. 28.
17. Thomas Merton, *Thoughts in Solitude* (New York: Farrar, Straus and Giroux, 1958), p. 17.
18. There are many materials available for persons interested in recovery programs. For example, see *The Twelve Steps, a Spiritual Journey: A Working Guide for Healing Damaged Emotions* (San Diego: RPI Publishing, 1994); *Prayers for the Twelve Steps—A Spiritual Journey* (San Diego: Recovery Publications, 1993); *The Twelve Steps for Christians* (San Diego: RPI Publishing, 1994); Martin M. Davis, *The Gospel and the Twelve Steps: Developing a Closer Relationship with Jesus* (San Diego: RPI Publishing, 1993); Jerry Seiden, *Divine Or Distorted: God as We Understand God* (San Diego: Recovery Publications, 1993); and Don Williams, *Jesus and Addiction: A Prescription to Transform the Dysfunctional Church and Recover Authentic Christianity* (San Diego: Recovery Publications, 1993).
19. Hadley Cantril, *The Psychology of Social Movements* (Huntington, N.Y.: Robert E. Kruger, 1941), pp. 147-48, in *The Twelve Steps, a Spiritual Journey: A Working Guide for Healing Damaged Emotions* (San Diego: RPI Publishing, 1994), pp. ix, x.
20. Ernest Kurtz, *Not God: A History of Alcoholics Anonymous* (Century City, Minn.: Hazelden Educational Materials, 1979), pp. 48-49, in *The Twelve Steps, a Spiritual Journey,* p. x.
21. See *The Twelve Steps, A Spiritual Journey.* The twelve steps are:

Step 1: We admitted we were powerless over [an addiction]—that our lives had become unmanageable.

Step 2: We came to believe that a Power greater than ourselves could restore us to sanity.

Step 3: We made a decision to turn our will and lives over to the care of God as we understood him.

Step 4: We made a searching and fearless moral inventory of ourselves.

Step 5: We admitted to God, to ourselves, and to another human being the exact nature of our wrongs.

Step 6: We were entirely ready to have God remove all these defects of character.

Step 7: We humbly asked God to remove our shortcomings.

Step 8: We made a list of all persons we had harmed and made amends to them all.

Step 9: We made direct amends to such people wherever possible, except when to do so would injure them or others.

Step 10: We continued to take personal inventory and when we were wrong promptly admitted it.

Step 11: We sought through prayer and meditation to improve our conscious contact with our God as we understood God, praying only for power to carry that out.

Step 12: Having had a spiritual awakening as the result of these steps, we tried to carry this message to other [addicts], and to practice these principles in all our affairs.

22. Edwin H. Friedman, *Generation to Generation,* p. 208.
23. Ibid., p. 212.
24. There are agencies and consulting firms that are available to assist you in working with dysfunctional congregations; for example, the authors are associated with Shawchuck & Associates, Ltd., a consulting company that works intensively in church conflict management.
25. George MacDonald, *365 Readings,* ed. C. S. Lewis (New York: Collier Books, MacMillan Publishing, 1947), pp. 46-47.

Introduction to Part Six

1. Donald A. Schon, *Educating the Reflective Practitioner* (San Francisco: Jossey-Bass, 1987), pp. 24-25.
2. Peter M. Senge, *The Fifth Discipline: The Art and Practice of the Learning Organization* (New York: Doubleday Currency, 1990), p. 23.

16. The Learning Congregation: Feedback, Reinforcing, Balancing, and Limits to Growth

1. M. Scott Peck, *A World Waiting to Be Born: Civility Rediscovered* (New York: Bantam Books, 1993), p. 11.
2. Peter M. Senge, *The Fifth Discipline: The Art and Practice of the Learning Organization* (New York: Doubleday Currency, 1990), p. 23.
3. Ibid., p. 17.
4. Ibid., p. 18.
5. Mary Walton, *The Deming Management Method* (New York: A Perigee Book, 1986), p. 3.
6. Ibid., p. 19.
7. Norman Shawchuck and Gustave Rath, *Benchmarks of Quality in the Church* (Nashville: Abingdon Press, 1994).
8. See Richard Luecke, *Scuttle Your Ships Before Advancing: And Other Lessons from History on Leadership and Change for Today's Managers* (New York: Oxford University Press, 1994), p. 67.
9. Ibid., p. 76.
10. Ibid., p. 68.
11. For a detailed discussion on these concepts, see Peter M. Senge, *The Fifth Discipline,* pp. 68-126.
12. Ibid., p. 79.
13. Tom Melohn, *The New Partnership: Profit by Bringing out the Best in Your People, Customers, and Yourself* (Essex Junction, Vt.: Omneo, an imprint of Oliver Wight Publications, 1994), p. 8.
14. Senge, *The Fifth Discipline,* p. 85.

15. Ibid., pp. 95-104. Senge defines reinforcing feedback, balancing feedback, and delays as the nouns and verbs in systems thinking. They become the simple building blocks of more complex archetypes that describe relationships in systems thinking, such as limits to growth (see pp. 94-95; 373-90).
16. Ibid.
17. Merv Thompson is an ELCA pastor. While he served Christ the King Lutheran Church in Burnsville, Minnesota, the congregation grew to become the second largest in the ELCA, 8,000 members.
18. Daniel Kim, Michael Goodman, Jennifer Kemeny, Charlotte Roberts, Art Kleiner, "Limits to Growth," in Peter M. Senge, Charlotte Roberts, Richard B. Ross, Bryan J. Smith, and Art Dleiner, *The Fifth Discipline Fieldbook: Strategies and Tools for Building a Learning Organization* (New York: A Currency Book published by Doubleday, 1994), p. 133.
19. Senge, *The Fifth Discipline,* 104-13.
20. Ibid., p. 104.
21. Daniel Katz and Robert L. Kahn, *The Social Psychology of Organizations* (New York: John Wiley & Sons, 1966), p. 21.
22. Ibid., p. 28.
23. Peck, *A World Waiting to Be Born,* p. 10.

17. Quality and Continuous Improvement: the Ultimate Test of Management

1. Richard Luecke, *Scuttle Your Ships Before Advancing: And Other Lessons from History on Leadership and Change for Today's Managers* (New York: Oxford University Press, 1994), pp. 69-70.
2. Lyle E. Schaller, *The Seven-Day-A-Week Church* (Nashville: Abingdon Press, 1992).
3. For a discussion of congregations and how they choose to be responsive or unresponsive, see Norman Shawchuck, et.al., *Marketing for Congregations: Choosing to Serve People More Effectively* (Nashville: Abingdon Press, 1992), pp. 68-78.
4. Peter M. Senge, *The Fifth Discipline: The Art and Practice of the Learning Organization* (New York: Doubleday Currency, 1990).
5. Books to help you begin quality efforts in your organization are: Norman Shawchuck and Gustave Rath, *Benchmarks of Quality in the Church: 21 Ways to Continously Improve the Content of Your Ministry* (Nashville: Abingdon Press, 1994); Norman Shawchuck, et al., *Marketing for Congregations: Choosing to Serve People More Effectively* (Nashville: Abingdon Press, 1992); Andrea Gabor, *The Man Who Invented Quality* (New York: Times Books, 1990); W. Edwards Deming, *Out of Crisis* (Cambridge, Mass.: Massachusetts Institute of Technology/Center for Advanced Engineering Study, 1982); and Richard Luecke, *Scuttle Your Ships Before Advancing,* pp. 57-81.
6. Bishop Richard Wilke, *And Are We Yet Alive?* (Nashville: Abingdon Press, 1986).
7. Senge, *The Fifth Discipline.*

Author Index

Topic Index